Tikkun
Olam

Tikkun Olam

Social Responsibility in Jewish Thought and Law

edited by David Shatz, Chaim I. Waxman, and Nathan J. Diament

Robert S. Hirt, Series Editor

The Orthodox Forum Series
A Project of the Rabbi Isaac Elchanan Theological Seminary
An Affiliate of Yeshiva University

JASON ARONSON INC.
Northvale, New Jersey
London

This book was set in 11 pt. Goudy Oldstyle by Alpha Graphics of Pittsfield, NH.

Library of Congress Cataloging-in-Publication Data

Tikkun olam : social responsibility in Jewish thought and law / edited by David Shatz, Chaim
   I. Waxman & Nathan J. Diament.
        p.   cm.
     Papers presented at the 6th conference of the Orthodox Forum, held March 13–14, 1994,
   in New York City.
     Includes bibliographical references and index.
     ISBN 0-7657-5951-9 (alk. paper)
        1. Judaism and social problems—Congresses.   2. Judaism and politics—Congresses.
   3. Orthodox Judaism—United States—Congresses.   I. Shatz, David.   II. Waxman,
   Chaim Isaac.   III. Diament, Nathan J.   IV. Orthodox Forum (6th : 1994 : New York, N.Y.)
   NH40.J5T54   1997
   296.3'87—dc20   96-28578

Manufactured in the United States of America. Jason Aronson Inc. offers books and cassettes. For information and catalog write to Jason Aronson Inc., 230 Livingston Street, Northvale, New Jersey 07647.

THE ORTHODOX FORUM

The Orthodox Forum, convened by Dr. Norman Lamm, President of Yeshiva University, meets each year to consider major issues of concern to the Jewish community. Forum participants from throughout the world, including academicians in both Jewish and secular fields, rabbis, *rashei yeshiva*, Jewish educators, and Jewish communal professionals, gather in conference as a think tank to discuss and critique each other's original papers, examining different aspects of a central theme. The purpose of the Forum is to create and disseminate a new and vibrant Torah literature addressing the critical issues facing Jewry today.

The Orthodox Forum
gratefully acknowledges the support
of the Joseph J. Green Memorial Fund
at the Rabbi Isaac Elchanan Theological Seminary.

THE ORTHODOX FORUM
Sixth Conference

March 13–14, 1994, 1–2 Nisan 5754
Congregation Shearith Israel, New York City

PARTICIPANTS

Rabbi Marc Angel, Congregation Shearith Israel, New York
Mr. Jeffrey Ballabon, Office of Senator Russell Danforth, Washington, D.C.
Dr. David Berger, Brooklyn College and Yeshiva University
Rabbi Jack Bieler, Hebrew Academy of Greater Washington
Dr. Rivkah Blau, Shevach High School
Rabbi Yosef Blau, RIETS/Yeshiva University
Dr. Judith Bleich, Touro College
Rabbi J. David Bleich, Benjamin N. Cardozo School of Law
Dr. Gerald J. Blidstein, Ben Gurion University
Rabbi Jay Braverman, Private Educational Consultant
Rabbi Michael Broyde, Emory University
Rabbi Shalom Carmy, Yeshiva University
Rabbi Zevulun Charlop, RIETS/Yeshiva University
Mr. Nathan Diament, Debevoise & Plimpton
Rabbi Mark Dratch, Shaarei Shomayim Congregation, Toronto
Dr. Yaakov Elman, Yeshiva University
Dr. Carl Feit, Yeshiva University
Dr. Marvin Fox*, Brandeis University
Rabbi Barry Freundel, Kesher Israel Synagogue, Washington, DC
Professor Martin Golding, Duke University
Mr. Morris Green, Board of Trustees, Rabbi Isaac Elchanan Theological
   Seminary

---

*Deceased

Rabbi Kenneth Hain, Congregation Beth Sholom, Lawrence, NY
Rabbi Nathaniel Helfgot, Frisch Yeshiva High School
Rabbi Basil Herring, Atlantic Beach Jewish Center
Rabbi Robert S. Hirt, RIETS/Yeshiva University
Dr. Jerry Hochbaum, Memorial Foundation for Jewish Culture
Mr. Malcolm Hoenlein, Conference of Presidents of Major Jewish
   Organizations
Professor Joshua Honigwachs, Yeshiva University
Dr. Arthur Hyman, Yeshiva University
Dr. Ephraim Kanarfogel, Yeshiva University
Professor Eliyahu Kanovsky, Yeshiva University
Dr. Norman Lamm, Yeshiva University
Mr. Howard Lasher, Law Offices of Howard Lasher
Dr. Sid Z. Leiman, Brooklyn College and Yeshiva University
Dr. Aaron Levine, Yeshiva University
Mr. Nathan Lewin, Miller, Cassidy, Larroca & Lewin
Rabbi Jay Marcus, Young Israel of Staten Island
Dr. Harold Nierenberg, Yeshiva University
Rabbi Yaakov Neuberger, RIETS/Yeshiva University
Professor Moses Pava, Yeshiva University
Mr. Yossi Prager, Avi Chai Foundation
Mrs. Smadar Rosensweig, Touro College
Rabbi Michael Rosensweig, RIETS/Yeshiva University
Rabbi Yonason Sacks, Yeshiva University
Dr. Jacob J. Schacter, The Jewish Center & Yeshiva University
Dr. Alvin Schiff, Yeshiva University
Dr. David Schnall, Yeshiva University
Mr. Carmi Schwartz, Beth Din of America
Dr. David Shatz, Yeshiva University
Dr. Michael Shmidman, Yeshiva University
Dr. Moshe Z. Sokol, Touro College
Mr. Marc Stern, American Jewish Congress
Professor Suzanne Stone, Benjamin N. Cardozo School of Law
Rabbi Moshe D. Tendler, RIETS/Yeshiva University
Rabbi Aaron S. Tirschwell, RIETS/Yeshiva University
Dr. Chaim I. Waxman, Rutgers University and Yeshiva University
Rabbi Simcha Weinberg, Lincoln Square Synagogue
Dr. Joel Wolowelsky, Yeshiva of Flatbush High School
Dr. Walter Wurzburger, Yeshiva University

In loving memory of

Rabbi Dovid and Rabbanit Tzipporah Lifshitz
Meyer and Lillian Shatz
Rabbi Nissan Waxman
תנצב"ה

Contents

Introduction

"*Tikkun olam*," variously translated as "repairing," "mending," or "improving" the world, is an elusive and amorphous concept. In halakhic sources the term is not defined, yet it is invoked in the Talmud as the justification for a variety of rabbinic edicts.[1] In our liturgy, most notably in the second paragraph of *Aleinu*, *tikkun olam* is connected to a messianic era in which all the world will know and serve God (*le-takken olam be-malkhut Shad-dai*). In the last century, the expression was employed in neo-kabbalistic discussions of the endeavor to bring God into this world.[2] In contemporary America, *tikkun olam* has been invoked by former New York Governor Mario Cuomo,[3] California Congressman Henry Waxman,[4] and, most conspicuously, writer and editor Michael Lerner[5] to link progressive politics with Jewish tradition. In the most general sense, however, *tikkun olam* is associated with the thesis that Jews bear responsibility not only for their own moral, spiritual, and material welfare, but for the moral, spiritual, and material welfare of society at large.

---

[1]Several *mishnayot* in *Gittin* 4 refer to legislation enacted for the sake of *tikkun olam*. Note that the legislation in question takes place within Jewish society, whereas in later usage the term refers to actions toward non-Jewish as well as Jewish society.

[2]See R. Yitzchak Nissenbaum, *Derushim ve-Homer li-Derush, Kinyanei Kedem, b-Reishit*; R. Yitzhak ha-Kohen Kook, *Orot hakodesh* (Jerusalem: Mossad HaRav Kook, 1985), vol. 1, sec. 125, p. 143.

[3]Stated on a broadcast of *Charlie Rose*, PBS.

[4]E.g., remarks on the 1992 Election Campaign, Hebrew Academy of Nassau County, October, 1992.

[5]See Lerner's "Founding Editorial Statement: To Mend, Repair and Transform the World," *Tikkun* 1:1 (1986): pp. 3–13. Lerner is editor of *Tikkun*.

1

The sixth conference of the Orthodox Forum, held in March 1994, brought together scholars and professionals from a variety of disciplines and fields to explore and debate this latter proposition. Utilizing both theoretical and practical approaches, participants sought to define the nature and scope of the Jewish community's responsibility to the non-Jewish society in which it lives. The discussion proceeded along a rich variety of dimensions: halakhic, theological, philosophical, legal, political, sociological, economic. In this volume, we are pleased to present the fruits of that conference.

The topic of *tikkun olam* has special resonance for Jews who believe that integrating Judaism with general culture constitutes an ideal. This ideology, variously known as *Torah u-Madda*, *Torah im derekh eretz*, *Torah ve-hokhmah*, is more complex than generally appreciated. The complexity we refer to emerges in a statement by Rabbi Abraham Isaac Kook in his address at the dedication of the Hebrew University in 1925:

> Two tendencies characterize Jewish spirituality. One tendency is internal and entirely sacred; it serves to deepen the light of Torah within. Such has been the purpose of all Torah institutions from earliest times, especially the fortresses of Israel's soul—the *yeshivot*. . . .
>
> The second tendency characterizing Jewish spirituality served not only to deepen the sacredness of Torah within, but also as a means for the propagation and absorption of ideas (*hotza'ah ve-hakhnasah*). It served to propagate Jewish ideas and values from the private domain (*reshut ha-yahid*) of Judaism into the public arena (*reshut ha-rabbim*) of the universe at large. For this purpose we have been established as a light unto the nations. It also served to absorb the general knowledge derived by the collective effort of all of humanity, by adapting the good and useful aspects of general knowledge to our storehouse of a purified way of living. Ultimately, this absorption too serves as a means of a moderated propagation to the world at large.[6]

Thus, not only does Jewish history reflect two tendencies, inner-directed and outer-directed, but the Jewish interaction with the outside world (what Rav Kook calls "the second movement") is itself dual. Jews absorb ideas from the outside; but they also transform those ideas and bring the new product to the outside world. The integration of Judaism with

---

[6]The translation is that of Shnayer Z. Leiman in *Tradition* 29:1 (Fall 1994): 89.

culture, then, can be interpreted in two ways, albeit no doubt compatible and indeed complementary. Integrationism entails *hakhnasah*, but
it also demands *hotza'ah*.[7]

As one surveys recent contributions to integrationism, it becomes clear
that their dominant note is *hakhnasah* rather than *hotza'ah*. Much has
been said about the salutary effect that secular study can exert on Torah knowledge and on religious sensibilities. We read that philosophy
deepens belief, history sensitizes us to providence, science inspires awe,
literature expands the spirit, and art stimulates feeling. These insights
strike us as valid and as well rooted in authoritative Jewish sources. But
in Rav Kook's conception, the interaction required between Torah and
culture is two-way. We ask not only what *madda* can do for Torah, but
also what Torah can do for *madda*. *Tikkun olam* is thus demanded by the
"outward" movement.[8]

The notion that Jews not only have a message for their surrounding
cultures but are obliged to convey it to their host societies and the world
at large is indeed echoed by several distinguished figures of the past two
centuries who advocated the integration of Judaism and culture. Among
them are Rav Samson Raphael Hirsch, Lord Immanuel Jakobovits, Rabbi
Jonathan Sacks, and Rav Joseph B. Soloveitchik. Corroboration for their
view emerges not only from the celebrated statement that Jews are "a
light unto the nations" (Is. 42:6, 49:6), but also, arguably, from such
classical sources as God's charge to Abraham in Gen. 12:2–3;[9] Jer. 29:7;[10]
Avot 3:2;[11] Maimonides' view that Jews are obliged to enforce Noahide

---

[7]Rav Kook is utilizing terms from the laws governing carrying on *shabbat*.

[8]Appreciating the notion of *hotza'ah* as a component of integrationism can
aid Yeshiva University graduates who wonder how to continue their integrated
existence after removing their graduation caps and gowns. If people are engaged
in full-time jobs outside of academic circles, where the purely intellectual manifestation of integration is unavailable, how do they actualize an integrationist
philosophy on a regular basis? *Tikkun olam* could be the appropriate rubric under
which they may seek integration.

[9]See especially the end of verse 3: ". . . and all nations of the world will be
blessed through you."

[10]"Seek the peace of the city to which I have exiled you and pray on its behalf to the Lord, because in its peace there will be peace for you."

[11]"Pray for the welfare of the government, for if not for fear of it, people would
be wont to swallow one another alive."

law;[12] and the latter's depiction of the messianic era.[13] One influence that is especially prominent in this book is Rav Soloveitchik's essay "Confrontation." While vocal in denying the propriety of theological dialogue between Jews and non-Jews, the Rav affirms that Jews are duty bound to join forces with all other human beings to advance the welfare of civilization. "We stand shoulder to shoulder with the rest of civilized society over against an order which defies us all." We must protect human rights and aid the needy, for such obligations are "implicit in human existence."[14] Indeed, all human beings incur this obligation; it devolves upon Jews not qua Jews, but qua human beings.

But *tikkun olam* need not be conceived solely as an antidote to religious isolationism. It is also a potent counterforce to a diametrically opposite tendency, namely, the secularism that dominates our culture. As R. Sacks notes:

> One of the most powerful assumptions of the twentieth century is that faith . . . belongs to private life. Religion and society are two independent entities, so that we can edit God out of the language and leave our social world unchanged.[15]

---

[12]See Maimonides, *Mishneh Torah, Laws of Kings*, 8:10.

[13]Ibid., chs. 11–12.

[14]Joseph B. Soloveitchik, "Confrontation," *Tradition* 6:2 (1964): 5–29. All of the sources alluded to in this paragraph are subjected to rigorous examination in this volume. See especially the papers by J. David Bleich Gerald Blidstein, Jack Bieler, Marc D. Stern, and Jeffrey Ballabon.

[15]Jonathan Sacks, *The Persistence of Faith* (London: Jews College, 1990), 27. See also David Shatz, "Practical Endeavor and the Torah u-Madda Debate," *The Torah u-Madda Journal* 2 (1992): 98–149, esp. 112–22, 129–31. The well-known philosopher Alasdair MacIntyre has described the phenomenon of privatization in a more general context:

> Any contemporary attempt to envisage a human life as a whole, as a unity . . . encounters two different obstacles . . . The social obstacles derive from the way in which modernity partitions each human life into a variety of segments, each with its own norms and modes of behaviour. So work is divided from leisure, private life from public, the corporate from the personal . . . The philosophical obstacles derive from . . . the tendency to think atomistically about human action and to analyze complex actions and transactions in terms of simple components . . . [as well as the tendency to make a] sharp separation . . . between the individual and the roles that he or she plays . . . (*After Virtue* 2nd Ed. [Notre Dame, 1984], p. 204).

The lack of appeal of *Torah u-Madda* in our time is a symptom of one of the most devastating effects of secularization: *the privatization of religion.* Judaism is experienced as a phenomenon of private life. . . . But we are far less sure what Judaism might mean in the public domain.[16]

Privatization is unacceptable if we seek to fulfill *ve-khol ma'asekha yihyu le-shem Shamayim* (all your actions should be for the sake of Heaven).[17] Time spent outside the synagogue and study hall is not a necessary evil foisted upon us by Adam's sin—but a context in which to seek redeeming activities and values mandated by a religious ethic. To hold otherwise is to partly concede the argument advanced by both secularists and isolationists that modernity is incompatible with orthodoxy.[18]

Because these considerations are so powerful, some members of the Orthodox Forum on *tikkun olam* initially expected that the forum's deliberations would simply confirm that *tikkun olam* is a religious obligation and then ultimately would galvanize the modern Orthodox community to engage in social action.[19] As it turns out, however, the papers that were presented and now are assembled here pervasively demonstrate that matters are more complicated than these initial suppositions recognized. The papers raise four fundamental issues: (1) whether there actually is an obligation upon Jews to work for the moral, spiritual, and/or pragmatic progress of the world; (2) if so, what the sources of this obli-

---

[16]Sacks, "Torah u-Madda: The Unwritten Chapter," *L'Eylah* 30 (September 1990): 14.

[17]Mishnah, *Avot*, 2:15.

[18]See Sacks, *Tradition in an Untraditional Age* (Vallentine, 1990). To compartmentalize our daily lives and enjoy the full bounty and range of activities without a more unified and consistent infusion of integrationist values also invites the charge that *Torah u-Madda* and "Modern Orthodoxy" are nothing more than convenient and savvy justifications for pursuing material and aesthetic pleasures which *halakhah* might otherwise frown upon. For an entertaining and provocative discussion of those cases, see the exchange between Shalom Carmy and David Singer, *Tradition*, 21:4 (Fall, 1985): 27–51. (Singer, "Is Club Med Kosher?: Reflections on Synthesis and Compartmentalization"; Carmy, "Rejoinder: Synthesis and the Unification of Human Existence.")

[19]Agudath Israel, which does not advocate *Torah u-Madda*, has been active in shaping American legislation and social policy to conform to Jewish values and law. Even if the theory behind their doing so is to promote the Jewish *self-interest* in a more moral society, rather than to fulfill an obligation to the world at large, theirs is a model that commands our attention.

gation are—are they textual, moral, halakhic, theological, or merely pragmatic—that is, to advance Jewish interests; (3) how Jews should carry out this obligation if it exists; and (4) what specific message Judaism brings to the world in which we live.

Gerald J. Blidstein discusses "Jewish responsibility for the welfare of society" in a broad, inclusive sense, relating it to spiritual advancement, social welfare and material progress. Focusing on "the structure and substance of our destiny itself," Blidstein claims that there is a significant and perennial position in Jewish tradition that urges Jews to accept responsibility for the welfare of society. To be sure, Blidstein notes that even if Jews ought to make an impact on the world, one might argue (and some sources suggest this, e.g., writings by R. Jacob Ettlinger and R. Samson Raphael Hirsch) that they best exert this impact when they serve God with devotion and probity, rather than when they busy themselves with the spiritual and material welfare of the world. (J. David Bleich's essay deals with such views as well.) Also, one could maintain that God might be the one to bring about the final spiritual enlightenment of all. Nevertheless, Blidstein believes that enough models exist to ground active and direct involvement. Abraham pleads for the lives of the people of Sodom and, according to the *aggadah*, calls all men and women to the service of God; thus, Abraham represents a fusion of concern for both the physical and spiritual life of humanity as a whole. In addition, Maimonides expects Jews to take an active role in the spread of true belief. The activist interpretation of Jewish responsibility to the world reaches a modern peak in the views of R. Joseph B. Soloveitchik described earlier.

In the course of his inquiry, Blidstein engages such topics as *kiddush ha-Shem*, conversion, kabbalistic teaching, the Reform notion of the Jews' mission, and the implications of Zionism, thereby demonstrating the rich range of classical materials that bear on the subject of *tikkun olam*. At the end of his essay, however, Blidstein adduces other, more general bases for Jewish involvement in the welfare of society. When Jews live in a democratic polity, they are obligated to that society because of mutuality: it is "unfair, ugly, and eventually impossible to make claims on society without feeling part of it and making one's contribution."[20] Also,

---

[20]Blidstein suggests that mutuality is inherent in the concept of *darkhei shalom* (the ways of peace).

silence and inaction reflect "an acquiescence in the evils and abuses to which other human beings are subject." This theme, that *tikkun olam* is partly rooted in general moral impulses, appears as well in other essays in the volume.[21]

J. David Bleich's essay combines theological reflection with halakhic analysis and practical assessment. According to Jewish law, the "Sons of Noah" (non-Jews) are obliged to observe seven commandments, among them prohibitions against idolatry, blasphemy, theft, murder, sexual immorality, and a positive injunction to set up a system of courts. (*Sanhedrin* 58a ff.) The provisions of the Noahide Code, Bleich contends, are not designed simply for the benefit of humanity—to regulate human conduct and prevent anarchy—but to fulfill a divine mission. Hence, the Jewish people, elected to serve God, are obligated to assure that God is served by all His creatures. Does this mean, Bleich inquires, that Jews are obligated to provide Noahides with detailed instruction about provisions of the Noahide Code? Or merely that they have a general obligation to secure commitment to Noahide law? Drawing upon rulings by Maimonides and also by the Hatam Sofer, Bleich argues for a middle position, namely, that Jews have an obligation to set an example and also to impart specific knowledge to Noahides *upon the latter's request.* However, he remarks that the paucity of rabbinic literature dealing with Noahide laws makes it difficult to know precisely how to counsel gentiles in concrete instances. This uncertainty is evident with regard to issues like the propriety of neutering pets, the permissibility of abortions to save the mother's life, active euthanasia, and the application of capi-

---

[21]In addressing the topic of political engagement by the Jewish community, Rabbi Aharon Lichtenstein (Audiotape, *The Interface of Religion with Politics,* 1992) has pointed to *Shabbat* 54b as an indication that our level of obligation is a function of our capability. The Talmud states: "Any person who is able to rebuke the members of his household and fails to, is accountable for [the misdeeds] of the members of his household; [if he is able to rebuke] the citizens of his city, he is accountable for the [misdeeds of the] members of his city; [if he is able to rebuke] the entire world, he is accountable for the [misdeeds of the] entire world."

Rabbi Lichtenstein reasoned that if responsibility falls upon those who are in a position to chastise potential misdoers with words, how much more responsibility falls upon those who can actually influence and shape the course of society's conduct.

tal punishment. In some cases, (abortion, for example) the uncertainty may be resolved by applying halakhic canons; in others the issues require the concerted attention of rabbinic authorities. Complicating matters still more is the need to create *one* public policy for both Jews and non-Jews; for policies that are acceptable for non-Jews according to *halakhah* may not be acceptable for Jews.

Notwithstanding these difficulties in implementing the concept of *tikkun olam*, and quite apart from Jewish obligations vis-à-vis Noahides, Bleich maintains that Jewish self-interest militates against our permitting society to degenerate morally. He cautions against allowing the historical association of social action with Reform Judaism to deter Orthodox Jews from enunciating Jewish teachings to the world. Bleich bemoans the lack of legislative campaigning and lobbying on the part of Orthodox groups with respect to such issues as abortion and gay rights, and he issues a call for responsible Jewish responses to social problems on the contemporary agenda.

Extending the halakhic aspect of Bleich's discussion, Michael Broyde offers an analysis of whether Jews are obligated to enforce the seven Noahide commandments and/or any other rules that gentiles must keep according to Jewish law. The *Sefer Hasidim* (thirteenth century) submits that "when one sees a Noahide sinning, if one can correct him, one should," for God sent Jonah to Nineveh to warn its non-Jewish inhabitants that their misdeeds would be punished. Furthermore, Maimonides holds, as we have mentioned, that Jews must compel non-Jews to observe the Seven Commandments. However, many authorities reject Maimonides' ruling and deny that individual Jews are obligated to ensure that Noahides observe their laws. Based on the verse "do not place a stumbling block before the blind" (Lev. 19:14) it is biblically prohibited to entice a gentile to violate Noahide laws if without the Jew's assistance the law would not be violated. However, when the Noahide is in a position to violate the law without the Jew's assistance, many authorities, including the Rama, rule that the prohibition against allowing a Noahide to sin is not violated, and one may even assist the Noahide in sinning.[22] Broyde notes the position of R. Menahem Mendel Schneerson that Jews are obligated to teach and persuade Noahides to observe the

---

[22]Though "pious people," according to Rama, will in certain instances act more strictly.

seven commandments, but he judges it to be contrary to the opinion of most authorities.

Notwithstanding the results of this halakhic analysis, Broyde, in a postscript, finds other grounds for Jews trying to influence the conduct of non-Jews. First, he observes that the halakhically permissible is not identical with the morally laudatory. God's compassion embraces all of humanity; Jews ought to show compassion for victims of evil. Second, echoing Bleich, Broyde cautions that moral disintegration in society threatens Jewish self-interest. Yet the fact that there is no technical obligation to enforce Noahide law is not without practical consequences. Absent a technical obligation, Jews may desist from seeking to enforce Noahide law if doing so would harm Jewish interests. Thus, for example, an abortion law in the United States that is consistent only with Noahide law would cause situations to arise in which *halakhah*'s mandates cannot be fulfilled. That would surely be contrary to Jewish interest. Similarly, Jewish agitation against gay rights might jeopardize protections against discrimination that have been extended to Jews; Jews are therefore advised, according to Broyde, to weigh these factors.

Jack Bieler perceives a discrepancy between modern and classical treatments of Jewish responsibilities to society. Whereas R. Hirsch, R. Kook, R. Joseph Soloveitchik, R. Aharon Soloveichik, the Lubavitcher Rebbe, R. Jakobovits, and R. Sacks, all accent the existence of these responsibilities, primary sources in pre-modern Judaism do not expressly formulate an obligation for Jews to affect the moral and spiritual welfare of society. (On this point Bieler's essay contrasts somewhat with Blidstein's). However, Bieler then suggests, this scarcity of texts could be due to the fact that until recently Jews did not have the opportunity to participate actively in the policymaking of their host societies.[23] Bieler believes that recent work by political scientists and philosophers furnish us with models that encourage participation. For example, the concept of a *berit* (covenant) highlighted by Daniel Elazar can be used to analyze the relationships between groups who bear responsibilities to one another. (This idea is akin to Blidstein's appeal to mutuality.) At the end of his essay, Bieler broaches two difficult problems: how we can create an

---

[23]Rabbi Soloveitchik, too, contrasts the possibilities of social action in the more distant past to those in recent times: see "Confrontation."

agenda for involvement in social causes; and how we can interest the
world in hearing our perspective.

Marc Stern analyzes some of the same texts as Blidstein and Bieler.
He, too, highlights Rav Soloveitchik's "Confrontation" as encapsulat-
ing an argument for *tikkun olam*. Also like Blidstein and Bieler, Stern
appeals not only to Jewish texts but to the nature of a democracy: citizens in a democracy bear a moral responsibility for what government does
in their name, since they have the power to change government policy.
Having agreed *that* Orthodox Jews should take a role in political affairs,
however, Stern goes on to consider when Orthodox Jews should look
for guidance on social policy and also *what* they should say on particular
social issues.

Should Jews seek to ban all taking of interest? Should Jews oppose
gay-rights bills, or instead push for religious exemptions to be incorporated into these bills? How, in general, does one balance the need to make
a moral statement with practical realities? Citing R. Nissim of Gerona
(the Ran),[24] Stern maintains that "there is no necessary one-to-one correspondence between *halakhah* and what is appropriate for the civil
political order." In other words, halakhists recognize extra-revelational
standards of ethics and policymaking. Thus, Stern states that with regard to whether there should be a single-payer system of medical care,
or whether the United States should invade Bosnia, "it is difficult to
envision what halakhic sources would be controlling here," let alone
envision what might prove compelling to people who reject the authority of *halakhah*. He points out that this problem is tied to another, namely
who settles these questions. But even when halakhic sources are readily
adducible, religious groups often have to urge their positions on "secular" grounds in order for them to win adherents. Stern recommends
against Orthodox Jews running to enlist in the ranks of the Moral
Majority.

Stern's essay introduces another dimension into our discussion. Contemporary philosophers and legal theorists have debated whether religion ought to play a role in public life and, if so, what that role should
be. Liberal thinkers such as Bruce Ackerman, Thomas Nagel, John Rawls,
and David Richards, along with Stanley Hauerwas from a Christian point
of view, oppose bringing religion into public debate; Stephen Carter, Kent

---

[24]*Derashot ha-Ran* 11, which deals with the powers of a Jewish king.

Greenawalt, Richard John Neuhaus, and Michael Perry, albeit to different degrees and on varying grounds, allocate a place for religion. Stern regards it as schizophrenic for a deeply religious person to put aside who he or she is in order to participate in public life. The right of religious individuals to speak to public issues on a religious basis has been affirmed by Supreme Court justices, many of whose key decisions and opinions Stern canvasses. However, in the end, he believes that Orthodox Jews "have done astoundingly well under secular democracy" and that "it is precisely the secular nature of government that enables Orthodox Jews to participate on equal terms with their fellow citizens without a serious threat of religious persecution."

The essays by Martin P. Golding and Nathan J. Diament are in part comments on Stern's. Golding sheds further light on the contemporary philosophical debate about the place of religion in society, to which Stern had alluded. Specifically, he relates the issue of *tikkun olam* to the concept of citizenship as it is treated by philosophers today. According to many theorists of the liberal democratic state—represented, for instance, by Harvard philosopher John Rawls—citizens are barred from introducing religious convictions into debates on issues of public principle or policy. This proposition clearly poses a problem for Jews who wish to promote *tikkun olam* from a Jewish perspective. Yet it seems paradoxical, as Rawls says, that citizens thinking about the most fundamental political questions should honor the limits of "public reason" and cannot appeal to the "whole truth" as they see it. Golding briefly describes and criticizes the development of Rawls's liberal theory and his dissolution of the paradox, then reacts explicitly to the papers by Broyde and Stern. No adequate theory of citizenship in a religiously diverse democracy has yet been formulated, he suggests, that takes into account actual "selves" and what they deeply care about.

Stern's praise of the secular state as benefactor of religious citizens and his suggestion that a secular state is demanded by the U. S. Constitution prompts a brief response by Nathan Diament. Diament notes that although the position described by Stern is the one that American Jewish organizations have traditionally espoused, its truth is the subject of great debate. Legal scholars and Supreme Court justices have called into serious question the assumption that the religion clauses of the Constitution require the current strict separation between church and state. Diament also raises for our consideration the possibility that not only does American constitutional theory welcome religious citizens and organizations to the public square, but our subject of *tikkun olam*, properly understood, might demand such actions from the religious citizen as well.

Jeffrey Ballabon's essay returns us to the central question of whether *tikkun olam* is an obligation. Like Jack Bieler, he doubts that sources such as talmudic *takkanot mi-penei tikkun olam* furnish a precedent for extensive programs of social action. Ballabon suggests a different basis for social action, based upon the approach of R. Abraham Grodzinksi in his *Torat Avraham*: a human being is obligated to work on behalf of whatever *sekhel* requires. Ballabon then turns to specifics of social policy. He observes that unlike Agudath Israel, whose means of social policymaking is a rabbinic consensus, modern Orthodoxy lacks the authority structure to make this model feasible for itself. Nevertheless, he suggests that a program for modern Orthodox social involvement can be built around such areas as commitment to Israel and free exercise of religion, where agreement is attainable. He also argues that self-interest is an appropriate motive for political involvement. A former legislative aide to a United States Senator, Ballabon draws on personal experience to analyze some conflicts that can arise between Jewish interests and ethical interests, as well as some that can arise for an individual public servant between his personal religious commitments and his commitment to the U. S. Constitution.

The essays by Meir Tamari, Aaron Levine, and Barry Freundel shift our focus from theory to practice. Each offers a model for how Jewish values and principles can be applied to particular social issues.

Tamari and Levine were asked to articulate whether and how such obligations as charity should be incorporated within a capitalist economy according to Jewish principles. According to Tamari, the Jewish view of the marketplace "is neither capitalist nor socialist but an 'ism' of its own." Judaism seeks to instill the qualities of mercy and righteousness; accordingly, Jewish law requires Jews to give charity to those in need— be they Jews or non-Jews. The community is empowered to enforce this obligation by such means as taxation and price controls. At the same time, Judaism distinguishes charity from welfare. Aiding others is an obligation; there is no accompanying right to live off welfare. Thus, for example, recipients must not squander loans and must repay them. Tamari evaluates a range of marketplace issues from the perspective of the duty of charity. He asserts, for example, that Judaism opposes un-employment benefits which remove the incentive to work and the use of a poverty line based on average standards of living rather than objec-tive need; he also states that Judaism does not distinguish between de-serving poor and undeserving poor (the latter being those whose foolish ways brought them into poverty). He also maintains that employers have an obligation to provide employment to redundant workers even when this is not economically feasible, and to help redundant workers find alternative employment. As against the contention that religious values should not motivate economic policies, Tamari responds that other approaches in economics, such as welfare economics, likewise are rooted in particular values and philosophies. Consequently, Jews ought not feel awkward or uncomfortable when they utilize religious values to construct economic theories and policies.

Levine's paper explores several aspects of the ideology of capitalism from the perspective of Torah values. In the capitalist system, the profit motive drives production. Capitalism provides no mechanism, however, that forces market participants to pause and assess the inherent worthi-ness of their livelihood by criteria that are not economic. Drawing upon Rav Soloveitchik's insights into the mandate *milu et ha'aretz ve-kivshuha*, "fill the earth and conquer it" (Gen. 1:28), Levine develops the notion that an economic activity should be considered worthy if it enhances human dignity and raises the human being's sense of responsibility. This criterion carries implications for the ranking of livelihood activities and for identifying perversions of the *kibbush* mandate.

Levine develops further similarities and differences between capital-ist and halakhically based systems. In the capitalist ethic, donating cor-porate funds to charitable organizations or committing corporate re-sources for socially responsible projects violates the presumptive desire of an owner to maximize profits. Perhaps surprisingly, Levine presents a halakhic argument *against* corporate altruism based on the idea that such use of funds might not accord with the shareholders' intentions. Mov-ing to another issue: the capitalist ethic adopts a non-judgmental atti-tude toward conspicuous consumption, but Torah values provide objec-tions to such conduct. Finally, in the capitalist ethic, charity giving is best left to individual decisionmaking in the private sector. Government taxation for this purpose violates economic freedom and interferes with the incentive system of the marketplace. In sharp contrast, Judaism calls for a dual system to deal with societal welfare, a system comprising both private and public sectors. The contrasts between Tamari's and Levine's positions about social responsibility command the reader's attention.

Barry Freundel's paper treats the topic of health-care reform, which was hotly debated in the United States. Indeed, Freundel regards this subject as a model for how Jews, by drawing upon halakhic and historical precedents, can help create a better society. Arguing that Jewish law never anticipated a risk-free society, the paper discusses the limits that society must impose on itself in expending resources for a life-preserving cause. Just as one individual cannot be asked to give up his life for another, so, too, individual and societal expenditures to help the sick must not result in the impoverishment and endangerment of others. Health-care planning must be done within appropriate limits set by an accurate understanding of the economic impact of any proposed plan.

Once limits are set, the question of rationing must be faced. Freundel argues that, as each life is infinitely valuable, decisions to withhold care based on age or similar criteria are immoral. The only rationing permissible would be in the initial allocation of resources to different areas of medical care, with patients then being treated on a first-come, first-served basis as long as supplies remain available. Because the prospect of running out of supplies is horrific, significant efforts to avoid reaching that limit should be implemented. Jewish historical models suggest malpractice and tort reform; pricing structures for physicians' fees, drugs, and medical paraphernalia; assumption of some measure of personal responsibility for one's unhealthy activities; and preventive care. Finally, Freundel describes a mixed model of care that covers the poor while retaining free-market incentives to care for those not covered by the other measures described.

Many issues of implementation are yet to be addressed. Thus, we raise the following questions for further thought and consideration:

1. How are we to assess the spiritual costs and benefits of different projects as our community attempts to balance competing demands and scarce resources?

2. What is to be the method of analyzing issues and developing plans of action for our community to pursue? Should an institution be established on behalf of the community to conduct research and analysis and advocacy to government bodies? Should it be staffed only by observant Jews? What role should leading rabbinic authorities in our community play in policy formulation?
3. How should the mission of *tikkun olam* be integrated into our educational curricula?
4. What role should the rabbinate and synagogues play in educating the community and mobilizing it?
5. How are "conflicts questions" to be evaluated? a. How do we evaluate support for a politician who supports some positions that we concur with and opposes others? b. How do we approach entering into alliances with other groups, especially religious groups, if we agree on a policy position? c. How should the individual modern Orthodox Jew deal with conflicts? Should one work for a legislator who is pro-Israel and supports homosexual marriage rights?

Blending theory and practice, examinations of texts with assessments of tactics, the essays that follow should stimulate a dialogue within the Orthodox community over the power of Judaism to transform a morally tenuous world. But for all their diversity and scope, they are only a beginning.

It is a pleasure for us to express gratitude to Rabbi Dr. Norman Lamm, President of Yeshiva University, who created the Orthodox Forum and convenes it each year. Thanks to his unflagging support and leadership, the Forum has grown in exciting ways. Its efforts, including the five previous volumes of the Orthodox Forum series, have been warmly received by both the scholarly and lay communities.

Rabbi Robert S. Hirt, Vice President for Administration and Professional Education of the Rabbi Isaac Elchanan Theological Seminary, an affiliate of Yeshiva University, and the editor of the Orthodox Forum series, is intimately involved in all aspects of every Forum meeting. He provided us with wise counsel, prompt assistance, and much encouragement at every stage. We are profoundly appreciative.

Rabbi Aaron Tirschwell of the Max Stern Division of Communal Services (M.S.D.C.S.) provided invaluable assistance in arranging the sixth conference. Mrs. Marcia Schwartz of M.S.D.C.S. greatly facilitated both the planning of the conference and the preparation of this volume. Steven Palmé, Production Editor for Judaica at Jason Aronson Inc., supervised publication and provided valuable guidance. Malka Gold and Rochelle Graubard furnished typing assistance. To all of them, our thanks.

1

Tikkun Olam

Gerald J. Blidstein

I

It might seem superfluous to make an issue of "Jewish responsibility for the welfare of society." Historians have long agreed that Judaic ideas were a formative factor in Western civilization and that Jews were central, as individuals, in its development, especially in modern times. Some have bewailed this phenomenon, and others have celebrated it—but few have denied it. The facts on the ground are that Jews and Judaism have been involved, indeed disproportionately involved, in advancing or attempting to advance the welfare of society.

I take it, then, that our question is not historical and descriptive, but normative and prescriptive. The crucial term is "responsibility." We are asking: What does Judaism, as a self-conscious entity, say? What do our normative materials teach us about this involvement? Do they impose this responsibility on us? And on a more pragmatic and specific level: How are we best advised to pursue this responsibility? What priority does it claim vis-à-vis other responsibilities and norms? We should be prepared to consider the possibility that "responsibility for the welfare of society" is not self-evident, that the interface between historical reality and normative ruling is problematic, or at least complex.

I propose to discuss *tikkun olam*,[1] "Jewish responsibility for the welfare of society at large," as the conveners of this conference define the term, in a foundational sense. By this, I mean to exclude the specific halakhic aspects of the topic as well as its practical implications for any given Jewish community in the world. I hardly intend to diminish the significance of either of these parameters. Rather, I mean that a foundational discussion has to begin elsewhere and discuss issues that are not properly halakhic in the normal, concrete sense of that discipline. So, too, as regards the practical implementation of *tikkun olam*, which, while of immense import, integrates the specific and variable situation in which Jewish society finds itself politically, historically, and morally. I wish, rather, to go back to the structure and substance of our destiny itself, insofar as it concerns our responsibilities to the human community at large. I shall deal with the broad, universalistic thrust within Judaism, against the backdrop of contemporary Jewish integration into modern Western society.

The phrase, "Jewish responsibility for the welfare of society at large," is nonetheless subtly problematic, or at least suggestive, especially as it compares with the Hebrew *tikkun olam*. *Tikkun olam* assumes (as we shall see in section II) that the acting party—whether it be an individual or a community—is one with the *olam*, or the society, whose benefit he seeks. At times, this society is the Jewish community itself, in other instances, it is the general human community. I sense, though, that the phrase "Jewish responsibility for the . . . welfare of society at large" carries a different linguistic implication, that it dissociates the actor, ever so subtly, from the "society" for whom he might (or might not) be responsible, by balancing "Jewish" against "at large" while claiming that one is responsible —a term that suggests both involvement and alienation—for the other. Compare the above formulation, for example, with something like "responsibility as part of society at large," and the point becomes clear.

Now it is possible that this perception is central to the topic as a whole. Perhaps the basic issue boils down, in large measure, to the question of the relation between the people Israel and humanity as a whole, a ques-

---

[1]For the terms, see G. Blidstein, "The Import of Early Rabbinic Writings for an Understanding of Judaism in the Hellenistic-Roman Period," in *Jewish Civilization in the Hellenistic-Roman Period*, ed. S. Talmon (Sheffield: Academic Press, 1991), 64ff.

tion that is one of the most sensitive topics in modern Jewish life, and one that obviously transcends by far the topic which I am discussing here. To indulge in the imagery of R. Akiva: Do we base our identity on our being created, with mankind as a whole, in the image of God, or do we focus solely on our unique status as Sons of the Lord, ever since Sinai? Clearly, we will get different results if we consider ourselves part and parcel of the human community, or if we consider ourselves independent of it (though I must admit that different political philosophies require different degrees of responsibility even towards the group to which one belongs).

It is therefore apt to note here how Rabbi Soloveitchik dealt with this topic in his essay, "Confrontation." The Rav declared, in principle, for a "double confrontation." On the one hand, the people Israel must maintain its own unique and autonomous relationship with the God of Israel. On the other hand, the people Israel must take part in the "universal confrontation" of man with the cosmos, a theme developed as well in "The Lonely Man of Faith." Indeed, the Rav asserts that "the limited role" heretofore played by the Jewish people in that universal confrontation was a function of historical reality, not ideological choice; and he suggests that this phenomenon has been reversed in modern times.[2]

The Rav unambiguously asserted that the Jew was to particpate fully in the civilizing efforts of humanity. "Created in the image of God, we are charged with responsibility for the great confrontation of man with the cosmos"; we are "involved with the rest of mankind" in that confrontation; we "co-ordinate our efforts"; "we stand shoulder to shoulder with mankind . . . for the welfare of all."[3]

As clear and unambiguous as the Rav's discussion is, it is marked by two underlying tensions. I do not refer, of course, to the basic thesis of "Confrontation" itself—that the Jew answers to two distinct imperatives, one calling for a unique covenantal intimacy with God, the other call-

---

[2]Joseph B. Soloveitchik, "Confrontation," *Tradition* 6:2 (1964): 5–29. The explicit discussion relates primarily to technological progress, but the reality of cooperation between members of different faith communities, which provided the actual context of "Confrontation," primarily concerns political and social processes. As I have contended elsewhere, Adam I functions on a political, collective, level as well as on the more explicit technological one.

[3]"Confrontation," 20–21.

ing for a universal mutuality with all humankind. There is no ambiguity in this thesis. Rather, my point relates to the universal responsiblity of the Jew alone. It seems, on the one hand, that this responsibility originates in our identity as "human beings, sharing the destiny of Adam in his general encounter with nature," as "human beings committed to the general welfare and progress of mankind." We are not commanded, then, as Jews, but as human beings. This argues for an organic relationship with gentile humanity. Operationally, it would also mean that this responsibility is ours as individual citizens in the various polities to which we belong. Elsewhere in the essay, though, it seems that the Rav addresses the Jewish community as such, and the Jew as a member of that community (as though humanity acts through its varied communities). Operationally, then—and we must recall that "Confrontation" offers concrete guidance on the parameters of Jewish communal involvement with the gentile faith communities—it seems that the Rav speaks of a communal responsibility.

Perhaps the point is that the Jew must answer to the human imperative both as individual and as community, that both aspects of this imperative are to be heard and answered. Be this as it may, the major point remains that the Jew stands "shoulder to shoulder" with all men and women in working for the "welfare of all." It is a joint project in which all humanity participates.

The problematic nature of the interrelationship of the people Israel and humankind, even on the level of the contribution this people is expected to make towards humanity, is a basic biblical topic. The Bible, as we all know, begins on a strikingly universalistic footing, narrowing its concerns to Abraham and his family in Gen. 12; from then on, its proper subject is the destiny and experience of the Jewish people. Now it is possible to read this structure as the Bible's final word. God has either lost hope in the rest of humanity, or He has destined the people Israel to be Adam's true descendants from the very beginning.[4] For most readers, though, mankind remains present throughout the Bible (even if we exclude Wisdom literature) in at least two basic senses.

---

[4]S. Japhet, *Emunot ve-De'ot be-Sefer Divrei ha-Yamim* (Jerusalem: Magnes Press, 1977), 104–111, and see the references to Eichrodt and Von Rad in Japhet's n. 335. For a (late) midrashic expression of this position, see *Midrash Bereshit Rabbati,* ed. Ch. Albeck (Jerusalem: Mekitzei Nirdamim, 1940), 18–19.

First, the narrowing of the universalistic perspective is not the last biblical word on the subject but is rather a prelude to a different ultimate goal: the ultimate regaining of the universalistic heights in the End of Days, when humankind will all worship the God of Creation and Exodus. On the "Day of the Lord," God will once again relate to all nations. And while this encounter is largely devoted to squaring accounts with those who have persecuted the people of God, it also ushers in a period when all humankind will participate in a renewed world on both a material and spiritual level.

Second, the narrowing perspective does not necessarily reflect an abandonment of humanity, but rather a recognition that mankind can best be affected—even over a very long duration—by God's workings through a single people, Israel, and in many different ways. And so, the biblical history of the people Israel is hardly restricted to the happenings internal to the people or to its relationship with God. Abraham, founder of the people Israel, pleads for the lives of Sodom's men and women, perhaps risking his own life to do so. As Ramban describes it, God expected Abraham to plead for them, for "how could a righteous man be so cruel to his nearby neighbors as not to pity them or pray for them at all?"[5] From the very outset, Israel constantly rubs shoulders with the human world around it. This is true of the patriarchs, each in his own way: Abraham and Isaac have dealings with the rulers of Egypt and the Philistines, and Abraham and Jacob deal with prominent gentiles as individuals. Joseph is a parade example of Jewish involvement with the non-Jewish world. This pattern is even more marked when we move to the birth of the people as such. This takes place, of course, in Egypt, in a series of events that concern and involve the gentile kingdom no less (almost) than the people Israel itself. It is clear as well that both the Patriarchal history and that of the Jewish experience in and with Egypt

---

[5]It is instructive to note how differently classical commentators have understood God's motive for notifying Abraham of the imminent destruction of Sodom (thus prodding him to act). Rashi (to Gen. 18:17) cites what are in effect two distinct reasons: (1) since the land and its cities have been promised to Abraham, he must be advised of anything about to happen to it; (2) since Abraham is called "father of many nations," he must be told of what is about to happen to his sons. Rashbam develops the first, national, motif further; Ramban deepens the universalistic thrust.

are paradigmatic. They are not merely singular happenings; rather, they will be formative, collective memories serving as touchstones and cata-lysts for centuries, even as regards the nature and modality of the Jewish contribution to the human community.[6]

My discussion of Jewish responsibility for the welfare of humankind will focus, in the sections immediately following, on the spiritual wel-fare of men and women. But it is not always easy to distinguish between spiritual and material; and more to the point, the responsibility for the one can imply and entail responsibility for the other—if responsibility is also a function of care and concern, and not only a formal norma-tive requirement.

II

The Exodus—beginning with Egyptian slavery and culminating in the destruction of the hosts of Egypt in the Red Sea—has two apparent purposes. The first is to create a people through the dual experience of bondage and redemption, all the while educating the people to the en-tire process and its significance for Israel: the meaning of slavery and freedom, of God's love and concern for them, of their radical debt to God and its implications. This transformation, both political and spiritual, lies at the heart of the Exodus. Yet there is a second, albeit minor purpose, this too educational. It is to demonstrate to Egypt the power and nature of God. The history of Israel is, indeed, a stage on which the reality of God is bodied forth before the world.

Several examples will make the point. The orchestration of the Exo-dus (perhaps, indeed, the Exodus itself) is justified: "But I will harden Pharaoh's heart, that I may multiply my signs and marvels in the land of Egypt. . . . And the Egyptians shall know that I am the Lord, when I

---

[6]See, e.g., M. Greenberg, "Mankind, Israel, and the Nations in the Hebraic Heritage," in *No Man Is Alien*, ed. J. R. Nelson (Leiden: E. J. Brill, 1971), 15–40; M. Buber, "*Behirat Yisrael*," in M. Buber, *Darko shel Mikra* (Jerusalem: Mosad Bialik, 1978), 88–99. Upon completion of this essay, I reread M. Greenberg's *Al ha-Mikra ve-al ha-Yahadut* (Tel Aviv: Am Oved, 1985), 68–76, and noted that my paper resembles (recalls?) Greenberg's discussion both in thrust and in materials, though significant differences remain.

stretch out My hand over Egypt and bring out the Israelites from their midst" (Ex. 7:4–6). Similarly with the catastrophe at the Red Sea: "Then I will stiffen Pharaoh's heart and he will pursue them, that I may assert my authority against Pharaoh and all his host; and the Egyptians shall know that I am the Lord" (Ex. 14:4). Moses' insistence, therefore, that by destroying His people the Lord will be perceived by "the nations which have heard Your fame" as "powerless to bring that people into the land which He had promised them" (Num. 14: 15–16), does not merely point to a problem on the level of public relations, but to the possible derailing of God's pedagogic purpose in history, or at least a fundamental challenge to that purpose.

This pattern is, I believe, writ large and in varied ways in biblical literature. At the outset, the divine strategy seems successful: "For we heard how the Lord dried up the waters of the Sea of Reeds for you when you left Egypt. . . . When we heard about it, we lost heart . . . for the Lord your God is the only God in heaven above and on earth below" (Josh. 2:10–11). Early Israelite history has apparently fulfilled its preordained purpose, educating the peoples of Canaan to the singularity of God. (Of course, God's punishment of His people for their evil ways could have much the same demonstrative power.)

But this early success—beginner's luck, as it were—fades; or so it seems from an Israelite perspective. Israel appeals to God on the basis of the same Mosaic logic but with additional pathos:

Do not hold our former iniquities against us . . .
Save us and forgive our sin,
    for the sake of Your name.
Let the nations not say, "Where is their God?" . . .
Pay back our neighbors sevenfold
    for the abuse they have flung at You, O Lord. (Ps. 79:8–12)

O God, do not be silent; . . .
For Your enemies rage. . . .
They plot craftily against Your people. . . .
Cover their faces with shame
    so that they seek Your name, O Lord. . . .
May they know
    that Your name, Yours alone, is the Lord,
    supreme over all the Earth. (Ps. 83:2–19)

The logic has not changed. If God saves His people, He demonstrates His reality and power to the world; if He abandons them to their enemies, His reality is denied. God, so to speak, desecrates His name and foils His own purposes.

In all this, God's name is spread among mankind, ultimately, by God Himself, using the history of Israel as His medium. "Praise the Lord, all you nations; / extol Him, all you peoples, / for great is His steadfast love toward us; / the faithfulness of the Lord endures forever" (Ps. 117:1–2).

This pattern, Harry Orlinsky has argued, lies at the heart even of all the passages (which were to have so different a modern career!) in which the people Israel are described as a "light unto the nations." The full context of these prophecies indicates that their point is that God's redemption of the people signals His justice and goodness to all humankind, not that Israel is itself a beacon of light.[7] Of course, I shall have to return to other passages of redemption, such as the messianic Isaiah 2, which suggest a much more dynamic role for Israel and/or its leaders; but the basic point is well made.

These thoughts lead rather quickly to the instructive, perhaps sobering realization that—as Avraham Holz wrote—the Bible knows of Israel's ability to desecrate God's name in the world, but not of our ability to directly sanctify His name.[8] See how carefully Lev. 22:32—the classic text of *kiddush ha-Shem*—is phrased: "You shall not profane My holy name, that I may be sanctified in the midst of the Israelite people. . . ." Man can profane God's name directly; but he sanctifies that name only indirectly, by not profaning it.

---

[7]H. Orlinsky, "'A Light Unto the Nations,' A Problem in Biblical Theology," *Seventy-Fifth Anniversary Volume of the J.Q.R.* (Philadelphia: Jewish Quarterly Review, 1967), 409–428. Orlinsky's position dovetails fully with that of the traditional medieval commentaries—see Rashi, Radak, Mezudot, to the verses discussed. The same point had been made in broader terms by Y. Kaufmann, *Toledot ha-Emunah ha-Yisra'elit*, 8 (Jerusalem: Mosad Bialik, 1956), 97, 103, 116, 151, and especially 154–155 (c.f. *Shir Ha-Shiriōm Rabbah*). For another example of how exegesis reflects ideology, see the discussion of *berakhah* in section IX.

[8]A. Holz ("Kiddush Hashem and Hillul Hashem," *Judaism* 10:4 [1961]: 360–367), who also cites earlier work in this direction, and deals with the single counter-example of Num. 27:14. See as well, Is. 8:13; and J. Milgrom, *Leviticus 1–16* (New York: Doubleday [Anchor Bible], 1991), 601–604.

This point is made more dramatically by Ezekiel. Ezekiel first describes the effect of Israel's living among the nations: "But when they came to those nations, they caused My holy name to be profaned, in that it was said of them, 'These are the people of the Lord, yet they had to leave His land.' Therefore I am concerned for My holy name. . . ." It is God, then, who will redress the balance and redeem His people so as to restore His name's sanctity: "Not for your sake will I act, O House of Israel, but for My holy name, which has been profaned among the nations. . . . And the nations shall know I am the Lord . . . when I manifest My holiness before their eyes through you" (Ezek. 36:20–23). Israel does not desecrate God's name by its behavior (as is sometimes thought), but by its historical fate—even when this fate is deserved, as has been true since the Mosaic instance—and God will renew the sanctity of His name through the history of His people. Here too, it is worth noting how the terms *hillul ha-Shem/kiddush ha-Shem* function.

All this might seem a rather perverse way to introduce a discussion of the Jewish contribution to the welfare of humanity, spiritual or material. But I believe the pattern to which I call attention is significant, even if it must be modified, refined, and revised. It raises the paradoxical possibility that Israel best fulfills whatever responsibility it has for the welfare of mankind by acting in devotion and probity before the Lord, rather than by busying itself in attempting to directly affect the spiritual or material state of the world.

Occasionally, I might even say rarely, the Jewish example is not spiritual in the narrow sense of the term (though it does relate to the deepest conditions of human existence). The *Mekhilta* tells that Pharaoh feared the Israelite release from Egypt because he knew that it would demonstrate to other nations that Egyptian domination could be successfully resisted.[9] The Egyptians stand in for Rome, and the *midrash* is telling of Jewish hopes that a (successful) Bar Kokheba revolt would show the world that the Roman yoke could be thrown off, perhaps even that true worship of God militates against political subjugation. The Jew sees himself, in this case, as the political liberator of mankind. But note, once again, that all this is done by example, by humanity learning from the Jewish experience, not by the direct involvement of the people Israel.

---

[9]*Mekhilta de-Rabbi Yishma'el* to Ex. 14:5, ed. Horowitz-Rabin, (Frankfurt am Main: J. Kauffmann Verlag, 1928–31), 87.

A similar problem is suggested by the varied uses of the term *tikkun olam* itself. It is found in its most universal sense in the second half of *Aleinu,* where it refers to the renewal of the world as the Kingdom of God. This renewal is the expressed hope of our prayer, but it is God who is expected and urged to bring it about.[10] Now *tikkun olam* refers also, in the Mishnah, to the goal of halakhic legislation. And there, it clearly means activity for the good of society—activity undertaken by humanity, by the courts of the Jewish people, which are obviously fulfilling their responsibility by so doing.[11] This parallel usage is emblematic of the halakhic enterprise as a whole, which works to achieve the Kingdom

---

[10]While the usage *"le-takken olam"* is slightly ambiguous in context, I think the phrase is correctly referred to divine activity; this is the pattern of the eschatological prayers in the liturgy of the *yamim noraim* as well. The kabbalistic tradition does take the phrase to refer to human activity, to be sure, but it removes the description from the realm of the historical and refers it to man's theurgic potential in bringing about *tikkun* within the divine spheres.

Another appearance of this phrase warrants our attention, and that is the well-known Maimonidean passage in *Hilkhot Melakhim* 11, 4, which reads, "and he [that is, the messianic king described earlier] will prepare the whole world to serve the Lord . . . [this is the translation of M. Hershmann in the Yale Judaica Book of Judges (New Haven, 1949), 240, of the Hebrew: *ve-yetakken et ha-olam kulo la'avod et ha-Shem. . . .*]. The phrase, here, does describe human, historical, activity. But, as is well-known, our printed editions present a severely mutilated version [even the Mossad ha-Rav Kook edition of *Rambam la-Am* is bewildering at this point] of this passage. In the original, uncensored, version (found in manuscripts and the Constantinople printing), this expression follows a long excursus on the functions of Christianity and Islam in the divine plan of history; these have come about so as to "smooth the way for the anointed king and prepare the world . . .", and the activity of the king himself is not mentioned at all. Though the result is the outcome of human activity, Maimonides describes a process that is clearly orchestrated by God. This passage itself provides an interesting parallel to the analysis of Yehuda Halevi which I cite in section VI.

[11]Mishnah, *Gittin* 4–5:3; other forms of *tikkun*—also intra-Jewish—are then cited in *mishnayot* 4–7. The phrase *"le-takken olam"* does have a universal meaning in *Midrash ha-Gadol* to Exodus 21, 1 (M. Margaliot, ed. [Jerusalem: Mosad HaRav Kook, 1956], 452), where it describes human activity after the great deluge. This *aggadah,* which deals with the origins and legitimacy of political authority, is well worth attention, incidentally.

of Heaven subtly, gradually, step-by-step, and particular by particular. Injustices are wiped out one by one, not in one fell swoop. At the same time, we note that these *takkanot* all concern the inner workings of Jewish, not general, society.[12] Is this dual usage—God is responsible for universal reform while the Jew is responsible for his own society—paradigmatic? Or is this scheme too simplistic?

We praise God for "bringing bread out of the earth," but we know that the dirty work will be done by the farmer. On a more significant level, or at least one closer to our topic, we know that God is always described as "making peace," yet we also recall that we are commanded to work for peace, and indeed pursue it. This problem, as we now see, is pervasive; it is found in areas affecting the particularistic Jewish experience no less than in areas relating to the Jewish-gentile encounter. Often raised in the context of Maimonidean texts, it really inheres in our religious literature from a much earlier date, though without the scholastic baggage. Perhaps the basic question is whether the classic dichotomy between transcendence and immanence, between God as acting and man as acting, is really all that firm. Alternatively, perhaps the description of God as actor reflects man's humble certainty that only God can fully achieve ultimate goals—yet that man must always act in the service of these same goals. In any case, these different perspectives alternate throughout this essay, adding no little confusion, I fear, to an already complex topic.

III

And so, several other models should be brought into play at this point. Man—or the Jew—is covenanted to God, and he is also expected to imitate God. The first model—the covenantal one—stresses that man and God are partners who share a common task and commitment; it also suggests that God transfers to man's responsibility goals that He has set. The second model, imitatio dei, also posits a common ground on which man and God meet. As is well known, the attributes of God that man is commanded to emulate are those of morality—even more markedly,

---

[12]Legislation relating to gentiles, which is given in *mishnayot* 8–9, is justified differently, as being "the ways of peace," and will be discussed in section X, below.

mercy and compassion: "Just as God clothed the naked, as it is written: 'And the Lord God made garments of skins for Adam and his wife and clothed them,' so you too ought clothe the naked . . ."[13] and so on. (I recall once hearing Rabbi Soloveitchik explain that the morning blessings, *birekhot ha-shahar*, begin with our thanking God for meeting our physical needs in universal terms, so as to set out an ethical program: we, too, are obliged, this day, to clothe the naked and free the captive.) Do these models have any implications for our topic?

On the aggadic level, God clothes Adam and Eve—humanity itself; and it is this that we are obliged to imitate. *Hesed*—and of a most physical, material, kind—thus seems to be a norm that we are to concretize on a universal scale. A more specific discussion of social intervention is found in the conversation of R. Akiva and Tinius Rufus. When the Roman taunts R. Akiva that aiding the poor, in effect, undermines God's providence, which consigned the poor individual to his poverty, R. Akiva replies that God Himself would really aid the poor—"His son whom He placed in prison"—but for the fact that He wishes to allow the Jew the merit of the act.[14] Here again, *hesed* is a divine value that man is privileged to bestow. In this case, though, the universal aspect of the norm is problematic: God's sons, in context and prooftext, are

---

[13]*Sotah* 14a and parallels. One occasionally encounters other rabbinic materials that speak of Jewish involvement in the welfare of society. Thus Gen. 33:18 ("He was gracious to the city") is explicated: "Rav said, 'He instituted coinage for them'; Samuel said, 'He instituted markets for them'; R. Jonathan said, 'He instituted baths for them'" (*Shabbat* 33b). The precise meaning of these statements (as well as the motivation behind these activities) might be modified by comparison with the parallels, but the general intent is clear: Jacob brings civilization to the alien city. (From that point of view, comparison with the tannaitic discussion, which appears earlier on *Shabbat* 33b, as to the material benefits brought by Roman culture to the Land of Israel is also suggestive.) But other midrashic materials to Gen. 33:18 see Jacob as functioning in a purely Jewish context: see the continuation in *Shabbat* and especially the comments in *Bereshit Rabbah* 79:6. These materials might provide another example of the kind of rabbinic debate about Jewish activism noted at the close of this section.

[14]*Bava Batra* 10a. This summary leans heavily on the discussion of I. Twersky, "Some Aspects of the Jewish Attitude Towards the Welfare State," *Tradition* 5 (1963): 139–141.

the people Israel, and it is not at all obvious that humanity as a whole is intended, though it is possible to transfer the discussion to that plane.[15]

A substantial step in that direction was taken by Maimonides, who wrote: "it . . . appears to me that one ought treat the *ger toshav* with humanity (*derekh eretz*) and *hesed* as one does a Jew, for we are commanded to sustain them."[16] *Ger toshav* remains a difficult category, however, and not merely because of the ostensible limit on who may qualify for that status, and when—a problem that might not be as intractable as it sometimes appears. Another issue is that *ger toshav* can be defined, primarily, as a resident of the Land of Israel. The people Israel's responsibility for him might then be a function of its national, landed existence and not a universal moral obligation. If this is so, the relations between Israel and its *gerei toshav* could provide a symbol of the universal scope of the Jew's concern, not a rule for global activity. It must be admitted, though, that this last problem does not surface in halakhic discussion, and the "landed" quality of *ger toshav* does not pre-empt the category even for Rabad.[17]

Maimonides then continues to deal with the obligations legislated by the Sages as regards even pagans, obligations generated under the rubric of "the ways of peace": "One buries their dead with the dead of Israel and supports their poor among the poor of Israel." And rather than relying on the talmudic category alone, Maimonides cites a biblical prooftext:

---

[15]However, see Twersky, above.

[16]Maimonides, *Mishneh Torah, Hilkhot Melakhim* 10, 12.

[17]See, for example, the discussion of Rabbi N. Rabinowich in his edition, *Mishneh Torah im Perush Yad Peshutah, Sefer Ahavah* (Jerusalem: Feldheim, 1984): 2: 1222–1225. Meiri, as is well known, found a different way to apply this Maimonidean ruling in contemporary times. On the "landed" quality of *ger toshav*, see Rabad to *Hilkhot Avodah Zarah* 10, 6. Maimonides does not limit the application of this term to residents of the Land, to the best of my knowledge; see as well *Hilkhot Melakhim* 10, 10. Without necessarily extending the responsibility for *ger toshav* to include *gemillat hesed*, as does Maimonides, Ramban explains that we are obliged to "preserve [him] and save him from evil, so that if he is drowning in a river or buried in a landslide we work with all our might to save him, and if he is sick, we work to cure him" (Additions to *Sefer ha-Mitzvot, aseh* 16).

"For it says, 'God is good to all and His mercy is on all his creatures.'"[18] Whatever the talmudic pedigree of these regulations, they have now been assimilated to a pattern of imitatio dei, which is of universal scope.

Taken as a whole—and granting the full significance of Maimonides' joining the obligations towards the *ger toshav* with the broader concern for all humanity based on Ps. 145:9—these passages deliver an imperative that is surely relevant to our discussion. And since it seems niggardly to read Maimonides narrowly, as though he spoke of individual behavior alone, his remains an authentic call for broad Jewish involvement with the welfare of society as a whole. Naturally, though, it cannot decide either concrete questions of prudence and priority; nor can it provide any guidance to religionists who do not wish simply to be swept along by the faddish social current of the day.

This responsibility is taught on an even broader, global, level. R. Yohanan ben Zakkai said that "if God said of the stones of the altar, which neither see nor hear nor speak, but do bring peace between Israel and their father in heaven, 'You shall not wield an iron tool over them,' is not it obvious that no harm will come to one who brings peace between a man and his fellow, a man and his wife, between cities, between nations, between rulers, and between families?"[19] It is likely that this teaching reflects R. Yohanan's opposition to the revolt against Rome; yet it clearly preaches the broad virtue (if not quite the responsibility) of bringing peace between all men and even all polities.

We ought not to be surprised to learn, though, that these sentiments (or others like them) were not always acceptable or relevant. Thus, Hillel's advice that one ought be a "disciple of Aaron, loving peace and pursuing it" was explained in two subtly different ways. One version has it that "he who brings peace to the earth is praised as though he brought peace to heaven," a divine task itself. The other version says, though,

---

[18]Ps. 145:9. This principled affirmation of *darkhei shalom*, which is here anchored in the imitation of God's behavior, should be contrasted with *Hilkhot Avodah Zarah* 10:6, which restricts it to situations when the people Israel lack power and sovereignty. This latter instance, moreover, is a halakhic ruling, unlike *Hilkhot Melakhim* 10:12 (and *Hilkhot Hannukah* 4:14), in which *imitatio dei* is simply aggadic underpinning. See my discussion, "*Le-Ma'amado shel Ger Toshav be-Mishnat ha-Rambam*," *Sinai* 101 (1988): 48–49.

[19]*Mekhilta de-Rabbi Yishmael* to Ex. 20:22 (ed. Horowitz-Rabin, 244).

that a person ought to love "peace in Israel," that is, among Jews, much as Aaron loved peace "in Israel."[20] These comments do not rule each other out; yet the very difference between them, and the fact that no version gives both comments, leads me to think that their authors understood "loving peace and pursuing it" in different ways. For one, Israel's task is universal; for the other, it is national and local, basically personal—at least in the period at hand.

<h1 style="text-align:center">IV</h1>

The halakhic and aggadic meanings of *kiddush ha-Shem* go far beyond the biblical parameters I have sketched; man is given an active role in the process of sanctifying God's name, a role indicated in the new terminological construct itself.[21] But the fundamental biblical posture is retained. The Jew sanctifies God's name in the world by remaining devoted to God and His Torah, even if he must pay the greatest price—the sacrifice of life itself. Mankind is expected to learn the lesson such devotion teaches; to be impelled towards the Lord who inspires such total love in His adherents, to learn why this is so. *Kiddush ha-Shem* is not achieved only by martyrdom, of course; it comes, perhaps primarily, with the leading of an exemplary ethical life. This is even clearer in the case of its opposite, *hillul ha-Shem*, which generally means the desecration of God's name generated by the base living of those associated with Him, though the term also functions in situations where martyrdom is called for.

Yet, all in all and on a popular level, *kiddush ha-Shem* evokes the idea of martyrdom. It is worth recalling, therefore, that this term originates—probably in Maccabean times—from the Greek *marturein*, "to testify for,"

---

[20]*Avot de-Rabbi Natan*, Version B, chap. 24; *Avot de-Rabbi Natan*, Version A, chap. 12 (ed. Schechter [New York: Feldheim, 1945] p. 48). Note as well the same usage in the continuation of ADRNB, p. 49, *s.v.* "*sha'al*," where it might have a different meaning. The possibility of consistent, systemic differences between these "versions" has been discussed.

[21]See Holz, above. For a rich collection of rabbinic sources, see "*Kiddush Hashem*," *Entziklopedyah Talmudit*. See, as well, H. G. Friedman, "*Kiddush Hashem* and *Hillul Hashem*," *Hebrew Union College Annual* (Cincinnati: Hebrew Union College, 1904): 193–214.

and most likely reflects Israel's vocation of witnessing for God: "[y]ou are My witnesses, says the Lord" (Is. 43:10; 44:80).[22] The Jew testifies to the goodness of God in his life and in his death; the world is expected to pay attention, especially because it frequently provokes or invites that sacrifice. Not infrequently, too, the world is asked to learn the virtues of Judaism and, indeed, the Jewish people, because it is difficult to differ-entiate between the people and its God. Fundamentally, the Jew and his people represent God in the world.

Kiddush ha-Shem attaches itself, by and large (I would say "is parasitic upon," were the phrase not so disagreeable), to other functioning norms or standards; it is, so to speak, the "added value" generated by these norms in specific contexts. It does not create new norms, designed especially to affect the non-Jew or to instruct him. This is true even in the "hard case," when this behavior is directed at a gentile. Take the well-known story of Simeon ben Shetah's returning the precious jewel to its gentile owner, who responded, "Blessed be the Lord of Simeon ben Shetah," thus identifying his behavior with the God to Whom he was devoted;[23] or the halakhic norm that lost objects must be returned even to their idolatrous owner if God's name is thereby sanctified.[24] True, the return of lost objects, an act of *hesed*, is not required towards gentiles, and is done—in the last case at least—for its pedagogic effect. Nonetheless, the return of lost objects is part and parcel of Jewish morality; it is not a norm invented purely for its educational value.

It is worth probing this point a bit further. What are the bounds of *kiddush ha-Shem*? Can it require or justify behavior that is otherwise counter to halakhic standards? Is it an autonomous value? And, to sharpen the question (and make its contemporary relevance obvious!):

---

[22]S. Lieberman, *Tosefta ki-Peshutah*, 3 (New York: Jewish Theological Semi-nary, 1962), 263. See also W. H. C. Frend, *Martyrdom and Persecution in the Early Church* (New York: Anchor Books, 1967), pp. 65–67. This understand-ing of Jewish responsibility as a form of witnessing (exemplifying Is. 43:12) is indeed found in *Va-Yikra Rabbah* 6, 5 (ed. M. Margaliot [Jerusalem: Ministry of Education, 1953], 142).

[23]*J. T. Bava Metzia* 2, 5. The *tanna*, it is said, did not want to be taken for a barbarian ("*barbaros*")—an interesting acknowledgement of a universal moral standard.

[24]Maimonides, op. cit., *Hilkhot Gezelah ve-Avedah* 11:3.

Ought *kiddush ha-Shem* to generate behavior that is valued largely by the gentile? I think these questions—honed further—are worth additional research; I do not claim to have a definitive answer. *Kiddush ha-Shem* does, obviously, require the sacrifice of life, when otherwise the effective norm would be *va-hai ba-hem*, "You shall live by them." And, in the second example given above, return of a lost object to an idolator is, for Maimonides at least, a forbidden act ("for you thereby strengthen the arms of the wicked of the world"), unless *kiddush ha-Shem* is achieved.[25] It would seem, then, that *kiddush ha-Shem* does overrule other normative standards. But we have also noted that in the cases cited, it is not the only operative standard. On the contrary: it supports or gives additional weight to norms that already exist within the tradition, whether it is the return of lost objects, or the specific *mitzvot* for which life is being sacrificed. It redistributes value within the system; it does not import a totally alien standard, even if God's name would be sanctified thereby. In a sense, this is coherent with the logic of *kiddush ha-Shem* itself, which ultimately refers to the devotion of the Jew to God through His Torah, which remains a stable standard of the good.

Despite the attractiveness of this formulation, I am not sure that it is not a bit glib, or pat. The distinctions, even in the cases cited, are rather fine. The identity of "alien standards" is also a rather fine judgement. Certainly, more research would be necessary in order to form a definitive opinion.[26]

---

[25]The full Maimonidean statement is most instructive: "But if he returns it in order to sanctify God's name, so that Israel should be praised and all should know that they are honest—that is praiseworthy." Two further points can be made about this text: (a) the strengthening and appreciation of the people Israel's standing is frequently a central aspect of *kiddush ha-Shem*; (b) in this context, the strengthening of this status counters the dysfunctional "strengthening of the arms of the wicked" and allows the return of the lost object.

[26]A suggestive instance is found in the opinion of R. Asher, *Bava Kamma* 10, 14. According to talmudic law, the testimony of two witnesses is necessary in order to take money from a defendant; consequently, a Jew may not testify as a single witness against another Jew in a gentile jurisdiction which would take the money on the basis of his testimony alone. However, R. Asher rules that he may so testify if a gentile made him a witness to a transaction for that purpose. This ruling is based on the value of *kiddush ha-Shem* in these circumstances,

The *aggadah* provides a provocative, somewhat atypical case in telling of King David's turning over seven of Saul's children for execution by the Gibeonites, who had been sinned against by Saul. This was done though it involved having the children suffer for the sins of the father and, eventually, allowing their corpses to hang unburied—violations of Jewish ethics and scriptural norms both. The talmudic justification is that it was done as *kiddush ha-Shem*—to demonstate to the Gibeonites, and to other prospective *gerim*, how justice would be done for their benefit, even at the expense of a royal family. But it is clear that the "justice" done would not be justified by Jewish criteria, which it in fact violated.[27] If value is merely being "redistributed" here, it is being done in a rather radical and unsettling way. I recall an interesting point of historical fact made by Mordekhai Breuer in his book on Frankfort Orthodoxy. For Breuer, periods that see greater rapprochement (or attempts at such) between Jews and their gentile neighbors see more reliance on *kiddush ha-Shem* as an operative halakhic category.[28] This observation, if true, has very interesting implications.

V

A more direct mode of Jewish responsibility for the welfare of humanity—still remaining within the parameters of spiritual, cultural, welfare— might be found in the idea of *giyyur*, that is, conversion or proselytism. Prima facie, at least, it would seem that the people Israel undertakes, in this context, to teach the way of God, the *mitzvot*, to mankind. But here too, a more careful examination of the topic indicates that matters are not so straightforward or simple.

I shall focus on several different but related issues. Is the people Israel responsible for the process? Is it expected to induce it actively?

---

though money is being transferred contrary to Jewish law through his testimony. To be sure, matters of civil law can be handled with greater flexibility than other topics, yet this ruling is suggestive.

[27]*Yevamot* 79a.

[28]M. Breuer, *Edah u-Dyukenah* (Jerusalem: Merkaz Zalman Shazar, 1991). One instance of this point is found on pp. 223–224; I am not presently able to locate the broader generalization.

Or, conversely, is the Jewish people to receive others who wish to adopt the teachings of our tradition, even teaching that tradition to gentiles who initiate the process—but no more? Are Jews those who "bring" the Torah to humanity by simply having accepted it at Sinai, thus providing for its entry into the world and its continuous presence in that world? Are they those who, going one step further, are responsible for the dissemination of that Torah in the world, culminating in the conversion of humanity? Or are they only to be ready to process and eager to embrace those gentiles who wish to adhere to the Torah, which is accessible in principle to all mankind? Attitudes and opinions on this topic are actually more varied that is commonly assumed.

One can speak of gentile acceptance of *mitzvot* in two distinct contexts. There is, of course, "conversion" as commonly used to designate entry into the Jewish people and acceptance of all 613 *mitzvot*. But there are also the seven basic *mitzvot* of Noahide law.[29] I do not think, however, that the Jewish people bears fundamental responsibility (or receives fundamental credit) for the bringing of Noahide law to humanity, at least from a normative point of view.[30] Biblical *peshat* presents these laws as known to early mankind, which is punished for their violation, as were, for example, the generation of the flood for its violence and the people of Sodom for their social vices. *Hazal* derive these commands midrashically from God's first words to Adam, stressing, as it were, that one is not human if they have not been heard. Even the halakhic reception of the gentile into the category of *ger toshav* by a body of Jewish scholars does not undermine this claim, as "reception" is a fairly passive act and, more significantly, *ger toshav*—who lives in the Land of Israel, impinges directly on Jewish existence.

The true issue at hand, rather, relates to conversion to Judaism. And here, as I have indicated, matters are far from simple. One must sort out different opinions, as well as remain aware of the impact of historical circumstance on actual experience. Let me say at the outset that, contrary to much popular opinion, contrary to many many centuries of historical

---

[29]The seven commands include the bans on murder, idolatry, incest and adultery, eating a limb torn from a living creature, blasphemy, robbery, and the command to institute law.

[30]This presentation is rather non-Maimonidean; a Maimonidean perspective is provided in section VI.

practice, and contrary to what the reader may expect given the way I have developed the overall topic until this point, it seems that the people Israel was expected, by some, to take an active role in the conversion of mankind. The question posed to those who held that position is: Do they intend proselytism, an actual mission to the gentiles? For others, of course, even that question does not arise.

It will be useful here, I believe, to distinguish between aggadic and halakhic perspectives. The "activist" perspective is developed in some (not all!) aggadic materials; it is not developed, so far as I know, in halakhic discussions. Now I do not at all wish to maintain that *aggadah* and *halakhah* are two hermetically sealed categories. On the contrary; one finds frequent instances where the boundary is permeable, where ideas flow in both directions. I do not refer to subterranean connections or influences, to the organic (but merely implied) interrelations of the normative and the axiological—these are legion. Rather, I refer to the actual utilization of aggadic materials as base for halakhic rulings. An example or two will make my meaning clear: the rule that one does not plead for the *mesit* is derived from God's not pleading the primeval serpent's innocence; the height of a *sukkah* is derived from a discussion of how high God hovered above Sinai; and the *sukkah's* very character is related to the nature of the *sukkot* in the desert wanderings—were they physical constructs or "clouds of glory."[31] On our question, how-ever, *aggadah* and *halakhah* do not impinge on each other. For talmudic *halakhah*, the people Israel accepts the proselyte who approaches; for some talmudic *aggadot*, however, a much more active role is projected.

Perhaps the richest lode of teachings in this connection concern the activities of Abraham and Sarah. These teachings, significantly, are them-selves varied; they range from the characterization of Abraham and Sarah as active missionizers, to their portrayal as Jews who attract others to the faith by their radiant example, to their description as waiting to accept gentiles who turned to them. The student ought to approach these materials carefully and read with sensitivity; subtle distinctions could be intended by their variety. Indeed, I suspect that a fuller study than the brief sketch I can give would be very rewarding.

---

[31]*Sanhedrin* 29a; *Sukkah* 4b–5a; *Sukkah* 11b–12a. Upon analysis, these three instances will be found to be methodologically different, but their general im-port is clear; and more examples could be given.

A cluster of exegetic and historiographic traditions does describe how Abraham and Sarah actively pursued the potential proselyte, suggesting that they ought to be seen as models for emulation. *"Thou shalt love the Lord thy God:* Make Him beloved to humanity, as did our father Abraham in the matter referred to in the verse, 'And the souls they had gotten [lit., "made"] in Haran.' But is it not true that if all the creatures in the world were to convene in order to create a soul, they would not be able to do so? Hence we learn that Abraham converted people, thus bringing them under the wings of the *Shekhinah.*"[32]

It could be argued, of course, that even this statement merely describes how Abraham radiated a spirituality that attracted men and women to the worship of God, and then accepted them as Jews. But the force of the active verbs ("made beloved," "converted"), indeed the very praise heaped on Abraham for these conversions, belie this reduced understanding. So, too, does the story of how Abraham and Sarah fed hungry travellers and then directed their thankfulness to God, the ultimate source of food; Abraham and Sarah are not polemical missionaries, but they do consciously direct men and women to God.[33] Finally, we should note that Abraham's activity is cited in *Hazal* as normative; it serves as model for the new reading of *ve-ahavta* as *ahavehu* ("make Him beloved"), a biblical norm that commands every Jew. This midrashic understanding is also used as an explanatory gloss to the somewhat vague Mishnah in *Avot* 1:13: "Be of the disciples of Aaron . . . loving mankind and bringing them nigh to the Torah." And, according to *Avot de Rabbi Natan,* at least, Hillel the Elder did take this *mishnah* in its activistic, Abrahamic, sense.[34] So the behavior of Abraham and Sarah was not left completely in the realm of legend.

---

[32]*Sifrei* to Deuteronomy 6:5, sec. 32 (trans. R. Hammer [New Haven, 1986], p. 59). In the version given in ADRN (version A, chap. 12; version B, chap. 26), Sarah is mentioned along with Abraham: he converts the men and she converts the women. In *Yoma* 86a Abbaye takes the imperative to "make God beloved through you" as independent of the norm of conversion.

[33]*Tanhuma, Lekh Lekha* 12.

[34]ADRNA, chap. 12 (I take *le-kape'ah et ha-beriyyot* in the sense of vigorous argument, as in the phrase: *le-kapeheni be-halakhot*); ADRNB, chap. 26 (it is not fully clear that Hillel encountered gentiles in the story told; the question would also be whether the phrase *le-hakhnis tahat kanfei ha-shamayyim* can also refer to the education of Jews, as it apparently does in *Tosefta Horayot* 2, 7 [ed. Zukermandel, Trier: Lintz, 1881, p. 476]).

These traditions notwithstanding, talmudic *halakhah* did not adopt
an activist policy on conversion. It did not require or even recommend
that Jews missionize among their neighbors (though it did teach that the
process of conversion, once begun, should not be unnecessarily prolonged, lest the convert change his mind!); and this stance probably
describes the overall historical situation as well.[35] This reticence could
be rooted in pragmatic considerations. Most likely, it expresses principled
preference as well. If one accepts the position that the righteous among
the gentiles have a share in the World to Come, then the altruistic pressure to convert them is reduced; indeed, gentile spirituality and morality are themselves valued. Furthermore, conversion itself is sometimes a
mixed blessing, as it confers responsibilities (and all that entails) as well
as privileges, and perhaps the conscientious Jew ought to do no more
than warmly receive the gentile who wishes to adhere, but not pursue
him. One can find many *aggadot*, too, that describe the Jewish people as
attracting the gentile implicitly, by radiating goodness and spirituality,
but no more.[36]

Some of this material concerns Abraham himself. Thus, the famous
teaching that God directed Abraham to leave his homeland and travel

---

[35]This topic has been discussed extensively. For a recent summary, see S. J.
D. Cohen, "Was Judaism in Antiquity a Missionary Religion?," in *Jewish Assimilation, Acculturation and Accommodation*, ed. M. Mor (Lanham, Maryland:
University Press of America, 1992), 14–23. L. H. Feldman's extensive survey
("Proselytism by Jews in the Third, Fourth, and Fifth Centuries," *Journal for the
Study of Judaism* 24:1 [1993]: 1–58), also proceeds on the assumption "that we
are speaking not of active organized missionary activities by Jews but rather of
readiness to accept proselytes" (p. 4); at the same time, even he speaks of "Jewish outreach," which implies active—if not necessarily organized—initiative,
by Jews (though not necessarily by rabbis). Note the carefully honed teaching
of R. Eliezer in *Mekhilta de-Rabbi Yishmael* to Ex. 18:6 (ed. Horowitz-Rabin,
p. 193): ". . . when a person comes to you and wishes to convert, and he comes
sincerely, bring him close and do not push him away."

[36]See, e.g., *Sifrei* to Deut. 33:18, sec. 354 (trans. Hammer, pp. 370–371):
"They [the nations] would . . . go up to Jerusalem and observe the people of
Israel worshiping only one God and eating only one kind of food. . . . So they
would say, 'There is no better nation for us to cling to than this' . . . the nations
would not budge . . . until they became proselytes."

to the Land of Israel so that "your name might become great in the world," much as one spreads the odor of a perfume, is most suggestive.[37] On one level, it is merely Abraham's reputation that is at stake. More profoundly, though, one notes that Abraham's reputation is magnified by the example of his good deeds, the "perfume" of his life. What is God's purpose in magnifying Abraham's reputation? Is it, perhaps, intended to attract others to him and his faith? It could well be that some of the midrashic teachings on the *Akedah* ought to be read in much the same way.

The virtue of exile—for Abraham was exiled, in a sense, from his father's home to the Land of Israel—probably reflected the self-understanding of the Jewish people in their historic exile. But the point was also made explicitly: "God dispersed the people Israel among the nations only so that proselytes should adhere to them . . . for a person sows a *se'ah* only so that he should reap many *kor*."[38] The Jews are not described as missionaries, to be sure; it is the gentile convert who joins them. The "responsibility" for conversion, then, is with the gentile—or with God. But Israel is expected to radiate a light that attracts, at the least.

A few talmudic comments hostile to conversion and suspicious of the convert do exist, but they are precisely that—a small proportion of the overall material. Most discussions suggest care in conversion, to be sure, but are nonetheless happy—indeed, eager at times—to welcome the convert into his new people. The experience of Ruth, who sought out Naomi and Boaz, their people and faith, and was received by them in love and admiration, is the paradigm.[39]

---

[37]*Bereshit Rabbah* 39:2. A most interesting instance is found in the Yemenite *Midrash ha-Gadol*. Whereas *Bereshit Rabbah* 39:7 has Abraham fearful of leaving his father Terah for the land of Canaan because of the *hillul ha-Shem* attached to abandoning an aged parent, *Midrash ha-Gadol* to Gen. 12, 1 (ed. M. Margaliot [Jerusalem: Mosad HaRav Kook,1967], p. 216), has him fearful of people saying, "This is he who brings men and women under the wings of the *Shekhinah* [i.e., converts them], and now he abandons his aged father and goes off."

[38]*Pesahim* 87a. See also *Menahot* 110a.

[39]See B. J. Bamberger, *Proselytism in the Talmudic Period* (Cincinnati: Hebrew Union College Press, 1939), esp. 149ff and 274ff.

VI

The perspective developed thus far, according to which the Jewish people does not bear direct "responsibility for the welfare of mankind," was challenged significantly by two major figures even before modern times. I refer to Yehuda ha-Levi and, more significantly, Rambam. Both portray a Jewish people actively involved—though to varying degrees—in ameliorating the spiritual welfare of humanity. Maimonides clearly makes this a matter of normative concern.

(A)

Yehuda ha-Levi: There is, first and most strikingly, the very story-frame of the *Kuzari* itself. This book not only includes the conversion of the king, but presents the Jewish sage as an active partner in the process. Formally, of course, the *haver* merely defends the Jewish faith and its people; moreover, he does not initiate the dialogue but is invited by the king to respond—and who can refuse a royal invitation? But even if there is some truth to these caveats, the fact remains that the book presents the king's conversion as a desirable goal, present from the very outset in his dream-vision; and the sage argues his ultimately proselytizing case vigorously and uncompromisingly. Without the Jewish sage—who continues, as it were, the process initiated by God Himself—it is doubtful if the king would have found his way to Judaism and God.

The second point lies in a single, but powerful and broadly conceived text:

> . . . God has a secret and wise design concerning us, which should be compared to the wisdom hidden in the seed which falls into the ground, where it undergoes an external transformation into earth, water, and dirt, without leaving a trace for him who looks down upon it. It is, however, the seed which transforms earth and water into its own substance, carries it from one stage to another, until it refines the elements and transfers them into something like itself. . . . The original seed produced the tree bearing fruit resembling that from which it had been produced. In the same manner the law of Moses transforms each one who honestly follows it, though it may externally repel him. The nations merely serve to introduce and pave the way for the ex-

pected Messiah, who is the fruition, and they will all become His fruit. Then, if they acknowledge him, they will become one tree. . . .[40]

This is an extremely complex passage, and the student is hard pressed to tease out a consistent reading. (Luckily, we need not interpret it all.) From a literary point of view, the parable has many echoes, among them the talmudic teaching cited earlier about the divine purpose of the dispersion of Israel in the world, a teaching that also suggested the travail implicit in the career of a seed and explicit in the dispersion of a people. For my purposes, suffice it to say that Israel is the seed that, though seemingly reduced to nothingness—let us not forget ha-Levi's national agenda—is actually the catalyst, if not more, of all future development. It transforms all else. Now ha-Levi does not make it clear how this happens. Are we to take the parable of the seed literally, in which case Israel "acts" by its mere presence, but not consciously? Certainly, the nations do have a conscious choice to make. One suspects that these questions are not of much interest to ha-Levi. What he does want to assert is that the Jewish people, which he elsewhere describes as "the heart" of the human organism, is the vital spiritual center of mankind, the source through which spiritual development will emerge, as it has until now (and as the *haver* has functioned for the king, by and large). So even though ha-Levi does not prescribe, with some exceptions, how the Jewish people is expected to fulfill this specific role, he does offer an interpretive key to the historical process—past, future, and present. The last, of course, is of more than theoretical interest. In the context of our topic we should recall, though, that social ethics do not seem a very high priority for ha-Levi, who suggests that they are a universal value without which even a gang of thugs could not exist. The image of the seed is meant for other, more spiritual, realities.

I know full well that there are other passages in Halevi that virtually rule out the possibility of any transformative role for the people Israel. These—and they are many—present a rigidly hierarchical model of existence, one in which Israel is as inherently different from the rest of humankind as humankind is from the rest of the animal kingdom. This

---

[40]*Kuzari* 4:23 (trans. H. Hirschfeld [London: Routledge and Sons, 1905], 226–227). See also *Kuzari* 2:16.

analogy to different levels of being, an analogy which is made in different forms throughout the book, not only posits superiority of some sort; it also suggests a permanent arrangement. It is seemingly impossible to square these passages with the parable of the seed. Improbable as it may seem, Halevi may sometimes have conceived of his hierarchical models as more flexible, at least in a messianic future, than would appear. Whatever the inconsistencies, the parable of the seed also has its place in the *Kuzari*.

(B)

Maimonides: Maimonides' construction of world history has been dealt with in several studies, and adding another discussion here would, in any case, take me far beyond the scope of this essay. I shall focus, then, on that topic closest to my concern: the Jewish responsibility for the welfare of mankind. In contrast to ha-Levi, Maimonides places his attitudes in a normative context; he speaks in terms of obligation, and of how the Jew is expected to achieve his goal. At the same time, we are not at a complete loss for an expression of Maimonidean vision. Maimonides' son, R. Abraham, explains Ex. 19:6 ("you shall be to Me a kingdom of priests and a holy nation") as follows: "You shall be, through observance of my Torah, leaders of the world. You will be to them as the priest to his flock. The world will follow after you, imitating your acts and walking in your path. This is the explanation of the verse which I received from my father and master, *z'l*."[41]

Israel, then, is priest to the world. These are not Maimonides' own words, of course, and we do not know in what context his comment was made, exegetic or homiletic. Nonetheless, these words do provide an adequate grounding for the normative texts. Israel does have a mission, though the Maimonidean reading suggests that the Jew does not actively engage his gentile neighbor, but is rather a model for emulation.

But Maimonides' activist perspective is expressed in a range of texts. He asserts that "Moses . . . commanded . . . [us] to compel all human beings to accept the commandments enjoined on the descendents of Noah"; even assuming that this broad comment is to be taken in con-

---

[41]*Perush ha-Torah le-Rabbi Avraham ben ha-Rambam*, ed. A. Weisenberg (London: S. D. Souson, 1959), 2:35.

text as referring to gentiles living in the Land of Israel, as I have argued elsewhere, the Maimonidean posture is still unusual, both in its specific provisions and in its broad statement of ideological policy, a policy which dovetails with the well-known Maimonidean provision that Noahides are to accept their law as given through the Torah of Moses. Maimonides also rules that it is a Jewish court—or a court appointed by Jewish authority—that enforces obedience. Though this, too, presumes a situation of Jewish power—though not necessarily a Jewish polity in the Land of Israel—its ideological thrust is clearly to create Jewish responsibility for gentile morality.[42]

Although Noahide law is to be enforced in the Land of Israel and perhaps wherever possible, Maimonides sees teaching and persuasion as the mode by which Jewish responsibility is expressed in the world as a whole. Indeed, he does not speak so much of "responsibility" as of the irrepressible overflow of love. Citing the rabbinic understanding of Abraham's activities in drawing humanity closer to God, Maimonides writes: ". . . this Commandment [to love God] . . . includes an obligation to call upon all mankind to serve Him and to have faith in Him. For just as you praise and extol anybody whom you love, and call upon others to love him, so, if you love the Lord . . . you will undoubtedly call upon the foolish and ignorant to seek knowledge of the truth which you have already acquired. . . . [J]ust as Abraham, being a lover of the Lord . . . by the power of his conception of God, and out of his great love for Him, summoned mankind to believe, you . . . must love Him as to summon mankind unto Him."[43]

---

[42]*Hilkhot Melakhim* 8:10. See my "Holy War in Maimonidean Law," in *Perspectives on Maimonides*, ed. J. Kraeamer (Oxford: Oxford University Press, 1991), 209–220. The other, not unlikely perspective, is presented in D. Hartman, "Pilosofeyah ve-Halakhah ke-Shtei Derakhim . . . ," in *Mehkerei Yerushalayim be-Mahshevet Yisra'el* 7 (1988): 319–338. For enforcement of Noahide Law, see *Hilkhot Melakhim* 10, 11 (and compare Nahmanides to Gen. 34:12). Maimonides here empowers *beit din shel Yisra'el* (a court of the people Israel) to enforce these laws, lest society be destroyed (*yeshahet ha-olam*). All this does not seem to necessarily take place in the Land of Israel.

[43]Maimonides, *Sefer ha-Mitzvot, aseh* 3 (trans. C. Chavel, *The Commandments*, I [London: Sorcino Press, 1967], p. 4). This perspective is not repeated in the Code, though note *Hilkhot Avodah Zarah* 1:4 on Abraham. See A. Feintuch, *Pekudei Yesharim* (Jerusalem: Maaliyot Press, 1992), 80–82; H. Kreisel, "Maimonides' View of Prophecy," *Da'at* 13 (Summer, 1984): xxi–xxvi.

From a formal point of view, it is love—the acquisition of knowledge—
that is commanded; Maimonides argues that the lover of God will of
necessity summon others to Him. But on the concrete level, which is
what interests me here, Maimonides asserts that the Jew is expected to
promote the knowledge of God actively among all men and women.

Maimonides does not specify how this is to be done, beyond saying
that the Jew is to "call upon the foolish to seek knowledge of the truth"
and to "summon mankind unto Him"; in the analogy given, he speaks
in slightly different terms of the "praise" of the beloved to be found in
the mouth of the true lover. It is clear, in any case, that Maimonides
expects the Jew to take an active role in the spread of true belief. This
thrust is found elsewhere in *Sefer ha-Mitzvot*, where he writes that the
purpose of *kiddush ha-Shem* is that we "make this true religion known
among the multitudes, fearlessly. . . .";[44] in that instance, martyrdom is
the form this testimony takes. Interestingly, Maimonides does not return to this theme in *Mishneh Torah*.

Of no less interest is the actual content of the Maimonidean mission.
Maimonides does not urge the Jew to spread the Jewish religion among
mankind; he speaks consistently of Jewish responsibility for mankind's
beliefs and spirituality. This is systemically appropriate, inasmuch as the
love that impels the mission and is expressed through it is rooted in
knowledge. But it could even be the case that Maimonides had a positive attitude towards proselytizing in the classic sense (much as his positive attitude towards sincere converts is well documented). Discussing
the teaching of Bible to gentiles, he distinguished between Christians
and Muslims; Christians, he argued, accept the textual integrity of the
Tanakh, and so no danger can come of teaching them. Indeed, "it is
permissible to teach them the *mitzvot* and draw them to our religion."[45]

So far, I have discussed Maimonides' view of the spiritual responsibilities of the Jew. He might well have thought that the responsibility of
the people Israel extends beyond the spiritual. Describing the functions

---

[44]Ibid., *aseh* 9.

[45]Maimonides, *Responsa*, ed. J. Blau, I (Jerusalem: MeKitzei Nirdamin, 1958),
no. 148, pp. 282. See my *Ekronot Mediniyyim be-Mishnat ha-Rambam* (Ramat
Gan: Bar-Ilan University Press, 1983), 227–233, and M. Kellner, *Maimonides
on Judaism and the Jewish People* (Albany: SUNY Press, 1991).

of the king, Maimonides writes, "His sole aim and thought should be to uplift the true religion, to fill the world with righteousness, to break the arm of the wicked, and to fight the battles of the Lord."[46] Note the second phrase in the list: "to fill the world with righteousness," a phrase that implies the active pursuit of justice on a global scale. And since Maimonides is speaking of a political leader, not of a prophet or sage, it does not seem likely that the king is functioning as an educator. In a sense—certainly on a pragmatic level—this passage is part of a messianic ideal; indeed, we shall see that this motif is fully developed in the messianic context. At the same time, both literary structure and the very content of the text itself indicate that Maimonides describes the normative goals and responsibilities of Jewish politics in the pre-messianic world.

VII

Sooner or later, of course, the messianic theme must surface, as it just has in passing. It might seem likely for the "Jewish responsibility for the welfare of society" to be germane to Jewish messianic efforts, efforts to improve the world so that universal redemption follows. This assumes that the people Israel is entrusted with the bringing of the messiah through human means in history and that this task will be accomplished, in part, through the improvement of the peoples of the world. The first claim has been, historically, a matter of great debate and is currently held by some elements within religious Zionism; in any case, it is never conceived of—except in more radical versions, one of which I shall note further on—as the total responsibility of the people, or fully within their ability. But even this messianic activity is, on the whole, inner-directed: greater piety, more social justice ("Zion shall be redeemed with justice . . ."), or even the political renaissance of the people.

Rather, if one speaks of the "Jewish responsibility for the welfare of the world" as a messianic category, it is literally that: the exercise of Jewish responsibility as a universal category in an already redeemed world and as part of that reality. Here, one is on solid biblical ground:

---

[46]Maimonides, op. cit., *Hilkhot Melakhim* 4:10; and see my *Ekronot*, 97–102.

And it shall come at the end of days
That the mountain of the Lord's house shall be
    established as the top of the mountains . . .
And all nations shall flow unto it.
And many peoples shall go and say:
"Come ye, and let us go up to the mountain
    of the Lord, And He will teach us of His ways. . . ."
For out of Zion will go forth the law,
And the word of the Lord from Jerusalem.
And He shall judge between the nations,
And shall decide for many peoples. . . . (Is. 2:1–4)

This passage speaks, it is true, of God's activity in a time of redemption: *He* will teach us. Perhaps, too, even the Torah, which goes forth
from Zion, is spread not by Israel, but by God (though we are accustomed
to the human teaching of Torah). But we also read:

And it shall come to pass in that day,
That the root of Jesse, that standeth for an
    ensign of the peoples,
Unto him shall the nations seek,
And his resting place shall be glorious. (Is. 11:10)

Certainly, Maimonides portrays the messianic king as fulfilling this
universal teaching role: "That king who will arise from the seed of
David will be of greater wisdom than Solomon; and a great prophet
approaching Moses our teacher. . . . [A]nd all the nations will come to
hear him. . . ."[47]

But this motif is not truly relevant here. The role of Israel in a redeemed reality is not the topic, much as it is not our situation. We do
not live in a redeemed world, and that makes all the difference. Our
present concern ought to be, perhaps, with our own needs and goals—
tasks more than large enough for our energies—much as these are the
concerns of all other peoples. The fact that the world community is always
described as seeking Israel's guidance in these texts is simply a symptom
of the gap between that projected time and our own, an indication of
how a redeemed world will differ from the one we now inhabit.

---

[47]Ibid., *Hilkhot Teshuvah* 9:2.

On the other hand, it could be that all messianic descriptions are meant as guides to activity in the here-and-now, that Israel embodies the messianic germ in historical time, for the people Israel must fulfill the tasks described as being God's, that it is His prophet and messenger. This position was articulated most forcefully by Steven Schwarszchild: "If . . . you transform into actuality all of God's will for the world—this is, or this causes, the Messianic advent." Menachem Kellner has pithily summarized (and moderated) his teacher's position: "to make the Messiah's coming possible, we must act now as if the Messiah has already come."[48] If I may be allowed a Maimonidean analogy, let us recall Rambam's view of *olam haba* as a spiritual possibility—for this life as well as the "next," after death.

Schwarszchild's doctrine, which was based on a rich (though obviously debatable) interpretation of both Jewish sources and neo-Kantian idealism, demanded and was in fact translated into a broad program of social involvement on a global level. The idea is found as well in more pedestrian thinkers, where it comes to resemble the liberal Christian notion of the Social Gospel. Thus Solomon Schechter: "For if the disappearance of poverty and suffering is a condition of the kingdom of the Messiah, or in other words, of the kingdom of God, all wise social legislation . . . must help towards its speedy advent." But Schechter makes it clear, in the continuation, that it is the people Israel's own fortunes—physical and spiritual alike—with which he is concerned: "Israel is the microcosm in which all the conditions of the kingdom are to find expression."[49]

Another topic that falls into the messianic problem is the case of the conversion of the gentiles, which, as Y. Yovel and A. Grossman have shown, is a definite component of the messianic vision of *ge'onim* and some medieval sages.[50] Are we to say that this phenomenon to-

---

[48]See M. Kellner, ed., *The Pursuit of the Ideal: Jewish Writings of Steven Schwarszchild* (Albany: SUNY Press, 1990), 10. The quotation from Schwarzchild is on p. 210; see also 134, 221, 248–249, and much else.

[49]S. Schechter, *Some Aspects of Rabbinic Theology* (New York: Macmillan, 1909), 114.

[50]Y. Yovel, "Ha-Nakam ve-ha-Kellalah, ha-Dam ve-ha-Allilah," *Ziyyon*, 58, 1 (1993): 45–50; A. Grossman, "Ha-Ge'ulah ha-megayyeret," *Ziyyon* 59, 2–3 (1994): 325–342. The materials cited do indicate a specifically messianic provenance. See the materials cited at the beginning of section IX, as well.

tally reflects messianic times, and does not teach us anything about Israel's responsibility in the present age? Or are we to see in this another testimony to the responsibility of Israel in all times, with the proviso that it does not necessarily imply an active posture, but perhaps only the duty of serving as an example and accepting the gentile who wishes to adhere?

VIII

The kabbalistic tradition is a most suggestive resource for our topic, and by this I refer primarily to imagery and metaphor rather than doctrine. In a sense, in fact, the doctrine might severely restrict the possibilities of the imagery, as we shall see.

In kabbalistic imagery, to put the matter simply, *keneset Yisrael* clusters organically with *Shekhinah* and *Shabbat*. Whatever other functions and meanings this structure might possess, it also communicates the idea that all these are conduits by which *shefa*, the benificent divine overflow, reaches the world and elevates it. On a popular level, this is reflected in *Lekhah Dodi*, where *Shabbat* is called *mekor ha-berakhah*, the source (much as a fountain is a "source" of the water it releases) of blessing. Other images serve much the same function; the *Shekhinah*, for example, is called *even shetiyyah*, the central stone, which nourishes the world; or the "hind," which distributes food to all creatures.[51]

Now this imagery can be interpreted in numerous ways or, more precisely, it can suggest numerous translations. What is the overflow? And what does it mean to say that it passes "through" Israel in one of her varied images?

Certainly, it is not unrealistic to see in the "overflow" all the good that reaches the world, whether spiritual, social, or physical. Describing the modality by which Israel "transmits" this "overflow" to the world, or humanity, is a more difficult task, as several interpretive strategies suggest themselves. The people of Israel could function indirectly, as an instrument used by God, so that the improvement and elevation of Israel then refracts on the world; or, it could be an active, purposeful agent. In terms already familiar to us, Israel—or the Jew—could be expected to

---

[51]See I. Tishbi, *Mishnat ha-Zohar*, 2 (Jerusalem: Mosad Bialik, 1965), 226–228.

serve as exemplar to the world, or going beyond that, to be a dynamic force, either by teaching or working for good in the world in more direct ways.

Examination of the career of this theme discloses, though, that it fre-quently functioned differently. Rather than describing Israel or the Jew as serving the destiny of mankind, it virtually reversed the equation. The presence of the *Shekhinah* in the world is exclusively due to the exis-tence of the Jewish people, to begin with; and all good that comes to the world must work through Israel, much as all physical blessing came to the world by the agency of the Temple, according to some *aggadot* (or, to choose Yehuda ha-Levi's image, different as its message might be: Israel is the heart of humanity). In a sense, an ironic sense to be sure, given historic realities, the *Shekhinah* as *matrona* is merciful and benevolent mother, but also powerful queen.

This aspect of the matter comes to the fore in some kabbalistic thought. Thus, *Sha'arei Orah* of R. Joseph Gikatilla[52] describes the people Israel (*malkhut*) as directing the "overflow" to the nations of the world, who then subject themselves to her and serve her (an interesting example of the political implications of the "mission" idea, which we shall shortly explore). Y. Tishbi's analysis of redemption in the system of the Ari, R. Isaac Luria, is even more extreme: "the presence of Israel among the nations mends the world, but not the nations of the world . . . it does not bring the nations closer to holiness, but rather extracts the holiness from them and thereby destroys their ability to exist. . . . [T]he purpose of the full redemption is to destroy the vitality of all the peoples." Even this can be understood in several ways, but when coupled with a hostile rejection of conversion, the fundamental thrust of the Ari, according to Tishbi, is to reject the idea that Israel serves to elevate the rest of humanity.[53]

---

[52]Y. Ben-Shlomo, ed., *Sha'arei Orah le-Rabbi Yisra'el Gikatilla*, I (Jerusalem: Mosad Bialik, 1981), *sha'ar* 6:215–216; and Ben-Shlomo's "Introduction," 35.

[53]I. Tishbi, *Torat ha-Ra ve-ha-Kelippah be-Kabbalat ha-Ari* (Jerusalem, 1942), 139–142. A similar perspective is found, overall, in the work of Gershom Scholem; see "The Messianic Idea in Kabbalism," in *The Messianic Idea in Juda-ism* (New York: Schocken, 1971), 46–48; *Major Trends in Jewish Mysticism* (New York: Schocken, 1941), 273ff. My appreciation to my colleague, Dr. Haviva Fedayah, who called some of these materials to my attention.

Despite all this, it seems likely that the potential of these basic images is hardly exhausted. They can, I believe, legitimately inspire a totally different—and positive—relationship between the Jew and mankind (though the superior station of the people Israel remains intact). It is possible that Rav Kook, whose description of this relationship will be noted in the next section, found some of his inspiration in these materials—understood differently.

IX

The very phrase, "the Jewish responsibility for the welfare of mankind" evokes, willy-nilly, the idea of the "Jewish mission." I assume that the proponents of "Jewish responsibility" do not wish to attach to this notion the baggage attached to the "Jewish mission," which became a total explanation or justification of Jewish existence in the modern world. Nor do they wish to adopt the assumptions underlying the non-Jewish idea of mission, I am sure. "Jewish responsibility," as it is used in our discussion, is meant to be and remains a very limited aspect of Jewish existence, normative or historical. But even acknowledging these reservations, I think it is still instructive to ponder the career and implications of the idea of a "mission"—Jewish or non-Jewish.

The doctrine of a national "mission" is a fairly pervasive idea found in both ancient and modern contexts. It is closely allied with the idea of "chosenness," and it is a common aspect of modern nationalism. I will merely note several chapter headings as a stimulus for further thought and discussion.

Two well-known and ultimately similar doctrines that embody the idea of a national mission are the ancient Roman assumption that it, as a "chosen people," was entrusted by the gods with the mission of bringing universal peace to the world and ruling it. Imperialism, indeed, is frequently conceived of as a mission. A second, more limited form of "mission" was the nineteenth-century British concept of the "white man's burden," which, of course, also mandated imperial rule. Chosenness, in both these cases, went hand in hand with the assumption of empire. It might come as a surprise to learn that the idea of Jewish chosenness, which we generally associate with duty and responsibility, was on occasion also interpreted as implying political rule. *Targum Onkelos* to Num. 24:17 asserts that Israel is destined to rule the world, and the amoraic *midrash* not infrequently claims that the people Israel will succeed Rome as the "fifth empire." This motif was hardly dominant—but neither was it an eccentricity. Political rule and spiritual superiority were not mutually exclusive; indeed they could often dovetail, and the idea that God rules through His people is also found.[54] The combination is found, in different forms, to be sure, from Second Commonwealth times through the medieval period. With this background in hand, one can read the end of Maimonides' *Hilkhot Melakhim* and its rejection of Jewish imperial ambition more perceptively.[55]

The idea of "mission" also dovetails with the idea of nationalism, especially in the modern period. Both Hans Kohn and Jacob Talmon have focussed on the close relation between these two ideas; Talmon has gone so far as to claim that it is the "sense of mission that generates national consciousness" rather than the reverse. And it is this sense that forms a basic component of "political messianism," as he argues in his book by that title.[56] Most significant for my purposes is the character and content of that mission. With virtually no exception, Talmon continues, "the mission . . . involves service to a universal ideal rather than the assertion of an exclusive national ethos."[57]

The assertion of a "Jewish mission" has taken several forms in modern Jewish history, but it could well be that all are indebted in some degree to the modern idea of nationalism (as perhaps that idea itself is indebted to Jewish notions of chosenness and mission!) or bear a functional similarity to the ancient idea of mission. This is a rather paradoxical state of affairs, of course, inasmuch as one form of the "Jewish mission" insisted on the dissolution of Jewish national existence.

---

[54]See my essay, *"La-Shilton Behartanu?"* in *Ra'ayon ha-Behirah*, ed. S. Almog (Jerusalem: Merkaz Shazar, 1991), 99–120.

[55]See my essay, *"Al ha-Shilton ha-Universali be-Hazon ha-Geulah shel ha-Rambam,"* in *Arakhim be-Mivhan Milhamah*, ed. A. Blum et al. (Jerusalem, n.d.), 155–172; and the study of Yovel cited above.

[56]H. Kohn, *The Idea of Nationalism* (New York: Macmillan, 1944), 44–45; 67, 585; J. C. Talmon, *The Unique and the Universal* (New York: George Braziller, 1965), 16, 31; *Political Messianism* (London: Secker of Warburg, 1960), 175, 242, 265, 270, 279.

[57]Talmon, *The Unique*, 16.

The most common referent of the "Jewish mission" is the idea, associated with nineteenth-century Reform, that Jews must lead a non-nationalistic diaspora existence so as to fulfill their mission, the instruction of mankind in monotheism and its ethical, humanitarian implications. (It appears that R. Samson Raphael Hirsch shared this view in its essentials, as even a reading of his *Nineteen Letters* indicates, though Hirsch spoke more of the Jew as an example than as an active instructor.) In a sense, this claim can be associated with the Maimonidean texts on the love of God and its implications (see section VI above), but this is clearly a misleading analogy. For Reform thinkers, the "idea of mission" was a way to justify the very continuation of Jewish existence, and it assumed that Jewish existence was to be led, ideally, outside the Land of Israel and without political expression. Maimonides, of course, needed no justification for Jewish existence; and *galut* was hardly his ideal. To proceed a step further, Reform "mission" functioned in much the same way that the doctrine of mission functioned generally: to justify a state of affairs encouraged for quite other reasons—as was the case with Roman rule or British imperialism.[58]

Interestingly, the critique of Reform "mission"—even the traditionalist critique—did not focus only on its abandonment of *mitzvot* but also reacted to the role it assigned the Jewish people. The Jewish people, it was argued, is not expected to undertake the spiritual reform of mankind actively; that responsibility is the proper task of God and the nations themselves. Y. M. Pines claimed that Providence worked in its own, indirect, ways; and R. David Hoffman wrote that to be a "kingdom of priests," a verse frequently enlisted by proponents of the universal Jewish mission (and understood similarly by Hirsch in his commentary to the *Humash*), meant to lead a holy life.[59] In essence, Pines and Hoffman were saying that Jewish existence is autonomously justified; the ultimate goal of such existence is not the concern of the people itself. Nor were

---

[58]See, for example, I. Schorsch, "Editor's Introduction," to H. Graetz, *The Structure of Jewish History* (New York: Jewish Theological Seminary, 1975), 14–17, and the materials cited in nn. 6–7 above.

[59]Pines' opinions on this topic are discussed by N. Rotenstreich, *Ha-Mahshavah ha-Yehudit ba-Et ha-Hadashah* (Tel Aviv: Dvir, 1945), 1:150–151; Hoffman is cited in D. Schwartz, "Historiyah ve-Historiographiya," *Ziyyon* 45, 2 (1980): 109 n. 54; and see n. 2 in section 6 above.

religionists the only opponents of the "mission" idea. Ahad Ha'am forcefully opposed the dissolution of Jewish nationhood implied by Reform
by asserting that no healthy national body need justify its existence by
reference to the service it renders to another (though he clearly expected
the people Israel to serve as a universal model of justice). Max Wiener
put it acerbically: "So long as Jews considered themselves as a living reality, a self-sustaining organism desiring to perpetuate itself, they conceived of no particular 'mission' to the world."[60]

Zionism, in both some of its religious and secular manifestations,
preached a different form of "Jewish responsibility," which combined traditional Jewish motifs and the newer ethos of European nationalism. The
Jewish people, its national and indeed political existence, was to serve
as an example for humanity. This position was faithful to the earlier critique of the Reform mission both in that it did not reduce this responsibility to the teaching of a deracinated monotheism alone and in that it
did not require the Jew to pursue the gentile actively with his message.
In this latter sense, it was also faithful to the traditional posture on
proselytism, which, as we saw earlier, preferred to have the Jew teach by
example and not actively missionize. Finally, the Zionist position assumed
that the national state was the major framework of human existence in
modern times; it both organized most of human life and also caused the
most significant moral issues. Consequently, creation of a model polity
and society to serve as a "light unto the nations" would be the way to
have the most significant impact on human life. Once again, incidentally, "responsibility" or "mission" serves to justify a goal—in this case,
the renewal of Jewish political existence—perhaps desired for quite other
reasons.

This line of argument is expressed in much ideological writing, from
Ahad Ha'am and Buber to Rav Kook (each in his own way, of course).
Ahad Ha'am envisaged a new Jewish reality in Palestine as the model of
justice; Buber wrote that we want the Land of Israel not for the Jews
alone but for humanity, which would benefit from the realization of

---

[60]For Ahad Ha'am, see A. Simon and Y. Heller, *Ahad Ha'am* (Jerusalem:
Magnes Press, 1956), 184–187; M. Wiener, "The Conception of Mission in
Traditional and Modern Judaism," *YIVO Annual of Jewish Social Science* 2–3
(1947/8): 9–24. This apparent denial of all purpose to national existence does
not seem true to the traditional consciousness.

Judaism in the world; and Rav Kook proposed that all the cultures of the world would be renewed through our spiritual renewal, a renewal that would be rooted in a renaissance in the Land of Israel. For Rav Kook, of course, kabbalistic materials could provide no mean basis for this idea, but even this basis was wondrously expanded in the light of modern reality and possibilities.

One biblical instance will illustrate this new perspective. In both Gen. 12:3 and 18:18, Abraham is blessed that "*ve-nivrekhu be Kha kol mishpehet ha-adamah*." This rather opaque phrase was explained in ancient and medieval times in several ways: Abraham was to serve as the model by which other men would bless their sons; he was to bestow the blessing of prosperity on all people, or all peoples were to share in the blessing which would come to the world for his sake; the nations of the world would fuse with the Jewish people, children of Abraham. Both Buber and Rav Kook articulated a new understanding of this verse: all the nations of the world are to be blessed spiritually and culturally through the life to be led by the Jewish people in its land, which would be a teaching for all humanity.[61]

The idea of a Jewish "mission" devoted to the propagation of monotheism in the diaspora seems quite outdated today, as monotheism is either the heritage of all mankind or, alternatively, it is an idea that today bores all mankind. Yet the Jews are assigned—or claim—another function in modern civilization, and I think it could be useful to see this, basically, as a variation of the idea of a Jewish "mission." Quite frequently, we hear that the Jew, being the quintessential "outsider," is also the quintessential social and moral critic of society, a position of both great privilege and great danger. The Jew is the perennial revolutionary. This claim shares with the idea of a Jewish "mission" its assumption that the Jew

---

[61]Buber, as cited in section I above; Rav Kook in *Orot* (Jerusalem: Mossad HaRav Kook, 1961) 17; and *Orot ha-Kodesh* (Jerusalem: Mossad HaRav Kook, 1963), 1:155. These passages and others are discussed in R. Yaron, *Mishnato shel ha-Rav Kook* (Jerusalem: The Jewish Agency, 1964), 285–288. See, as well, Y. Bin-Nun, "*Le-Umiyyut ve-Enoshut u-Keneset Yisra'el,*" in *Yovel Orot*, ed. Binyamin Ish Shalom and Shalom Rosenberg (Jerusalem: World Zionist Organization, n.d.), 169–208. Buber cleverly connects his interpretation of *ve-nivrekhu* with the ethical content of the verse continuing. It might be possible to find this interpretation in *Targum Onkelos*, but I do not think that is his meaning.

has a unique message to bestow upon mankind or a special function within culture, and also that Jewish existence must be diaspora, non-political existence. For when the Jew lives in a national polity of his own, he ceases to be an outsider, and he inexorably loses his peculiar moral and intellectual vantage point. In a sense, he ceases to be a Jew. George Steiner is a good example of this interpretation of Jewish existence.

X

Patient readers are doubtless rather put out by now; they are irritated and even plain angry. This discussion does not seem to be what was intended by the question of the "Jewish responsibility for the welfare of general society." The topics presented are remote and far from the obvious sense of the question posed. They are too "spiritual"; they deal with much larger issues—the conversion of mankind, say—than we associate with the term "welfare of . . . society." That phrase suggests a social melioration, step-by-step intervention and improvement, not total reorganization. Perhaps readers also feel a sense of irresolution. Different voices have been heard on a variety of topics, but no decisive claim has been entered.

To place matters in focus, I think we can safely say that "responsibility for the welfare of general society" is not the highest priority in our scheme of things, at least on the day-to-day level. The people Israel seems called upon primarily to keep its house in order and to care for its own, to serve God and witness to Him. At the same time, this exemplary life ought to have an overall incremental impact on mankind as a whole. Although we have only infrequently seen ourselves as directly reforming humanity or even educating it, we have more frequently believed that we would be a model to be imitated. And a more activist pattern exists, too, ranging from aggadic comments to Maimonidean statements to the broad vistas articulated by Rabbi Soloveitchik.

There is no reason to deny Judaism's commitment to humanity. The Jewish contribution flows rather naturally from the situation of our being part of the human fraternity, and it needs much less ideological justification than is usually thought, assuming, of course, that this contribution stays in healthy and sensible balance with other pursuits and commitments.

On a personal level, Jews, including pious Jews, will naturally want to participate in the full range of human activities if these are open to them. The variety of human talent and the legitimacy of its expression has been lauded from earliest times. To put the matter more concretely, I doubt that Shmuel ha-Naggid, Don Isaac Abravanel, or, for that matter, Yosef ha-Tzaddik, found it necessary to justify their involvement in the economic or diplomatic realities of their time. The same is true of the Jew's utilization of his scientific/technological talents. We all know that the Rav, *zt"l*, read Gen. 1:28 (". . . Fill the earth and subdue her . . .") as a norm, much as *Hazal* read " . . . be fruitful and multiply," with which the sentence begins. Somehow, I am even satisfied to take these words as a description of the legitimate, indeed blessed energies and drives encoded in humanity—Jews included.

Moreover, it is patent that "general society" in the modern world includes Jews. This integration, a result of technological and political realities as much as of ideological preferences, results in a situation where even those activities not directed specifically at Jews or designed to benefit them will in fact have an impact on them. This is true of all medical and technological processes, obviously; it is also true of much social structuring. Political structures and power determine the distribution of resources.

But the impact of "general society" on the Jew goes far beyond the crude question of who gets what. Jews who are open to their human surroundings—and this situation obtains today not only for the "centrist Orthodox," all denials to the contrary—are willy-nilly affected by them culturally and even spiritually, and consequently they have a stake in their content and quality. This is true for the culture of the street as well as the culture of the library.

Finally, being a part of general society implies human mutuality. It is unfair, ugly, and eventually impossible to make claims on society without feeling part of it and making one's contribution. This, incidentally, seems to me a more correct understanding of *darkhei shalom*, a value that focuses on the harmonious relation among a variety of different groupings (priests and Israelites; children and adults; neighbors; the more pious and the less) than the cynical explanation usually given. Mutuality has pragmatic value, to be sure, but it also expresses a value of the spirit.

These last two paragraphs describe a situation that is quite remarkable in the history of the Jewish encounter with the world, as the Rav pointed out. For even periods in which Jews held great power, or places in which the doings of general society impinged powerfully on the Jewish condition, were ultimately different. Society and state were stratified by religion, class, people; they did not see the kind of integration (or, from the conservative's point of view, breakdown) that defined, for the time being at least, the place of the Jew and his community in the general scheme of things. And it was often difficult even to conceive, let alone urge, the Jew's taking an active role in the history of general society. So perhaps we must exercise our moral and spiritual imaginations as well as our erudition.

This change in historical and sociological reality carries various implications. Obviously, it is now possible to act in ways that were inconceivable before; and this possibility creates responsibility. But the matter cuts more deeply. Since the Jew is able—as individual and perhaps as community—to participate in the processes that govern democratic societies as a whole, his silence and inaction reflect an acquiescence in the evils and abuses to which other human beings are subject. This raises the issue of *hillul ha-Shem* in an overall sense, as we project an image of apathy to suffering. No less acute, though, is the fact that this image is true to reality, that our passivity in the face of societal challenges means that we do condone evil and that we do not really care about our fellow human beings. What happens to the divine image within us if we remain unmoved by indecency, if we are not outraged by wrong? And if we are part of the society in which all this happens, it is difficult to see how we can deny our share of responsibility for its character.

Certainly, the exercise of judgment is required, especially on a communal level. Questions of prudence and policy will always be on the agenda. So, too, will questions of priority and resource management. Even the most idealistic of rationales, and I shortly revert to some of these, require balanced concretization. Hillel taught that the rich person who has fallen from his station must be restored to it, and he even served as herald before one such man. But I doubt that Hillel would have made this his priority if he had to choose between buying a horse for an erstwhile nobleman, and feeding ten hungry men and women. And to choose an example more appropriate for our topic: Despite the rule, "*aniyei irekha va-aniyei ir aheret—aniyei irekha kodemim*" (between the poor of your own town and the poor of another town—your poor come first),[62] it is unlikely that a Jewish community would devote its resources completely

---

[62]*Bava Metzia* 71a; Me'iri on that passage relates to the position of the gentile.

to its own needs and thoroughly refuse the poor of its neighbors. Here, too, considerations of comparative need must be factored in, as well as the literal parameters of the phrase *kodemih* (come first).

Israeli Jewry, for better or for worse, bears the burden of Jewish political identity. Its community will be part of the world community of nations, whatever degree of mutuality that invites. And, if we use the terminology of *kiddush ha-Shem*, Israeli Jewry will appear as the global representative of Jewry as a whole, in moral terms at least. The universal interest generated by the kibbutz movement some years back is an indication of how open many people are (theoretical as this openness might have been), all over the world, for new solutions and standards. Today, the basic issues concern the underprivileged classes and persons and ethnic minorities. Can Israel become a model in these areas? I spoke earlier of the vocation of teaching by "doing your own thing" as an expression of non-imperialist mission; Israel, as state and as society, is well situated to do this, if it can. Perhaps these are among the issues on which we shall be tested.

We have seen statements urging the Jew to work for peace in the world, to bestow *hesed* on all creatures, to call all men and women to the love of God, to be the conduit through which physical and spiritual good reach humanity, to teach, to share. It is difficult to argue with the person who acts on (as he experiences) Rav Kook's vision: "The love for Israel (*ahavat Yisra'el*) implies the love of humanity (*kol ha-adam*)." Or, in more lyrical terms: "There is a person who sings the song of his own soul . . . there is one who sings the song of his people . . . there is one whose soul expands until it spreads beyond the limits of Israel and sings the song of humanity . . . and there is one who goes even higher until his soul joins with all existence, with all creatures, with all the worlds, and he sings with them."[63] Are these ideals more easily appropriated by individuals than by the community as a whole? Perhaps, if one believes Reinhold Niebuhr; but the opposite could be true as well.

It is difficult, if not impossible, to provide the person who lives the ideal with a prudential calculus, or even a rational one. At times, indeed, one feels the need to adopt more of the ideal, even if it means compro-

---

[63]*Orot*, p. 149; *Orot ha-Kodesh* (Jerusalem: Mossad HaRav Kook, 1961), 2:444.

mising one's own justifiable needs. Recall that after Rav explains why one may prefer one's own loss to the *avedah* of one's neighbor and even urges one to do so, he then concludes that a person who always takes this prudential path, will eventually come to the same poor state from which he fled.[64] Perhaps this applies to spiritual, human poverty no less than to the economic kind?

---

[64]*Bava Metzia* 33a.

2

Tikkun Olam: Jewish Obligations to Non-Jewish Society

J. David Bleich

Every person is created for his telos and that is his "service." Likewise, Israel was created to be an illumination unto the nations and to cause them to achieve knowledge of the Lord of the universe.

—Haamek Davar, Ex. *12:51*

The phrase "Therefore do we place our hope in You . . . to perfect the universe through the sovereignty of the Almighty" serves as a focal point of the latter portion of the *Aleinu* prayer uttered by Jews thrice daily. This is an expression of yearning, not simply for the perfection of Israel but, as reflected in the very next phrase, "and all mortals will call upon Your name," a yearning for the perfection of all mankind. Thus, perfection of mankind in the service of God is the acknowledged telos of human existence. Less obvious but, nevertheless, as will be shown, widely accepted among rabbinic scholars, is the recognition that the nation of Israel is charged with facilitating the perfection of mankind as a whole. However, the nature and parameters of that obligation on the part of Israel vis-à-vis the nations of the world require careful elucidation.

Any examination of the obligations of Jewry with regard to *tikkun ha-olam* in the sense of perfection of society must perforce proceed from an understanding of the nature of that *tikkun*—i.e., what it is that the Creator expects of mankind at large. That understanding, in turn, must begin with a thorough awareness of the ramifications and applications of the Seven Commandments of the Sons of Noah.

I

Judaism is at once both universalistic and particularistic. The very existence of two religio-legal codes of widely disparate content side by side, i.e., the Sinaitic Covenant and the Noahide Code, is itself reflective, at the very minimum, of differing standards of moral and devotional responsibility. Any thinking person will perceive that the establishment of differing standards of religio-legal responsibility is either the product of capricious whim on the part of the divine lawgiver or is a correlative of disparate capacities, talents or potentials with which different peoples have been endowed or of disparate missions with which they have been charged. Any attempt to explicate the nature of Jewish responsibility vis-à-vis the nations of the world must proceed from a clear perspective of the differing roles played by Jews and the community of nations in the divine scheme of creation. From this perspective is born an assessment of the nature of the human telos, that, in turn, leads to explication of the concept of *tikkun ha-olam*.

The concept of the election of Israel may indeed serve as a thesis unifying manifold provisions of *Halakhah*. Nevertheless, it is hardly central to the philosophy of *Halakhah*. Theologically, it is probably most significant as a means of understanding divine intervention in shaping history. It is only in Christianity that the concept assumes supreme doctrinal significance only to be redefined in order to allow for the supplanting of the children of Israel by members of another faith community as the subjects of this election. Nevertheless, for good and sufficient reason, the concept of the election of Israel is indeed a focal point in Jewish liturgy and a dominant factor in popular thought, attitudes, actions and reactions of the Jewish populace throughout the course of millennia.

The election of Israel is certainly manifest in the covenantal relationship established by God with the people of Israel, a covenantal relationship inaugurated with the *berit bein ha-betarim* (covenant between the parts) entered into with Abraham and reaffirmed in subsequent covenants. Israel is twice described in the Pentateuch as the "chosen" people: "... the Lord your God has chosen you to be His treasure ... out of all the peoples that are upon the face of the earth" (Deut. 7:6); and "... the Lord has chosen you to be a treasure to Him out of all the people that are upon the face of the earth" (Deut. 14:2). Similar descriptions occur in Ps. 33:12, Ps. 135:4 and elsewhere. Scriptural passages repeatedly refer to Israel as an "*am segulah*." In addition to the earlier citation of biblical references to "chosenness," the term "*segulah*" occurs in the verse "and you shall be a treasure to me from all the nations" (Ex. 19:5) and in the verse "And the Lord has avouched you this day to be unto Him a treasured nation" (Deut. 26:18), while in Ps. 33:12 there occurs a reference to the choice of Israel as a divine *nahalah*. The rendering of "*segulah*" as "treasure" and "*nahalah*" as "inheritance" in standard English translations, although not inaccurate, is nevertheless less than totally faithful to the concepts connoted by the Hebrew terms employed. In biblical Hebrew the terms overlap as nouns describing a *res* that is the subject of a property interest. Thus, in each of these passages, Israel is described as chosen by God for the purpose of being made the subject of some type of proprietary interest vested in Him as is otherwise expressed in the verse "... for unto Me are the children of Israel slaves" (Lev. 25:55). The latter verse serves to make explicit the notion of a proprietary interest in the sense of a personal servitude requiring the rendering of particular services, i.e., performance of divine commandments.[1]

Asserting the existence of such a relationship between Israel and the Deity is straightforward and unambiguous. Less clear is why Israel, rather than some other nation, is chosen for this servitude. The biblical references as well as the liturgical formulae "You have chosen us out of all the peoples," "who has chosen us from [among] every people," "who has

---

[1]See the comments of R. Samson Raphael Hirsch in his *The Nineteen Letters of Ben Uziel*, Fifteenth Letter: "The Bible terms Israel *segulah*, a peculiar treasure, but this designation does not imply, as some have falsely interpreted, that Israel has a monopoly of the Divine love and favor, but on the contrary, that God has the sole and exclusive claim to Israel's devotion and service; that Israel may not render Divine homage to any other being." (*The Nineteen Letters of Ben Uziel*, trans. Bernard Drachman [New York: Bloch Publishing Co., 1942], 142.)

chosen us from [among] all the peoples and given us His Torah," and "for us have You chosen" seemingly connote a unilateral choice on the part of the Deity. The concept of choice connotes, in turn, the existence of alternative possibilities. The choice of x over y by an intelligent being will, of course, be predicated upon carefully weighed rational and/or pragmatic considerations but nevertheless implies the existence of an alternative option that, albeit not optimal, is nevertheless viable.

Rambam, in *Guide of the Perplexed*, Book II, chapter 25, apparently agrees that the election of Israel represents a choice of that nature. In a very brief comment he asserts that it is impossible for us to understand why God should have revealed His will to one particular nation; in the words of Rambam, man can say only "[God] willed it so; or His wisdom decided so." From the human perspective, the question is totally unanswerable. In answering the same question from the divine perspective, Rambam is equivocal. The election of Israel is the product either of divine wisdom or of divine will—of which, we cannot tell. If the choice is born of divine wisdom, the reasons are of a nature that we cannot discern on the basis of human intelligence. But unlike his position in rejecting Sa'adyah's view that *mitzvot* may be based upon the arbitrary will of God and need not proceed from divine wisdom, Rambam is perfectly willing to accept the possibility that the election of Israel is an arbitrary determination of divine will. Perhaps he regards determination of the particular recipients of revelation to be analogous to other matters with regard to which there is no reasoned basis for choosing between available alternatives, with the result that it is logically necessary to choose between making an arbitrary determination or suffering the paralysis of inaction. An example of such a choice is the determination of the species of animal or the specific number of animals to be sacrificed. In the latter case, argues Rambam, the quest for a rationale is pointless.[2] Some determinate number must be selected; there need not be a reason for choosing one rather than another. Assuming, as Rambam certainly does, that God has good and sufficient reason for revealing the Torah, Rambam may find it pointless to ask why it was revealed to one people rather than to another. One nation must be chosen—perhaps to serve as the vehicle for transmission to all of mankind. There need be no particular reason, then, for the choice of one people over another.

---

[2]See Rambam, *Guide of the Perplexed*, 3:26.

A sharply contrasting picture emerges from the comments of *Sifrei* 20:2 upon the verse, "The Lord came from Sinai, and shined forth from Seir unto them: He radiated splendor from Mount Paran" (Deut. 33:2). The verse itself cries out for clarification. Moses begins his valedictory blessing with a reference to the giving of the Law at Sinai. There is no biblical reference to any divine activity at either Seir or Paran prior to that event, nor is there any perceivable nexus between any event that took place in those locales and the giving of the Torah at Sinai. In identifying the events to which allusion is made, *Sifrei* comments:

> When God revealed [Himself] to give the Torah to Israel, He did not reveal Himself only to Israel but to all the nations. First He went to the children of Esau and said to them, "Do you accept the Torah?" They said to Him, "What is written therein?" He said to them, "Thou shalt not kill." They said to Him, "The very essence of that ancestor was that of a murderer as it is said 'but the hands are the hands of Esau' [Gen. 27:22] and such was the promise of [Esau's] father 'And by your sword shall you live' [Gen. 28:40]."
>
> He went to the children of Ammon and Moab and said to them, "Do you accept the Torah?" They said to Him, "What is written therein?" He said to them, "Thou shalt not commit adultery." They said to Him, "Sovereign of the universe, [ours] is the very essence of sexual relations as it is said, 'And the two daughters of Lot were with child of their father [Gen. 10:36].'
>
> He went and found the children of Ishmael. He said to them, "Do you accept the Torah?" They said to Him, "What is written therein?" He said to them, "Thou shalt not steal." They said to Him, "Sovereign of the universe, the very essence of our father was armed robbery as it is said, 'and he shall be a wild man' [Gen. 16:12]."
>
> There was no nation among the nations to which He did not go and speak and knock on the door to [see] if it could agree to accept the Torah . . . even the Seven Commandments that the Sons of Noah accepted they could not sustain with the result that [the Seven Commandments] were removed [from them] and given to Israel . . .[3]

---

[3]See *Bava Kamma* 38a and *Avodah Zarah* 2b. The Gemara renders Habakkuk 3:6, "*ra'ah va-yatter goyim*," as "He saw and He released the nations" and interprets the passage as declaring that God saw that gentiles did not observe the Noahide Code and "released" them from it. The Gemara then proceeds to explain that the nature of the "release" is such that they do not receive the reward for observance of those commandments that is vouchsafed to the commanded. Cf. *Or Same'ah, Hilkhot Isurei Bi'ah* 14:7.

The comments of *Sifrei* are paraphrased in a parallel comment recorded in the Gemara, *Avodah Zarah* 2b: "What did [God] seek in Seir and what did He seek in Paran? Said R. Yohanan, 'This teaches [us] that the Holy One, blessed be He, offered the Torah to every nation and every tongue but they did not accept it until He came to Israel and they accepted it.'"[4]

Read literally, the scenario depicted by the *Sifrei* does not reflect a free choice on the part of the Deity from among a number of potential recipients. Quite to the contrary, "There was no nation among the nations to which He did not go and speak and knock on the door." God did not choose to make Israel the recipient of the Torah; He chose each and every other nation in turn only to be treated as a rejected suitor. It appears that, as it were, God is reduced to peddling His wares and can find no nation willing to give Him entrée—save Israel. Language describing the "chosenness" of Israel seems highly inappropriate. It would seem that it would be far more accurate to speak of Israel choosing to accept the Torah than to speak of God as choosing Israel as its recipient.

But, of course, such aggadic statements are not to be taken literally. Moreover, acceptance of any of the classical philosophical analyses of the nature of the prophetic experience makes it difficult to accept the

---

The opinion of *Teshuvot Penei Yehoshu'a*, I, *Yoreh De'ah*, no. 3 and II, *Even ha-Ezer* no. 43, to the effect that the prohibitions of the Seven Commandments have been rescinded "but they will be judged for not having fulfilled them" is rejected by *Teshuvot Hatam Sofer, Hoshen Mishpat*, no. 185; *Beit Yehudah, Yoreh De'ah*, no 17; and *Sedei Hemed, Ma'arekhet ha-Vav, klal* 26, sec. 22. That view is also contradicted by *Teshuvot ha-Rema*, no. 10.

[4]This is also the theme of yet another midrashic statement, cited by R. Jacob Ettlinger, *Minhat Ani, Parashat be-Midbar*. The *midrash* states: "Why was the Torah given in the month of twins? So that the nations of the world would have not have grounds to complain, 'If He had given us the Torah we would have observed it.' The Holy One, blessed the He, said to them, 'Behold I give you the Torah in the third month which is the month of twins, of Jacob and of Esau. If you wish to accept [the Torah] come and accept [it].'"

The heavens are divided into the twelve signs of the zodiac. Each of the twelve *mazalot*, or constellations of the zodiac, bears a distinctive name and representation in the form of a sign. The sign of the third month, the month in which the Torah was revealed at Sinai, is Gemini, i.e., *te'omim*, or "twins," representing Esau and Jacob.

phenomenon of a dialogue between God and each and every nation—in effect, all of humanity—in a literal sense. Undoubtedly, the description of the proffered offer of the Torah to each of the nations of the world *seriatim* must be understood not as an actual offer, but as a constructive offer. As such, it follows that the refusal of the offer was constructive as well.[5]

Edom could not accept the Torah because it was constitutionally incapable of renouncing bloodshed; Ammon and Moab could not possibly purge themselves of a proclivity for sexual licentiousness; and Ishmael could not sustain itself other than by preying upon other innocent peoples. Collectively, the nations of the world could not find it within themselves even to abjure activities proscribed by the provisions of the Noahide Code. It is both pointless and unjust to bind a people to acceptance of additional commandments that they will undoubtedly be incapable of observing. By the process of elimination, Israel was the only candidate for meaningful acceptance of the Sinaitic Code.

Since this was known to God, any actual offer to other nations would have been superfluous. But this is known to God not simply because He is omniscient; it is known to Him because, as the Creator of all flesh, He knows the nature of His creatures. God is assuredly aware of the capacities and limitations of His creatures precisely because He imbued them with those capabilities and limitations. Thus, from the moment of creation, Jews—and only Jews—were destined to become the beneficiaries of revelation at Sinai. Hence, Jews are indeed "chosen" not arbitrarily or capriciously, but in the sense of having been purposefully endowed with the qualities necessary for obedience to divine law.

The comments of *Sifrei* constitute eloquent support for the doctrine of the election of Israel set forth by R. Judah ha-Levi in his *Kuzari*.[6] As explained by R. Judah ha-Levi, Adam was endowed with particular and superior physical and intellectual traits and represented a supreme state of human perfection. Adam was possessed of a diminished sensual and corporeal nature by virtue of the fact that he was directly created by the hand of God. Moreover, since he was not the offspring of human parents he was not heir to the deficiencies of their constitution, nor did he suffer the adverse effects of food and climate to which other mortals are

---

[5]Cf., Maharal of Prague, *Tiferet Yisra'el*, chap. 1.
[6]Part I, secs. 27–43, 95, 101–103.

subjected during the period of their growth and maturation. Those distinctive qualities, asserts R. Judah La-Levi, were not shared equally by
all of his progeny. They were transmitted first to Abel, then to Seth, and
then passed on to but a single individual in each generation. The chain
of transmission included Noah, Shem, Ever and, finally, Abraham. The
heir of Abraham was Isaac and the heir of Isaac was Jacob. Only with
the birth of the sons of Jacob do multiple heirs appear. These qualities
are then transmitted to the entire seed of Jacob and become the inheritance, albeit in varying degrees, of the entire people of Israel.[7]

The spiritual and psychological qualities described by R. Judah
ha-Levi serve a teleological purpose. Creation of a people endowed with
such a nature constitutes a necessary aspect of the creation of a universe
in conformity with the divine blueprint. Centuries later, R. Joseph Ber
Soloveichik[8] in his *Beit ha-Levi*, similarly commented that the rabbinic
teaching regarding the existence of the Torah prior to creation of the
world reflects a teleological view of the universe. This concept is similarly reflected in the dictum "The Holy One, blessed be He, scrutinized
the Torah and created the world."[9] The Sages sought to emphasize that
God did not first create a universe and then devise a legal and religious
code tailored to the needs of the universe that He created. Quite to the
contrary, first God composed a Torah and only then did He proceed to
create a universe in which fulfillment of the provisions of the Torah would
be possible as well as advantageous.

The practical effect of this perspective is to engender a Copernican
revolution in perception of the relationship of the Torah to the conditions
of human life. In effect, the Sages tells us: Do not ask whether the Torah
is relevant to the world in which you live, but whether the world in which
you live is relevant to the Torah. If the world in which you live is not relevant to the Torah, it is not the Torah that requires modification; rather
it is human mores, values, economic policies, political structure and/or
social institutions that require modification so that they become meaningful and relevant in implementation of biblical laws, norms and values.
According to R. Judah ha-Levi, it was in order to provide for the empiri-

---

[7]See also the comments of R. Israel Lipschutz, *Tiferet Yisra'el, Avot, Bo'az*
3:1. For a kabbalistic exposition of the unique nature of the Jewish soul see
Tanya, chaps. 1–2.

[8]*Beit Ha-Levi, Parashat Bo*, s.v. *"ve-higadta."*

[9]*Zohar, Parashat Terumah*, p. 161b.

cal possibility of implementation of the provisions of the corpus of law contained in the Torah that God found it necessary to create a people imbued with the requisite psychological and spiritual qualities.

R. Samson Raphael Hirsch's depiction of the *"Israel-Mensch"*[10] is effectively an expansion of the categories posited by medieval philosophers in describing the constituents of the created world and serves to provide appropriate nomenclature for expression of what is, in actuality, the seminal thesis propounded by R. Judah ha-Levi. Medieval philosophers divided the world into four categories: inanimate objects (*domem*), vegetable life (*tzome'ah*), animal life (*hai*) and rational creatures, i.e., man (*medabber*). To these R. Hirsch, in effect, adds a fifth category, *viz.*, *Israel-Mensch*. R. Hirsch underscores the fact that both the role and the function of Jews in the scheme of Creation are fundamentally different from those of other rational beings. Diverse categories of created entities are assigned differing roles and functions and are designed to achieve distinct purposes. Animate life is a necessary but not sufficient condition of the human state; reason is required in order for man to function in the role assigned to human beings. Similarly, reason and intelligence are unique to mankind, but these are necessary rather than sufficient conditions for fulfillment of the unique mission assigned to Israel. The *Israel-Mensch*, unlike the rest of mankind, is imbued with the metaphysical qualities necessary for fulfilling his designated purpose.

It is the idiosyncratic spiritual quality described by R. Judah ha-Levi or, as some would categorize it, their religious disposition that renders Israel capable of obedience to the will of God. God's election of Israel is then nothing more, and nothing less, than the shaping of that spiritual disposition. Once created, this spiritual quality must be nurtured and preserved. This unique disposition is delicate in nature and must be protected as is so clearly evident from the comments of *Midrash Tanhuma*, *Parashat Shemini* on the verse "He saw and made the nations tremble" (Hab. 3:6). There are a number of diverse rabbinic interpretations of the phrase "*ra'ah va-yatter goyim*" based upon translation of "*va-yatter goyim*" as "and He released the nations" or "and he permitted to the nations" rather than "and he made the nations tremble."[11] *Tanhuma* comments:

---

[10]See Hirsch, *Nineteen Letters*, Twelfth Letter.

[11]For a differing rabbinic interpretation based on the translation "and he released the nations" see *Bava Kamma* 38a and *Avodah Zarah* 2b. See supra, note 3.

R. Tanhuma ben Haglia'i said: He permitted to them the forbidden, detestable creatures and swarming creatures. To what is the matter to be compared? To a physician who goes to visit two patients. He perceives that one
of them is in grave danger and tells the members of his family, "Give him any
food that he requests." He perceives that the other will survive [and] tells
[the members of his family], "Such and such food he may eat; such and such
he may not eat." They said to the physician, "What is the meaning of this?
To this one you say he may eat any food that he requests and to the other
you said he may eat such and such." The physician said to them, "To the
one that will live I said 'This you may eat and this you may not eat' but [re-
garding] the one which will die I said to them, 'Give him anything that he
requests.'" Similarly the Holy One, blessed be He, permitted detestable creatures and swarming creatures to gentiles. But to Israel who are destined for
life He said, "And you shall be holy for I am holy; do not defile yourselves"
[Lev. 11:44]; "This you shall eat" [Lev. 11:21], and this you shall not eat
[Lev. 11:4]; "do not make yourselves unclean with them that you become
impure through them" [Lev. 11:43]. Why? Because they are destined to life
as it is said "But you who cleave unto the Lord your God are alive every one
of you this day" [Deut. 4:4].[12]

Thus, the relationship between the propensity for observance of
divine commandments and actual observance of those commandments
is seen as reciprocal in nature. Taken as a unitary corpus of law, divine
edicts can be observed only by a people endowed with the requisite
nature for doing so; by the same token, at least some of these commandments are designed to preserve and secure that nature.

The "chosenness" of Israel as their election for instrumental purposes
rather than as an intrinsically elect nation is reflected in *Avot* 3:14 in
the declaration: "Beloved is man for he was created in the image [of God].
It is indicative of greater love that it was made known to him that he
was created in the image [of God], as is said: 'For in the image of God
did He make man' (Gen. 9:6)." The term "man" is used as a reference to
all of humanity as evidenced by the very next statement "Beloved are
Israel who are called children of God." As noted by the author of *Tiferet
Yisra'el*, in his commentary *ad locum*, the juxtaposition of the terms "man"
and "Israel" makes it abundantly clear that the two terms are not employed synonymously but that "man" is used in a generic sense as a reference to all human beings.

---

[12]Cf., *Shemot Rabbah* 30:18.

This does not at all imply that the Creator chose to deny gentile nations a role in His service by making obedience to His law constitutionally impossible for them. Quite to the contrary, as understood by a number of the classic commentators, the statement of the Mishnah in *Avot* establishes a similar, albeit more limited, role for gentile nations as well. *Tosefet Yom Tov* astutely questions why the Mishnah cites Gen. 9:6 in establishing that man is created in the image of God, since man is earlier described in precisely the same terms in Gen. 1:26–29. Citing Rashi's comment to *Avot* 3:14, "Man is beloved because he was created in the image [of God]; therefore, it is incumbent upon him to perform the will of his Master," *Tosefet Yom Tov* points out that the reference in Gen. 9:6 occurs in the context of God's issuance of a command to Noah. The love bestowed upon man is expressed in endowing man with the divine image— that is, godlike qualities making it possible for him to obey the divine commandments. Thus, creation in the "image of God" does not represent status or privilege but is a description of human capacity to obey the divine will. The obligations of gentiles are, of course, limited to observance of the Noahide Code while Jews are bound by 613 commandments. Although both Jews and gentiles share in participation in the "image of God," additional proclivity is required for acceptance of the yoke of the 613 commandments, a responsibility for which Israel alone was chosen.

II

Noteworthy is an *obiter dictum* introduced by the author of *Tosefet Yom Tov* in his elucidation of the words of the Mishnah (in *Avot* 3:14) that goes beyond explication of the text to formulate an implied behavioral principle. Since gentiles are described as "beloved" by virtue of the fact that they have the capacity to obey the divine will ". . . we are commanded (*nitztavinu*) to coerce them by means of words to draw their heart to the will of their Master and the desire of their Rock, may they be remembered for good." Were the provisions of the Noahide Code designed simply for the benefit of mankind, i.e., to regulate human conduct and to prevent anarchy, non-observance on the part of gentiles might be of no concern to Jews unless, of course, they were directly affected by negative forms of social conduct. But since the raison d'être of gentile nations lies in the fulfillment of a divine mission, Jews also have an obligation to assure that God is served by all of His creatures.

The obligation incumbent upon Jews to assure the moral perfection of non-Jews is greatest in the Land of Israel. That is not at all surprising. The Land of Israel was designated as the homeland of the people of Israel, i.e., as the soil upon which the divine plan for realization and perfection of the purpose of creation might be maximally effected.[13] Observance of Torah was designed to be maximized in the Land of Israel both in the sheer number of applicable commandments and in the quality of observance. Reciprocally, or at least concomitantly, divine providence is manifest most intensely within the boundaries of the Land of Israel.[14] Consequently, even for gentiles, the possibility of adherence to higher standards is greater in the land of Israel. Hence, demands upon the spirit may be pressed more adamantly in that land. Moreover, the deleterious effects of immoral conduct, were such conduct to be tolerated, would inevitably mar the near-utopian moral climate to which the inhabitants of the land of Israel must aspire. Thus, Rambam, in *Hilkhot Melakhim* 8:10, records that Moses was commanded to compel all the nations of the world to accept the Noahide Code, while in *Hilkhot Melakhim* 8:9, he rules that a peace treaty cannot be concluded with any gentile city within the Land of Israel unless the inhabitants "subject to our jurisdiction" (*tahat yadeinu*) renounce idolatry and accept the Noahide Code. Again, in *Hilkhot Melakhim* 10:11, Rambam rules that the *beit din* is obliged to establish a judiciary for the purpose of administering and enforcing the Noahide Code.

The obligation to compel non-Jews to accept the Noahide Code is limited to places and epochs in which non-Jews are subject to the absolute authority of a Jewish commonwealth. As a practical matter, such authority does not exist in our age even in the modern-day State of Israel. Upon promulgation of the Balfour Declaration, R. Me'ir Simhah of Dvinsk, author of *Or Same'ah* did indeed write, "The fear of the oaths has departed."[15] However, in light of the attendant exigencies of Realpolitik, the prayerful anticipation of untrammelled sovereignty has

---

[13]See *Kuzari*, Part II, secs. 8–16.

[14]See, for example, Deut. 11:12 and Rashi, ad loc.

[15]The reference is to the oaths cited in *Ketubot* 111a which include an undertaking not to rebel against the nations of the world. For the text of R. Me'ir Simhah's statement see Z.A. Rabiner, *Toledot R. Me'ir Simhah* (Tel Aviv, 5727), p. 164.

not yet been realized. Indeed, a political climate in which imposition of the Noahide obligations upon non-Jewish nationals will become possible is not likely to arise prior to the advent of the messianic era. Rambam, in *Hilkhot Melakhim* 10:4, enumerates the conditions that must be fulfilled by a putative messiah in order to substantiate a claim of messiahship with certainty. Among them are that he must "wage the wars of God" and "perfect the entire world (*ve-yetaken et ha-olam kulo*) to serve God together." It is in that context—and in that context only—that Rambam refers to the concept of *tikkun ha-olam*.

Nevertheless, as reflected in the previously cited comments of *Tosefet Yom Tov*, absence of an obligation to compel acceptance of Noahide obligations does not imply abnegation of less drastic means of achieving the same effect. To be sure, the nature of that obligation is far different from similar obligations vis-à-vis fellow Jews. The obligation of *arevut*, or "surety," renders a Jew culpable for preventable transgressions of a fellow Jew. That obligation flows from a reciprocal covenant entered into by all Jews prior to entry into the promised land and consequently is limited to members of the Jewish faith-community. Responsibility of Jews for one another's conduct is rooted in the unique covenantal relationship described in Deut. 9:9–14 and is accordingly limited to those who have entered into that covenant.

Rambam's formulation of Jewish responsibility vis-à-vis non-Jews serves to define the obligation as limited to achievement of a general acceptance of Noahide commandments (*le-kabel mitzvot she-nitztavu benei No'ah*) by non-Jews rather than as an obligation to prevent particular infractions of the Noahide Code.[16] For most authorities, the obligation

---

[16]See *Teshuvot ve-Shev ha-Kohen*, no. 38; R. Yitzchak Zev ha-Levi Soloveitchik, *Hiddushei Maran Riz ha-Levi* (Jerusalem, 5723), p. 164; R. Yosef Shlomoh Kahaneman, *Shem Olam* (Wickliff, 5745), pp. 382–384; R. Moshe Sternbuch, *Edut*, no. 7 (II Adar 5749), pp. 27–31; and R. Shmu'el Tuvya Stern, *Teshuvot ha-Shavit*, VIII, *Hoshen Mishpat*, no. 3. Cf., however, R. Menachem Mendel Schneerson, *Ha-Pardes*, Iyar 5745, pp. 7–11. The view cited by Rema, *Yoreh De'ah* 151:1, permitting sale to a non-Jew of items to be used in conjunction with idolatrous practices when such sale involves no technical violation of *lifnei iver* appears to be incompatible with an obligation to prevent infractions of the Noahide Code. The suggestion of Rabbi Stern, *Teshuvot ha-Shavit*, VII, *Orah Hayyim*, no. 1, note 2, that, assuming such an obligation does exist, it cannot mandate financial expenditures or loss of profit is without support.

to prevent a particular infraction (*le-afrushei me-issura*)[17] on the part of a fellow Jew[18] is born of the responsibility of *arevut*;[19] for others, the obligation is subsumed in the commandment "You shall surely rebuke your fellow" (Lev. 19:17).[20] Neither of those considerations applies to conduct vis-à-vis a non-Jew.[21] Accordingly, *Shakh, Yoreh De'ah* 151:6, rules

---

Sefer Hasidim, sec. 1124, declares: "If one sees a gentile committing a transgression, if he can protest, he should protest for the Holy One, blessed be He, sent Jonah to Nineveh to cause them to repent. Because when the Holy One, blessed be He, is angry it is not a time of favor before Him." The chastisement advocated by *Sefer Hasidim* is clearly an act of piety, not a normative obligation, as evidenced by reference to God's concern for non-Jews rather than to a normative halakhic provision. The consideration advanced by *Sefer Hasidim* regarding God's anger and the absence of "a time of favor" is clearly extra-halakhic and in the nature of Jewish self-interest. Cf., however, the comment of the editor of the Mosad ha-Rav Kook edition of *Sefer Hasidim* (Jerusalem, 5720), *ad locum*, and R. Yitzhak Ya'akov Weisz, *Teshuvot Minhat Yizhak*, IV, no. 79, sec. 4.

[17]*Mishnah Berurah, Sha'ar ha-Ziyun* 347:8, and *Maharatz Hayes, Shabbat* 3a, maintain that this obligation is biblical in nature. See also *Sedei Hemed, Ma'arekhet ha-Vav, klal* 26, sec. 3. A host of authorities maintain that this obligation is rabbinic in nature. See *Tosafot*, Rosh and Rashba, *Shabbat* 3a; Ran, *Shabbat* 3a and *Avodah Zarah* 6b; and *Rabbeinu Yeruham, Netiv* 12, *halakhah* 5.

[18]See, however, *Rabbeinu Yeruham, Netiv* 14, *halakhah* 7, who apparently denies the existence of such an obligation. This is apparently also the view of *Teshuvot Radbaz*, III, no. 535; see R. Yitzchak Teib, *Erekh ha-Shulhan, Yoreh De'ah* 151:1. Cf., *Turei Even, Hagigah, Avnei Milu'im* 13a, who analyzes the apparently similar position of *Tosafot* and Rosh, *Avodah Zarah* 6b. Cf. also, Ritva, *Avodah Zarah* 6b. For possible resolutions of the seemingly contradictory positions of some of these authorities see *Shakh, Yoreh De'ah* 152:6; *Teshuvot Binyan Zion*, no. 15; and *Teshuvot Meshiv Davar*, II, no. 31.

[19]See *Teshuvot Hatam Sofer, Yoreh De'ah*, no. 19; *Teshuvot Maharash Engel*, VIII, no. 219; *Teshuvot Beit Yehudah, Yoreh De'ah*, no. 17; and R. Aaron Moses Kisilev, *Mishberei Yam*, no. 10.

[20]See *Teshuvot Ketav Sofer, Yoreh De'ah*, no. 83; and *Maharatz Hayes, Shabbat* 3a, who imputes this view to Rambam, *Sefer ha-Mitzvot, mitzvot aseh*, no. 205. Cf., Rashi, *Sanhedrin* 75a, s.v. "*ve-'im ita*," who states that "your fellow" excludes even a *ger toshav*.

[21]See *Teshuvot Meshiv Davar*, II, no. 31, who states, "With regard to a non-Jew, we do not find that we are obligated to prevent him from transgressing." See also *Mishberei Yam*, no. 10, who maintains that the obligation *le-afrushei me-issura* is rabbinic in nature but nevertheless maintains that no obligation was imposed to prevent non-Jews from transgressing.

that there is no obligation to prevent a non-Jew from committing a trans-gression.[22] Accordingly, the obligation to secure a general commitment to the binding nature of the Noahide commandments is entirely distinct from any obligation to prevent infractions.[23]

The obligation to secure commitment to acceptance of Noahide law may not, in and of itself, entail an obligation to provide detailed instruc-tion with regard to the minutiae of that code. Nevertheless, the matter is more complex than it may appear. "Ignorance of the law excuses no man" is a legal maxim whose counterpart was first enunciated in Jewish law in the context of Noahide obligations. The Gemara, *Makkot* 9b, declares that a non-Jew is culpable even if he acts in ignorance of Noahide prohibitions because "he should have learned, but did not learn." The conceptual problem is obvious.

Rambam, in his *Commentary on the Mishnah, Hullin* 7:7, declares that commandments announced prior to revelation at Sinai that are still bind-ing today do not derive their binding authority from the original com-mand but from reiteration at Sinai. Thus, circumcision is practiced today not because of the divine command addressed to Abraham, but because God commanded us through Moses to practice circumcision as it was practiced by Abraham; we are forbidden to eat the sciatic nerve not be-cause it was forbidden to Jacob but (as was Rambam's reading of the text of the Mishnah) because it was forbidden at Sinai.[24] Similarly, declares

---

[22]Cf., however, *Teshuvot Tashbatz*, III, no. 133, who declares that assistance to a non-Jew in committing a transgression that is not in the category of "plac-ing a stumbling block before the blind" is nevertheless forbidden since "there is an obligation to prevent them [from sinning]." That position is apparently con-tradicted by Rema, *Yoreh De'ah* 151:1 (see supra, note 16 and is clearly contra-dicted by *Shakh, Yoreh De'ah* 151:6; *Teshuvot Meshiv Davar*, II, no. 31; and *Mishberei Yam*, no. 10.

[23]Ramban, in his *Commentary on the Bible*, Deut. 23:18, states, "for we are not commanded with regard to the nations other than with regard to idolatry." Ramban seems to imply that there is an obligation *le-afrushei me-issura* with regard to non-Jews in the limited case of idolatry. Cf. idem, Num. 15:26 and Deut. 20:18.

[24]The Mishnah records a dispute between the Sages and R. Judah with re-gard to whether the prohibition includes the sciatic nerve of unclean species. R. Judah argues that the prohibition occasioned by Jacob's encounter with the angel as recorded in Gen. 32:33 was announced before unclean species were prohibited and hence encompasses such species as well. The Sages respond that

Rambam, the prohibition concerning eating flesh torn from living animals is not binding upon us because it was commanded to Noah, but because it was confirmed through Moses at Sinai. This is true not only for the contents of the Noahide Code that remain binding upon Jews but is true as well for the Noahide Code as it pertains to non-Jews. Put somewhat differently, all pre-Sinaitic legislation was abrogated at Sinai with the result that, to the extent that any such legislation remains binding, whether upon Jews or non-Jews, it is because of reenactment by divine fiat at Sinai. That this is true also with regard to the Noahide law as it pertains to non-Jews is clear from Rambam's statement, *Hilkhot Melakhim* 8:15, in which he declares that, in order to achieve eternal reward, non-Jews must accept and observe the Noahide Code as the command of God. Rambam, however, does not content himself with stating that the commandments must be accepted as the product of dogmatic revelation rather than on the basis of human conviction, but adds that they must be accepted because of revelation at Sinai that they had been commanded to Noahides by God. Noahides, then, have no independent binding revelation concerning the Noahide Code. Jews are the bearer of the *mesorah*, not only of the 613 commandments addressed to Jews and recorded in the Sinaitic Code, but of the Noahide Code as well.[25]

But if non-Jews are not the recipients of an independent source of revelation and were not present at Sinai to receive the Noahide Code,

---

the sciatic nerve was prohibited at Sinai but recorded in the appropriate place in the historical narrative. A literal reading of the Mishnah would yield a controversy with regard to whether there was at all a prohibition in the interim period between Jacob's encounter with the angel and revelation at Sinai. Rambam seems to indicate that the Sages concede that the prohibition was indeed announced at the earlier time but that the original commandment and the circumstances attendant thereupon are irrelevant since, if not for reiteration at Sinai, the commandment would have been completely abrogated. Rambam, *Hilkhot Melakhim* 9:1, also states that the *gid ha-nasheh* was forbidden at the time of Jacob.

[25]See R. Yitzhak Ze'ev ha-Levi Soloveitchik, *Hiddushei Maran Riz ha-Levi al ha-Torah* (Jerusalem, 5723), *Parashat va-Ethanan*, s.v. "*ve-ameru*," who interprets the verse "for this is your wisdom and your understanding in the eyes of the peoples who will hear all these statutes and say, 'surely this great nation is a wise and understanding people'" (Deut. 4:6) in consonance with the principle that Jews are the bearers of the *mesorah* of the Noahide Code.

how can they be responsible for its contents? "A Noahide is executed because he should have learned, but did not learn," declares the Gemara, *Makkot* 9b.[26] However, as Rambam emphatically declares, the Noahide Code is not to be observed on the basis of an a priori moral awareness, but as the product of revelation. How can nonparticipants in the phenomenon of revelation become familiar with its contents other than through instruction by a teacher? Assuredly, matters of doubt and ambiguity can be resolved only by application to the bearers of the *mesorah*, i.e., Jews. Logically, then, the Jewish scholar must be under some reciprocal obligation requiring him to impart knowledge to the Noahide. Although there may be no obligation to volunteer information or to seek out Noahides in order to teach them the contents of the Noahide Code, there must be, at the minimum, an obligation to respond to a request for information. "The Holy one, blessed be He, does not deal with his creatures with trickery" (*Avodah Zarah* 3a). "He should have learned" can be a normative legal principle only if such learning is a possibility in reality. It can be a possibility only if there are teachers who are under a concomitant obligation to teach. Accordingly, if information or advice is solicited there must be a definite obligation to respond.

Apparently, one rabbinic authority expressly recognized an independent obligation of that nature at least with regard to Jews. R. Moses Sofer, in *Teshuvot Hatam Sofer, Hoshen Mishpat,* 164, propounds a remarkable thesis. A former student had accepted a rabbinic position but apparently his community was unwilling or unable to provide compensation at a level sufficient to keep body and soul together. It appears that the student sought Hatam Sofer's advice with regard to the propriety of engaging in some form of "work action." Hatam Sofer responds to his interlocutor by stating unequivocally that, if he must indeed seek some mundane form of securing a livelihood, he is under no obligation whatsoever to interrupt gainful activities in order to respond to halakhic queries or to sit in judgment in monetary disputes. Nevertheless, Hatam Sofer admonishes the student that every Jew is obligated to devote the lion's share of his time to Torah study.

---

[26]The problematic comments of *Kometz le-Minhah* that are apparently contradicted by this source are discussed in J. David Bleich, *Contemporary Halakhic Problems* (New York: Ktav, 1983), II, 331, note 38. The resolution there suggested has now also been advanced by R. Isaac Elijah ha-Kohen, *Lifnei Ivver* (Ofakim, 5749), p. 108.

And, continues Hatam Sofer, "during such time dedicated to Torah and
[divine] service, if a person comes to learn something from him or [re-
quests that he] judge between man and his fellow or render a decision with
regard to a matter of ritual law, he is obligated to do so without compensation and he is not permitted to accept any remuneration even though
his own study is diminished thereby for, with regard to this [matter], that
of his fellow takes precedence over that of himself."[27]

Hatam Sofer carefully and precisely spells out three areas of obligation:
1) to teach a particular matter with regard to which information is sought;
2) to rule in response to a halakhic inquiry; and 3) to serve as a judge in a
financial or interpersonal dispute. The first obligation is relatively easy to
comprehend: "And you shall teach them to your children" (Deut. 6:7) is
understood by Hatam Sofer as prioritization of the obligation to teach others
over the obligation of Torah study that is of benefit only to oneself. But
the declaration "*mutar*" ("permitted") or "*asur*" ("forbidden") and most
certainly the adjudication of financial disputes does not constitute fulfillment of the *mitzvah* of *talmud Torah* as evidenced by the halakhic provision codified by Rema, *Orah Hayyim* 47:4, to the effect that a halakhic
ruling unaccompanied by an explanation may be issued prior to recitation
of *birkat ha-Torah*.[28] What, then, is the nature of the obligation to interrupt one's own Torah study in order to issue a halakhic ruling? The issuance of a ruling, or of a decision in a monetary dispute, certainly constitutes the transmission of the *mesorah* and, apparently, Hatam Sofer posits
an obligation to transmit the *mesorah* that is quite independent of the
mitzvah of *talmud Torah*.[29] If so, it may cogently be argued that Jews, as
bearers of the *mesorah* regarding the Noahide Code are also duty-bound

---

[27]Cf. the apparently conflicting position of R. Eliyahu David Rabinowitz-
Teumim (Aderet), *Seder Eliyahu* (Jerusalem: Mossad HaRav Kook, 5744),
pp. 62 and 65.

[28]The contradictory opinion of *Bi'ur ha-Gra, Orah Hayyim* 47:4, is predicated
upon that authority's antecedent view that not only oral study, but also mental
study, requires *birkat ha-Torah* and is based upon recognition that a halakhic
determination cannot be reached other than upon at least silent deliberation.

[29]The source of that obligation is elusive. The Gemara, *Shabbat* 23a, questions the appropriateness of the liturgical formula "who has sanctified us through
His commandments and has commanded us" with regard to the blessing pro-
nounced prior to performance of a rabbinically commanded *mitzvah*: "Where
have we been commanded?" queries the Gemara. The Gemara proceeds to cite

to respond to solicitation of information with regard to elucidation of the provisions of the Noahide Code.[30]

III

The corpus of the Noahide Code consists of only seven commandments, as opposed to the 613 commandments binding upon Jews. Yet resolution of any particular matter of doubt regarding ramifications of the Seven Commandments, or of any novel or heretofore unaddressed problem of Noahide law, is vastly more difficult than resolution of similar matters pertaining to the 613 commandments. When confronted by a question involving a matter of Jewish law, the rabbinic decisor, if he does not already know the answer, has available to him vast libraries of codes and compendia, commentaries and supercommentaries, responsa and essays, dealing with every facet of Jewish law. Even if the particular question that he must address has not previously been dealt with explicitly, it is

---

two alternative sources: "You shall not turn aside from the matter they shall declare unto you" (Deut. 17:11) and "Ask your father and he will declare unto you, your elders and they will tell you" (Deut. 32:7). Although the latter verse is not cited in this context by Rambam, *Hilkhot Berakhot* 11:3, Hatam Sofer may have regarded that verse as being of halakhic import connoting, not an obligation with regard to obedience to rabbinic legislation, but an obligation upon the father and the elders to transmit the *mesorah* by responding to solicitation of information.

[30]Hatam Sofer himself, in *Teshuvot Hatam Sofer, Hoshen Mishpat*, no. 185, states: ". . . it is a *mitzvah* to teach them as recorded by Rambam, chap. 10 of [*Hilkhot*] *Melakhim*." There is, however, no such explicit statement in Rambam. [Cf., R. Menachem Mendel Schneersohn, *Ha-Pardes*, Iyar 5745, p. 8. The statement to which that author refers, even if his interpretation is accepted, does not appear in chapter 10 of *Hilkhot Melakhim*.] Rambam, *Hilkhot Melakhim* 10:12, rules: "Two gentiles who come before you to adjudicate according to the laws of Israel and both wish to adjudicate accenting to the law of the Torah, we adjudicate." Rambam's term, "we adjudicate" (*danin*), must presumably be understood as meaning "we are *obligated* to adjudicate." That statement, then, reflects the position later enunciated by *Teshuvot Hatam Sofer* concerning the obligation to serve as a judge in financial disputes and signifies an obligation to serve in that capacity even when the litigants are gentiles. As has been argued, the "teaching" described is the transmission of the *mesorah*.

most likely that diligent research will uncover principles and precedents leading to a resolution of the problem. Not so with regard to the Noahide Code. The task of a rabbinic decisor confronting a question of Noahide law is formidable because of the paucity of rabbinic literature dealing with even fundamental problems confronting Noahides on a daily basis.

Every student of the Talmud is aware of recorded controversies between *tanna'im* and *amora'im*. Those controversies were adjudicated by the codifiers of Jewish law, at times with unanimity and at times without. Occasionally, early-day authorities disagree with regard to whether or not ostensibly disparate talmudic discussions represent conflicting views and, if so, which discussion is to be regarded as normative. Thus, to take a well-known example, Rambam, contra the position of the tosafists, seemingly posits a controversy with regard to the explicitly formulated principle "There is nothing permitted to Jews that is prohibited to gentiles" (*Sanhedrin* 59a; *Hullin* 31a). Upon the severing of the trachea and the esophagus, internal organs are deemed to be "as if placed in a basket (*ke-manha be-dikula damya*)," torn from the yet living animal and reposing within its skeletal structure. Such organs are rendered permissible to Jews by virtue of ritual slaughter but would be forbidden to non-Jews as organs torn from a living animal save for the principle "There is nothing permitted to Jews that is prohibited to gentiles." Rambam, however, apparently regarded the validity of that principle to be the subject of a talmudic dispute and accordingly, in *Hilkhot Melakhim* 9:11, apparently rules that organ meat of a ritually slaughtered animal is prohibited to non-Jews as meat of an organ torn from a living animal.[31] Whether non-Jews should be counselled on the basis of the tosafists' position or advised to abstain from such meat, as is Rambam's view, is not immediately clear. A further ramification of Rambam's position is that a Jew may not sell or serve such meat to a non-Jew. The internal organs of an animal defectively slaughtered by a ritual slaughterer, and hence forbidden to Jews, would apparently be prohibited to non-Jews according to all authorities as "organs torn from a living animal." No doubt due to their frequent impact upon Jews engaged in the sale of meat,

---

[31]Cf., however, *Mirkevet ha-Mishneh, Hilkhot Melakhim* 9:11, who understands Rambam as forbidding such meat to a non-Jew only as long as the animal is yet alive on precisely the grounds that at such time the animal is prohibited to Jews by virtue of the prohibition "Thou shalt not eat of the blood" (Lev. 19:26).

those questions have received significant attention. Surprisingly, in dealing with actual situations, even the latter question is resolved in a permissive manner by no less a personage than R. Moses Sofer in his *Teshuvot
Hatam Sofer, Yoreh De'ah*, 19. Yet it is probably fair to assume that, since
Hatam Sofer's responsum is not widely quoted, most candidates for a
rabbinical diploma are unaware of its existence; since it is not cited in
later halakhic précis, those who are familiar with its contents may well
be perplexed with regard to whether or not Hatam Sofer's responsum
represents the final word regarding this matter.[32]

Other, far more prevalent, problems pertaining to *"kashrut"* of meat
for non-Jews are no less difficult to resolve, and indeed even the existence of those problems is hardly common knowledge. One who has studied the tractate *Hullin* is probably aware of the view espoused by a number of early-day authorities deeming the meat of an animal that has died

---

[32]More perplexing is the fact that R. Joel Schwartz, *Or la-Amim* (Jerusalem,
5743), p. 131, despite his generally wide-ranging citation of sources in a work
devoted to Noahide law, ignores *Hatam Sofer*'s position entirely.

[*Hatam Sofer*'s conclusion is indeed debatable. It is based on the empirical
contention that all miscarriages of the process of ritual slaughter result in doubtful
(*safek*) *neveilah* rather than certain (*vadai*) *neveilah*. For Jews, doubtful *neveilah*
is treated as certain *neveilah* because of the animal's prior forbidden status as an
unslaughtered animal (*hezkat einah zevuhah*). Noahides are not bound by the
commandment concerning ritual slaughter and hence, insofar as Noahide law
is concerned, there is no *hezkat einah zevuhah*. Accordingly, argues *Hatam Sofer*,
since for Noahides, the animal's prior status was that of a permitted animal,
Noahides should be permitted to partake of its flesh unless there is positive
evidence that the animal has been rendered impermissible.

An objection may be raised to this line of reasoning on the basis of the fact
that the internal organs of an animal slaughtered in the ritual manner would
always be forbidden to Noahides as organs "torn from a living animal" if
not for the principle that all things permitted to Jews are also permitted to
Noahides. The animal in question is clearly not permitted to Jews. The fact
that it is forbidden to a Jew for a reason having no bearing upon the Noahide
Code should be irrelevant. Since, in the final analysis, the animal is not permitted to a Jew there appears to be no applicable halakhic provision negating
the status of the animal's internal organs as organs "torn from a living animal." Cf., *Likkutei He'arot al She'elot u-Teshuvot Hatam Sofer*, III (Jerusalem,
5736), *Yoreh De'ah*, no. 19, sec. 5.]

of natural causes to be forbidden to Noahides.[33] More problematic is the question of whether an animal killed by hunters by means of a rifle shot is permitted to non-Jews.[34] Nor, for that matter, is it at all certain that a non-Jew is permitted to cause pain to an animal simply for sport.[35]

Oddly enough, a rabbinic scholar might feel far more comfortable and confident in counseling a gentile with regard to certain esoteric matters, such as sacrificing an animal on an altar, than with regard to perfectly common matters, such as whether he may retain lost property even if it came into his possession after *ye'ush*, i.e., after the owner has lamented his loss. The first matter involves an activity permitted to non-Jews but prohibited to Jews. A rabbinic scholar whose advice is sought with regard to incidental questions pertaining to Noahide sacrifices will find such matters addressed in great detail in *Mishneh le-Melekh*, in his commen-

---

[33]See Rashi, *Hullin* 92b, s.v. *"be-mekulin"* (but cf., Rashi, *Sanhedrin* 57a, s.v. *"le-meisheri"*); *Tosafot, Hullin* 91a, s.v. *"ke-man de-amar"* and *Tosefot Rabbeinu Peretz, Sanhedrin* 56b. See also *Pesikta Zutrata*, cited by Rema of Panu, *Asarah Ma'amarot, Ma'amar Hakor Din* part 3, chap. 21, p. 103. Cf., R. Samuel ben Hofni Ga'on, introduction to his commentary on the Pentateuch, and *Nahal Eshkol, Hilkhot Treifot*, 15:15. Cf., however, R. Ya'akov Kahana-Shapiro, *Teshuvot Ne'ot Ya'akov*, no. 11; R. Meir Dan Plocki, *Hemdat Yisra'el*, "Kuntres Ner Mitzvah," no. 28, s.v. *"lakhen,"* who maintain that, even according to those authorities, this prohibition was abrogated at Sinai. An opposing view to that of Rashi and *Tosafot* on *Hullin* is held by *Sefer ha-Eshkol, Hilkhot Treifot*, no. 15, and by *Tosafot, Sanhedrin* 56b, s.v. *"akhal."*

[34]*Tosafot, Hullin* 92a, s.v. *"ke-man,"* seems to require slaughter by means of *nehirah* to render animals permissible to non-Jews. See commentaries of Reshash, Maharatz Chajes and *Dor Revi'i*, ad locum. Cf., however, *Be'er Sheva*, ad locum. Rashi, *Hullin* 28a, s.v. *"le-taharah"*and *Hullin* 81b, s.v. *"ve-ha-moher,"* depicts *nehirah* as involving the trachea and esophagus. According to Rashi, severance of those structures in any manner satisfies the requirement of *nehirah*. Indeed, Rashi, *Hullin* 17a, defines *nehirah* as a vertical perforation of those structures. See *Dor Revi'i*, introduction, nos. 1–2. However, Rashi, *Hullin* 85b, s.v. *"noharo,"* defines the process as strangulation (*honko*). Cf., however, R. Ovadiah of Bartenura, who, in his commentary on the Mishnah, *Hullin* 4:2, defines *nehirah* as an incision made at the site of the nostrils and *Tosefet Yom Tov*, ad locum, who comments that *nehirah* does not at all involve the trachea or the esophagus.

[35]See R. Yaakov Zev Kahana, *Toledot Ya'akov* (Vilna, 5667), *Yoreh De'ah*, no. 33.

tary on Rambam's *Hilkhot Ma'aseh ha-Korbanot*. Adjudication of the provisions of the Noahide Code regarding ownership of lost property has not received such detailed attention.[36]

Issues that impact upon broader social policies are even more murky. To offer as an example a matter that perhaps is of relatively minor societal significance, there exists a talmudic controversy regarding whether or not Noahides are forbidden to castrate animals. That controversy is mirrored in a dispute among early-day authorities who differ with regard to adjudication of the issue. The impact of that controversy upon the propriety of neutering pets and upon related matters of animal husbandry is obvious. Assuming that surgical sterilization of female animals is prohibited by rabbinic decree, does such rabbinic legislation extend to non-Jews as well? Of course, the much broader issue is the question of whether Noahides are subject to rabbinic legislative authority.[37] Here, again, the implication with regard to the spaying of household pets is obvious.

---

[36]See the sources cited by R. Ya'akov Blau, *Pithei Hoshen*, I, *Hilkhot Aveidah*, chap. 1, note 55, and his accompanying inconclusive discussion.

[37]*Semak*, cited by *Shakh*, *Yoreh De'ah* 55:11, rules that rabbinically prohibited extensions of *ever min he-hai* are forbidden to non-Jews as well as to Jews. *Peri Hadash*, *Yoreh De'ah* 55:16, challenges this position and asks in astonishment, "Since when did the Sages promulgate edicts for gentiles? And [gentiles] themselves, do they then obey?" *Mishneh le-Melekh*, *Hilkhot Melakhim* 10:7, and *Reshash*, *Sanhedrin* 58b, assert that the Sages did not enact prohibitions binding upon Noahides. Indeed, it is not clear that there exists authority for enactment of such edicts. Rabbinic authority to promulgate legislation binding upon Jews is derived by the Gemara, *Shabbat* 23a, from biblical sources. Since those sources are not rooted in Noahide commandments the source of rabbinic authority vis-à-vis non-Jews would require further elucidation. Nevertheless, *Sedei Hemed*, *Ma'arekhet ha-Vav*, *klal* 26, sec. 20, and ibid., *Pe'at ha-Sadeh*, *Ma'arekhet ha-Gimel*, sec. 10, cites authorities who maintain that all rabbinic edicts pertaining to commandments included in the Noahide Code are also binding upon non-Jews.

Teshuvot Hatam Sofer, *Hoshen Mishpat*, no. 79, s.v. *"pesik ha-shem ha-revi'i,"* develops the thesis that competition that interferes with the ability of another person to earn a livelihood constitutes a biblical transgression. In establishing that point *Hatam Sofer* cites the ruling of *Teshuvot ha-Rema*, no. 10, prohibiting a non-Jew from engaging in such competition. *Hatam Sofer* clearly assumes that such a prohibition could not be made binding upon gentiles by rabbinic decree.

Other such uncertainties have much more profound implications for the development of a Jewish position regarding matters of topical concern.

If, however, the prohibition against such activity is regarded as rabbinic in nature, as would be assumed upon a literal reading of the comments of *Beit Yosef*, *Hoshen Mishpat* 157, *Teshuvot ha-Rema* must be regarded as affirming the principle that rabbinic extension of prohibitions included in the Noahide Code are binding upon gentiles as well as upon Jews.

It seems to be certain that Noahides enjoy the authority to promulgate binding edicts in order to strengthen adherence to the Noahide code as evidenced by the statement of the Gemara, *Avodah Zarah* 36b, indicating that Tamar was sentenced to death for violation of an enactment of the *beit din* of Shechem prohibiting intercourse with an idolator. *Or ha-Hayyim*, Gen. 38:24, comments, ". . . and perhaps they possessed a tradition [authorizing] them to promulgate edicts and to execute one who transgresses the edict." There is, however, no evidence of a tradition explicitly granting Jews the power to legislate on behalf of Noahides. An alternative explanation of the source of the authority of the *beit din* of Shechem and of other Noahide judicial bodies to promulgate edicts may be found in Rambam's analysis of the commandment of *dinin*. Rambam, *Hilkhot Melakhim* 9:14, regards the seventh of the Noahide commandments as imposing an obligation upon non-Jews to establish a judiciary, not only for the purpose of punishing transgression of the provisions of the Noahide Code, but also "to admonish the populace." It may be suggested that legislation to provide a "fence" around the law is a legitimate exercise of the mandate requiring judges "to admonish the populace." [Indeed, this thesis, if correct, may serve to resolve a difficulty inherent in Rambam's formulation of a duty "to admonish the populace" as integral to the *mitzvah* of *dinin*, viz., the identification of a talmudic source for that statement. On the basis of the foregoing it may be postulated that Rambam deduced that conclusion from the authority ascribed to the enactment of the *beit din* of Shechem. That au-thority, Rambam may have reasoned, could be derived only from an anteced-ent premise to the effect that the commandment of *dinin* includes an obligation "to admonish the populace," i.e., to prevent transgression of the Noahide Code. The phrase employed by Rambam, "to admonish the populace" (*le-hazhir et ha-am*), has the connotation of a general admonition rather than simply the injunction of an individual. That phraseology may well be understood as including the obligation to issue general admonitions in the form of edicts binding upon all that are designed to prevent transgression. Thus, if Rambam derives his analysis of *dinin* from the talmudic

It can be definitively stated that, for Jews, a fetus that, if carried to term, would cause the demise of its mother may, and indeed must, be destroyed. *Tosafot* express doubt with regard to whether such a principle exists in the Noahide Code. How is that doubt to be resolved in terms of practical guidance of non-Jews?[38] Assuming that such intervention is generally proscribed, does Jewish law recognize a double-effect theory as a valid principle within the Noahide Code with the result that excision of a cancerous uterus would represent an exception to the general rule?[39]

The talmudic narrative concerning R. Hananyah ben Teradion and his executioner, in which R. Hananyah assures his executioner of a portion in the World to Come in return for adding additional fuel to the fire presents a highly perplexing problem precisely because of an absence of elucidation by early-day authorities. Does the narrative stand for the proposition that hastening the death of an already moribund person, i.e., active euthanasia, does not constitute homicide in the Noahide Code,

---

reference to the powers of the *beit din* of Shechem, that precedent reflects exercise of the authority, not simply to restrain individual malfeasors, but also to enact prophylactic legislation binding upon all.] In addition, Rambam, *Hilkhot Melakhim* 10:11, declares that Jews have an obligation to establish a judiciary to administer the Noahide Code on behalf of *gerei toshav* subject to Jewish sovereignty. Rambam further declares that, if the "*beit din* of Israel" chooses to do so, it may appoint Jewish judges to sit on Noahide courts for the purpose of passing judgment upon Noahides. If it is accepted that the duty "to admonish the populace" gives rise to authority to promulgate general legislation for that purpose, that power might no doubt also be exercised by Jews sitting as members of Noahide courts. Accordingly, it might be argued that rabbinic authorities have the right to constitute themselves as a Noahide court and invoke that court's duty "to admonish the populace" as authority to promulgate legislation binding upon Noahides.

[38]It would appear to this writer that, particularly in the absence of a conflicting statement by any early authority, overt intervention must be eschewed on the grounds that "doubtful" homicide cannot be countenanced even for the purpose of rescuing a human life. Nevertheless, at least one contemporary rabbinic writer is less than unequivocal with regard to this matter. See *Or la-Amim*, p. 128.

[39]For a discussion of this question see J. David Bleich, *Contemporary Halakhic Problems*, III (New York, 1989), 7–9.

as is the expressed view of several contemporary rabbinic authorities,[40] or does it reflect an entirely different principle?[41]

Formulation of a Jewish policy position with regard to capital punishment similarly presents highly complex questions of Noahide law whose resolution is fraught with difficulty. On the one hand, the Noahide Code provides for capital punishment for a number of crimes. Moreover, according to Rambam, imposition of capital punishment, when prescribed by the Noahide Code, is mandatory rather than discretionary. The crux of the problem is the standard of evidence required for imposition of such punishment by Noahides. In practice, most convictions resulting in the death penalty are obtained, not upon the unimpeached testimony of at least a single eyewitness, but upon circumstantial evidence. It must be remembered that, from the vantage point of Jewish law, fingerprints, forensic evidence and the like must be categorized as forms of circumstantial evidence. Sources from which a resolution of the question of whether or not non-Jewish courts may convict on the basis of circumstantial evidence are far from obvious.[42]

Issues of Noahide law are often extremely difficult to resolve. More significantly, the Jewish obligation with regard to *tikkun ha-olam* does not end with determination of particular points of Noahide law. It is clear that in the society in which we live there cannot be one public

---

[40]See R. Samuel Baruch Werner, *Torah she-be-al Peh*, 18 (5736), 42 and R. Schneur Zusha Reiss, *Ha-Ma'or* (Iyar-Sivan 5734), pp. 19–20. R. Moses Feinstein, *Ha-Pardes* (Shevat 5736), p. 12 and idem. *Iggerot Mosheh, Yoreh De'ah*, II, no. 174, *anaf 3*, cites this narrative as "perhaps" reflective of a halakhic provision permitting a non-Jew to perform mercy killing if a mortal wound has already been inflicted by human hands. Cf., however, a later responsum, *Iggerot Mosheh, Hoshen Mishpat*, II, no. 73, sec. 3, in which Rabbi Feinstein cites his earlier responsum as leaving the issue unresolved and declares R. Hananyah ben Teradion's action to have been a *hora'at sha'ah*. Cf., Ran and Rosh, *Nedarim* 22a; and R. Shelomoh Kluger, *Nidrei Zerizin, Nedarim* 22a.

[41]For diverse and conflicting analyses of the halakhic import of this narrative see R. Eliezer Waldenberg, *Ziz Eli'ezer*, IV, no. 13, chap. 2, sec. 7; R. Isaac Liebes, *Teshuvot Beit Avi*, II, no. 153; R. Menasheh Klein, *Mishneh Halakhot*, VII, no. 282; R. Saul Israeli, *Amud ha-Yemini*, no. 32, sec. 2; R. Moshe Dov Welner, *Ha-Torah ve-ha-Medinah*, 7–8 (5715–5717): 318; and *Yam shel Shlomoh, Bava Kamma* 8:59. See also, Ya'akov Weinberger, *Dine Israel* 7 (5736): 117.

[42]See *Contemporary Halakhic Problems* II:341–367.

policy for gentiles and a different public policy for Jews. The result is that Jewish endorsement of policies that from the Jewish perspective, are perfectly acceptable for non-Jews will inevitably lead to effects not acceptable for Jews. Support for the neutering of stray dogs will lead to transgression, knowingly or unknowingly, of a biblical prohibition by Jewish veterinarians. Support for personal autonomy and freedom of choice with regard to withholding of medical treatment will inevitably result in contrahalakhic withholding of treatment from Jewish patients. Criminalization of conduct deleterious to the moral welfare of society and increasing the severity of punishment for acts already branded as criminal will undoubtedly impact upon Jewish malfeasors. Yet, rabbinic sources are far from unequivocal in recognizing the authority of gentile authorities to impose penal sanctions upon Jewish nationals.[43] Successful Jewish advocacy of social policies pertaining to matters involving a disparity in Jewish law between Jews and non-Jews must affect members of the Jewish community. Consideration of such consequences must be judiciously factored into any analysis of Jewish obligations to promote *tikkun ha-olam*.[44]

IV

Although non-Jews are not formally bound other than by the Seven Commandments and Jews have no obligation to impose any higher morality upon gentiles, nevertheless, there are sources indicating that the divine intent is that, at least with the passage of time, the nations of the world will adopt the standards that are normative for Jews. The most authoritative of these sources is R. Jacob Ettlinger, who eloquently developed this thesis in his homiletic work, *Minhat Ani, Parashat be-Midbar*:

---

[43]See J. David Bleich, "Jewish Law and the State's Authority to Punish Crime," *Cardozo Law Review*, 12:3–4 (February–March, 1991): 829–857, reprinted in *Contemporary Halakhic Problems*, vol. IV (New York: Ktav, 1995), pp. 67–91.

[44]For example, I am convinced that the patently specious argument advanced by the representative of Agudath Israel in the Polish Sejm in opposition to capital punishment was not intended as declarative of principles by which Noahides should be bound but motivated by concern for execution of Jewish nationals. See *Contemporary Halakhic Problems*, II, 366, note 35.

the Torah is therefore termed an "illuminating light" and proceeds bit by bit until it illuminates all inhabitants of the universe under all the heavens. And Israel will be the priests of God into whose hands has been given the banner of the Torah to carry unto all corners of the earth. . . . This is explained at the conclusion of the midrashic comment[45] in the statement "'and in the waste, a howling wilderness' [Deut. 32:10]—The universe was [as] night.[46] As soon as Israel accepted the Torah the world lit up, as it is said, 'For *mitzvah* is a lamp and Torah is light' [Prov. 6:23]." This indicates that not for [Israel] alone did the Torah become a light illuminating the darkness but rather for the entire world. Therefore Israel gives thanks to its Father in Heaven saying, "He delivered me because He wanted me" [2 Sam. 22:20], [i.e., He wanted] to give the light of His Torah into my hands to illuminate the entire world through it.[47]

The comments of R. Jacob Ettlinger serve to establish two distinct points.

First, the moral principles embodied in the Sinaitic laws, although not normatively binding upon non-Jews, serve to establish a morality to which they should aspire. Moreover, this aspiration will become actualized, at least in the eschatological era. Quoting a midrashic statement underscoring the fact that the Torah was given in the month of "twins," thereby symbolizing that the Torah was "offered" to both Esau and Jacob,[48] *Minhat Ani* adds that, although the original offer to Esau was in vain, "nevertheless the word of God does not return empty in that in the end of times the light of Torah will illuminate even Esau and his compatriots."

Secondly, the role of Israel in achieving that goal is entirely passive, at least in so far as "outreach" activity directed toward the nations of the world is concerned. There is no hint whatsoever in either *Minhat Ani*'s comments or in the midrashic source upon which they are predicated indicating that Jews have any particular obligation to assure that such a goal is achieved. Apparently, the role of Israel is to teach by ex-

---

[45]*Minhat Ani*'s quotation is actually a paraphrase of *Be-Midbar Rabbah* 2:5.

[46]The midrashic interpretation is based upon rendering "*yelel*" as a form of "*lel*," meaning "night," rather than as a form of "*yelalah*" meaning "wail" or "howl."

[47]These comments are advanced by *Minhat Ani* in elucidation of *Yalkut Shim'oni*, II Samuel, no. 161.

[48]See supra, note 4.

ample. Obviously, the greater the quality and the purity of the example, the greater the effect. The more intense the "light of Torah," the brighter the illumination that it will cast.

Noteworthy also are the comments of R. Naphtali Zevi Yehudah Berlin, popularly known as "the Netziv," in his *Kidmat ha-Emek*, introducing his commentary on the Pentateuch: ". . . it is the desire of the Holy One, blessed be He, that [gentiles] study Scripture and for that reason the Holy One, blessed be He, commanded that it be translated into seventy languages." An even clearer and more forceful statement of the obligations of Jews vis-à-vis non-Jews occurs in Netziv's introduction to his *Haamek Davar* on *Sefer Shemot*. In those comments Netziv develops the thesis that the Book of Exodus is actually the complement to the Book of Genesis in that it constitutes the concluding portion of the story of creation. As Genesis records the efficient cause of creation, Exodus records the final cause, or *takhlit*, of creation: *viz.*, the notion that the world was created on account of "*reshit*," i.e., "on behalf of Israel which is termed *reshit*'" (Rashi, Gen. 1:1).[49] This goal, Netziv tells us, was not fulfilled "until Israel exited from Egypt and *achieved their telos that they be fit to be an illumination unto the nations to cause them to arrive at knowledge of the Lord of the universe*" (emphasis added).

The theme is further developed by Netziv in his commentary on Ex. 12:51. The final phrase of the verse "And it came to pass the selfsame day that God brought the children of Israel out of the land of Egypt *al tzivotam*" is generally understood as meaning "by their hosts." Netziv understands the term "*tzava*" in the sense of "service" as in the verse "Is there not a time of service to man upon earth" (Job 7:1), i.e., "every person is created for his telos and that is his 'service.'"[50] The telos for

---

[49]Cf., *Pesikta Zutrata* 1:1 and *Midrash Tanhuma* (ed. S. Buber), *Parashat Bereishit* 3 where the phrase appears as "in the merit of Israel."

[50]Netziv's interpretation of this term is not as imaginative as might appear. The term "*kol yotzei zava*," occuring in Num. 1:21 and frequently thereafter, is translated "all that are capable of going forth to war." The term "*zava*" in that context clearly denotes an armed force. However, an armed force is a "host" in which every individual has an assigned duty. Thus, the term "*zava*" may well have the connotation of both "host" and "assignment" or "service." It is certainly in the latter sense that the term is used in Job 7:1. Accordingly, Netziv understands the phrase "*al ziv'otam*" as having an identical connotation.

which Israel was created, continues Netziv, is "to be an illumination unto the nations to cause them to arrive at knowledge of the Lord of the universe." Only upon undergoing circumcision[51] and their subsequent exodus from Egypt "did [the children of Israel] attain their service, i.e., that for which they were created on earth."

Netziv is silent with regard to how this task is to be achieved. He neither declares that Israel's role is passive in nature nor does he take issue with the earlier published views of R. Jacob Ettlinger and demand that Israel play an active role in providing instruction to non-Jews. With regard to Netziv's remarks in *Kidmat ha-Emek* concerning translation of the Bible, it may be observed that God commanded that the Pentateuch be translated into seventy languages but not that it be taught in seventy languages. The Torah is to be made available by means of translation, but there is no obligation to establish a Jewish Gideon Society. The Torah is to be made available by means of translation, but there is no concomitant obligation actively to disseminate even the Written Law among non-Jews.

The passive nature of Israel's mission to mankind is expressed at even greater length by a disciple of R. Jacob Ettlinger, R. Samson Raphael Hirsch. R. Hirsch's comments are verbose and perhaps infelicitous to the contemporary ear, but they are entirely unequivocal. As stated by R. Hirsch:[52]

> When, in the choice of Abraham, the foundation-stone of this people was laid, God, Who did it, pronounced its significance: "and in thee shall all families of the earth be blessed" [Gen. 12:3], and explained the blessing that came from this choice: ". . . For I know him, that he will command his children and his household after him, and they shall keep the way of the Lord, to do justice and judgment" [Gen. 18:18]—meaning that Abraham's descendants should follow with love and justice in the ways of God and by this silent

---

[51]Netziv asserts that realization of this telos became possible only subsequent to circumcision to which reference is made in Ex. 12:44 and 12:48. Although he does not offer an explanation or rationale for the connection between circumcision and Israel's role as "an illumination unto the nations" he points to a parallel connection in the command to Abraham to circumcise himself and Abraham's role as "the father of the multitude of nations" in bringing them nigh to the service of God.

[52]*Horeb*, no. 613.

example become a blessed monument to God and humanity among the peoples of the earth, so that they should be "a kingdom of priests, and a holy nation" [Ex. 19:6].

As the priest among the people, so should they among mankind uphold the vision of God and humanity and by so doing be a holy nation, raised above every injustice, profaneness and hardheartedness, as becomes the bearers of such a message. . . . Let us live our Jewish life quietly and modestly, illumine and strengthen mind and soul through the teachings of the Torah; perpetuate these teachings for ourselves and others by observing our Festivals of Commemoration, fulfil them by a life of justice and love towards every creature that bears the seal of God's creating, as our religion teaches us. If, thus, we were truthful, just and holy and loving in mind and soul, in possession and enjoyment, in word and deed, if then God would let this promise of salvation grow out of our fate and our life: that the whole of mankind, awakened by its own experience, enlightened anew and uplifted by our destiny and life, should, in unity with us, turn to the One and Only—and if thus we would fulfil our vocation as priests to humanity—what bliss there would be . . . ![53]

Despite his assertion that the mission is essentially passive in nature, R. Hirsch recognizes that is was necessary to seize opportunities to teach by example. Thus, he writes:

Do not shirk the social obligations of pulsating modern life; do not regret that today's nations, in their struggle for enlightenment, have invited also the sons of Jewish Law to participate in their social aspirations and that they have opened for the sons of Israel the gates to scientific and civil endeavors and achievements.[54]

However, carrying out these responsibilities should never result in compromise of halakhic obligations, nor should an individual seek a role or occupation which, while furthering Israel's mission to mankind, might create pitfalls with regard to the individual's own religious observance. R. Hirsch cautions, "Your only purpose in trying to acquire property . . . should be to . . . work for the advancement of your people and humanity: . . . In the choice of an occupation the guiding consid-

---

[53]Loc. cit.

[54]*The Collected Writings*, vol. VIII (New York and Jerusalem: Philipp Feldheim, Inc., 1995), p. 325.

eration should be which one involves the least danger to your loyalty to God's law. . . ."[55]

In defining Israel's mission as an obligation to teach by example, R. Hirsch develops at some length the corollary theme that Israel is admonished to abjure conduct that would have the opposite effect:

> But because Israel has such a high and sacred vocation, because, for the working out of this destiny, every son and every daughter of Israel is obliged to contribute thereto by their behavior in their own humble circle—how careful do we need to be in our behavior, in particular in the way in which we conduct ourselves towards non-Jews, so that they may see in our lives really only a reflection of the Torah of truth, of justice and of love!

Indeed, R. Hirsch asserts such negative conduct constitutes a form of profanation of the Divine Name:

> Therefore, once more so urgently to *all of us* goes out the call: Do not profane My Holy Name! Do not destroy, through your way of living, the recognition of the all-holy God and His word in the minds of the nations among which you live! . . .
>
> Therefore our Sages say: "The crimes of stealing and injustice are greater towards a non-Jew than towards a Jew"; for towards a Jew it is the simple violation of a commandment, "Thou shalt not steal," etc. But in the case of a non-Jew, as well as being that, it is also that great crime which can only be expiated by death: the *chillul HaShem*, profanation of the Divine Name. Every Jew who deceives or cheats a non-Jew commits this greatest of all crimes, and, indeed, it is said: "and those that remain of Israel shall not commit injustice, shall not speak false things, neither shall their lips utter words of deceit!" And here, again, avoid not only real injustice, real hardheartedness, but even the semblance of them . . . towards your non-Jewish brethren; for the semblance is the crime as much as the actual sin, because it—as with the sin itself—breeds contempt for that very thing which it is your task to maintain as holy. . .[56]

---

[55]*Horeb: A Philosophy of Jewish Laws and Observances*, tr. I. Grunfeld (New York: Soncino Press, 1962), pp. 392–93. See also *The Collected Writings*, VII, 12.

[56]*Loc. cit.* Cf., R. Me'ir Simhah ha-Kohen of Dvinsk, *Meshekh Hokhmah, Parashat Mishpatim*, s.v. "*ve-yetakhen*," who finds halakhic expression for the thesis that the murder of a non-Jew is more heinous than the murder of a Jew in that it involves, in addition to the crime of homicide, a transgression in the nature of profanation of the Divine Name.

R. Hirsch's development of this thesis is paralleled and, in a sense, extended by R. Naftali Tzvi Yehudah Berlin in the preface to his *Haamek Davar* on the Book of Genesis. Joshua 10:23 and 2 Samuel 1:18 refer to a certain *Book of Yashar*. The Gemara, *Avodah Zarah* 25a, queries: "What is the *Book of Yashar*? R. Hiyya ben Abba said in the name of R. Yohanan, 'It is the book of Abraham, Isaac and Jacob who were called "righteous" (*yesharim*), and of whom Scripture says, "Let me die the death of the righteous and let my last end be like his." '"

Citing this statement *Haamek Davar* comments,

> This was the praise of the Patriarchs, that in addition to being righteous, pious and lovers of God in the greatest manner possible, in addition they were righteous (*yesharim*) that is, that they conducted themselves with the nations of the world even with repugnant idolators . . . with love and with concern for their benefit since that is what sustains creation. Thus we see how much our father Abraham put himself out to pray for Sodom . . . This is precisely as "the father of the multitude of nations" for even though the son does not tread in straight paths nevertheless he is concerned for his welfare and benefit. And our father Jacob, although he was sorely vexed by Laban who intended to eradicate him . . . nevertheless [Jacob] spoke soft words to him . . . and quickly became reconciled with him.[57]

Haamek Davar asserts that recognition that the nations of the world are necessary to "sustain Creation" constitutes a motivating force for active concern for their welfare. Recognition that the nations of the world, too, play a significant role in actualization of the divine blueprint for human destiny renders it "righteous" for Israel to contribute to, and hasten, the actualization of the divine plan.

The function of Israel as a role model for the nations of the world is further developed by R. Hirsch in his *Nineteen Letters*. R. Hirsch describes the moral degeneration of mankind depicted in the opening chapter of Genesis as the process of abjuring a theocentric existence and supplant-

---

[57]This concept is echoed in an etymological observation advanced by R. Hirsch and applied as a categorization of Jews as a people. Deut. 33:26 employs the term "*Yeshurun*" as a cognomen for the people of Israel. Hirsch, in his commentary on Deut. 5:17, understands the term to be derived from "*yashar*," meaning "straight" or "just," and comments: ". . . in their intercourse with other people [Jews] are to show themselves as *yashar*, as the straightest, most honest, most upright nation amongst the nations."

ing service of God with a desire for material possessions and hedonistic pleasure. In the Seventh Letter, R. Hirsch asserts that "it became necessary that a people be introduced into the ranks of the nations which through its history and life should declare God the only creative cause of existence, fulfillment of His will the only aim of life; and which should bear the revelation of His will . . . *unto all parts of the world* [emphasis added] as the motive and incentive of its coherence."[58]

In the same letter R. Hirsch makes it abundantly clear that fulfillment of the original purpose of Creation is not restricted to Jews but that, at least ultimately, all of mankind will rededicate itself to fulfillment of the divine plan. In a footnote appended to the Fifteenth Letter, R. Hirsch, in what must be understood in a homiletical vein, observes that the rabbinic dictum "The pious of the nations of the world have a portion in the World to Come" may be interpreted as meaning that "all nations will help to work out the historical destiny of humanity." In the interim, Jews, in their meticulous observance of God's commandments, keep that goal alive and serve as an exemplar for emulation by others. As a people, Israel "must remain alone and aloof, must do its work and live its life in separation, until, refined and purified by its teachings and its example, universal humanity might turn to God and acknowledge in Him the only Creator and Ruler. That attained, Israel's mission will have been accomplished."[59]

The essentially passive nature of this educative function is underscored by R. Hirsch in the Ninth Letter: "If in the midst of a world which reveres wealth and lust . . . if we were, if we would become, what we should be—if our lives were a perfect reflection of our laws—what a mighty engine we would constitute for propelling mankind to its final goal of all human perfection! More quietly, but more forcefully, and profoundly, would it affect mankind . . ."[60]

The prophet Isaiah testifies that in the end of days there will be a pervasive thirst for the word of God and, ultimately, non-Jews will turn to Jews in their quest to become familiar with the law of God: "And it shall come to pass in the end of days . . . And many nations shall come

---

[58]*The Nineteen Letters*, pp. 66–67.

[59]See also S. R. Hirsch, *The Collected Writings*, vol. I (New York: Feldheim, 1984), pp. 175, 348, 371.

[60]*The Nineteen Letters*, pp. 85–86.

and say, 'Come ye, and let us go up to the mountain of the Lord, to the house of the God of Jacob and he will teach us His ways [*derakhav*] and we will walk in his paths [*orhotav*]'" (Is. 2:2–3). Malbim, in his commentary on this passage, notes that elsewhere the Hebrew term "*derakhav*," translated as "His ways," denotes major roads or highways while the term "*orhotav*," translated as "His paths," refers to secondary roads. Thus, according to Malbim, Isaiah speaks of Jews teaching the nations the "roots and principles" of divine service and prophesies that, in the end of days, these nations will seek even greater edification and will, of their own accord, seek to discover even the byways and footpaths, i.e., the details and minutiae, of the Torah.

R. Hirsch returns both to an elucidation of the mission of Israel and its essentially passive nature in his commentary on Ps. 126:5. The verse "Those who sow in tears will reap in exultation" is understood by Hirsch as referring to the sowing and harvesting of a spiritual crop. The exile, declares R. Hirsch, turned Israel into "the sowers of God," i.e., those whose task was "to disseminate the seeds of truth concerning God and the destiny of mankind into the fields of man's future." This mission is apparently developed by Israel simply by virtue of its presence and example. As stated by R. Hirsch:

> And Israel has fulfilled this vocation as "God's sower" through the Divine Book which nations everywhere have accepted from its hands, as well as through the living commentary which it has given to the doctrine taught in this Book by virtue of its conduct in private and public life alike. For every aspect of Israel's life was directed to all that was spiritual, humane and pure, and ran its course with self-sacrificing devotion in morality and loyalty to duty.

Those seeds are sown together with, and despite, the tears of persecution. But ultimately "the seed sowed with tears will open in the form of ever-growing homage paid on earth to truth and right, morality and mercy as the duty and destiny of mankind." Then, and apparently only then, the "'sowers of God' . . . will be allowed to rejoice and exult in this harvest."[61] That is so, at least in part, because we ourselves are not aware of

---

[61]S. R. Hirsch, *The Psalms*, trans. by Gertrude Hirschler (Jerusalem and New York: Feldheim, 1978), commentary on Ps. 126:5, vol. II, p. 385.

our own success in fulfilling this mission and will not fully appreciate our accomplishment until:

> our return to Zion, then we shall awaken as if from a dream. It will seem to us that we had lived through the long, long years of our exile as in a dream, a long nightmare during which, absorbed in ourselves, we had taken little notice of the changes which had gone on round about us, and of the impact which, unknown to us, our wanderings had had upon the nations with which we had come in contact during our dispersion.[62]

V

This is yet another consideration that must inform policies adopted by the Jewish community vis-à-vis the general society. The earlier-cited rulings of Rambam address only the obligations of Jews to secure general acceptance of the Seven Commandments bestowed upon the nations of the world. They do not at all address the question of punishment for particular transgressions of the Noahide Code. However, in *Hilkhot Melakhim* 10:11, Rambam writes, "The *beit din* of Israel is obligated to establish judges for these resident strangers in order to judge them on the basis of these ordinances in order that the world not be destroyed (*she-lo yishahet ha-olam*)."

Rambam's formulation is somewhat problematic. According to Rambam's own formulation, in *Hilkhot Melakhim* 9:14, of the last of the Noahide commandments, *viz.*, *dinin*, obligates Noahides to establish a judiciary in order to enforce the Noahide Code and to punish transgressions thereof. The commandment of *dinin*, however, is addressed to Noahides, not to Jews. The commandment addressed to Jews with regard to establishment of *batei din* is couched in the words "Judges and officers shall you establish *to yourself* in all your gates" (Deut. 16:18). Yet Rambam explicitly declares that there exists an obligation incumbent upon the Jewish *beit din* to establish a judicial system for Noahides. It is precisely because there is no explicit commandment giving rise to such an obligation that he finds it necessary to append an explanatory comment indicating the rationale un-

---

[62]Ibid., commentary on Ps. 126:1, vol. II, p. 384. See also Hirsch's commentary on Ps. 149:1, ibid., pp. 492–93.

derlying this ruling, *viz.*, "so that the world not be destroyed." The ruling and its rationale are not based upon any explicit talmudic text. Rambam maintains that the obligation is self-evident and a priori. Lawlessness and anarchy, even if limited to non-Jews, are bound to have a deleterious effect upon Jews. Immorality is contagious and its effects are inescapable. Disintegration of the moral fabric of society affects everyone. Particularly in our age, we cannot insulate ourselves against the pervasive cultural forces that mold human conduct. Jewish self-interest requires that society not be allowed to become morally degenerate.[63]

VI

The foregoing notwithstanding, there is no question that, historically, the Jewish community has not engaged in any concerted effort to influence non-Jews to abide by the provisions of the Noahide Code nor has it attempted to influence society to reflect the mores of the Noahide Code in its laws and institutions. The reasons, I believe, can better be elucidated by social historians than by students of *Halakhah*. The relevant factors, however, are not difficult to discern. Until fairly recently, Jewish influence upon the dominant society was virtually nil. No one was listening to us and certainly no one was asking us. Moreover, given the burden of a long and arduous *galut*, other internal concerns were much more pressing. Those concerns demanded commitment of time and human resources to such an extent that focus upon obligations vis-à-vis society at large was precluded.

In the twentieth century, disenchantment with the nations of the world grew as anti-Semitism reared its ugly head in the 1930s and reached its height during and after the Holocaust. The poet Uri Zevi Greenberg voiced the disillusionment of the members of his generation:

> Between us and the nations of the world lie the slaughtered of our family . . .
> Deathly poison is the spirit of Europe . . .[64]
> We were as dreamers of a reality that is not and shall not ever be.

---

[63]See also the comments of *Sefer Hasidim* cited supra, note 16.

[64]*Rehovot ha-Nahar: Sefer ha-Iliyut ve-ha-Ko'ah* (Jerusalem: Schocken, 1950), p. 172.

The world of the nations is a night forest of beasts and they in it are wild animals.[65]

In the wake of the Holocaust he came to regard non-Jews as entirely bereft of a capacity for humaneness and declaimed:

The time has come to examine the concept of "European culture" in the light of the furnace, in the light of reality, and to effect two departures at one time, from Europe and from its culture. . . . There are two types of person in the world, circumcised and uncircumcised; that is the reality.[66]

In many circles any hope of educating or refining the nations of the world was written off as a utopian endeavor incapable of realization in premessianic times.

Finally, in the modern age, social action became a dominant concern of the Reform movement with the result that such activity quite incorrectly became suspect within the traditionalist sectors of our community. Reform theology stressed the universal and abnegated the particular. The two paragraphs that together constitute the *Aleinu* prayer are vastly different in content. The theme of the first paragraph underscores Jewish particularism, extols Jewish chosenness and distinctiveness and expresses gratitude to the "Master of everything," who "has not made us like the nations of the lands and has not emplaced us like the families of the earth; for He has not assigned our position like theirs nor our lot like all their multitudes." In contrast, the second paragraph of the prayer outlines Judaism's universalist teachings, reiterates hope for the universal recognition of the supremacy of God, expresses the aspiration "to perfect the universe through the sovereignty of the Almighty—*le-takken olam be-malkhut Shadai*" and heralds the dawn of an era in which "all the world's inhabitants will recognize and know that to You every knee should bend, every tongue should swear."

The first paragraph, with its unambivalent emphasis on the motif of Jewish chosenness, was profoundly disconcerting to the liturgists of Reform and Liberal Judaism. Accordingly, over the decades, several Re-

---

[65]Ibid., p. 176.

[66]Uri Zevi Greenberg, oral remarks cited in Aaron ben Or, *Toledot ha-Sifrut ha-Ivrit be-Doreinu* (Tel Aviv: Israel Publishing House, 1958), I, 277.

form rites completely omitted the comparative phrases from the *Aleinu* prayer and thereby entirely eliminated any particularist tone. Some Reform prayerbooks retained the original Hebrew but paraphrased or altered the translation. Other Liberal prayerbooks emended the Hebrew text by stating the particularist teachings in positive terms and eliminating the negative references to other nations.[67]

However, while many Reform prayerbooks include an attenuated version of the beginning of the *Aleinu* prayer, the second paragraph usually appears in its entirety and without the slightest alteration. This universalist paean was greatly beloved by the very Reform liturgists who found the opening words of the *Aleinu* so embarrassingly chauvinistic. Indeed, at times, the relative length of this Hebrew passage is striking, appearing as it does in some Reform rites in its pristine form as one of the lengthier Hebrew selections to be found in the prayerbook.

Reform teaching did indeed extol the mission of Israel "*le-takken olam*—to perfect the world*." But neither the predilections of our separated brethren, nor, *le-havdil*, the contemporary zealotry of Habad emissaries with regard to teaching the Seven Commandments of Noah to non-Jews,[68] should serve to deter us from enunciating Jewish teaching even if, at times, it has made the propagation of such teachings somewhat more difficult. We are not about to abandon our belief in the coming of the Messiah because of our embarrassment at the spate of advertisements in the media erroneously announcing his advent as an already accomplished fact. Public teaching of the subject may suffer, for the nonce, but surely, as hallowed by tradition, no *darshan* will hesitate to conclude his sermon with the age-old prayer for the coming of the Messiah speedily in our day!

---

[67]For a discussion of this topic and an outline of revisions in the *Aleinu* text in thirty-six different Reform prayerbooks see Jakob J. Petuchowski, *Prayerbook Reform in Europe: The Liturgy of European Liberal and Reform Judaism* (New York: World Union for Progressive Judaism, 1968), pp. 298–306.

[68]See the censorious comments of R. Eliezer Schach, "Le-Hitrahek me-Kat ha-Yedu'ah: Le-Hasir Mikhshol," *Mikhtavim u-Ma'amarim*, III (Bnei Brak, 5748), 101, directed against a sect that conducts a "campaign regarding the Seven Commandments of the Sons of Noah as if only this is presently lacking to us." The letter originally appeared in *Yated Ne'eman*, 7 Shevat 5747. Cf. also R. Moshe Sternbuch, *Edut*, supra, note 16.

VII

Jews committed to *Halakhah* have only rarely, and only recently, taken positions *qua* Jews on matters of public policy. Despite the democratic institutions of this country, Jews whose roots were in a totally different environment were apt to view themselves as living on sufferance even on these shores. In many circles it was felt that a low profile should be maintained lest latent anti-Semitism be aroused. Some argued that political influence should best be husbanded and held in reserve for matters of more vital concern to the Jewish community. Nor should it be overlooked that in earlier periods of American Jewish history, the sector of the Jewish community that was concerned with matters of *Halakhah* could boast of few articulate spokesmen with a mastery of the vernacular.

In recent years, the Orthodox community has matured, but it has still chosen to remain silent on most public issues. When it *has* spoken it has done so not out of a desire to impose halakhic standards upon the community at large but for entirely different reasons. Abortion legislation is a case in point. But the fact is that no Orthodox group has mounted a legislative campaign or lobbied for the enactment of restrictive measures. Testimony before legislative committees and public statements were forthcoming because they were specifically requested and because the teachings of classical Judaism had been distorted in public forums. But the issue simply did not cause Jews to buttonhole legislators, generate a barrage of telegrams, or march on Washington.

The so-called gay rights bill enacted in New York City by the City Council did occasion a flutter of opposition on the part of some Jewish groups. Here, too, the expressed concern was not the desire to impose halakhic norms upon society at large. The concern focused particularly upon the presence of professed homosexuals in the classroom as authority-figures whose lifestyle and mores might serve as a role-model for youngsters in their formative years. Since Judaism does not view homosexuality as an acceptable alternative lifestyle, those groups perceived the proposed legislation as boding a moral danger to themselves and their families. They were hardly concerned with legislating *Halakhah* for society in general.

Personal liberty and the rights of the individual are strongly rooted as cardinal values of Western philosophy. Systems of thought that view the rights of individuals as paramount and inalienable find it difficult to accommodate the concept of a state that requires its citizens to surrender basic freedoms and to sublimate individual self-interest for the sake of the welfare of society. Much of Western social and political philosophy is devoted to the formulation of an intellectual matrix designed to justify extension of the powers of the body politic to spheres beyond the simple protection of its members against evildoers. Thus, eighteenth- and nineteenth-century European thought gave rise to various forms of social-contract theory. Inherent in many such theories is the concept that, at least ideally, the state should maintain a laissez-faire attitude toward its citizens insofar as possible.

Jewish thought—and law—is based upon an entirely different set of premises. Judaism views man as his brother's keeper. Man is bound by divinely imposed imperatives that oblige him to be concerned with the needs—and morals—of his fellow. Jewish law recognizes that the human condition requires that the governing authority, acting as the representative of society as a whole, be endowed with the broad powers necessary for the promotion of social welfare and moral conduct.

This is, of course, sharply at odds with the posture of contemporary Western society which, despite its abandonment of the laissez-faire doctrine in the arenas of economic and social welfare, tends to view a hands-off policy as the ideal to be pursued in areas of personal morality. Within a libertarian framework, the positions of Mill, Hart, *et al.* are eminently consistent and logical. But one can hardly use the philosophical systems of these thinkers as a backdrop for the formulation of halakhic or quasi-halakhic policies. By the same token, one must recognize that if any legislation is to pass a judicial test of constitutionality it must reflect some defensible social interest over and above the furtherance of personal morality.

It is the strong inclination of this writer that there should be a Jewish response to many of the social problems on the contemporary agenda. Any responsible response requires careful assessment of the principles herein outlined and, above all, dare not suborn violation of the Noahide Code. Advocacy in the public and political arenas should be an expression of cogent and principled positions reflecting halakhic norms applicable to non-Jews as well as to Jews. There should emerge carefully articulated policy statements regarding such topical issues as abortion, health-care plans and sexual mores as well as capital punishment and legislation addressing rights of homosexuals.

We live in an age of searching and seeking. We should certainly not hesitate to make the teachings of Judaism as they bear upon contemporary issues more readily accessible to our fellow citizens. At the very minimum, that would be one way of imparting knowledge of Torah to our fellow Jews. Beyond that, it would quite likely serve to improve the moral atmosphere in which we all live.

3

The Obligation of Jews to Seek Observance of Noahide Laws by Gentiles: A Theoretical Review[1]

Michael J. Broyde

When one sees a Noahide sinning, if one can correct him, one should, since God sent Jonah to Nineveh to return them to his path.
—Sefer Hasidim (*Wistinetski edition [Frankfurt, 1924], Section 1124*)

INTRODUCTION

This paper will address the scope of *halakhah*'s mandate upon Jews to enforce the seven Noahide commandments, as well as any other rules

---

[1]Rabbi Howard Jachter commented on a version of this article, and his comments were appreciated. For excellent works surveying issues concerning Noahide law generally, see Rabbi J. David Bleich, "*Mishpat Mavet be-Dinei Benei No'ah*," *Jubilee Volume in Honor of Moreinu Hagaon Rabbi Joseph B. Soloveitchik*, eds., S. Yisrachi, N. Lamm, and Y. Rafael (Jerusalem: Mosad Ha-Rav Kook, 1984), 1; 193–208; Rabbi J. David Bleich, "*Hasqarat Poshei'a Yehudi Shebarah*

Jewish law mandates that gentiles should keep.[2] It will do so from a purely theoretical perspective, without any attempt to apply the rules devel-

---

le-Eretz Yisrael," *Or Ha-Mizrah* 35 (5747):247–269; Nahum Rakover, "Jewish Law and the Noahide Obligation to Preserve Social Order," *Cardozo Law Review* 12 (1991):1073–1136; Nachum Rakover, "*Ha-Mishpat ke-Erekh Universali: Dinim bi-Benei No'ah*" 15–57 (5748); *Entziklopedyah Talmudit*, "*Ben No'ah*" 3:348–362; Aaron Lichtenstein, *The Seven Laws of Noah*, 2d ed. (New York: Rabbi Jacob Joseph School, 1986). (As a general matter, I have tried to provide citations to both English and Hebrew versions of works, when both exist, for the convenience of some readers.)

I do not address the merits of alternative rationales for enforcing the Noahide commandments, such as, for example, to teach and direct the Jewish community. In a famous story, often recounted, Rabbi Yisra'el Salanter favored the translation of the Talmud into German and its introduction in the curricula of German universities; when asked to explain his support, he replied that if the gentiles thought Talmud study is important, maybe the Jews would study it also! For a detailed discussion of this issue, see Dov Katz, *Tenu'at Ha-Musar* (Tel Aviv, 1945–56) 1:22–25 and Rabbi J. David Bleich, *Contemporary Halakhic Problems* (New York: Ktav, 1983), 319–320. So, too, that rationale could be advanced to support enforcement of the seven commandments. See also the postscript for more on this issue.

The term "Noahide" is used in the rabbinic literature to denote anyone who is not Jewish. See generally Rashi, *Nedarim* 31a and R. Aaron Kirschenbaum, "The Covenant with Noahides Compared to the Sinai Covenant" *Dinei Israel* 6 (5735): 31–48. More specifically, as noted by Ritva, *Makkot* 9a, "Noahide" denotes a gentile who keeps the Noahide commandments," "*ger toshav*" denotes a gentile who formally accepts the commandments, and "gentile" denotes one who has done neither. An *eved kena'ani* ("Canaanite slave") is generally not thought to be a Noahide; see Rashi, *Sanhedrin* 58b. See also Rabbenu Gershom, *Keritut* 9b and *Me'iri* 48a, both of whom appear to classify a *ger toshav* as a partial convert; see also Rabbi Howard Jachter, "*Kedushat Yisra'el la-Hatzain*" *Beit Yitzhak* 24 (5742): 425–428.

[2] As noted by *Sefer ha-Hinukh* 416, although classically referred to as "seven" commandments in the Talmudic literature (see Tosefta A.Z. 9:4 and *Sanhedrin* 56a), these commandments include far more than seven obligations. As noted in *The Seven Laws of Noah* supra note 1, at 90–91, these seven commandments correspond to nearly 60 of the 613 *mitzvot* given to the Jews, or one in four of those obligations practical since the destruction of the Temple and exile from the Land. Even the Talmud readily acknowledges this fact; see *Hullin* 92a. In

oped to America in the 1990s or any other particular (factual) setting.[3] Rather, the purpose of this article is to determine which options concerning enforcement are halakhically *acceptable*. In the field of "Jewish public policy," the first question that must be asked is which (if any) of the theoretical options are prohibited by Jewish law. After that question is answered, one can consider which of the remaining options most closely accomplishes whatever Jewish goal is sought.[4]

Part 1 of this article outlines what are the Noahide commandments, and identifies their place in a halakhic system. Part 2 discusses the obligation of both Jews and Noahides under the rubric of the commandment called *dinim* (literally: "laws" or "justice"). Part 3 reviews the various opinions on the obligation of Jews to enforce the Noahide commandments. Part 4 considers not only whether enforcement must be sought, but whether in situations where enforcement is not possible, Jewish law mandates Jews to seek to persuade Noahides to obey their commandments. It considers also whether—when persuasion fails—Jewish law,

---

my opinion, there is a dispute on how to understand this talmudic section. Are the thirty obligations mentioned there explanations and elaborations on the seven, or are they additional commandments not included in the seven? Rabbi Menahem Azaria Mifano, *Asara Ma'amrot, Ma'amar Hoker Din* 3:21 clearly understands them as mere explanations. On the other hand, Shmuel ben Hofni Ga'on seems to understand them as additional commandments; see his commentary on Gen. 34:12; see also Jerusalem Talmud, *Avodah Zarah* 2:1, which states "These thirty commandments Noahides will accept upon themselves in the future." This distinction leads to some very practical differences; see Rabbi J. David Bleich, "Divine Unity in Maimonides, the Tosafists and Meiri," in *Neoplatonism and Jewish Thought*, ed. Lenn E. Goodmann (1992), 237–254; he uses the opinion of Shmuel ben Hofni to explain an insight of Me'iri which has practical ramifications.

[3]As with any specific halakhic ruling, but even more so in this one, that application requires evaluation of the impact on society at large. Thus, there might be no halakhic obligation to seek enforcement when it is clear that there is no possibility of success (however defined) or that profound harm would befall the Jewish community if enforcement was sought; for more on this, see postscript. For a discussion of this issue in the context of enforcement of Jewish law within a Jewish community, see *Tehumin* 7:107–144 (articles by Rav Moshe Malka, Rav Yitzhak Zilberstein, Rav Simha Kook, and Rav Yisra'el Rosen).

[4]For more on this issue, see postscript.

at the minimum, requires that one may not assist a gentile in violating the Noahide commandments.

THE NOAHIDE LAWS

Preliminary Issues

Before one can explore the obligation upon Jews to enforce Noahide law, it is necessary to determine if Jewish law accepts that these commandments are still binding on Noahides. The Talmud recounts, as one possible resolution of an unrelated tort law problem, that "God observed the gentiles of the land—What did He see? He saw that the seven commandments He gave the Noahides were not observed and thus He permitted these seven commandments to them."[5] Based on this assertion, Bah,[6] Rabbi Hayyim Abulafia,[7] *Penei Yehoshu'a,*[8] Maharit[9] (and perhaps *Hatam Sofer*[10] and a version of Tosafot[11]) all indicate that gentiles are no longer legally obligated even to keep the Noahide commandments and those who do keep them would be in the status of one "not obligated and observing."[12] This can perhaps be inferred from the comments of Rashi,

---

[5]*Bava Kamma* 38a. For a use of this talmudic text in a different context, see Responsa of Rabbi Hildesheimer, *Yoreh De'ah* 259.

[6]*Haggahot ha-Bah, Hagigah* 13a. The reference in Bah to *Ein Ya'akov* is to the version of Tosafot printed in *Ein Ya'akov* on *Hagigah* 13a. See also *Responsa Rama Mefano* 30.

[7]*Sefer Etz Haim,* beginning of Gen. 37, quoting Maharash Algazi from *Ahavat Olam.*

[8]*Responsa Penei Yehoshua, Yoreh De'ah* 1:3 and *Even Ha'ezer* 2:43.

[9]Quoted in *Makrai Kodesh* 63a. For a discussion of the opinions of Rabbi Haim Abulafia, *Penei Yehoshua* and Maharit, see *Yabi'a Omer, Yoreh De'ah* 3:17(10).

[10]Commentary on *Orah Hayyim* 39; but see Hatam Sofer *Hoshen Mishpat* 185, where he indicates that he does not, in fact, accept this theory as correct.

[11]Tosafot on *Hagigah* 13a quoted in *Ein Ya'akov* on *Hagigah* 13a. I have no explanation for the differences between the Tosafot on *Hagigah* 13a in *Ein Ya'akov* and the version of Tosafot in all of the various talmudic sources. The version of Tosafot found in *Ein Ya'akov* is not found in the other alternative versions of Tosafot commonly consulted.

[12]See *Kiddushin* 29b–30b for a discussion of this status.

as well.[13] As noted in *Penei Yehoshu'a*, if these commandments are no longer binding on Noahides, the problems associated with assisting a violation or not encouraging observance would greatly decrease. And, indeed, *Penei Yehoshu'a* rules that the only thing that would still be prohibited would be actually enticing them to do something that Noahides cannot do without the assistance of a Jew.[14]

Most authorities reject this insight and accept that the Noahide commandments are fully binding.[15] They argue that it is difficult to accept that all of the talmudic discussions concerning Noahide law are predicated on the *unstated assumption of the abrogation of the Noahide obligation* or even the abrogation of the biblical obligation.[16] Indeed, this position appears to be rejected by every single one of the early authorities (*rishonim*) who codified the Noahide laws[17] and the numerous later authorities (*aharonim*) who did so.[18] It is safe to state that Jewish law treats

---

[13]*Avodah Zarah* 6a.

[14]He understands even this only as a rabbinic prohibition; but see page 129–134 of this article, which indicates that it is normally considered a biblical prohibition.

[15]*Responsa Beit Yehuda Yoreh De'ah* 17; *Sedei Hemed* 6:26:22 (in the name of numerous authorities); *Yabi'a Omer Yoreh De'ah* 2:17(10); *Yad Eliyahu* 48 and many others.

[16]Whether there could be any Noahide obligation based on a rabbinic commandment is subject to some debate; see *Sedei Hemed* 2:32–33. To me, it would seem logical that there can be no rabbinic obligation on gentiles to keep the Noahide laws, as there is no obligation on gentiles to keep rabbinic rules. That does not, however, mean that there can be no rabbinic decrees ever governing Noahides; see ibid. However, the central obligation to observe cannot be rabbinic; Rashi, *Sanhedrin* 58b (*ve-likelal yisra'el lo ba*) clearly indicates that a rabbinic decree cannot govern one who is not Jewish. This issue is perhaps related to the question of whether Noahides must follow majority rule. Compare *Peri Megadim, Yoreh De'ah, Sha'ar Ha-Ta'arovet* 1:1(3) with *Noda Be-Yehudah, Tinyana, Even ha-Ezer* 42 with *Hatam Sofer, Yoreh De'ah* 70 and Maharam Shick, *Orah Hayyim* 104.

[17]See e.g., Maimonides, *Kings* chapters 7–9 and various other *rishonim* discussed in parts II–V of this article who refer to the seven commandments in a way which indicates that they are biblical in origin.

[18]See e.g., *Arukh ha-Shulhan he-Atid Kings* 78 and the numerous *aharonim* cited in parts II–V of this article, all of whom discuss the issue of Noahide obligation assuming that it is biblical in nature.

the Noahide laws as binding.[19] Indeed, there are numerous discussions within the *Shulhan Arukh* and its commentaries, which simply assume that the Noahide laws are fully binding.[20]

A second preliminary issue is whether the unintentional violation of one of the Noahide commandments leads to legal culpability in Jewish law. Based on a statement of Maimonides,[21] *Minhat Hinukh* rules: "When is it prohibited to hand a Noahide something forbidden to him? This is only when he knows that it is prohibited; but when he does not know that it is prohibited, there is no prohibition, since in this case there is complete unintentionality (lit: *shegagah gemurah*) and a Noahide violates no rule when his violation is completely unintentional."[22] If this *Minhat*

---

[19]I am inclined to read the authorities cited in notes 6 to 10 (and the related Talmudic text) as perhaps standing for a lesser proposition: Noahides are only obligated to obey the seven commandments based on logic or natural law, and they are released from adhering to them solely because of a divine revelation. This perhaps can be implied from Tosafot, *Hagigah* 13a (which seems to indicate that observance of the seven commandments is possible independent of the study of Torah), Rabbeinu Nissim Ga'on in his introduction to Talmud (printed as the preface to *Berakhot*) (which discusses the obligations upon all people to obey logical rules) and Maimonides, *Kings* 8:11 (which discusses whether Noahides who rationally observe the commandments are acting meritoriously assuming the text is changed from *ve-lo* to *ela*, as indicated by Maharam Alshikh). Supporting this alternative reading of Maimonides, Rakover, "Jewish Law and the Noahide Obligation to Preserve Social Order," *Cardozo Law Review* 12 (1991):1073–1136, fn 28, states in part: "The reading, 'of their wise men,' ('*ela mehakhmeihem*') is to be found only in manuscripts and not in printed editions of Maimonides' Code. The same reading may be found at Y. ben Moshe, Introduction to Ma'aseh ha-efod (1403) (Rabbi Yitzhak ben Moshe is also known as Profiat Duran halevi of Catalonia); and at Y. ben R. Shem Tov, Kevod Elokim 29:1 (1556). See also Z. Hayyot, [1 Kol Sifrei Maharatz Hayyot 61], at 66; Maharatz Hayyot, 2 Kol Sifrei Maharatz Hayyot 1035 . . . ; A. Kook, Iggerot Re-iyah, Iggeret no. 89, 100."

[20]See, for example, Rama, *Orah Hayyim* 156:1; *Shulhan Arukh Yoreh De'ah* 169; *Even Ha-Ezer* 5:14 (and comments of *Helkat Mehokek*). Many such citations could be brought.

[21]See *Kings* 10:1, which states "a Noahide who unintentionally violates one of the *mitzvot* is excused from them all."

[22]*Kometz ha-Minhah* 232 (reprinted as part of the text in the new *Minhat Hinukh* 232).

Hinukh is correct, a case could be made that Noahides are, in fact, *better served* by not teaching them laws.[23]

Many authorities disagree with the *Minhat Hinukh* and limit the permissive ruling to a situation where the Noahide recognizes the category of activity as prohibited, but merely does not recognize this particular action as in violation.[24] However, when the Noahide does not recognize the whole category of activity as prohibited, his actions still rise to the level of legal culpability.[25] Others simply reject the whole insight of the *Minhat Hinukh* and base their view on an explicit passage in the Tosafot,[26] which appears to do the same.[27] These authorities rule that Noahides are always obligated to obey the law and culpability is thus always present. Thus, it is well established that gentiles benefit from being taught the Noahide laws.

The Content of Noahide Laws

Having established that the Noahide commandments are binding on gentiles, and that lack of knowledge does not excuse obligation, it is necessary to explore what the commandments are. The Talmud[28] lists

---

[23]See also *Peri Megadim Orah Hayyim* 443:5 and 444:6, which is argued with by *Derishah Yoreh De'ah* 297(1–2).

[24]For example, it would be permissible for a Noahide to eat a piece of flesh from a living animal in a situation where he did not know that this meat comes from a living animal, but knows that if it had, he would not be allowed to eat it.

[25]For example, it would be prohibited for a Noahide to eat a piece of flesh from a living animal in a situation where he knows that this meat comes from a living animal, but is unaware that this flesh is prohibited.

[26]See Tosafot, *Bava Kamma* 79a.

[27]See *Avenei Melu'im Even ha-Ezer* 5; *Sedei Hemed* 5:26:13; *Terumat Ha-Deshen* 299; *Arukh ha-Shulhan Yoreh De'ah* 62:6; *Responsa Rav Betzalel Ashkenazi* 3 (in the name of Radvaz also).

[28]*Sanhedrin* 56a. Indeed, the source for these laws plays a role in their interpretation. As noted by Rama, responsum 10 (to be discussed infra): if the sources for these rules are biblical verses directed at Adam or Noah, they are to be interpreted independently of the subsequent revelation at Sinai. Rama states: "It is recounted in *Sanhedrin* 56b. Rabbi Yohanan states that the seven Noahide laws were given based on the verse 'God commanded Adam stating: from all the trees in the garden you may eat' [Gen. 2:16]. "*Va-yetzav*" is the source for

seven categories of prohibition: idol worship, taking God's name in vain, murder, prohibited sexual activity, theft, eating flesh from a living animal, and the obligation to enforce laws. These seven commandments are generalities that contain within them many specifications—for example, the single categorical prohibition of sexual promiscuity includes both adultery and the various forms of incest.[29] As has been noted already, these Noahide laws encompass nearly 60 of the 613 biblical commandments incumbent on Jews, which is nearly one in four of those biblical commandments generally applicable in post-Temple times.[30] What might sometimes make the practical application of the Noahide laws difficult is the frequently wide divergence of opinion found within the various Jewish authorities concerning details of many Noahide laws. A simple example illustrates this.

The Jerusalem Talmud recounts that there is no formal divorce according to Noahide law.[31] The *rishonim* understand this in three completely different ways. Some claim that this means that divorce is legally impossible for a gentile and once married there is no way to end the marriage.[32] For others, the talmudic passage means that there is no formal process of divorce, and either spouse can end the marriage by simply leaving the family unit.[33] Still other authorities insist that,

---

dinim since it states . . . "*Elokim*" is the source for *birkhat ha-Shem*, since it states. . . .' Contrary to this is the opinion of Rabbi Yitzhak who states that '"*Va-yetzav*" is the source for the prohibition of idol worship; "*Elokim*" is the source for the *dinim.* . . .'" Rama continues: "Rabbi Yohanan, who learns *dinim* from '*Va-yetzav*,' understands that Noahide law obligates only observing the customs of the community and judging people . . . However, Rabbi Yitzhak has a completely different approach and he learns *dinim* from '*Elokim*' as a *gezerah shaveh* from the verse 'and the litigant shall approach the judge ("*Elokim*")' [Ex. 20:3]. He rules that Noahide laws are the same as those laws commanded to the Jews at Sinai, and thus he learns them from a verse announced at Sinai."

[29]According to Shmuel ben Hofni, 30 specific commandments are included; see generally appendix to *Entziklopedyah Talmudit* 3:394–396 and supra note 2.

[30]See Lichtenstein, *The Seven Laws of Noah*, 90–91.

[31]Jerusalem Talmud *Kiddushin* 1:1; see generally *Kings* 2:16.

[32]See *Hiddushei ha-Ran Sanhedrin* 58b; see also *Penei Yehoshua, Kiddushin* 13b, which insists that this applies even after the death of the spouse.

[33]Maimonides, *Ishut* 1:1–2 and *Kings* 9:8.

in Noahide law, a man may never divorce his wife—but she may divorce him at will.[34] Similar disputes touch many core areas of Noahide law, leaving the resolution of many cases very difficult to determine.[35] Before one seeks to apply the details of Noahide law to issues in current society, then, it is necessary to determine what precisely is the Noahide obligation.[36]

However, disputes about the details should not be allowed to undermine the clarity of the general principles. The application of Noahide law to many general areas is relatively clear. Homosexuality is forbidden,[37] as are adultery[38] and bestiality.[39] Murder is prohibited, and subsumed in the prohibition of murder is abortion.[40] So, too, most forms of theft are prohibited, as is eating the flesh of a living animal.[41] Indeed, the general Noahide laws share a common base of "ethics," which most religious peoples would share.[42]

---

[34]Opinion of Rabbi Yohanan, *Bereshit Rabbah* 18:5; see also commentary of Rashi on *id.* for an elaboration on this.

[35]For example, the nature of the monotheistic obligation and its application to contemporary religions; see *Entziklopedyah Talmudit*, supra note 1, at 350–351 or the obligation of *dinim* discussed in part III; whether Noahides are prohibited to perform castrations or grow *kelayim*; *Entziklopedyah Talmudit*, supra note 1, at 356–357, and many others.

[36]This paper is not the place to address the details of the Noahide laws. For such an analysis, see Lichtenstein, *The Laws of Noah*, supra note 1.

[37]*Entziklopedyah Talmudit*, supra note 1, at 353–354.

[38]*Entziklopedyah Talmudit*, supra note 1, at 353–354.

[39]*Entziklopedyah Talmudit*, supra note 1, at 354.

[40]*Entziklopedyah Talmudit*, supra note 1, at page 351. As noted by Rabbi Waldenberg, *Tzitz Eliezer* 9:51 (page 239), what flows from this assertion is that if a Jewish woman is permitted to have an abortion according to Jewish law, it is preferable that the doctor performing the abortion be Jewish and not a Noahide.

[41]*Entziklopedyah Talmudit*, supra note 1, at pages 354–55.

[42]However, many things that are considered general wrongs by both Jewish law and the general Western legal codes, are not considered violations of the Noahide code. For example, various forms of incest considered wrong by most Western legal systems and Jewish law are permitted in the Noahide code; see *Entziklopedyah Talmudit*, supra note 1, at 351–2.

THE OBLIGATION OF "LAWS" OR "JUSTICE"[43]

The final commandment in the Noahide code is *dinim*, commonly translated as "laws" or "justice." Two vastly different interpretations of this commandment are found among the early authorities. Maimonides rules that the obligations of *dinim* require only that the enumerated Noahide laws be enforced in practice. "How are [Noahides] obligated by *dinim*? They must create courts and appoint judges in every province to enforce these six commandments . . . for this reason the inhabitants of Shekhem [the city] were liable to be killed[44] since Shekhem [the person] stole[45] [Dinah], and the inhabitants saw and knew this and did nothing."[46] According to Maimonides, it is logical to assume that other types of regulations that society might make are subsumed under the rubric of either "laws of the land" or "laws of the king." Their binding authority is quite different.[47]

Nahmanides argues with this formulation and understands the obligations of *dinim* to be much broader. It not only encompasses the obligations of society to enforce rules, but also obligates society to create general rules of law governing such cases as fraud, overcharging, repayment of debts, and the like.[48] Within the opinion of Nahmanides, there is a secondary dispute as to which substantive laws Noahides are supposed to adopt. Rama, writing in his responsa,[49] states that according to Nahman-

---

[43]For an excellent review of the Noahide commandment of *dinim*, see Rakover, supra note 1 (both articles).

[44]See Gen. 34.

[45]As to why Maimonides uses the word "stole" see *Sanhedrin* 55a and Hatam Sofer *Yoreh De'ah* 19.

[46]*Kings* 10:14.

[47]See generally *Teshuvot Hakhmei Provence* 48, which clearly distinguishes between regulations based on the Noahide laws and regulations based on the law of the land or the law of the king. For more on this distinction, see Arnold Enker, "Aspects of Interaction Between the Torah Law, the King's Law, and the Noahide Law in Jewish Criminal Law," *Cardozo Law Review* 12 (1991) 1137–1156.

[48]Commentary of Nahmanides on Gen. 34:14.

[49]Responsa of Rama 10. His ruling is also accepted by Hatam Sofer *Hoshen Mishepat* 91 and R. Ya'akov Linderbaum (R. Yaakov mi-Lisa), *Responsa Nahalat Ya'akov* 2:3.

ides, in those areas of *dinim* where gentiles are supposed to create laws, they are obligated to incorporate Jewish law into Noahide law unless it is clear contextually that it is inappropriate. Most authorities reject this interpretation and accept either Maimonides' ruling or that, according to Nahmanides, those rules created under the rubric of *dinim* need be only generally fair and not identical to Jewish law.[50] I cannot find even a single *rishon* who explicitly accepts the ruling of Rama, and one can find many who explicitly disagree.[51]

The dispute concerning the nature of the commandment called *dinim* is extremely relevant in explaining the obligation of Jews to provide guidance and seek enforcement of the Noahide laws. It seems to me that Maimonides accepts that the biblical commandment of *dinim* (or some Noahide cognate of it) compels enforcement by all—Jews as well as gentiles—of these seven laws, perhaps because Jews, too, are bound by them.[52] In his explanation of the laws of *dinim*, he does not limit them to

---

[50]See Rabbi Y. Elhanan Spector, *Nahal Yitzhak Hoshen Mishpat* 91; R. Abraham Isaiah Karelitz, *Hazon Ish al Hilkhot Melakhim* 10:10 and *Bava Kamma* 10:3; R. Isser Zalman Meltzer, *Even ha-Azel, Hovel u-Mazzik* 8:5; R. Yehiel Mikhael Epstein, *Arukh Ha-Shulhan he'Atid, Law of Kings* 79:15; R. Naftali Tzvi Yehudah Berlin, *Ha-amek She'alah* 2:3; R. Abraham Kook, *Etz Hadar* 38, 184; R. Tzvi Pesah Frank, *Har Tzvi, Orah Hayyim* II, *Kuntres Mili de-Berakhot* 2:1; R. Ovadia Yosef, *Yehaveh Da'at* 4:65; R. Yitzhak Ya'akov Weiss, *Minhat Yitzhak* 4:52:3. For a more complete analysis of this issue see N. Rakover, "Jewish Law . . ." (n. 1 above) 1098–1118, and app. 1 and 2.

[51]Most authorities do not accept Nahmanides' opinion; see e.g., Maimonides, *Kings* 10:10; R. Yom Tov Ashvealli (Ritva), *Responsa* 14 (quoted in *Beit Yosef Hoshen Mishpat* 66:18); Tosafot, *Eruvin* 62a ("Ben No'ah"). The comments of Albo are also worth citing: "One finds that although Torah law and Noahide law differ in the details, the principles used are the same, since they derive from the same source. Moreover, the two systems exist concurrently; while Jews have Torah law, the other peoples abide by the Noahide code" (*Sefer ha-Ikkarim* 1:25).

[52]Maimonides asserts in his commentary on the Mishnah (*Hullin* 7:6) that the reason why these seven commandments are obligatory is that God commanded these seven laws as part of the divine revelation at Sinai. Based on this, the Ba'al Haturim notes that 620 commandments were revealed at Sinai, which he remarks is hinted at by the 620 letters in the Ten Commandments. Interestingly, *Mahzor Vitri* notes that only 606 commandments were given to the Jews

Noahides only. Writing much more recently, Rabbi Yosef Engel,[53] Rabbi
Me'ir Simhah Devinsk, Rabbi Yehiel Ya'akov Weinberg, Rabbi Shlomo
Zalman Auerbach,[54] and Rabbi Moshe Feinstein[55] all seem to indicate
that there is some residual jurisdictional impact upon Jews from their
Noahide obligation. For example, Rabbi Me'ir Simhah says that if a Jewish child who is not yet a bar or bat mitzvah (and thus not an adult according to Jewish law) comprehends the nature of right and wrong,[56] he
or she[57] is obligated according to Torah law in the Noahide commandments; according to Noahide law, he or she is an adult.[58] In a similar

---

at Sinai, because the Jews were already commanded in the Noahide laws prior
to that; this is also noted by Gera (R. Elijah Gaon) as derived from the word
"*rut*," whose value is 606, which Gera asserts is the additional commandments
that Ruth became obligated in. See also Maimonides, *Sefer ha-Mitzvot, aseh*
176–177. For a general discussion of the Noahide laws and the counting of commandments, see Naomi Cohen, "Taryag and the Noahide Commandments,"
Journal of Jewish Studies, 43, 1 (Spring 1992): 46–57.

[53]See Rabbi Yosef Engel, *Beit Otzar Ma'arekhet* 1–1:7, 9. "The seven Noahide
commandments are still obligatory to Jews, and their authority derives from their
pre-Sinai obligation. The Torah . . . merely added to Noahide laws . . ."

[54]Rabbi Pinhas Hayyim Schienman, "Teshuvah be-Inyan Yeladim mefaggerim
le-Gabbei Hinukh u-Mitzvot," *Moriah* 11:9–10 (1982):51–65. (This article contains an appendix written by Rabbi S. Z. Auerbach.)

[55]*Iggerot Moshe, Yoreh De'ah* 1:6. Rabbi Feinstein there discusses whether one
who is legally excused from observance of commandments generally because of
blindness (according to one opinion) is nonetheless obligated in the Noahide
laws.

[56]Is a *bar de'ah* (understands right and wrong).

[57]Although this goes almost without saying, there is no general difference in
level of obligation in Noahide law between men and women; see *Entziklopedyah
Talmudit*, supra note 1, at page 348.

[58]*Or Same'ah, Isurei Biyah* 3:2. This presupposes the correctness of the *Minhat
Hinukh's* famous assertion (*Minhat Hinukh* 190; also found in Hatam Sofer, *Yoreh
De'ah* 317) that Noahides become adults—and thus obligated in obedience of
the law—not when they reach any particular age, but when they reach intellectual maturity. It is likely that the correctness of this assertion is itself in dispute between Rosh and Rashi; compare *Teshuvot Ha-Rosh* 16:1 and Rashi commenting on *Pirkei Avot* 5:21. See also *Yabi'a Omer, Yoreh De'ah* 2:17.

See also *Sefer ha-Mikaneh* 1:8(5) which states "for violations of the seven
commandments Jews certainly are to be punished . . ." Perhaps similar senti-

vein, Rabbi Weinberg states that a marriage between two Jews that is technically invalid according to Jewish law could still be valid as a Noahide marriage.[59]

The opposite claim could be made according to Nahmanides (as interpreted by those who disagree with Rama). Because the obligation to create *dinim* includes in it other obligations clearly not applicable to Jews (such as the creation of a general civil or secular law system governing all except Jews), Nahmanides could not accept a Jewish obligation to participate in *dinim*.[60] This is not to say that Jews need not obey *dinim* or other aspects of the Noahide code, according to Nahmanides. It is clear that several authorities find some connection between the obligation of *dinim* and the halakhic mandate of *dina de-malkhuta dina*, the obligation of Jews to obey the secular law.[61] If Noahides are obligated in the creation of general secular law and not only the enforcement of these six specified commandments, it would seem logical that Jews, too, must obey these *dinim*, at least in interactions with Noahides.[62] But a crucial observation must be made. Merely because Jewish law rules that one is obligated to obey Noahide law does

---

ments are expressed by Rav Kook when he states "in our time, when Torah is not upheld . . . still it seems that the principles of fairness applied by force of Torah law of *dinim* to Noahides applies, because we are no worse than they" (*Etz Hadar* 42).

[59]*Seridei Eish* 3:22; Rabbi Menasheh Klein, *Mishneh Halakhot* 9:278, also agrees with this.

[60]I have found no authority who explicitly notes this in the name of Nahmanides. However, it would appear logical to this author that there is no obligation to participate in the creation of a legal system that is not binding on one who creates it. Other factors, such as *lifnei ivver* or its analogues, would be in place according to Nahmanides to prevent Jews from enticing Noahides to violate; indeed, even *dina de-malkhuta* might be such a rule.

[61]See Rashi, *Gittin* 9b, and Rabbi Bleich, "Jewish Law and the State's . . ." 856.

[62]See for example, Rashi, commenting on *Gittin* 9b. Rabbi Isser Zalman Meltzer, *Even Ha-azel*, *Nizkei Mamon* 8:5 freely mixes as near synonyms the terms *dina de-malkhuta*, *din melekh*, *din benei No'ah metzuveh al ha-dinim* in a discussion about why a Jew must return property lost by another when it is required by secular law and not *halakha*. See also Rabbi Me'ir Dan Plotzki, *Hemdat Yisra'el*, *Ner Mitzvah* 72 *mitzvah* 288. See also the discussion on pp. 134ff, below, of the position of Rabbi Menahem Mendel Schneerson on this issue.

not mean that one is necessarily obligated to *assist in its enforcement*.[63] The two are not necessarily interrelated.[64]

According to Hazon Ish, Jewish law requires respect for Noahide legal pronouncements even when the Noahide judges themselves do not fully observe Noahide law.[65] Hazon Ish was asked about the obligation

---

[63]This article does not address one very significant issue—the scope of a gentile's obligation (both as an individual and as a society) to enforce Noahide law. As is clear from Maimonides' formulation (cited in text accompanying note 46), gentiles are obligated not only in formulating a legal system, but also in actually enforcing it; after all, the inhabitants of Shekhem were punished because they declined to *enforce* the law. On the other hand, as noted by many authorities (see sources cited in notes 90, 158 and more generally the sources cited in notes 90 to 99) it is clear that Noahides need not punish all violations with death. Indeed, a claim can be made that a Noahide system of law fulfills its mandate as a system of justice (*dinim*) even if it were to occasionally decline to punish criminally a clear violation of Noahide law (such as theft of a nickel). So too, it is reasonable to suppose that Maimonides's formulation of the difference between the obligations of an individual to enforce law and the obligation of society to enforce law (see *Rotze'ah* 1:5) has some place in the Noahide system also. This is even more apparent according to the approach of Nahmanides, which incorporates vast amounts of general law into Noahide law. Clearly, not every violation of this general law requires death or even criminal punishment. On the other hand, it is reasonable to assert that the Noahide obligation is not fulfilled merely by legislative action without any enforcement activity. What is missing from this discussion is the halakhic parameters of the discretion, and that task shall be left to another time.

[64]This was first noted in a different context by Rabbi Bleich, supra note 61, at 856, who was commenting on the permissibility to assist in the punishment of criminals.

> Nevertheless, one point requires clarification. Punishment of malfeasors may be a royal prerogative. That, however, does not establish an obligation [for Jews] to assist the king in exercising that prerogative. . . . Reason demands that a murderer be brought to justice and punished. Reason similarly demands that punishment be carried out only in accordance with legal procedures and only by duly constituted authorities, because the alternative would similarly lead to a breakdown of the social order. Just as reason forbids a person to take the law into his own hands, it also mandates that there be no interference with the administration of justice by properly constituted authorities.

[65]Something that would be completely unacceptable in a Jewish court, where complete observance is mandated for service as a judge; see generally, *Hoshen Mishpat* 35–37 for a list of disqualifications.

to accept legal pronouncements from a Noahide court that does not generally observe (or enforce) all of the seven commandments but "observes the law concerning sanctity of life and theft of property." He replied that if they are enforcing even a section of the Noahide laws properly, it is halakhically necessary to respect those pronouncements.[66] Respect does not necessarily mean, however, that full participation is mandatory.

In sum, there certainly is an obligation upon Noahides—at the minimum—to create a legal system designed to enforce Noahide law. Jews

---

[66]Hazon Ish, *Bava Kamma* 10:15.

A similar situation is also discussed in *halakhah*: Does Jewish law recognize the right of the Noahide government to punish Jewish violators of the Noahide code? Two distinctly different approaches have been taken by the authorities on the permissibility of a Jew aiding the secular government in criminally punishing Jews; for an excellent analysis of this issue, see Rabbi J. David Bleich, "*Hasgarat Poshei'a* . . ." The dispute revolves around the proper understanding of *Bava Metzia* 83b–84a which states in part:

> R. Eleazar son of R. Simeon met a police officer. R. Eleazar said to him, "How can you detect the thieves . . . ? Perhaps you take the innocent and leave behind the guilty." The officer replied "And what shall I do? It is the king's command." [R. Eleazar then advised this policeman how to determine who was a thief and who was not] . . . A report was heard in the royal court. They said, "Let the reader of the letter become the messenger." R. Eleazar son of R. Simeon was brought to the court and he proceeded to apprehend thieves. R. Joshua son of Karhah, sent word to him, "Vinegar, son of wine! How long will you deliver the people of our God for slaughter?" R. Eleazar sent the reply, "I eradicate thorns from the vineyard." R. Joshua responded, "Let the owner of the vineyard come and eradicate his thorns."

Rabbi Eliezer was rebuked for assisting the government in the prosecution of criminals, thus indicating that this conduct is not proper or at least the subject of a dispute between Rabbi Eleazar and Rabbi Joshua.

Several commentaries advance an explanation for this reprimand which changes its focus. Rabbi Yom Tov Ashvelli (Ritva quoted in *Shitah Mekubetzet* on *id.*) states that even Rabbi Joshua admits that it is only scholars and rabbis of the caliber of Rabbi Eliezer and Rabbi Yishmael who should not assist the government as prosecutors or police officers—and even for these individuals such conduct was not prohibited, but only frowned upon. Many authorities agree with this explanation; see Ran, commenting on *Sanhedrin* 46a; Rabbi Shimon ben Adret, *Teshuvot Rashba* 3:29; Rabbi J. Karo, *Beit Yosef, Hoshen Mishpat* 388; Taz, *Yoreh De'ah* 157:7–8; R. Tzvi Hirsh Eisenstadt, *Darkhei Teshuva*, commenting on *Yoreh De'ah* 157:1; R. Me'ir Simha Midevinsk, *Or Same'ah, Kings* 3:10; R.

have an obligation to recognize and respect this system, even if it is incomplete in its observance of Noahide law. According to many, there is a residual impact of Noahide law in Jewish law.[67]

Moshe Shick, *Teshuvot Maharam Shick, Yoreh De'ah* 50. According to this analysis, it is only the pious who should not engage in this type of work as it is undignified for scholars also to be government agents—but all others may, since the secular government has "jurisdiction" over Jewish violators of its laws. Additionally, Rashi, commenting on the Talmud, seems to argue that any action which the secular government may take within the scope of the rule of *dina demalkhuta dina* (the law of the land is the law) which is binding on Jews, the government may enforce; See e.g. Rashi commenting on *Gittin* 9b ("*dinim*"). Keeping law and order is unquestionably one such function. A proof to this proposition can perhaps be found in Rabbi Feinstein's decision allowing one to be a tax auditor for the government in a situation where the audit might result in the criminal prosecution of Jews for evading taxes; *Iggerot Moshe, Hoshen Mishpat* 1:92.

The second approach rejects the opinion of Rabbi Eleazar, and states that Rabbi Joshua, who rebuked Rabbi Eleazar, represents the normative opinion which prohibits this conduct; this approach can be found in Meiri, *Bava Metzia* 83b and can be implied from Maimonides, *Hilkhot Rotze'ah* 2:4 and *Tosafot, Sanhedrin* 20b; R. Moshe Sofer, Hatam Sofer *Likkutim* responsum no. 14. If Rabbi Joshua's opinion is the one accepted by Jewish law, then the only time it would be permitted to assist the secular government in criminal prosecutions is when the criminal poses a threat to the community through his conduct. This is based upon the rules of *rodef* (pursuer); see R. Shimon Duran, *Tashbetz* 3:168 and Rabbi Isserless, (Rama), *Hoshen Mishpat* 388:12. Obviously where the criminal poses a threat to the community through his conduct, it is proper to apprise the secular authorities of his activities; see e.g., R. Shmuel Demidina, *Responsa Maharashdam, Hoshen Mishpat* 55:6; Rabbi Moshe Sternbuch, *Teshuvot ve-Hanhagot* 1:850. This threat need not be limited to the possibility that the criminal will actually harm another, but includes such factors as the possibility that in response to a Jew being apprehended committing a crime, other Jews will be injured or anti-semitism will be promoted; see Rama commenting on *Shulhan Arukh, Hoshen Mishpat* 388:12, 425:1. According to this approach it is only when there is a likelihood that the lack of punishment of this criminal will lead to other crimes, that the secular authorities should be informed. One authority has argued that on a functional level there is no difference between the two approaches because disobedience of the law generally will surely lead to anarchy and crime, and thus all significant violations of the law can be punished

THE OBLIGATION TO TEACH OR JUDGE NOAHIDES

Maimonides states: "Moses, our teacher, only willed Torah and *mitzvot* to the Jewish people, since it states 'An inheritance to the community of Jacob.'[68] . . . One [who is not Jewish] who does not wish to, we do not compel to accept Jewish law. So too, *Moses our teacher was commanded by God to compel the commandments to the Noahides. All who do not accept are killed.* One who accepts them [voluntarily] is called a *ger toshav* [literally: resident alien] . . ."[69] So, too, Maimonides says: "A Jewish court [*beit din*] is obligated to appoint judges for *gerei toshav* [literally: resident aliens] to judge them in order that the world not be destroyed. If the Jewish court wishes to appoint judges from within their midst, it may; if it wishes to appoint judges from the Jews, it may."[70] Finally, Maimonides rules: "One who takes an adult slave from an idol worshiper, and the slave does not wish to be circumcised one may delay up to twelve months

---

under the pursuer rationale. Rabbi Tzvi Hirsch Hayyot (Maharatz Hayyot), *Torat Nevi'im*, chap. 7. For more on this, see Michael J. Broyde, *The Pursuit of Justice and Jewish Law* (Yeshiva University Press, 1996).

[67]Perhaps among the most significant impacts is whether Noahides are valid witnesses as a matter of biblical law or not; for more on this, see "Goy," *Entziklopedyah Talmudit* 5:337–343.

[68]Deut. 33:4.

[69]Maimonides, *Kings* 8:10. In explaining the source for this ruling of Maimonides, Rabbi Karo states in *Kesef Mishnah*, *Milah* 1:6 that "Rabbeinu learned this rule from what is stated in *Sanhedrin* 57a"; see also *Yevamot* 48a. The dispute between Maimonides and others revolve around the talmudic statement (*Sanhedrin* 57a) that "on seven commandments Noahides are killed." Maimonides understands this as not limited to judaical punishment in a court of 23 when the Sanhedrin is functioning (as is required to execute a Jew for a violation) but includes "extra-judaical" activity. Those who argue (see section 2) limit this statement to judicially sanctioned executions.

[70]Maimonides, *Kings* 10:11. As noted by Radvaz, commenting on Kings 10:14, *le-ha-tehillah* (*ab initio*) it is preferable that Noahides serve as judges on their own tribunals. It is only *be-diaved* (after the fact) that Jews should seek such roles. I would suggest that the rationale for that assertion is that it is generally better that a *mitzvah* be done by the principal and not through an agent. In this case the *mitzvah* is *dinim*, the Noahide is the principal, and the Jew is the agent. It is worth noting that Maimonides explicitly adopts a universalistic formulation of the obligation to love our Maker in his *Sefer ha-Mitzvot*, Aseh 3.

. . . If one agreed concerning this slave with his previous owner not to circumcise him, it is permitted to keep the slave uncircumcised; however, the slave must keep the seven commandments obligatory on Noahides and if not, he is killed immediately."[71]

This article will address three basic issues that flow from the formulation of Maimonides. They are: (1) Is there an obligation upon each individual Jew to coerce compliance? Or is the obligation only on *beit din*? And if so, which court? Or perhaps classical *halakhah* rejects this ruling of Maimonides.[72] (2) When a Noahide violates these rules no matter what posture Jews take, may Jews assist in the sin? Or, at the least, must a Jew decline to assist in a violation of Noahide laws? (3) Is there an obligation to induce or persuade a Noahide to comply with the Noahide laws, or even to teach Noahides about their obligations? Or, if there is an obligation, is it limited to the obligation to coerce? The answer to each of these three interrelated questions is in dispute, and each of these disputes is central to many of the issues raised in this paper.

The Obligation to Compel Observance

Maimonides' Approach

A simple reading of the rules of Maimonides would indicate that Jews or Jewish courts are obligated in (at the minimum) coercing Noahides to observe their laws. This is not the only way, however, to interpret Maimonides' statements. Maharatz Hayyot, in his responsa,[73] seems to adopt a formulation of Maimonides' ruling, which makes this law a mere historical recounting of facts. He states (quoting the Rashbash[74]):

---

[71]Maimonides, *Milah* 1:6. Ravad notes "Nowadays we cannot kill a person." See pp. 124ff, below, for a discussion of Ravad's assertion.

[72]It is clear that, once a person is actually a full *ger toshav* (resident alien), there is an obligation to judge that person (at least in Israel). Most likely, no such people exist in the United States. This paper will limit its discussion to Noahides. For a discussion of who is a *ger toshav*, see Rabbi Berel Wein, *Hikrei Halakhot* 5–45 (Mossad Harav Kook, 5748) and *Arukh Ha-shulhan, He'atid Yovel* 49.

[73]*Responsa* 2.

[74]Rabbi Shlomo Ben Shimon Duran (Rashbash) 543.

Sanhedrin 56b recounts that the Jews were commanded in ten command-ments at Marah;[75] these ten commandments were the seven laws of Noah, the Sabbath laws, *dinim*, and respect for one's parents. Why did the Jews need to be commanded again [on the seven Noahide laws], because Jews were already commanded from the time of Adam and Noah . . . Because we con-clude that commandments that were given prior to Sinai to Noahides, and not repeated at Sinai, are obligatory only for Jews, the seven commandments had to be repeated at Sinai *to obligate Noahides*.[76] Based on this Rashbash, the assertion of Maimonides that "Moses, our teacher, willed only Torah and *mitzvot* to the Jewish people, because it states 'An inheritance to the com-munity of Jacob.'" . . .[77] and his assertion that "Moses our teacher was com-manded by God to compel the commandments obligatory to the children of Noah" appears logical. Why was Moses also the messenger to the rest of the world to compel observance of the seven commandments? Perhaps they are obligated by Adam or Noah? Rather, we see that Moses being commanded at Marah on the seven Noahide commandments, even though gentiles were already commanded, was done to make Noahides obligated in the *mitzvot* even now.

Thus, according to Maharatz Hayyot, there is no obligation for any specific Jew, in any circumstance, to compel observance by a Noahide. Maimonides is merely explaining the jurisprudential basis for the obli-gation of Noahides to their seven commandments—absent Moses' re-commandment at Sinai, only Jews would have been obligated in Noahide law. The most that one could claim, according to Maharatz Hayyot, is that perhaps Moses himself was obligated to compel observance of the Noahide laws; Jews currently are not—neither in the context of a *beit din* nor in the context of any specific individual. Maharatz Hayyot would then limit Maimonides' rule obligating Jews to establish courts and ap-point judges to those Noahides who formally accept the obligations of a *ger toshav* (resident alien), who live in the Jewish community, and who

---

[75]See "*Dinim*" *Entziklopedyah Talmudit* 7:396–397 for a discussion of this issue.

[76]The general rule is that commandments apparently directed to all that are recounted in the Bible prior to revelation at Sinai are binding only on Jews; commandments that are listed twice in the Bible, once before revelation and once after are binding on all. See generally *Entziklopedyah Talmudit*, 3:359–360.

[77]Ellipses are by Maharatz Hayyot.

are dependent on it for law and order "lest the world be destroyed."[78] In the diaspora, certainly, there are few communities of Noahides like that;[79] if there were, and they could not see fit to enforce the law themselves, a Jew should guide them.[80] Similar claims that Maimonides' rules do not create a practical, legal obligation can be found in *Arukh Ha-Shulhan*,[81] the writings of Rabbi Yehuda Gershuni,[82] Rabbi Sha'ul Yisra'eli,[83] and

---

[78]Maimonides, *Kings* 10:11.

[79]Although some Noahide communities do exist. See e.g., "Ex-Christians Drawn to Noah's Law," *San Jose Mercury News*, Saturday January 26, 1991, p. 11D. The article reads in part:

> Some are former Christian clergymen who no longer consider themselves Christians. They use many Jewish practices, but don't convert to Judaism. About 250 of them met in Athens, Tenn., recently, reports Ecumenical Press Service. James D. Tabor, member of an advisory council, says members tend to be "disenfranchised former Christians" who "do not denounce belief in Jesus" but the "most they would say is that he was a great teacher." Tabor says members want to identify with the "ethical monotheism" of Judaism without converting to it. He says they uphold the "laws of Noah," such as those against idolatry, blasphemy, bloodshed, sexual sins and theft.

It is worth noting that these communities do seek rabbinic guidance; see "Tennessee Church Studies Judaism," *Sun Sentinel*, 31 May 1991: 5E, discussing involvement of a local Orthodox rabbi.

[80]Whether this is obligatory depends on issues discussed in this paper and the additional issue of whether these communities have the status of *ger toshav* communities or merely Noahide ones. This is a classical dispute among Maimonides, Ravad, and many others. For a lengthy discourse on many details of *ger toshav*, see Wein, *Hikrei Halakhot* 9–46 and particularly pages 44–46, which discuss whether this status can currently exist.

[81]*Yoreh De'ah* 267:12–13. For more on the context in which *Arukh ha-Shulhan* is speaking, see infra, text accompanying notes 99 to 106. There is some tension between the remarks found in *Arukh ha-Shulhan, he-Atid Yovel* 49:1–3, *Kings* 78:10–11 and *Yoreh De'ah* 367:12–13. I would be inclined to assume that the remarks found in *Arukh ha-Shulhan, he-Atid* are not intended for current practical use, and while that is not stated explicitly in them, that flows logically from the nature of the work generally. (Although even that rule is not without exception, as *terumah* and *ma'aser* rules are found in *he-Atid*, notwithstanding their clear relevance even in my life.)

[82]Rabbi Yehudah Gershuni (*Mishpetei Melukhah*, 2d ed., 454–455) also understands Maimonides' rule so as to impose no real obligation. He understands

Rabbi Menahem Mendel Kasher,[84] the author of *Torah Sheleimah*, all of whom assert that the opinion of Maimonides itself is to be understood as limited to *yemot ha-mashiah* (or perhaps less ideally, full Jewish law in Israel).

All of these explanations of Maimonides' ruling are difficult, however, and the simple understanding of Maimonides is that (at the least) a person who is capable of forcing compliance, must. Although Rabbi Karo does limit the application of Maimonides somewhat, he clearly understands that Maimonides requires compulsion whenever possible, even by an individual.[85] This is similarly understood to be the opinion of

---

the force of the relevant rules as designed to *limit* what a Jewish court can do, and not to expand on it. He understands Maimonides as ruling that Noahides are commanded from Moses only in these seven laws; a Jewish court, though might think that it can impose on Noahides additional obligations or portions of the remaining 613 commandments, cannot. He argues that Maimonides' statement ("So, too, Moses our teacher was commanded by God to compel [only] the commandments obligatory to the children of Noah") should be understood as a limitation on that power. The same, he states, is true for the second example ("A Jewish court is obligated to appoint judges to *ger toshav* (resident alien) to judge them *for these laws* . . ."). This interpretation is quite novel and original to him.

[83]*Amud Yemini* 12:1:12. Rabbi Yisraeli posits that Maimonides cannot possibly mean that there is a general obligation to compel observance of the Noahide laws everywhere in the world as "where do we see that in the writing of the Sages." Rather he argues that Maimonides' rule must be limited to the Land of Israel itself, where there is a halakhic imperative to prevent violations of the Noahide law. Thus according to him, Maimonides' rule is inapplicable in the diaspora.

[84]*Torah Shelemah* 17:220. The most fascinating explanation for the opinion of Maimonides is found in *Responsa Maharam Shick*, where he avers that the primary motivation for this ruling is that if Noahides are allowed to sin unpunished, impropriety will occur in the Jewish community also; Maharam Shick, *Orah Hayyim* 144. Indeed, Maharam Shick indicates that the basis for this rule is that society cannot stand if the justice system cannot regulate a portion of the community. Similar insights are made by Rabbi Bleich in "*Hasgarat Poshei'a* . . . ," supra note 1. See also postscript.

[85]*Kesef Mishnah*, Milah 1:6. Similar sentiments as to the opinion of Maimonides can be found in *Lehem Mishnah* commenting on *Avoda Zarah* 10:1.

Maimonides in *Tzafenat Pane'ah*, in its lengthy discussion on this topic.[86]
A ruling similar to Maimonides' is found in *Hinukh* 192: "The rule is as
follows: In all that the nations are commanded, any time they are under
our jurisdiction, it is incumbent upon us to judge them when they violate the commandments."

The Approach of Ravad, Nahmanides, Tosafot, and so on

Many *rishonim* simply disagree with the opinion of Maimonides, ruling
that there is no obligation upon an individual Jew to impose Noahide
rules on gentiles. Included in this group are at least Ravad, Nahmanides,
Tosafot, and perhaps Rashi and Rashba. Ravad, in disagreeing with the
ruling of Maimonides that a slave who refuses to accept one of the seven
commandments ought to be killed, states that[87] "the slave should be sold.
We may not, now, kill a person." Although one could understand this
assertion as merely practical,[88] it is more likely that Ravad is limiting the
juridical power of the Jewish community in punishing Noahides for violations of the Noahide code.[89] Under this analysis, it would, according
to Ravad, take an authorized *beit din* of 23 functioning when the
Sanhedrin is legally empowered to impose capital punishment, to kill for
violations of the Noahide code.[90] Ravad disagrees with Maimonides,

---

[86]Rabbi Joseph Rosen, *Tzafenat Pane'ah*, Maimonides, *Milah* 1:6.

[87]Maimonides, *Milah* 1:6.

[88]As *Kesef Mishnah* does; see *Kesef Mishnah*, *Milah* 1:6.

[89]For an understanding of why that approach is "more likely," see *Tzafnat
Pane'ah* on *Milah* 1:6, Rabbi Aharon Soloveitchik, "On Noahides," *Beit Yitzhak*
19 (5747): 335–338 and Rabbi J. David Bleich, "*Mishpat Mavet . . .*"

[90]See Rabbi Aharon Soloveitchik, "On Noahides," supra note 89. Of course,
a person who violates the Noahide laws and thus poses a danger to others could
be killed using the pursuer rationale; indeed, even a Jew could be punished under
that rationale. However, a violation of the purely theological components of
the Noahide law cannot result in punishment according to this rationale. So,
too, it is likely that Jewish law recognizes as proper a Noahide law that provides
a sanction for violations other than the death penalty. Noahide law is authorized even to execute. It is not, however, obligated to execute for all violations.
See generally, Rabbi Aharon Soloveitchik cited above and Rabbi Bleich, "*Mishpat Mavet . . .*" (n. 1 above). See also *Helkat Yo'av Tinyana* 14. In particular this
must flow logically from the opinion of Nahmanides that *dinim* incorporates the
obligation to create a system of financial law.

therefore, and at least limits the obligation of Jews to impose law on Noahides to situations that do not now (and will not in the pre-messianic era) exist.

Proof that this is the approach of Ravad can be derived from his ruling in *Laws of Kings* 6:1, which allows the subjugation of Noahides to a Jewish nation in wartime without the imposition of observance of the Noahide commandments, as Maimonides requires.[91] This would make the positions of Maimonides and Ravad, in their writings in *Mila* and *Kings* consistent on this issue.

Similarly, Nahmanides agrees with Ravad and does not require the imposition of the Noahide commandments as part of a negotiated peace between Israel and its Noahide neighbors.[92] He indicates that the military goals alone determine whether peace terms are acceptable. According to Nahmanides, Jewish law would compel the "victor" to accept peace terms that include all of the victors' demands except the imposition of Noahide law on the defeated society; Maimonides would reject that rule and permit war in those circumstances purely to impose these laws on a gentile society. This indicates that Nahmanides, too, does not require the imposition of Noahide law by a Jewish government.[93]

Tosafot[94] also concur with the rulings of Ravad and Nahmanides and deny that there is any obligation upon even a Jewish government to impose the Noahide commandments on nations under their control.[95] No systemic obligation is present. Rashi, too, sides with Ravad on this issue.[96] So does Rashba, in his responsa.[97] "A similar approach is

---

[91]See Comments of Ravad on Kings 6:1 and *Isurei Bi'ah* 12:7–8.

[92]Commentary of Nahmanides on Deut. 20:(1) and (11). Although Nahmanides does mention subsequent adoption of Noahide laws by these nations, it is in the context of self-incorporation of these rules by these nations and not through compulsion.

[93]Except, as noted above, upon those who are *gerei toshav*.

[94]Tosafot, "*ve'lo moridin*," *Avodah Zarah* 26b. This can also be reinforced from the assertion of Tosafot, *Shabbat* 3a that there is no obligation to separate Noahides from sin. For more on this, see 129ff below.

[95]For a general discussion of this, see R. Yehudah Gershuni, *Mishpetei Melukhah*, 165–167.

[96]Commenting on Deut. 20:1, 11 which cites only the obligation of taxation, and deletes the obligation of observance of the Noahide commandments. This is also in harmony with Rashi's opinion (*Yevamot* 48a), which does not appear to require observance of Noahide laws by Noahide slaves of Jews. This too is

found in *Haggahot Ashrei*: "A Noahide, even though he violates the seven Noahide commandments, and his warning is his execution and he does not need formal witnesses and warning, nonetheless every moment prior to his conviction in *beit din*, he is not liable for the death penalty and it is prohibited to kill him."[98] This source clearly disagrees with the opinion of Maimonides discussed above and limits the obligation of a *beit din* to punish Noahides. Indeed, it would seem logical that the *beit din* needed for this punishment is the same type of *beit din* needed to execute Jews, which has not been extant since prior to the destruction of the Second Temple.[99] This approach would make the comments of *Haggahot Ashrei* identical to those of Ravad. Even if this opinion is not accepted, and any regular *beit din* can function in this role, it is clear that no obligation is imposed upon individual Jews to punish Noahides for violations.

In the two areas where this issue is codified into the *halakhah*, the obligation for Jews to compel observance by Noahides is clearly left out. In the laws relating to keeping slaves, there is an intricate discussion of the rules relating to the circumstances in which a Jew may keep a gentile slave who does not undergo (partial) conversion. This matter is fraught with disagreement beyond the scope of this paper.[100] However, one thing is clear: *Tur*, Rama,[101] and the classical commentaries on

---

consistent with Rashi's broad conception of *dina de-malkhuta* noted in *Gittin* 9b (see notes 61 to 63). Merely because there is an obligation to obey does not mean that there is an obligation to assist in enforcement. It is logical to infer that that concept is present in Noahide law also according to those who accept Nahmanides' general framework; see Nahmanides on Gen. 34:11.

[97]Responsa of Rashba 1:59; see also comments of Rashba to *Yevamot* 48b. In this responsa Rashba discusses at some length the status of slaves that do not observe Noahide law without giving any indication that ownership of these slaves is prohibited, thus indicating agreement with Ravad (for reasons that will become apparent once the next paragraph is read).

[98]*Haggahot Ashrei*, *Avodah Zarah* 64b. This source was referred to me by Rabbi Yehudah Herzel Henkin of Jerusalem, in his comments on a draft of this paper.

[99]See note 89 and sources cited therein.

[100]See generally *Arukh ha-Shulhan*, *Yoreh De'ah* 267 for a review of this area.

[101]The opinion of *Shulhan Arukh* itself is unclear. In *Yoreh De'ah* 276:4 Rabbi Karo appears to simply disallow any temporary slavery absent circumcision, and thus he does not even discuss the imposition of Noahide law. In *Beit Yosef* 267, R. Karo appears to accept the approach of Maimonides. However, in *Bedek*

Shulhan Arukh[102] do not quote the obligation to impose Noahide law upon gentiles living—either as a conditional slave[103] or as an employee—in the house of a Jew (and over whom presumably one could have considerable influence).[104] This is true even though the whole area is generally subject to codification.[105] *Tur* and Rama do quote and agree with the various other assertions of Maimonides found in *Milah* 1:6, but they

---

ha-Bayyit (on *id.*) he appears to retract this ruling and condition this whole issue on the presence of a *ger toshav* (resident alien), something which is impossible currently, in the opinion of R. Karo. Thus, the situation appears to be that *Kesef Mishnah* and *Beit Yosef* rule in accordance with Maimonides that these rules are applicable currently, whereas *Bedek ha-Bayyit* rules that (at the least) Maimonides' opinion is inapplicable currently or the *halakhah* is not in accordance with Maimonides. *Shulhan Arukh* is unclear. See generally *Hikrei Lev* 2:53 and *Sedei Hemed* 9:16 for a discussion of these types of situations in the writings of Rabbi Karo. Particularly given the discussion found in text accompanying notes 107 to 116, one is inclined to understand *Shulhan Arukh* as in agreement with Rama.

[102]Maimonides and Rama are both discussing a simple relevant case: May one employ household help that violates one of the Noahide commandments, or must one terminate the help? This issue is relevant even in the 1990s. Rama and the latter authorities indicate that there is no obligation upon a Jewish employer to compel observance of the Noahide laws by employees. It is difficult to assert that Rama left this law out as there was nothing they could do to compel observance because certainly, even in those times, one had the right to fire employees/slaves, if not more than that. Rather, Rama thought that there was no halakhic obligation to compel Noahides to observe the Noahide commandments.

[103]A slave acquired with the explicit condition that conversion not be done and whom Maimonides explicitly required to observe the Noahide laws. See *Milah* 1:6 for a description of this status.

[104]Given the secular law relating to servitude, indentured servants, and slaves found in Europe before the Emancipation, it is difficult to claim that Jewish law declined to address this issue because it was irrelevant. On the contrary, it was quite relevant, and employees/owners had considerable latitude in regulating the conduct of employees/slaves even in issues unrelated to their work; see generally Jonathan Bush, "Free to Enslave: The Foundations of Colonial American Slave Law," *Yale Journal of Law and the Humanities* vol. 5, (1993): 417–70, pp. 417–23.

[105]Unlike those rules found in *Kings* 8–11.

do not cite this one. Indeed, the notes to Rama clearly indicate that he accepts the rulings of Ravad on this matter.[106] The fact that Maimonides quotes an obligation to compel observance by Noahide slaves, which is deleted by the later authorities, is indicative that his opinion is not considered binding according to *halakhah*.[107]

So, too, when discussing the obligation to save gentiles who do not observe the Noahide laws from life-threatening dangers, both *Tur* and *Shulhan Arukh*[108] indicate that there is no obligation to punish violators of Noahide rules. For example, *Beit Yosef*[109] states that there is no obligation (*mitzvah*) to kill gentiles who do not obey the Noahide laws; similar sentiments can be found in *Tur*,[110] *Bah*,[111] and *Derisha*.[112] (Maimonides, in the sources cited above, clearly rejects this.) Rama, in *Darkhei Mosheh he-Arukh* adopts this posture also.[113] *Shulhan Arukh* explicitly incorporates it.[114] So, too, Shakh states "There is no obligation [*mitzvah*] to kill gentiles even if they violate the Noahide laws"[115]

---

[106]*Shulhan Arukh, Yoreh De'ah* 267:4. The notes to Rama were not written by Rama. A close read of *Iggerot Moshe, Yoreh De'ah* 3:103 (particularly the second-to-last paragraph) indicates that Rabbi Feinstein agrees with Rama on this issue.

[107]Further proof that Jewish law did not perceive an obligation to compel observance by Noahides (absent messianic times) can be found on pp. 129ff below, where once again, the approach of Maimonides is a minority opinion.

[108]*Tur* and *Shulhan Arukh, Yoreh De'ah* 158:1. Portions of this can be found in repetition in *Hoshen Mishpat* 425.

[109]*Yoreh De'ah* 158 s.v. "*mi-kol makom ravinehu*." For more on this, see the uncensored version of *Beit Yosef, Hoshen Mishpat* 425, which has recently been incorporated into various editions of the *Tur* (and is found in the new *Makhon ha-Tur*).

[110]*Yoreh De'ah* 158:1 (new *Tur* numbers).

[111]*Yoreh De'ah* 158 s.v. "*mi-kol makom ravinehu*."

[112]*Yoreh De'ah* 158:1. Similar sentiments can be found in Sema, *Hoshen Mishpat* 425:15–19 in his attempts to distinguish gentiles from heretics.

[113]*Yoreh De'ah* 158 s.v. "*ein moridin*." For a long discussion of this topic which reinforces this understanding of the *halakhah*, see the commentary of *Arukh Meshar* on *Darkhei Moshe*.

[114]*Shulhan Arukh* 158:1.

[115]Shakh, *Yoreh De'ah* 158:2. It is worth noting that he cites Yam Shel Shlomo's commentary on *Semak, mitzvah* 48 as in agreement with that. Nekudat Hakesef is equally clear on this issue.

and *Taz* agrees with this assertion.[116] This ruling—not mandating the punishment of gentiles for violating Noahide law—stands in clear contrast to the assertion in *Shulhan Arukh* encouraging and certainly permitting the punishment (and even killing) of one who (is Jewish and) defiantly rebels against Jewish law; this principle holds in the abstract, though definitely not in practice.[117] *It is thus clear that* Shulhan Arukh *and the other various commentaries rule (contrary to Maimonides' assertion) that gentiles need not be punished by Jews for violating Noahide law according to Jewish law.*[118] There is no obligation or duty to compel observance of Noahide law by gentiles.

On the other hand, even those authorities who reject the obligation could accept the assertion of *Sefer Hasidim*:[119] it is a meritorious thing to do, which imitates God's conduct towards the Noahides at Nineveh. Absent other factors, it is laudatory to instruct a Noahide of his obligations, both for reasons mentioned by Rabbi Yehuda he-Hasid, for those mentioned by Maimonides in *Kings* 10:11 and for those discussed in the postscript.

Although Maimonides is relatively clear that, when possible, Jews must impose Noahide law, one could reasonably conclude that most of the *rishonim* and codifiers disagree with that conclusion, asserting that there is no obligation for any individual Jew to compel a Noahide to cease violating the Noahide commandments or asserting that the obligation is limited to messianic times or to resident aliens.

When a Noahide Will Certainly Violate the Law, May Jews Assist in the Violation?

When the gentile will nonetheless perform an action that violates the Noahide code, no matter what a Jew or the Jewish tradition says or does, is there an obligation to withdraw from the situation? If there is an obligation to separate a Noahide from sin—as mandated by a broad reading of *Kings* 8:10 and *Milah* 1:6—one certainly may not assist him in sin.

---

[116]*Taz*, Yoreh De'ah 158:1. For a discussion of this issue, see Responsa *Beit Yehudah*, Yoreh De'ah 4.

[117]*Yoreh De'ah* 158:2.

[118]See also, for a recent reformulation, Rabbi Yitzhak Blau, *Pituhei Hoshen* 5:2(18).

[119]Quote at the opening of this article.

Pesahim 22b quotes the following statement of R. Natan: "R. Natan said from where do we know that one may not extend a cup of wine to a *nazir* nor *a limb of a live animal to a ben Noah?* The source is from the verse 'before a blind person thou shall not put a stumbling block.'" Thus, it is clear that one may not enable a Noahide to sin. If no violation could or would take place without the assistance of a Jew[120] it is a biblical violation of *lifnei ivver* for a Jew to assist a Noahide in violating his law.

But *Avodah Zarah* 6b quotes R. Natan's statement and limits its application to an instance of *terei ibra de-nahara* (literally "two sides of a river"). Only when the Noahide is on one side of a river and the flesh of a living animal is on the other side, so that he cannot obtain it on his own, is the one who extends it to him in violation of *lifnei ivver*. On the other hand, if the Noahide and the flesh are on the same side of the river (*had ibra de-nahara*), so that he could procure the meat on his own, the person who gives it to him is not in violation of *lifnei ivver*. The assumption is that the prohibition will be violated in any case; assistance does not enable the sin.

This discussion relates only to the biblical prohibition called "*lifnei ivver.*" But is there a rabbinic prohibition on assisting a Noahide to violate his seven commandments even when he can violate them independently of the helper? This issue is a crucial one, for it addresses whether there is a general obligation to separate a Noahide from sin. It is impossible to accept Maimonides' opinion that Jews must compel observance of the Noahide laws and simultaneously rule that one need not separate a Noahide from sin.[121]

---

[120]The *Mishneh le-Melekh* (*malveh ve-loveh* 4:2) states (perhaps reflecting his understanding of the Maimonides) that in order for the action to become permissible according to Torah law, it has to be doable by a gentile, or a person otherwise not obligated in this commandment of *lifnei ivver* generally, rather than be able to be done by any person. The *Mishneh le-Melekh's* approach is based upon his understanding of Tosafot (*Hagigah* 13a, *ein moserin*) that *had ibra de-nahara* ("one side of the river") means when the principal can do it on his own or through the assistance of a non-Jew. This makes sense only within the conceptual framework of Tosafot and the Ran (which will be explained below), as it seems irrelevant that others can aid in the prohibited act if they too are obligated not to do so.

[121]The reverse (which is not the contra-positive) is not true. See the discussion relating to the opinion of Ran, infra.

Two schools of thought exist. The first position is taken by Tosafot, *Mordekhai*, Rama, and Shakh. Each accepts that when one is not in a "two-sides-of-the-river" situation, there is no prohibition associated with assisting a Noahide who sins.[122] Rama states that there are those who rule that it is prohibited to sell Noahides supplies used for their idol worship only when others will not supply them; however, when others can supply them, there is no prohibition. He concludes by adding, "The tradition is in accordance with this opinion; pious people [literally: spiritual people] should conduct themselves in accordance with the stricter opinion." Shakh states this even more clearly: "In my humble opinion, all authorities agree with the opinion of Tosafot and *Mordekhai* that it is permissible to aid a Noahide . . .[123] [All those] who argue are discussing the case of a Jew whom one is obligated to separate from sin . . . This is not the case for a Noahide . . . whom we are not obligated to separate from sin."[124] This ruling has a significant impact on the issue of the Jew's obligation to prevent a Noahide from violating his seven commandments. Essentially, this school of thought accepts that once one cannot *actually prevent* the violation from occurring, there is no obligation to dissuade or convince a Noahide from violating the law. *Indeed, one may actively assist him by providing him with things that he could otherwise acquire on his own.*

This approach—which rules that there is no obligation to prevent sinning by a Noahide or convince a Noahide to cease sinning—is accepted by nearly all authorities, including *Magen Avraham*,[125] *Gra*,[126]

---

[122]Tosafot, *Avodah Zarah* 6b, s.v. *"minayin"*; *Mordekhai*, *Avodah Zarah* 6b; Rama, *Yoreh De'ah* 151:4; Shakh, *Yoreh De'ah* 151:6.

[123]The ellipses in this paragraph all refer to the case of a *mumar*, apostate, and assisting him in sin. That topic is beyond the scope of this paper; for more about it, see Michael Broyde and David Hertzberg, "Enabling a Jew to Sin: The Parameters," *Journal of Halacha and Contemporary Society* N. 19 (1990):7–32.

[124]Shakh, *Yoreh De'ah* 151:6.

[125]*Orah Hayyim* 347:4. *Magen Avraham* rules that it is prohibited to assist an unobservant Jew to sin even when he can do it without assistance; however, he clearly permits one to assist a Noahide in sinning.

[126]*Yoreh De'ah* 151:8. Gra rules that it is prohibited to assist an unobservant Jew to sin even when he can do it without assistance; however, he clearly permits one to assist a Noahide in sinning.

Levush,[127] *Beit Shmu'el,*[128] *Mahatzit ha-Shekel,*[129] *Dagul Merevavah,*[130] and *Birkei Yosef.*[131] It is important to realize that several authorities reach the conclusion that it is permitted to assist a Noahide but prohibited to assist an unobservant Jew. This is based on their observation that there is no obligation to separate a Noahide from sinning.[132] (The precise rationale to distinguish between an unobservant Jew and a Noahide is beyond the scope of this paper.)[133]

Although I have found no authority explicitly attempt to harmonize these rulings with Maimonides' ruling cited above,[134] one could easily do so by limiting Maimonides' ruling to a situation where one could literally compel observance of the law, which would then make the situation a "two-side-of-the-river" case. That would argue that the word "to compel" (*lakof*) used by Maimonides should be limited to just that situation.[135] Equally interesting, many of those *rishonim* who clearly argue with Maimonides concerning the obligation to enforce Noahide law discussed in section III, also clearly aver that there is no obligation to separate a Noahide from sin.[136] Their position, too, is consistent. This author would note that any authority who rules that a Jew may assist a Noahide in a violation of the Noahide

---

[127]*Yoreh De'ah* 151:3.

[128]*Even Ha'ezer* 5:18.

[129]*Orah Hayyim* 163:2.

[130]*Yoreh De'ah* 151.

[131]*Yoreh De'ah* 151. Rabbi Feinstein, *Iggerot Moshe* 3:90 states that this is obvious, "proper and true."

[132]Also, the harmonization of apparently inconsistent talmudic texts using this Noahide/*mumar* distinction to separate the various cases; see comments of Gra and *Magen Avraham* cited in notes 125 and 126.

[133]For a discussion of that issue, see Broyde and Hertzberg "Enabling a Jew . . .", (n. 123).

[134]It is worth noting that Shatih (*Yoreh De'ah* 151:6), in his list of authorities who he thinks agree with his assertion that there is no obligation to separate a Noahide from sin, leaves out Maimonides.

[135]Rabbi Menahem Mendel Schneerson unambiguously rejects this reading of Maimonides and accepts that Maimonides means that one should do anything in one's power, to encourage or compel observance. For more on his position, see pp. 134ff below.

[136]Thus, for example, *Tosafot, Shabbat* 3a clearly indicates that to be his rule, as does Nahmanides, cited by Ran in *Avodah Zarah* 7a.

rules (when the Noahide can do the violation without the Jew's assistance) *must* rule that there is no obligation upon any particular Jew to convince a Noahide to obey the commandments.[137]

The second position is taken by Rabbeinu Nisim ("Ran"). Ran states that there is a separate rabbinic prohibition, called *mesaye'a yedei overai aveirah* (literally: "aiding the hand of those who sin") to assist a person— Jew or Noahide—in sin even in situations where the person can do the sin without the help of another.[138] Though many authorities accept the opinion of the Ran concerning a Jew who is generally not observant,[139] as noted above, this opinion essentially is rejected in Jewish law[140] concerning a Noahide—the classical exception being *Tashbetz*, which rules that it is halakhically prohibited to assist a Noahide in sin, because Jews are obligated to separate Noahides from sin.[141]

---

[137]This is analogous to the tension between the obligation of *tokhahah* (rebuke) to an unobservant Jew and the permissibility to assist him in sin (according to *Shakh* and *Dagul Merevavah*). As noted by many, once one is permitted to assist a Jew in sin it is logical to assume that there is no obligation also to rebuke him.

[138]See Ran, *Avodah Zarah* 6b (1a in Rif pages). This author finds very difficult the assertion of Shakh that even Ran would agree that even for a Noahide there is no obligation to restrain him from sin, as Ran explicitly asserts this rabbinic obligation in the case of a Noahide. Most likely Shakh is referring to the opinion of Nahmanides cited in Ran, Rif pages 7a. This opinion of Nahmanides is consistent with the opinion of Nahmanides cited on page 125 above. Tosafot, too, are consistent on this issue.

[139]Among the commentaries, see *Magen Avraham, Orah Hayyim* 347:4 and Gra, *Yoreh De'ah* 151:8. Among the responsa, see R. Yaakov Ettlinger, *Binyan Zion* 1:15; R. Naftali Tzvi Yehudah Berlin, *Meshiv Davar* 2:32, R. Aharon Kotler, *Mishnat Rav Aharon* 1:6.

[140]See sources cited in notes 125 to 131. Perhaps one could claim that the opinion is accepted by Rabbi Karo himself writing in *Yoreh De'ah* 151:1, although as noted by Rabbi Ovadiah Yosef (*Yabi'a Omer, Orah Hayyim* 2:15[8–9]) this is difficult to prove.

[141]*Tashbetz* 3:133. It is worth noting that even Rabbi Ovadia Yosef cites no later authorities in agreement with Tashbetz on this issue. He too perceives him as standing alone; *Yabi'a Omer Orah Hayyim* 2:15(2–10). Perhaps a claim could be made that Tosafot *Yom Tov, Pirkei Avot* 3:14 agrees with Tashbetz (see postscript). This author is more inclined to read his remarks in the same light as those of *Sefer Hasidim* cited at the opening of this article and also note 146.

According to Ran's approach, Maimonides' ruling, cited above, could be understood in two different ways. When a Jew could compel observance of the law, that would be a biblical obligation. When compulsion would not work, there would be a rabbinic obligation at least not to assist. This position is neutral on the proper understanding of *Kings* 8:10 (which appears to compel observance), as even if there is no obligation to compel observance, one could readily imagine the Sages prohibiting actual assistance in a violation, even if there were no obligation to deter the sin. If one accepts Maimonides in *Kings* 8:10, one must at the minimum accept Ran's rule.

Maimonides, himself, however appears to be completely consistent. He rules that one may never aid a person—Jew or Noahide—who is attempting to violate the law even if, when one declines to aid him, another will do so. This is true whether or not the next person who aids him is also obligated to observe the law. Thus, his position rejects the approach taken in *Avodah Zarah* 6b and makes no distinction between one or two sides of the river.[142] Maimonides' position is completely consistent: he prohibits assisting another in sin in all situations and compels both Jews and Noahides actively to prevent others from violating Noahide law.[143]

The Responsa of Rabbi Menahem Mendel Schneerson

When a Jew contemplates violating Jewish law, there is an obligation upon Jews not only to prevent him from violating the law (physically, if necessary and possible). But there are also obligations to teach him or

---

[142]Maimonides would maintain that the statements by R. Natan in *Avodah Zarah* 6b represent only R. Natan's opinion, and are not accepted by most of the Amora'im; to support this he would cite the fact that this limitation on R. Natan is not quoted in the Talmud in any other place. Although Maimonides does not say so explicitly, this position can be inferred from several of his comments. First, in *Sefer ha-Mitzvot*, negative commandment 299, Maimonides does not limit the scope of the prohibition of *lifnei ivver* to situations where others cannot help. Secondly, he never quotes this limitation in any of the instances he deals with *lifnei ivver* in his primary work, the *Mishneh Torah*. In addition, this understanding of Maimonides is found in *Minhat Hinukh*, Negative Commandment 232:3, and *Melamed Leho'il* 1:34.

[143]See also *Havot Ya'ir* 137, who appears to adopt the opinion of Maimonides.

her about the law and to induce or persuade compliance.[144] Indeed, in a post-Emancipation society, limiting Jewish sinning is rarely done with coercion; it is typically done through persuasion and teaching. In my opinion, as noted above, the *halakhah* as generally understood by most authorities rules that there is no obligation to persuade and teach Noahides about the Noahide law. None of the classical commandments designed to deter sinning by Jews (except the biblical prohibition of *lifnei ivver*, which was discussed previously)[145] is generally thought applicable to Noahides. Thus, there is no obligation of *tokhaha* (to rebuke) a Noahide who sins,[146] there is no notion of *arevut* (cooperative activity) that compels collective responsibility,[147] and no obligation to separate a Noahide from sin.

One modern responsum stands out as advocating an approach completely different from that generally accepted by Jewish law. The strongest case that a Jew is obligated to teach and persuade gentiles to keep the seven commandments is found in the writings of Rabbi Menahem Mendel Schneerson of Lubavitch, in one of his classical responsa.[148] After

---

[144]For a general discussion of the parameters of this obligation, see R. Yehuda Moreal, *Be-Derekh Tovim* 124–129 and Moshe Weinberger, *Jewish Outreach: Halakhic Perspectives* (New York: Ktav, 19).

[145]In general, *lifnei ivver* is a different type of obligation, since it discusses assisting or enabling sin, which logic would indicate is more restricted than merely not preventing sin. Thus, the fact that one is under no obligation to teach a person that murder is wrong, does not mean that one can sell the person a gun to commit a murder or provide directions to the victim's house.

[146]See generally *Sanhedrin* 75a and Rashi (excluding even a resident alien). It has been claimed that Rashi, according to an alternative version not found in our text, maintains that there is an obligation of rebuke applicable to a Jew when a Noahide sins. See *Minhat Yitzhak* 4:79(4), who relates this to the sources cited in note 1. This author would be more inclined to understand the ruling of *Sefer Hasidim* as imposing an extra-halakhic moral duty; but see notes of Rabbi Meir Arik to *Sefer Hasidim* which cross-references this to Maimonides, *Kings* 8:10.

[147]For a lengthy discussion of this issue, see Aaron Kirshenbaum, "'Covenant' with Noahides Compared with Covenant at Sinai," *Dinei Yisra'el* 6 (1974):31–48, n. 37 (Hebrew).

[148]Rabbi Menahem Mendel Schneerson "*Sheva Mitzvot Shel Benei No'ah*," *Ha-Paredes* 59:9 7–11 (5745). This responsum has been reprinted in a number of places; see e.g. *Responsa Shavit* 7:1. For Rabbi Stern's reply, see *Responsa Shavit* 8:3 (asserting that Maimonides' ruling is limited to enforcing acceptance,

quoting Maimonides, *Kings* 8:10 discussed in part 1, Rabbi Schneerson states:

> It is obvious that this obligation [found in Maimonides, *Kings* 8:10] is not lim-
> ited only to a Jewish court, since this commandment is unrelated to the pres-
> ence of a *ger toshav* (resident alien), and thus what is the need of a *beit din*. . . .
> Thus, this obligation is in place in all eras, even the present, when no *ger toshav*
> can be accepted and it is obligatory on all individuals who can work towards
> this goal. So, too, this commandment is not limited to using force—where, in
> a situation we cannot use force, we could be excused from our obligation—
> since the essence of the obligation is to do all that is in our power to ensure
> that the seven Noahide commandments are kept; if such can be done through
> force, or through other means of pleasantness and peace, which means to ex-
> plain [to Noahides] that they should accept the wishes of God who commanded
> them in this rules. This is obviously what is intended by Maimonides. . . .
>
> In *Responsa Tashbetz* (3:133) it states that even in a case where there is no
> prohibition of *lifenei iver*, such as two sides of the river, still it is prohibited to
> assist Noahides who wish to sin, since "we are obligated to separate them from
> sin." In reality, we have no source for the obligation to separate a Noahide
> from sin, if it is not derived from the remarks of Maimonides discussed above
> [*Kings* 8:10] that we are obligated to coerce them into accepting command-
> ments, and thus, of course, we may not assist them in violating them.

Rabbi Schneerson concludes by stating:

> From all of the above, it is clear that anyone who has in his ability to influ-
> ence, in any way, a Noahide to keep the seven commandments, the obliga-
> tion rests on him to do so, since that was commanded to Moses our teacher.
> Certainly, one who has connections with Noahides in areas of commerce
> and the like, it is proper for him to sustain the connection in order to con-
> vince and explain to that person, in a way that will reach that person's heart
> that God commanded Noahides to keep the seven commandments. . .[149]

---

rather than observance). In this author's opinion, Rabbi Stern's distinction is
difficult to accept as Maimonides, in the three sources cited above, appears to
be speaking about observance as well as acceptance. Any other reading leaves
Maimonides internally inconsistent and not based logically on the Talmudic
source found in *Sanhedrin* 57a, as *Kesef Mishnah* states he is.

[149]However, even Rabbi Schneerson concedes that the obligation to induce
compliance is limited to situations where "no financial loss is caused, even the
loss of future profits." This limitation is itself a little difficult, as halakhah does
not recognize "loss of profit" generally as a claim.

In my review of the literature, the weight of halakhic authority is contrary to this analysis, although it certainly is morally laudatory (all other things being equal) to convince Noahides to keep and observe the Noahide laws. Three proofs can be adduced, indicating that the ruling of Rabbi Schneerson is not accepted by most authorities.[150] First, as he himself notes, his position assumes that there is an obligation to separate a Noahide from sin. As noted in detail previously, nearly all authorities reject that assertion. Second, it assumes the halakhic correctness of the opinion of Maimonides concerning the general obligation to compel observance by Noahides; this author suspects that the normative *halakhah* is codified in favor of those who disagree with Maimonides and thus rejects the rulings found in Maimonides, *Kings* 8:10.[151] Finally, it assumes that even within the position of Maimonides, the obligation to compel observance includes the obligation to persuade. No support is advanced for that proposition, and one could easily assert by analogy that merely because compulsion is mandatory (when possible) to prevent a violation, persuasion need not also be mandatory.[152] In addition, proof that there is no obligation upon any individual Jew to teach Noahides their laws can be found in the many responsa that *permit* the teaching of Noahides about their laws: these many responsa all *permit* this activity—but none rules it *obligatory or compulsory*.[153]

In addition, I believe that systemic jurisprudential concerns within *halakhah* for reciprocity (which are constantly present and which are

---

[150]Of course, Rabbi Schneerson—himself a preeminent authority of Jewish law—is quite within his purview to argue with the overwhelming weight of authorities.

[151]See pp. 124ff above.

[152]For example, in the area of *lifnei ivver*, if one's actions are needed to allow another to sin, there is a biblical prohibition in doing the activity; that is analogous to compulsion. On the other hand, if the sinner can sin without assistance, it is at best a rabbinic violation to assist the sinner; it might even be permissible. That would be analogous to persuasion.

[153]See, for example, *Melamed Leho'il, Yoreh De'ah* 77; *Yabi'a Omer, Yoreh De'ah* 17; *Seridei Eish* 2:92; *Teshuvot Maharil* 199 and *Zekan Aharon* 2:71. For a survey of this issue, see Rabbi Bleich, "Teaching Torah to non-Jews," *Contemporary Halakhic Problems*, 2:315–316. Even Maimonides, who permits the teaching of Scripture to Christians based on the rationale that they accept the divinity of the Bible, merely rules that one *may* teach them the proper commandments, and not that one *must; Teshuvot ha-Rambam* 1:149 (Blau).

beyond the scope of this paper) mandate a symmetry of obligation between Noahide and Jew. Jewish law certainly does not compel Noahides
to enforce their legal system on Jews and certainly does not authorize
Noahides to punish Jews for violations of Jewish law.[154] To impose a
non-reciprocal obligation upon Jews would violate jurisprudential norms
found in Jewish law, where systemic obligations to act for the benefit
of others are typically imposed only when those others would be obligated to do the same were the situation reversed. Noahides are not
obligated to enforce Jewish law; Jews are thus not obligated to enforce
Noahide law.[155]

CONCLUSION

This article started by reviewing the halakhic obligation of gentiles to
obey the Noahide commandments and concluded that notwithstanding a minority opinion to the contrary, *halakhah* accepts that gentiles are
obligated to keep the Noahide laws, and they are responsible even for
unintentional violations. So, too, *halakhah* recognizes that gentiles are
obligated to create a system of laws designed to—at the minimum[156]—
enforce the Noahide laws and punish Noahide[157] violators.[158] This article then continued by noting that Maimonides believes Jews as well as
Noahides are obligated to enforce the Noahide laws; but many authorities, early and late, including Rama, reject this rule of Maimonides and

---

[154]See generally Rashbatz, 1:158–162, 59–61. See also Shmuel Shiloh, *Dina de-Malkhuta Dina* (Jerusalem: Magnes Press, 1974) 422–32.

[155]This idea is a paper in and of itself; see Michael Broyde and Michael Hecht, "The Gentile and Returning Lost Property According to Jewish Law: A Theory of Reciprocity" forthcoming in the *Jewish Law Annual*.

[156]Perhaps even to create a general legal system, according to Nahmanides.

[157]See note 66.

[158]It is important to note that the overwhelming consensus of halakhic scholars is that there is no obligation upon Noahides to execute every violator of the
law. Within the rubric of *dinim* is the right to create a hierarchical system of
law, which invokes punishments other than death for violations; See Rabbi
Bleich, in *Mishpat Maveti* (n. 1), and Rabbi Aaron Soloveitchik, "On Noahides,"
Beit Yitzhak 19 (5747):335.

deny that there is a halakhic obligation on individual Jews to compel Noahides to observe their laws. Indeed, Rabbi J. David Bleich states unequivocally: "Jews as individuals are not required to secure compliance with the Noahide Code on the part of non-Jews."[159]

Finally, this article noted that whether there is (or is not) a halakhic obligation to enforce the Noahide laws, it is nonetheless still biblically prohibited to enable a Noahide to violate the Noahide laws (without a Jew's[160] assistance, the law would not be violated). In a situation where the Noahide is able to violate the law without the assistance of any Jew, however, nearly all authorities rule that there is no obligation to prevent a Noahide from sinning, and one may thus even assist the Noahide in sin. Clearly then, classical *halakhah* does not compel a Jew to persuade or entice a Noahide to observe the law. Rama rules that one may assist, but pious people should abstain from this activity. Shakh indicates that even pious people need not abstain from this activity. Rama's assertion that pious people should abstain from this activity can be supported both as a minority opinion within *halakhah* and as the ethical direction of *Sefer Hasidim* with which I began.

POSTSCRIPT

It is the conclusion of this paper that *halakhah* sees no technical obligation in most situations—even as it is morally laudatory—to ensure that Noahides obey their laws. Two observations must be made.

First, as with all issues, the outer parameters of that which is halakhically permissible do not establish that which is morally laudatory (or perhaps even halakhically encouraged). According to *Pirkei Avot*: "[Rabbi Akiva] used to say, Humanity is precious since people were created in God's image." The remarks of *Tosafot Yom Tov* are also relevant. "Rabbi Akiva is speaking about the value of all people . . . He wished to benefit all people including Noahides . . . Rabbi Akiva seeks to elevate all inhabitants of the world . . ."

---

[159]Rabbi J. David Bleich, "Teaching Torah to non-Jews" *Contemporary Halakhic Problems* 2:338.

[160]Or perhaps even any fellow Jew. See note 120.

Consider also the remarks of Rabbi Yehuda ha-Hasid, with which this paper opened.[161] Indeed, Rabbi Joseph B. Soloveitchik continues the theme of *Sefer Hasidim*, concerning Nineveh, when he states:

> There may be an additional reason for Jonah's association with Yom Kippur ᠈ . . . Nineveh was the capital city of pagan Assyria . . . It was a country which would later, under Sennacherib in 722 B.C.E. besiege Jerusalem and exile the ten tribes. Yet God's compassion embraces all of humanity . . . It is, therefore characteristic of the universal embrace of our faith that as the shadows of dusk descend on Yom Kippur . . . the Jew is alerted . . . that all of humanity are God's children. We need to restate the universal dimension of our faith, especially when we are sorely persecuted and are apt to regard the world in purely confrontational terms.[162]

In a similar vein are the remarks of the *Kuzari*, which indicates that the moral relationship of the Jews to the nations of the world is similar to that of the heart to the rest of the body.[163] Thus, there are many theological or halakhic reasons why it might be proper to teach Noahide laws generally. In fact, a claim can be made that *halakhah* obligates a truthful response to an honest query from a Noahide concerning his obligation under the Noahide code.[164]

---

[161]"When one sees a Noahide sinning, if one can correct him, one should, since God sent Jonah to Nineveh to return them to his path"; *Sefer Hasidim*, Section 1124.

[162]*Reflections of the Rav*, Volume 2: *Man of Faith in the Modern World* (adaptations of the lectures of Rabbi Joseph B. Soloveitchik by Abraham Besdin) (New York: Ktav, 1989), 142–144.

[163]*Kuzari*, 2:36; see also *Kuzari* 1:47 and 1:57 for similar insights. It is based on this *Kuzari* that Rabbi Yaakov Kamenetsky indicated that Torah Umesorah should close its various *yeshivot* on the day of President John F. Kennedy's funeral in 1963. (After citing the *Kuzari*, he stated "it is the role of the Jews to teach morality to the nations, and thus, whenever some terrible wrong occurs, we should feel implicated for not having completed our mission;") Yonason Rosenblum, *Reb Yaakov* (New York: Mesurah, 1993), 182–183. Rabbi Howard Jachter pointed out this source to this author. Similar thoughts can also be found in *Moreh Nevukhim* 3:51 concerning the role of the Jewish forefathers.

[164]Support for this proposition can be found in Seforno, commenting on Ex. 19:6, which clearly indicates that Jews must answer these questions from

Second, this paper has left unexplored many other rationales for seeking enforcement of Noahide law. The words of Maharam Schick should be quoted: "[I]t appears that any situation that involves judging violators, even if they are Noahides, is a Jewish people's concern, for others will learn from any wrong done in public and will follow suit and, in the least, the sight of evil is harmful to the soul. Thus, it is our concern. In any case, it is inconceivable that any person living among the residents of a given city be beyond the jurisdiction of the court."[165] Rabbi Bleich puts it a little differently.

Noahides. See generally comments of Maimonides, *Ma'aseh Korbanot* 19:16 and Meiri 59a. Rabbi Bleich states:

> It seems to this writer that while there exists no *obligation* to volunteer information (although it may well be laudable to do so), there *is* an obligation to respond to requests for information. Jews are commanded to disseminate Torah as widely as possible among their fellow Jews, but there is no obligation to seize the initiative in teaching the Seven Commandments to Noahides. Nevertheless, when information or advice is solicited there is a definite obligation to respond. When a non-Jew takes the initiative in posing a query, the Jew must respond to the best of his ability. (Rabbi J. David Bleich, *Contemporary Halakhic Problems* 2:339)

Limiting the obligation to respond to sincere solicitations relating to personal conduct (as Rabbi Bleich apparently intended), this can also perhaps be inferred from *Peri Megadim*, *Orah Hayyim* 443:5 and 444:6, whose assertion as to the obligation to remove passive obstacles might rise to the level of a "one side of the river" case when a particular Jew is asked by a Noahide what his law requires of him. This raises the question of whether *lifnei ivver* can be violated through passivity; for more on that see "Enabling Jews to Sin," supra note 123.

[165]Maharam Shick, *Orah Hayyim* 144. An example of this can also be found in the letter of Rav Moshe Feinstein sent to the New York State governor favoring the implementation of the death penalty for certain crimes; *Iggerot Moshe, Hoshen Mishpat* 2:68. So too, the mandate of *tikkun olam* might provide some direction; see generally R. Nissim, *Derashot ha-Ran*, 11 (which uses the term *tikkun siddur ha-medini* to refer to Noahide activity). For a brief discussion of this issue, see Suzanne Last Stone, "Sinaitic and Noahide Law: Legal Pluralism in Jewish Law," 12 (1990) *Cardozo Law Review*: 1157–1214. On the use of *tikkun olam*, it is also important to examine the way that term is used by Maimonides, in *Kings* 11:4 in the uncensored versions of his text (for example, see *Rambam le-Am*). This issue is quite crucial, as Maimonides' image of *tikkun olam* seems to be directed at the reason for religions other than Judaism; see also *Responsa Kol Mevasser* 1:47 and *Heikhal Yitzhak Orah Hayyim* 38.

Despite the absence of a specific *obligation* to influence non-Jews to abide by the provisions of the Noahide Code, the attempt to do so is entirely legitimate. Apart from our universal concern, fear lest "the world become corrupt," as Maimonides puts it, it is also very much a matter of Jewish concern and self-interest. Disintegration of the moral fabric of society affects everyone. Particularly in our age we cannot insulate ourselves against the pervasive cultural forces which mold human conduct. Jews have every interest in promoting a positive moral climate.[166]

Additionally, there is the issue of *hillul ha-Shem*, desecration of God's name. It is possible that there could be situations where public institutional silence by Jewish groups as to the propriety of a particular activity by government or other groups, particularly when other religious groups are protesting this activity as immoral, could lead to desecrations of God's name. On the other hand, the more clearly known it is that governmental policy is areligious in nature and that Jewish law imposes no obligation on Jews to protest, the less serious an issue this becomes.

Finally, there is the philosophical mandate to be a "light onto the nations of the world." As noted by Radak commenting on the words "*le-or goyim*" (Is. 42:6), "because of the influence of the Jews, the gentiles will observe the seven commandments and follow the right path." While this concept is beyond the scope of this paper, and deserves one of its own, a brief review of the use of the term "light onto the nations" indicates that it is normally used to mean that the Jews should behave in an exemplary manner such that gentiles will wish to imitate Jews, and not as a mandate to proselytize observance. This is exemplified by Is. 60:3; for examples of that in rabbinic literature, see *Bava Batra* 75a; *Midrash Rabbah Ester* 7:11; *Midrash BeReshit* 59:7 and *Midrash Tehilim* (Bubar) 36:6. For a sample of its use in the responsa literature, see *Tzitz Eliezer* 10:1(74); Yavetz 1:168 and particularly Hatam Sofer 6:84; see also responsa of Rosh 4:40 which is also cited in *Tur, Orah Hayyim* 59. None of these authorities uses the citation in a legal context to direct Jewish participation in gentile activities—all of the citations are homiletical (Maharit, *Even Ha'ezer* 2:18 does appear to use it in a legal context concerning a Jewish dispute; however upon further examination one sees that not to be so). This concept plays yet a more prominent note in kabbalistic literature; see *Sefer Resisei Laylah*, section 57 s.v. "*techlat*" and "*ve-zehu.*" For a defense of this beacon-like (i.e., Jews behave properly and this illuminates the world) understanding of the verse as the proper understanding of the literal meaning of the Bible itself, see Harry Orlinsky, "A Light onto the Nations: A Problem in Biblical Theology," *Seventy-Fifth Anniversary Volume of the Jewish Quarterly Review* eds., Abraham A. Neuman and Solomon Zeitlin (Philadelphia: Dropsie College, 1943 [1967]), 409–428. For an indication as to

There might be many practical reasons why it is a wise idea to teach vigorously the Noahide Code, or parts of it,[167] to gentiles.

On the other hand, the apparent absence of a general halakhic obligation upon Jews to increase observance of the Noahide code by gentiles allows for a balancing of Jewish interests to occur. The possibility that there might be circumstances where the unfettered teaching of the Noahide code in the United States, where distinctions based on religious affiliation may not be governmentally defended, could be deleterious to the observance of *halakhah* by Jews is not to be dismissed.[168] So, too, the possibility that a clearly Jewish attempt to seek enforcement of Noahide laws could result in vast antagonism and backlash toward Judaism from those groups whose conduct is categorically prohibited by Noahide law is not to be dismissed.[169] Long-term damage to broad Jewish interests might occur.

All of the concerns—on both sides of the issue—are real. How to weigh the likelihood of each scenario and its consequences is beyond the scope of this paper. Perhaps it varies from issue to issue and case to case—although once it is established that no technical halakhic obligation is present, a broad variety of realpolitik factors comes into play, each attempting to evaluate what will be in the long term best interest of the Jewish people. These political factors are much less relevant when technical halakhic prohibitions are on the line, but are certainly significant when discussing the advisability of undertaking discretionary conduct.

---

why Radak might use both the phrase "observe the seven commandments" and the phrase "follow the right path," see *Iggerot Moshe, Yoreh De'ah* 2:130 who indicates that the two are separate concepts.

[166]Rabbi J. David Bleich, "Teaching Torah to non-Jews" *Contemporary Halakhic Problems* 2:339. See also material cited in note 164.

[167]Rabbi Yehudah Gershuni, *Kol Tzofayikh*, 2d ed., where he discusses the possibility of selective teaching of the Noahide laws (unnumbered pages in the back of the book, seven pages after numbering ends).

[168]For example, the promulgation of an abortion law in the United States, consistent only with the Noahide code, would cause situations to arise where *halakhah*'s mandates could not be fulfilled.

[169]For a discussion of such a case, see this author's "Bullets that Kill on the Rebound: Discrimination against Homosexuals and Orthodox Public Policy," *Jewish Action* 54:1 (Fall 1993):52, 74–78 and the reply to it by Rabbis Goldberg, Stolper and Angel in *Jewish Action* 54, 1 (1993):53, 80–82.

4

A Religious Context for Jewish Political Activity

Jack Bieler

A conceptual framework that enables a broad consideration of the religious parameters for political involvement on the part of Orthodox Jews in American society can be found at the end of R. Joseph B. Soloveitchik's essay, "Confrontation."[1] Although the Rav was primarily addressing the specific issue of interfaith dialogue, we can extend his argument to the delineation of guidelines for proactive involvement in working for the improvement of American society. The Rav draws an analogy between the committed Jew who wishes to become significantly involved with "the community of the many" and the conduct of Ya'akov Avinu prior to his face-to-face meeting with his brother Esav (Gen. 33). Ya'akov instructed his messengers to anticipate a three-part question from Esav: "Whose are you, where are you going, and to whom belong these things?"[2] These questions are interpreted by the Rav as posing an existential challenge: that of defining one's values and allegiances on the one hand, and articulating how one sees one's ultimate goals and purpose for existence

---

[1] R. J. B. Soloveitchik, "Confrontation," *Tradition*, 6:2 (Spring/Summer 1964):24.
[2] Gen. 32:17.

on the other. Only after relative clarity is achieved in these two areas does the third issue—the extent to which we are permitted and perhaps even enjoined to "participate in every civic, scientific, and *political* [emphasis mine] enterprise"[3]—become capable of being defined.

Some writers suggest that the statement that Jews would serve as a "light unto the nations"[4] was meant as a prophecy rather than as an obligation and that it applies only when all Jews finally reside in Israel.[5] In effect, this exempts the Jewish people from any self-conscious actions beyond those that they are expected to observe anyway, whether or not they are defined as some sort of "light." Others, however, disagree. For example, R. S. R. Hirsch and R. Avraham Y. Kook are understood to have defined Judaism respectively as a preoccupation with a continual sanctification of God's Name[6] (*kiddush ha-Shem*) and an alignment with the thrust of history and Providence.[7] *Kiddush ha-Shem* cannot take place in a vacuum without onlookers, and history comprises all human events, not just those directly involving the Jewish people. Hence, proactive involvement with the non-Jewish world is being called for.

---

[3]R. Soloveitchik 24.

[4]Is. 42:6.

[5]Emanuel Feldman, "The Paradox of Separation," *Jewish Action* 50:4 (Fall 5751[1990]):27–8.

[6]The extension of the concept *kiddush ha-Shem* to areas beyond the limited legal definition implied by Lev. 22:32 *"be-tokh benei Yisrael"* (in the midst of *the Jewish people*) and delineated in telegraphic fashion by Rambam in *Mishneh Torah, Hilkhot Yesodei ha-Torah* 5:4, can be found both in the *Mishneh Torah* itself (ibid., 5:11, where the term *beriyot* [divine creations], taken from *Yoma* 86a, is used and probably includes both Jews and non-Jews), and much more extensively by S. R. Hirsch in "Profaning and Hallowing of the Holy Name" in *Horeb* (New York: Soncino Press, 1962) 463–8. However, the question can still be posed as to what is the intended effect of an act of *kiddush ha-Shem*. Is the point of a Jew acting in this manner to demonstrate how devoted he personally is to the tenets of his faith? Or is at least part of the desired outcome to inspire the observer of the act of *kiddush ha-Shem* to some higher moral, spiritual commitment of his own? Whereas the first formulation can be looked upon as an ennobled manner of gaining credibility for the integrity and commitment of the Jewish people, accompanied by little or no effect on general society, the second conception is a more appropriate complement to the idea of *"or la-goyim"*.

[7]Jonathan Sacks, "Torah U'Maddah: The Unwritten Chapter," *L'Eylah* 30 (Sept. 1990): 13–14.

R. Jonathan Sacks maintains that because Judaism is concerned with the perfection of general society, it is only logical that Jews must be involved as Jews within general society.[8] R. Aharon Soloveichik infers from one of the seven Noahide commandments which are binding on all peoples, that the need "to maintain humanity, decency and morality extends to the entire human race."[9] All peoples are expected to adhere to the requirement of having courts of law to adjudicate disputes, thereby maintaining fundamental humanity within the society. It follows logically that all members of society are owed courtesy and respect by all other members of this society.

R. Menahem Mendel Schneerson has given the amorphous concept of participating as role models in the general society even sharper halakhic definition: according to the Rebbe, it is obligatory for each individual to do everything in his power to influence the people of the nations to fulfill the seven Noahide commandments. Because this is the stated opinion of the Rambam (*Mishneh Torah, Hilkhot Melakhim* 8:10), and nobody contradicts him, this is certainly the *halakhah*.[10] R. Walter Wurzburger[11] infers from a different comment, appearing twice in Rambam's *Mishneh Torah* (*Hilkhot Melakhim* 10:12; *Hilkhot Avadim* 9:8), that there is a positive requirement that we interact in a moral and humane manner with the non-Jewish society surrounding us. Rambam cites Prov. 3:17, "And its ways are ways of pleasantness and all its roads lead to peace," and Ps. 127:9, "God extends goodness to all, and He grants mercy to all of His creatures," to establish that non-Jews should be the recipients of visits to the sick, burial assistance, charity, and sensitive treatment if they are enslaved to a Jew. Wurzburger suggests that if all Rambam wished to prove was that measures should be taken to stave off violent attacks and other animosity, the verse stressing *shalom* would be the clear justification. But if Rambam has taken care to add yet another verse to the codification of this commandment, stressing God's indiscriminate and uni-

---

[8]Ibid.

[9]Aharon Soloveichik, "Jew and Jew, Jew and Non-Jew," in *Logic of the Heart, Logic of the Mind* (Jerusalem: Genesis Press), 69–91.

[10]Menachem Mendel Schneerson, *Hiddushim u-Biurim be-Shas u-ba-Rambam*, (New York: Kehot, 1984), 2: 76; quoted by Arye Forta, in "The Role of Judaism in the Secular World," *L'Eylah* 34 (Sept. 1992):27–30. [For discussion of the Rebbe's position, see Michael Broyde's article in this volume—Eds.]

[11]Walter Wurzburger, "Darchei Shalom" *Gesher* 6 (1977–8):80–6.

versal goodness, then treating a non-Jew appropriately becomes a fulfillment of Deut. 28:9 "And you will walk in His Ways." R. Immanuel
Jakobovits boldly refers to the expectations that are made for the Jewish
people as the "Jewish Mission to the Nations."[12] The proof-text for Jews
serving as a "light unto the nations" was from the Prophets, considered
a lesser form of heavenly inspiration than that of the five books of Moses.
Jakobovits attempts to remove the possible objection; in the process, he
makes the case more compelling by providing Torah-based sources for
his approach, namely, Gen. 12:13, "And through you shall be blessed
all the nations of the earth," and Deut. 28:10, "And all the peoples of
the earth shall see the Name of the Lord is called upon you."

The fundamental problem with all of these highly creative attempts
to mandate direct action that will influence our fellow non-Jewish citizens, as well as the general society in which we all live, is that the authoritative texts of Jewish tradition hardly discuss the concept.[13] Those
who wish to gain the approval of the Jewish traditional world will have
to demonstrate that the silence of the Talmud and halakhic decisors re-

---

[12]Immanuel Jakobovits, "The Jewish Mission to the Nations," *Jewish Action*,
50:4 (Fall 5751 [1990]):29–30.

[13]Although the concept of *kiddush ha-Shem* is certainly ubiquitous throughout Jewish primary sources, the particular application that is suggested by Hirsch
in *Horeb* as well as Jakobovits (in, for example, "*Kiddush ha-Shem le-Einei ha-
Goyim be-Or ha-Halakhah*" in *Sefer Yovel li-Kevod R. Yosef Dov ha-Levi Soloveitchik*,
ed. S. Yisraeli, N. Lamm, Y. Rafael, [Jerusalem: Mosad Ha-Rav Kook, 1985], 1:
281–5), must be thought of as innovative. The anecdotes and general examples
provided for instances of the sanctification of God's name involve a single individual, and sometimes a group of individuals, who, due to a particular act of
kindness, honesty, or self-sacrifice, make an impression on a limited group of
onlookers. To extend this idea so that one calls for the presentation in various
public forums of Jewish ideas and Jewish life before general society, though certainly logical, does involve a significant act of interpretation. The single verse
that might be able to be cited as a support is Deut. 4:6 ". . . for it [the laws of
the Torah] are your wisdom and your understanding in the eyes of the nations,
who will hear all of these statutes and will conclude, 'this great nation is certainly wise and understanding.'" Even were it to be posited that the means by
which the nations are to come to learn about Jewish law is by way of its popular
presentation to general society, the verse implies that this will gain credibility
for the lifestyle and nature of the Jews rather than constitute a sanctification of
God's name per se. See n. 6 above.

garding this matter of *hashkafah* and *halakhah* indicates not opposition but mitigating circumstances during various historical periods. Sacks suggests that it is the Holocaust that has "driven Jewish concerns markedly inward in the last two decades from universalism to particularism, from 'example' to 'survival.'"[14] His comment implies that there was once a period when it was not only acceptable but perhaps even normative to look upon the broader world with concern and compassion, even to contemplate how to contribute to this wider world. But one is hard-pressed to demonstrate this universalistic sentiment during the years immediately preceding the Holocaust, let alone in the decades and centuries before.[15]

As for Judaism's messianic vision, a sharp distinction can be drawn between hopes and dreams for the messianic period (e.g., Is. 2:3, "And many nations will travel and they will say, 'Let us travel and go up to the mountain of God to the house of the God of Ya'akov, and He will teach us of His ways and we will go in His paths...'"; or Zech. 14:9 "And it will be that God will be the king over all the land, in that day He will be one and His name One") and the role that the Jewish people will play to bring these situations about. Even Rambam's depiction of why Jews are looking forward to the messianic period does not suggest that their reasons include the improvement of general society, independent of Jewish

---

[14]Jonathan Sacks, *Traditional Alternatives: Orthodoxy and the Future of the Jewish People* (London: Jews College, 1989), 5.

[15]Eliezer Schweid notes, after reviewing the perspectives of Spinoza, Mendelssohn, Maimon, Ascher, Samuel Kirsch, Krochmal, Hirsch, Frankl and Graetz—a list that includes many who were unorthodox in their Judaism, to say the least—that not a single one is understood to promote a positive approach to participating in and hopefully influencing the political state in which Jews reside. See Schweid, "The Attitude toward the State in Modern Jewish Thought before Zionism," in *Kinship and Consent: The Jewish Political Tradition and Its Contemporary Uses*, ed. Daniel Elazar (Ramat Gan: Turtledove Publishing, 1981), 127–47. This evaluation certainly supports the conclusion that Jews living in these European environments could not even imagine ever being in a position of true political influence, let alone having their own country. It would therefore seem that developing attitudes whereby Orthodox Jews would think that it is appropriate for them to wield political clout, beyond the context of group protection and interests, will constitute a major undertaking in terms of changing ingrained attitudes.

peace and security: "The [primary reason why] the scholars anxiously await the advent of the messiah . . . is in order to be able to completely devote themselves to the Torah and its wisdom, that there not be op-pressors or distractions [to disturb these Torah pursuits] and therefore in this way that they would merit life in the World to Come . . ."[16] Al-though Rambam does mention in the next *halakhah* that one feature of this epoch will be "that the exclusive preoccupation of the world at this time would be to come to know God . . ." there is no explicit indication in his words that the Jews will play a key role in disseminating this knowl-edge or that they will be particularly responsible for this stage in world history being achieved.[17]

Some have pointed to the instruction of Jeremiah, "Seek out the peace of the city where I have exiled you there and pray on its behalf to God because by virtue of its peacefulness, you will enjoy peace,"[18] along with the similar directive offered by R. Haninah, deputy High Priest in *Pirkei Avot*: "Pray for the welfare of the government, for lacking such political stability, people are wont to swallow one another alive."[19] Though these statements initially appear to reflect Jewish concern for the general non-Jewish society, this contention is difficult to defend on two counts: (a) The motivation of these sentiments appears to be primarily, if not ex-clusively, self-serving; peace and governmental strength are promoted to guarantee the safety and survival of the Jewish population of the com-munity, not to improve for its own sake the quality of life and moral level of society at large. (b) At least in the source in *Avot*, the Jews are in-structed at most to pray; we have here a call to metaphysical rather than political and/or social activism.

A case could be made, however, that the two terms employed by Jeremiah, "*ve-dirshu*" (and seek out, pursue) and "*ve-hitpallelu*" (and pray) are not synonyms, and therefore the former instruction is calling for more than prayer.[20] In fact, Hirsch takes the injunction to pray as *transcend-ing* that of mere "seeking out." "We are obliged not only '*lidrosh*,' to do everything to promote the welfare of the countries in which we live, but actually '*lehitpallel*,' to pray before God and as good citizens, with sin-

---

[16]Rambam, *Mishneh Torah, Hilkhot Melakhim* 12:4.
[17]Ibid. 12:5.
[18]Jer. 29:7.
[19]*Pirkei Avot* 3:2.
[20]See *Da'at Mikra* on Jer. 29:7.

cere devotion known and recognized as such by Him alone, to beseech Him for the welfare of the government.[21]

Nevertheless, the positive theological implications of "even" praying for a non-Jewish government should be balanced by the comment in *Sotah* 37a on Ex. 14:15, regarding the interchange between Moshe and God as the Jews were standing before the Sea of Reeds with the Egyptians bearing down behind them. *Ha-Kadosh barukh Hu* chastised Moshe for praying at great length rather than instructing the Jews to travel. Prayer is an important reflection of a religionist's concern and convictions; yet there are times when actions are also necessary in order to advance the cause(s) that are at hand.

R. Ovadiah Seforno[22] understands the salient point in the Mishnah in *Avot* to be that even corrupt rulers are better for the Jews than none at all. Reflecting upon the situations that informed this particular *tanna*'s

---

[21]S. R. Hirsch, trans. and comm. *Chapters of the Fathers* (Jerusalem: Feldheim, 1989), 40. I. Grunfeld, "S. R. Hirsch—The Man and his Mission," in *Judaism Eternal* (London: Soncino Press, 1956), 1: xxxviii–xli. Grunfeld presents us with a brief consideration of Hirsch's political activities. It is ironic, but altogether understandable in terms of the historical period in which Hirsch lived, that he himself had the opportunity to serve in the Austrian parliament in February 1849, following the 1848 revolution; rather than working for the concerns of the general society as he wrote in his commentaries one should, he became primarily a lobbyist for Jewish concerns. In addition to serving as Chief Rabbi of Moravia and western Silesia, Hirsch was a powerful parliamentary advocate for the ending of discrimination against the Jews, and publicized his ideas via speech-making and pamphlet writing. He was more successful in the pursuit of his cause than the leaders of the new government liked. Upon being told that the Imperial Chief Rabbi should concentrate upon "praying diligently and preaching," he responded as could be expected, that his concept of the Chief Rabbinate was "that working for justice and freedom in the country was just as much a part of religion as praying and preaching." This difference in opinion led to his resigning his post in 1851 and accepting a rabbinic position in Frankfurt. Although the principle of "*aniyei irkha kodmin*" (when considering priorities in the distribution of aid, you should help those closest to you first) might have informed Hirsch's political activities designed to assist primarily the Jews, it might be interesting to speculate whether he perhaps missed an opportunity to be perceived as also taking to heart issues that affected the society as a whole.

[22]*Kitvei Rav Ovadyah Seforno*, ed. Ze'ev Gotlieb (Jerusalem: Mosad Ha-Rav Kook, 1987), 365. The editor points out in footnote 4 that whereas Seforno

recommendation, we can reasonably assume that the society in general and the government in particular, which people such as R. Haninah Segan ha-Kohanim had to confront, were highly unsympathetic to Jews and could hardly be imagined to be open to Jewish active participation in the affairs of state. Nevertheless, the Rabbis had the perspicacity to take the realpolitik position that even a corrupt government is better for society than a totally anarchical situation.[23]

The question that consequently arises is whether and how Orthodox Jewish perspectives regarding active participation within the broader society might change, once the possibility presents itself to take part actively and vigorously in a political climate that lacks at least the overt anti-Semitism of the past, and which ostensibly does not discriminate against particular groups so as to bar them from the political arena. Because of these very changes, Sacks sees particular opportunities for observant Jews in the United States and Great Britain to make significant political contributions at this time: "As Hirsch hoped, Jews have reached prominence in the diaspora. In America they have reached higher educational and occupational levels than any other religious or ethnic group. In Britain, unprecedently, the former Chief Rabbi was elevated to the House of Lords. The vision that animated Hirsch's *Nineteen Letters*—of Jews as moral exemplars in the midst of humanity—may have been in retrospect desperately inappropriate to Germany. But it is hardly absurd given the receptivity to a Jewish voice in the United States and Britain."[24]

Jakobovits, who achieved the distinction described above by Sacks, also reflects upon the unique opportunities that are presenting themselves at this point in history. "The traditional approach of serving by

---

used as the example of corrupt government the kings during the Second Temple period, rulers who would have been familiar to the *tanna* R. Hanina, his real intention was to attack the monarchs of his own time. However, he decided that discretion was the better part of valor, particularly when the royal and church censors would review his work prior to publication.

[23]See Martin Sicher, "A Political Metaphor in Biblical and Rabbinic Literature," *Judaism*, 40:2 (1991):208–14. The author traces the imagery of people resembling fish as they swallow one another alive during times when government is weak, back to the period of the Flood, and even to the conflict between Cain and Abel.

[24]Sacks, "Torah U'Maddah," 14.

example is certainly incumbent upon every Jew. But some have the additional opportunity and therefore *obligation* [emphasis mine],[25] to teach and advance moral ideals directly."[26]

Once it is acknowledged that at least in some Western societies, among them the United States, Jews openly associated with traditional observance have not only the opportunity, but perhaps even the responsibility to participate in political activity, thought must be given to the nature of the goals of these activities and the manner in which this activity ought to manifest itself. It would appear that this question revolves around at least two issues: (a) Can a Jewish political tradition be defined based upon the fundamental ideas that make up the traditional Jewish world view? and (b) What agendas should be set in terms of the general society that traditional Jews engaged in politics could pursue?

Daniel Elazar has written extensively with regard to the political implications that emerge from the biblical concept of *berit*, or "covenant."[27] He defines this term as representing an arrangement "that is usually meant to be perpetual, between parties having independent but not necessarily equal status, that provides for joint actions or obligations to achieve defined ends (limited or comprehensive) under conditions of mutual respect, in such a way as to protect the integrity of all parties involved. A covenant is more than a contract because it involves a moral commitment beyond that demanded for mutual advantage, even involving the development of community among the partners to it."[28]

The paradigm of covenant can be informative on at least two levels in terms of developing political philosophy. On the one hand, covenant describes the parameters of the relationship between the governor and the governed, informed by the dynamics extrapolated from how the Divine interacted with the Jewish people, what He expected from them, how He nurtured them, the manner in which He attempted to educate them, and so on.[29] On the other hand, the nature of the biblical under-

---

[25]See n. 13 above.

[26]Jakobovits, "The Jewish Mission to the Nations," 29–30.

[27]E.g., Daniel Elazar, "Some Preliminary Observations on the Jewish Political Tradition," *Tradition*, 18:3 (1980):249–71; and "Covenant as the Basis of the Jewish Political Tradition," in *Kinship and Consent*, 21–56.

[28]Elazar, "Covenant. . .", p. 22.

[29]See *Shavu'ot* 39a-b; *Sanhedrin* 27b.

standing of covenant can be utilized to analyze the relationships that were set up among the individual groups constituting the governed by virtue of their joint responsibilities towards one another in order to satisfy collectively Divine expectations of them.

Covenants generate legal and moral expectations for mutual and collective responsibility, assistance, service, defense, and law enforcement among divergent religious, social, familial, and sexual groups. These can inform the development of a unique approach for working towards the formation of a particular kind of political community. Probably for some, the suggestion that we work towards creating a covenantal community that would include non-Jews—a form of political *arevut* (guarantorship) paralleling in some ways that mandated among Jews,[30]—would be discordant with their sensibilities. But the distinction that R. Aharon Soloveichik makes[31] with regard to "friendship" (defined by him to include living together, helping one another, guiding, comforting, and encouraging types of relationship that can and should be engaged in between Jews and non-Jews) as opposed to "fellowship" (joining together in the intimate facets of life, playing together, drinking together, seeking pleasure together, relegated exclusively to Jews) would provide a context in which, even though distinctions between communities are made, an overall "covenant" can still be sought as a goal for an Orthodox politically active individual.

This "covenantal" idea can be expressed in halakhic terms by means of the many social enactments that make up so much of the Jewish legal tradition. These enactments can in turn be translated into political goals that can be attained within society. When a person acknowledges that he comes from a system that attempts to enhance the moral nature of his own, immediate, ethnically homogenous society and is then afforded the opportunity to set agendas for general society, these models can serve him in good stead. Walter Wurzburger[32] identifies the umbrella phrases of "*tikkun olam*" (enactments designed to improve social welfare), "*darkhei shalom*" (legislation intended to enhance ways of peace and tranquility),

---

[30]See V. D. Segre's discussion of the particularly Jewish approach to the "legitimacy of power", in "Jewish Political Thought and Contemporary Politics," in *Kinship and Consent*, 298–9.

[31]Soloveichik, "Jew and Jew, Jew and Non-Jew", 84–5.

[32]Walter Wurzburger, "Law as the Basis of a Moral Society," *Tradition* 19:1 (1981):42–54.

"*Derakheha darkhei no'am*" (the assumption that the ways of Torah are informed by pleasantness) as fitting under the broader rubric of the Torah's call in Deut. 12:28: ". . . you will do the good and the straight in the eyes of the Lord your God." Ramban's understanding of this verse as, paradoxically, legally mandating going beyond the letter of the law (*lifnim mishurat ha-din*) would allow Wurzburger's approach to manifest the moral commitment and striving towards community of which Elazar writes.

A second approach for developing a specifically Jewish political philosophy is suggested by Ella Belfer and Ilan Greilsammer.[33] They conceive of Jewish tradition as pitting pairs of ideas against one another in a constant state of tension. Examples of these antithetical emphases include: particularism vs. universalism, the individual vs. the group, extremism vs. compromise, and revolution vs. conservatism.[34] The authors contend that to emphasize one aspect of this political tradition at the expense of the other would be dishonest to our heritage, and therefore all of these factors must be kept in healthy balance with one another. This mentality would assist traditional people opting to make political contributions to general society to maintain their personal loyalties and identity alongside commitments to their fellow citizens. In effect this becomes another means by which Ya'akov's charge to his messengers can be understood.

Once we accept the global idea that working to improve the quality of general society has value not merely in terms of self-preservation and personal comfort, but also in idealistic, spiritual terms (and even in terms of religious obligation), it would be logical to identify those areas that are most likely to be of greatest mutual interest to us and the different faith and ethnic communities we envision joining us in the creation of "community." R. Soloveitchik had written that once we recognize potential personal limitations arising from our historical, existential and religious uniqueness, we should be prepared and more than merely willing to "participate in *every* [emphasis mine] civic, scientific and political

---

[33]Ella Belfer and Ilan Greilsammer, "Political Theory," in *Contemporary Jewish Religious Thought*, ed. Arthur A. Cohen, Paul Mendes-Flohr, (New York: Free Press, 1987), 715–22.

[34]An additional tension that emerges from V. D. Segre's "Jewish Political Thought and Contemporary Politics" is the legitimacy of power vs. the opposition to power. See pp. 298–301.

enterprise."[35] An agenda of specific issues for advancement and advocacy would allow us, at least on an institutional and organizational level,
to focus our efforts and inspire change and improvement for everyone.
Perhaps it is unrealistic to expect a clear consensus with respect to a
specific list of issues that deserve close attention on the part of the
Orthodox community. But even several lists that loosely share specific
concerns would allow us to begin to make the significant contributions
that we might be obligated to try to make, given the opportunities currently available to Jews who wish to participate in the process of developing social and political policies.

To date, unfortunately, the contributions to general social discussions
and debates made by the Orthodox Jewish community have been reac-
tive. An individual is typically consulted or commissioned to offer an
opinion about a particular issue or dilemma that has already been developed and analyzed for some time in the public sector.[36] Consequently,
rather than being in the position to draw public attention to a particular
matter that has not been sufficiently explored or considered, those who
are dealing with Jewish perspectives on questions such as health care,
medical ethics, poverty, commercial practices, or social morality, are often
viewed as attempting to illustrate the relevance of traditional Judaism
to contemporary society, rather than directly participating in the social
debate over the issue. But what is the likelihood that other religious and
ethnic groups would be interested in the Jewish approach to shared
social and ethical dilemmas?

Suppose, by way of illustration, that Orthodox Jewry were to accept the
model offered by Nathan Rotenstreich for how Jews and their traditions
ought to contribute to the world: "Israel must take an Archimedean point,
intellectually, which will be faithful to its own principles on the one hand,

---

[35]See n. 3.

[36]An interesting early example of an apparent exception to the general trend
is noted in n. 1 to R. Norman Lamm's article "Self-Incrimination in Law and
Psychology: The Fifth Amendment and the Halakhah," in Lamm, *Faith and
Doubt: Studies in Traditional Jewish Thought* (New York: Ktav, 1971). Lamm's
essay published in *Judaism*, winter 1956, was quoted by Chief Justice Warren in
the case of Miranda vs. Arizona in 1966. It might be interesting to research how
this situation came about, in order to consider means by which Orthodox Jewish viewpoints could be made available to decision makers at present and in the
future.

and open-minded to the world on the other.[37] Such an Archimedean point can be derived from the basic Jewish outlook that man's life does not belong to himself . . . man is not master of the world, and yet his attitude to the world is not a passive one."[38] How can we "move the world" if the world is not interested in being moved in general, let alone by us in particular? R. Avraham Yitzhak ha-Kohen Kook took the rather drastic position that it was within the context of a world war[39] that general society would come to take Jewish values and ideas seriously:

> The structure of the world, which appears at this point to be tottering due to the terrible storms caused by the sword full of blood, requires the building of the Jewish nation. The building of the nation and the revelation of its spirit is identical, and it is all intertwined with the building of the world, which is presently fragmenting and is yearning for a force full of unity and spirituality, and all of this is to be found in the soul of the Congregation of Israel. The Spirit of God is full therein. It is impossible for the spirit of a person whose emotions of his soul course within him, to be still at this pregnant moment, to not call to all of the forces that lie hidden within the Jewish people: Arise and fulfill your obligations . . . World culture is tottering, the spirit of man is weakened, darkness envelops all of the nations . . . the time has arrived for the Light of God that is revealed via His people to shine . . .[40]

Even R. Kook was probably trying only to suggest a positive role for an otherwise horrific and traumatic life experience, rather than maintaining that a major conflict among the nations of the world is positive and even desirable because it advances non-Jewish interest in Jewish values and ideas. But R. Kook's thought could be useful on a metaphorical level

---

[37]Nathan Rotenstreich; quoted in V. D. Segre, "Jewish Political Thought and Contemporary Politics," in *Kinship and Consent*, 295.

[38]Archimedes, the philosopher of Syracuse, was noted for his statement that "with a lever long enough, and a point to stand upon, he could move the world." *The Compact Edition of the Oxford English Dictionary*, Vol. 1 (Oxford: Oxford University Press, 1971), p. 109, s.v. "Archimedes."

[39]In this essay that was published in 1924, Rav Kook was obviously reflecting upon his perceptions of WWI. The Jewish experience in WWII seemed to have lived up to anything but R. Kook's vision. See R. Tzvi Yehuda ha-Kohen Kook's Introduction to the volume, p. 7.

[40]R. Avraham Yitzhak ha-Kohen Kook, "Ha-Milhamah" in *Orot* (Jerusalem: Mosad ha-Rav Kook, 1966) 16.

if we posit that social conflict between clashing groups and interests, or the development of a siege mentality in light of the erosion of family values and escalation of violence and other criminal activity, might cause those seeking guidance and direction for the formulation of policy to turn urgently to sources that might previously have been overlooked or not taken sufficiently seriously. And even in the absence of what might be perceived as truly desperate circumstances, we ought to support efforts by scholars, scholarly institutions, and journals to explain and disseminate to the public halakhic principles that govern situations which presently daunt everyone collectively as well as individually.[41] These efforts would not only prove beneficial to general society, but would also constitute a possible fulfillment of our divine mandate as a people who is expected to be a *mamlekhet kohanim ve-goy kadosh*, a kingdom of servants of the Divine and a holy nation.

---

[41]Bernard Susser, in "On the Reconstruction of Jewish Political Theory," *Forum*, 45:69–77, comments upon why Jewish ethical and political thought has been relatively inaccessible to the non-scholar. The Jewish tradition, he says, "begins with the palpable existence of a kaleidescopic array of singular events, phenomena, etc., and proceeds to define, circumscribe, authorize, institutionalize etc. the specific entitlements of the various actors in particular instances. Rights are not abstractly postulated and then translated by jurists and legislators into the language of positive law, but rather first and foremost, fleshed out in all their existential variety without a view to subsequent philosophical abstraction" (p. 76). Susser categorizes the Jewish approach as asking "how," rather than the "what" questions that underlie Western political tradition, and he points to responsa literature as constituting the richest vein to be mined for these purposes. Perhaps the very reason why it is difficult to establish the philosophical orientation of Jewish tradition regarding political and ethical matters is what makes their presentation so compelling and potentially beneficial for consideration by general society. When these issues are tied very concretely to real cases and situations, rather than being linked to abstraction, the impetus to find means for implementation is more reality-based and can be understood to potentially have an optimistic, this-worldly resolution. Therefore, the importance of trying to disseminate relevant Jewish positions on issues of the day could prove to be truly informative and practical for society at large, as difficult and challenging as it may be to carry out.

5

Jews and Public Morality

Marc D. Stern

I

Life in the diaspora over two millennia did not offer frequent opportunities for Jews to expend their energies on disinterested political activity aimed at universal social and communal betterment. Largely as a result of the prevailing organization of politics along religious lines, "citizenship" was in most places and times delineated along religious lines. Most countries excluded Jews from full participation in the political life of the community. Moreover, the systematic pursuit of this activity presumes the existence of robust democracies. These were not at all common, even in rudimentary forms until the seventeenth century, and on a large scale until the American Revolution in the eighteenth century.

Even in the United States, full democracy did not come easily. The battle to enfranchise non-Protestants, then the landless, then women and blacks, took almost two hundred years. For Jews in the United States, equality came relatively easily with the separation of church and state and the prohibition on religious tests for federal public officials embodied in the Constitution and the Bill of Rights, and later in state constitutions.[1] These twin proscriptions reflect the idea that religious confor-

---

[1]Naomi W. Cohen, *Jews In Christian America: The Pursuit of Religious Equality* (Oxford University Press, 1993); M. Borden, *Jews, Turks and Infidels* (Chapel Hill, N.C.: University of North Carolina Press, 1984).

159

mity was neither the ideal nor the necessary organizing principle of political life and that, following Locke,[2] it was inappropriate for government to coerce religious belief.

What political influence Jews had in pre-Enlightenment times and
places was generally directed toward physical survival and eliminating
the most oppressive features of inferior political status (such as crushing
taxation). It was generally carried on not by a representative body of the
entire community, but by wealthy individuals. Their influence was the
product of their wealth. Perhaps those influential few rendered general
political advice to their non-Jewish patrons, but, as far as I can tell, this
was done for reasons of personal advancement, not out of any sense
of obligation to the general community. The sort of political activity
shtadlanim engaged in—protecting the community's immediate interests,
particularly from discriminatory legislation, expulsion or inquisition—
needed no justification in twelfth-century Germany, fifteenth-century
Spain or eighteenth-century Poland. It does not need justification in the
very different circumstances of the end-of-the-century United States.
Whatever one may think about government aid to parochial schools, no
one can question, and no one really does question, the legitimacy of a
religious community's advocacy of this aid.[3]

One must also carefully distinguish between advancing one's own
interests and pursuits that incidentally benefit the entire society on the
one hand, and on the other hand, a conscious effort to reform an iden-
tified evil because reform will make the world a better place. Jewish money
lending in the Middle Ages might have been responsible for general
economic growth, but it was undertaken as a way of making a living in a
hostile society, not as a religiously mandated plan for economic growth.[4]

There are three broad rubrics under which Jews could seek general
political involvement. One is a specific halakhic imperative, as in some
sort of *mitzvah* of *tokhahah* (rebuke) aimed not at Jews, but the world at

---

[2]Locke, *A Letter on Toleration* (1740).

[3]Not even those Supreme Court justices who have thought such aid impermissible have thought to argue that the fact that aid received its chief political
support from religious groups in any way tainted it. See text below at note 123.

[4]See *Bava Metzia* 71b–72a. H. Soloveitchik, *Halakhah, Kalkalah, ve-Dimuy
Atzmi* (Jerusalem: Magnes Press, 1985), 17; 25–26.

large. This is by no means an implausible argument, particularly as applied to the seven Noahide commandments (really, the seven categories of Noahide commandments). As others have addressed this problem, I do not deal with it.[5]

Second, one can argue persuasively that in Western societies, where egalitarian norms exert powerful cultural pressures, politics and life do not easily lend themselves to compartmentalizing between conditions that affect Jews and those that do not. This is particularly so for those Orthodox Jews who are economically, professionally, and (partially) culturally integrated into the larger society. This "spillover effect" is obvious in the case of relaxed sexual mores, but appears elsewhere as well.

If inner-city minority youth are disaffected and utterly without hope of a fair chance to enjoy society's benefits, and therefore more prone to violence, all who live in the society will be affected, Jews included. Perhaps as a result of accidents of demography Jews could in some places be marginally more affected by such crimes than others, but that is hardly likely, nor is it a terribly persuasive argument for specifically Orthodox Jewish involvement in ameliorating the pressing problems of the inner city.

Rather, the heart of the matter is that the entire society is hurt both by the isolation of the inner city and the intolerable anti-social behavior that follows in its wake. That isolation and desolation and their violent aftermaths rip at the heart of the social fabric to nobody's benefit and everyone's detriment. Self-interest, not as Jews, but as full members of the society, dictates concern for these problems. This is an instrumental argument for participation in the political life of the community, one without any substantial moral underpinnings.

Finally, there is an inherent ethical and religious value in making society better, fairer, more just, more righteous. In other words, the argument here is that all persons are commanded to make the world better; we are obligated to seek to improve the functioning of society not as Jews qua Jews, but simply as human beings.

This is one of the twin thrusts of Rabbi Soloveitchik's seminal paper "Confrontation."[6] In that essay, the Rav rejected the notion, which he

---

[5]See the essays of Rabbis J.D. Bleich and Michael Broyde in this volume.
[6]Rabbi J. B. Soloveitchik, "Confrontation," *Tradition* 6:2 (1964): 5–29.

ascribed to modern Westernized Jewry (but which today, ironically, is equally applicable to too much of Orthodox Jewry), that one must choose between the "universal and the covenantal."[7] The Rav insisted that "involvement in the [universal] creative scheme of things is mandatory" for all people.[8] Not often noticed is that the Rav insisted that Jews should participate in this task as "an inseparable part of humanity" and on the "basis of equality, friendship and sympathy, as human beings committed to the general welfare and progress of mankind, combatting disease, in protecting man's rights, in helping the needy."[9] Some of these are inherently political tasks ("protecting man's rights") and others can be realized or helped along through political action ("helping the needy"). These are, said the Rav, obligations "implicit in human existence."[10] They come, as any one who has read the essay knows, not from the Sinaitic revelation, but from God's charge to Adam and Eve,[11] "who typify all of humankind."[12] Jews, it would seem to follow, have neither a special expertise in solving these problems, nor a special dispensation to refrain from this endeavor.

It bears emphasizing that the Rav's commitment to political (and other socially protective) activity is not based on some unique Jewish particularism, on some "white man's burden" obligating Jews to act for the benefit of the less fortunate, unenlightened members of society. On the contrary, Jews are called to act simply as members of the human family on the basis of "equality, friendship and sympathy."[13]

These are radical sentiments for contemporary Orthodoxy. It is not surprising that "Confrontation" is today remembered mostly for its ban on interfaith dialogue on theological issues and secondarily for its endorsement of joint efforts of Orthodox Jewish and Christian groups aimed at social betterment (an understanding that assumes each group will retain its own individual identity and not merge in a common endeavor,

---

[7]Ibid., 66.

[8]Ibid., 69.

[9]Ibid.

[10]Ibid.

[11]Ibid.

[12]See also J. B. Soloveitchik, *Lonely Man of Faith*, (New York: Doubleday, 1992) (originally published in *Tradition* 1965).

[13]Soloveitchik, "Confrontation," 68.

which largely distorts the Rav's teaching). Such is a particularist's understanding of a paper with important universalist themes. It is a reading that says much of the current state of Orthodoxy, which insists on emphasizing Judah ha-Levi's tribal, quasi-racial notions of Judaism[14] as opposed to Maimonides' more universalist view, clearly visible in his eschatological vision.[15] It is perhaps not surprising that the Rav, so committed to Maimonides, would assert that Jews are also merely human and may—indeed must—act on that basis.

II

As noted, Jewish history does not abound with examples of Jewish involvement with politics for the purpose of advancing the general good. For some fifty or sixty years prior to World War I, German Orthodoxy took an active role in politics—in large part, of course, out of concern for advancing Orthodox Jewish interests. Dr. Joseph Breuer's comprehensive account of German Orthodoxy in this period reveals a split over whether it was better to work with Catholic religious parties that would protect Jewish religious interests (*e.g. shehitah* or aid to parochial schools) even if they harbored anti-Semitic views, or to join with more liberal, non-religious parties that were opposed to anti-Semitism even if they were unsympathetic to religion. This dichotomy repeats itself within Orthodoxy in the United States.[16] Polish Orthodoxy, mostly in the form of Agudath Israel, also engaged in political activity (over the objection of the Lubavitcher rebbe and Galician Hasidim who attacked the adoption of modern political methods in place of traditional devices[17] [such as the *shtadlan*]) but Agudath's program seems to have been primarily parochial.[18]

---

[14]Judah Ha-Levi, *Kuzari*, 1:27; 1:96; 2:36.

[15]See Menachem Kellner, *Maimonides on Judaism and the Jewish People*, (Albany: SUNY Press, 1991).

[16]Mordechai Breuer, *Modernity within Tradition: The Social Thrusts of Orthodox Jewry in Imperial Germany* (New York: Columbia University Press, 1992), 329 ff.

[17]M. Piekarz, *Hasidut Polin* (Jerusalem: Mosad Bialik, 1990), 23–31.

[18]Gershon Bacon, "Agudat Israel in Interwar Poland," in *The Jews of Poland Between Two World Wars*, ed. Israel Gutman, et al. (Hanover, N.H.: New England University Press, 1989), 20.

Given the absence of opportunities, it is not surprising that the traditional religious literature is relatively silent on the desirability of pursuing the general public welfare. "Confrontation" sought to meet this gap by reference to the Genesis account of Adam's placement in the Garden to "work it and guard it,"[19] but this is a novel approach not even hinted at in the traditional commentaries.

American Reform Judaism, which has put most of its religious eggs in the *tikkun olam* basket, as well as secular Jewish agencies such as the American Jewish Congress, National Jewish Community Relations Advisory Council (NJCRAC), and the like, frequently point to Jer. 29:7 as a mandate for Jewish political involvement. Historically, as even Reform Jewish historians now admit, this emphasis on social improvement, on *tikkun olam*, drew heavily from regnant liberal Protestant ethics.[20]

Jer. 29:7 is a part of an epistle from Jerusalem warning the exiled Jews of Babylonia not to heed the calls of the false prophets and to resist messianic speculation of an immediate return to Zion. In addition to urging on them the pursuit of economic and family goals instead of passively awaiting fulfillment of eschatological dreams, Jeremiah urges on the exiles a concluding obligation: "Seek (*dirshu*) the peace of the city to which I have exiled you and pray on its behalf to God, because in its peace there will be peace for you."

The entire dispatch does not generate much interest among the traditional Jewish commentators. Only the post-Emancipation commentary of one German Orthodox rabbi, Breuer,[21] interprets this verse as an imperative to do justice for the city as a whole; even he is unclear as to whether more than prayer is required. He writes that "God requires the *golah* to help promote, with selfless devotion, the welfare of the foreign land in which they dwell. The exiles are bidden to perceive their own welfare as so closely linked with that of their host nation that they will pray to God for a nation that has dealt them the most grievous wounds. Thus the exiles are to transform their sojourn in Babylonia into one of homage to the divine Providence."

---

[19]Gen. 2:15.

[20]Michael Meyer, *Response to Modernity: A History of the Reform Movement in Judaism*, (New York: Oxford University Press, 1988), 287–88.

[21]Joseph Breuer, *Commentary on Jeremiah*. Note that the Rav cited the verse for this purpose in "A Stranger and a Resident," in *Reflections of the Rav: Lessons in Jewish Thought Adapted from Lectures of Rabbi Joseph B. Soloveitchik by Abraham R. Besdin* (New York: Ktav, 1979), 170.

In textual context, the commentators' silence is not surprising. Jeremiah's letter is more focused on warning Babylonian Jewry that it cannot expect an imminent return to Zion than on the independent desirability of advancing the welfare of the city as a religious norm. Still, *ein mikra yotzei mi-yedei peshuto*,[22] the verse in *Jeremiah*, is to be interpreted according to its plain meaning. The most obvious reading is an injunction to seek out the welfare of the larger community, including the Babylonians responsible for the Temple's destruction. The Hebrew *"dirshu"* conveys a sense of urgency, passionately seeking the welfare of the city, not just making some passing effort.[23] This verse offers a religious justification for civic involvement without prescribing precisely how that should be done. It is a distortion of Jewish tradition to ignore that injunction, especially if it is overlooked solely to counter the emphasis placed by the Reform movement on *tikkun olam*[24] as the major thrust of Judasim.

It is also possible to understand *dirshu et shelom ha-ir* (seek the peace of the city) as simply the parallel to the phrase *"hitpalelu ba-adah"* (pray on its behalf). The *Metzudat David*[25] apparently so understands the verse, citing it as being the equivalent of the mishnaic exhortation to "pray for the welfare of the government."[26]

---

[22]*Shabbat* 63a.

[23]Compare *"Ki tidreshenu be-khol levavkha"* (Deut. 4:29); *"dirshu mishpat"* (Is. 1:17); *"dirshu Hashem bi-he-matzeo"* (Is. 55:6).

[24]The phrase *"tikkun olam"* is taken from the *Aleinu* prayer, where it has a plainly religious connotation: *"le-takken olam be-malkhut Shadai,"* to perfect the world under the rule of God. Of course, without question, a world filled with injustice is not God's kingdom, and so to "perfect the world under the rulership of God" necessitates eliminating raw social injustice. It cannot justify political activity designed to undermine God's kingdom by enthusiastically seeking policies at odds with God's revealed will.

In any event, the use of the phrase *"tikkun olam"* depends on the reading, apparently universally accepted today, of *"tikkun"* with a *kuf*. R. Sa'adiah Ga'on's *siddur*, however, spells the word with a *kaf*, with the apparent meaning of "to hold together," a reading that fits perfectly with what follows.

[25]Jer. 29:7.

[26]*Avot* 3:2. In his commentary to *Avot*, which cites a biblical source for each of the injunctions contained in *Avot*, the Vilna Ga'on cites a different verse as the source for this proposition. See *Perush ha-Gra*, ad loc., citing Hab. 1:14, a verse invoked for this purpose in *Avodah Zarah* 3b.

In a well-known responsum,[27] R. Moses Sofer (the Hatam Sofer) cites this verse as being the source of the custom of praying for the welfare of the government. But this responsum is apparently the only invocation of this verse in the entire responsa literature,[28] a fact that indicates the lack of an Orthodox Jewish commitment to social improvement as a religious imperative.

Now praying for the welfare of the government is surely something for believing Jews, but it is not active involvement in politics. It is an internal, quietistic act (even when engaged in collectively) that does not guarantee results and might have reference to little more than the need to avoid anarchy as a matter of self-protection. ("Pray for the welfare of the Government, since but for the fear of it we would swallow each other alive.") One is reminded of the quip attributed to the Kotzker Rebbe that people are unfortunately all too solicitous of other's souls and devote their tangible efforts toward their own material welfare, when they should in fact take an active and tangible interest in the material welfare of others and worry about their own spiritual welfare. Further, although my observations are purely anecdotal, it is my experience that the more "separatist" a congregation in general, the less likely it is to recite the traditional prayer for the secular government. The Rabbinical Council of America's *Art Scroll Siddur* contains the prayer for the American government; the ordinary *Art Scroll Siddur* does not.

Though almost any government might be superior to anarchy (though one wonders whether this was true for Hitler's Germany or Stalin's Russia) the notion that we are unconditionally obligated to pray for the government suggests that it is a matter of indifference to Jews which government obtains, how it treats its citizens, whether it adheres to minimal standards of decency, what it does in the moral realm (a category that today appears to exhaust itself with sex), the treatment of the poor, the environment, or dozens of other issues.

In a democracy, it is inaccurate to speak of the government as if it were wholly distinct and independent of the citizenry. True, government agencies have interests and agendas of their own. They sometimes pursue those agendas despite the countervailing interests of the public and

---

[27]*Responsa Hatam Sofer, Likkutim* 95.

[28]To be more precise, a computer search of the Bar-Ilan Responsa database turned up no additional references.

efforts at democratic control. Nevertheless, the sins of democratic government can be, and often are, the sins of its citizens. Citizens of a democracy bear moral responsibility for what government does in their name precisely because they have the power to change its policies. Passively praying for its welfare, without more, without any judgment about the character of any particular government, can constitute acquiescence in, and ratification of, its sins.

Finally, one can cite other sources suggesting a religious imperative to improve the world. The *Midrash ha-Hefetz* explains the seemingly meaningless repetition of the stories of Isaac and the wells he and his servants dug, stating that *"melamed she-ha-tzadikim osekim be-yishuvo shel olam"*—"this teaches that the righteous are involved with the civilization of the world," even where they do not benefit from their actions or even where the surrounding circumstances suggest that the efforts' success is not guaranteed.[29] Thus, while the sources are more noticeable for their silence than for what they have to say, they surely are not indifferent to the need for concern with the general welfare.[30]

III

The question of *whether* Orthodox Jews take an active role in political affairs that do not directly affect uniquely Jewish interests says nothing about *what* they say. If one insists that only halakhic answers, or other answers grounded in wholly religious sources will do, one set of constitutional and political concerns arises. If there are sources of political guidance other than *halakhah* that Orthodox Jews can rely on, such as reason, experience, history, and political preferences, then these questions take on quite a different coloration. The Rav's insistence that the obligation to improve the world is a universal one tends strongly toward the latter position, although the Rav also emphatically rejected

---

[29]*Midrash ha-Hefetz* to Gen. 26: 18. Rabbi Soloveitchik cites this comment in "The Universal and the Covenantal," in *Man of Faith in the Modern World*, adapted from the lectures of *Rabbi Joseph B. Soloveitchik* by Abraham R. Besdin (New York: Ktav, 1989), 75.

[30]In his paper in this volume, Rabbi Jack Bieler quite properly cites Jonah's mission to the gentile city of Nineveh as an additional source to this effect.

the view that human reason alone is a sufficient guide to ethical behavior.[31]

More importantly, if all answers must be halakhic and only halakhic, then only halakhic experts are competent to answer them. If other sources of moral and ethical guidance are legitimate, then it could well be that the rabbinate has no particular advantage in addressing questions of public policy. Indeed, because political decisions can be based on facts outside the competence of the rabbinate, rabbis might even be less qualified than others to determine communal policy.

At issue here is authority—that is, whether only those competent to make halakhic decisions may make binding decisions about public policy or whether the rabbinate has no special authority, only that of moral suasion.[32] This is not to say that *halakhah* cannot offer guidance to contemporary problems, but there is a world of difference between guidance, which suggests only preferred answers, and binding authority, which mandates a particular course of action.

It is important here to underscore how difficult it is to draw conclusions from the sources and translate them immediately to the political sphere. For example, *halakhah* makes assumptions about duties owed to neighbors and to God. American law makes assumptions about rights of individuals.[33] Translating the two legal systems so that one informs the other is not always easy.

Take double jeopardy; the rule that a person may not be tried for a criminal offense having been previously acquitted of that offense. It is easy enough to cite a biblical source for this rule—Ex. 23:7. But the biblical rule has a religious justification: "for I [God] will not acquit the

---

[31]See J. B. Soloveitchik, "The Ethical Emphasis in Judaism," in *Man of Faith in the Modern World*, 193–94.

[32]I leave aside the possibility of reference to *da'at Torah*. See, *e.g.*, Lawrence Kaplan, "*Daas Torah*: A Modern Conception of Rabbinic Authority," in *Rabbinic Authority and Personal Autonomy*, ed. M. Sokol (Northvale, N.J.: Jason Aronson, 1992), 1–60. See also, Walter S. Wurzburger, "Covenantal Imperatives," in *Samuel K. Mirsky Memorial Volume*, ed. Gersion Appel (New York: Yeshiva University Press, 1970), 10, for an explanation of what role *gedolei Yisra'el* ought to play for those who reject the concept of *da'at Torah* as a binding guide.

[33]For an early statement of this assumption, see Moshe Silberg, "Law and Morals in Jewish Jurisprudence," *Harvard Law Review* 75: (1961):306–331.

wicked," a point emphasized by the talmudic parable cited by Rashi of two murderers who happen upon the same inn.[34] But in a secular legal system that has denied itself this belief—and in whose unexpected acquittals (or convictions) it is difficult to discern God's hand—is the biblical double-jeopardy bar applicable? Is the divine promise applicable to any but a *sanhedrin*? Should Orthodox organizations nevertheless file *amicus* briefs with the Supreme Court, urging an expansive reading of the Double Jeopardy Clause of the Fifth Amendment?

The Torah sanctions the death penalty, but its use was not encouraged as an everyday affair.[35] What should we do when the State of Texas holds hundreds of people on death row? New York City has 2,000 murders a year. Should New York State have a death penalty? Is this an occasion to withdraw as the *Sanhedrin* did when murderers became numerous,[36] or, on the contrary, to use extra-judicial sanctions such as described in the Mishna?[37] Is a rabbi or a criminologist better suited to answer these questions? Perhaps the matter is so much in equipoise that it ought to be left to popular choice.

Even where the traditional sources speak with greater clarity, they frequently do not speak with sufficient detail to resolve twentieth-century dilemmas. Jewish sources speak of both protecting the dignity of the poor[38] and protecting the community against charlatans seeking charity.[39] How, then, do we decide whether, in order to discourage fraud, welfare recipients should be fingerprinted, a process associated in the public mind with criminal behavior? The Orthodox Jewish speaker of the New York Assembly opposes fingerprinting as an assault on the dignity of the poor;[40] I rather doubt that the bulk of the Orthodox community agrees with him.

Unfortunately, there is in some quarters a tendency to superficial, even dishonest, treatment of the sources—such that they appear to speak with

---

[34]Rashi to Ex. 21:13.

[35]Mishnah, *Makkot* 1:10.

[36]*Avodah Zarah* 8a; *Sanhedrin* 41b.

[37]*Sanhedrin* 81b; cf. *Sanhedrin* 46b.

[38]Mishnah, *Shekalim* 6:1.

[39]*Bava Batra* 8a.

[40]Kevin Sack, "New Speaker Recasting an Image," *New York Times*, 6 April 1994: B-1.

far greater clarity than they do—all in the pursuit of an identifiable secular ideology. Much of the popular Orthodox literature on the death penalty fits this genre. A recent op-ed piece in the *Wall Street Journal*[41] by an Orthodox rabbi "proves" that a tax rate of more than 10 or 20 percent is excessive, and that the recent Clinton-sponsored tax increase on the wealthy violates a biblical exhortation that "the children of Israel shall enjoy . . . the inheritance of his father,"[42] a use of the verse that sounds suspiciously like Reverend Jerry Falwell's invocation of the Bible to oppose the Panama Canal treaties. A 20 percent tax barely equals the mandatory agricultural tithes, let alone any tax to support the political or defense establishment (to say nothing of charitable contributions, which are a personal obligation, whether or not judicially enforceable). Presumably, the prohibition on falsifying the Torah applies to political conservatives as well as religious liberals.[43]

Moreover, if all answers must be halakhic or rooted in other traditional sources, whether a matter of obligation or preference, then we must grapple with the problem of applying the supererogatory norms of the Torah, intended as a special obligation to fellow members of the faith community, not to society at large. In Jewish law, the ban on taking interest does not reflect any moral default in the charging of interest, as the medieval church taught. Rather, the Torah enjoins the taking of interest from Jews as a special act of kindness towards fellow believers.[44]

Ours is an egalitarian society. Thus it is inconceivable to legislate against usury for Jews, but not non-Jews. No one in the Orthodox community has ever seriously suggested such dual-level legislation. Shall we seek to ban all taking of interest? The economy would collapse. Few of us could afford to purchase homes. The question, then, is which norms do we insist are binding on all of society—that is, which are universal norms? *Sha'atnez*? All of the *arayot*? Some of them? *Tzizit*? Theft? Usury? How do we decide, unless we draw the line at the Noahide commandments? Do we seek to move all of society towards the supererogatory

---

[41]D. Lapin, "A Higher Authority on Taxes," *Wall Street Journal*, 31 August 1993, p. A-10.

[42]Num. 36:8.

[43]See *Yam Shel Shlomo* to *Bava Kamma* 38a.

[44]See H. Soloveitchik, *Halakhah, Kalkalah, ve-Demuy-Atzemi* 18–21, citing Nahmanides to Deut. 23:21.

norms of the Torah, especially when it is unclear whether and to what extent even Jews are compelled to accept all supererogatory norms?[45]

Third, if only religious answers are acceptable, it is necessary to confront constitutional and theoretical issues that have arisen in regard to public advocacy resting explicitly on religious grounds. But what if Orthodox Jews are not under any general religious obligation to apply only halakhic norms? What if they are enjoined to "do good"? Even if they apply secular criteria—tempered, of course, by their religious imperatives and background—these objections are at least minimized and perhaps disappear.[46]

It is important to reemphasize that the question under discussion is how we respond to general political issues, not whether Orthodox Jews should respond to proposals that would require them to act in violation of *halakhah*. Thus, there is an obvious difference between the question of what position Orthodox Jews should take on the general question of abortion, and the question of what position they should take on a law that requires Orthodox institutions to provide insurance coverage for elective abortions (including those no halakhic authority would countenance), or a law or regulation that required Orthodox obstetricians to perform abortions. Our first priority must be to ensure the full practice of *mitzvot* both for our own sake and so that we can teach by example, putting our beliefs into practice in both individual and communal life.

It does not follow that any proposal containing halakhically problematic material must be opposed. It is often possible to obtain an exemption for religious observance. Under the newly enacted Religious Freedom Restoration Act,[47] there is a rebuttable presumption in favor of an exemption. Thus, in many cases the question will be whether to oppose

---

[45]Illicit interest is forcibly taken from the lender. But prohibitions on, for example, taking revenge (Lev. 19:18) are not judicially enforced. And it remains something of an open question whether and to what extent charity may be coercively exacted.

[46]It was objected at the Forum that this leads to a purely subjective ethic, as opposed to a purely "objective system of halakhah." Professor Golding correctly replied that there are objective ethical criteria other than revealed ones. Although this is not the place to fully explore the issue, I also doubt that *halakhah* is as strictly objective as is sometimes asserted.

[47]U.S.C. § 2000bb.

a bill because of its impact on society at large, notwithstanding the possibility of obtaining a specific, iron-clad exemption purchased at the cost of not opposing the rest of the legislation.

To answer the question in any particular case requires a close examination of political realities, not off-the-cuff political assumptions resting on pious hopes or casual political analysis. Take the effort to enact gay-rights legislation, both at the federal and local levels. Some years ago, I urged on a prominent Orthodox activist that the community downplay outright opposition to this legislation and seek, instead, generous exemptions for religious Jews and their institutions. That advice was rejected on the ground that I overestimated the likelihood of the passage of these bills. I countered that in the current climate, passage was ultimately inevitable but that religious exemption was not, a prediction that unfortunately was borne out three years ago by Supreme Court decision.

Now, there is pending a proposal for a federal gay-rights bill. Since my initial conversation with that Orthodox activist, the Supreme Court has refused to recognize a constitutional right to homosexuality.[48] However, the lower federal and state courts have increasingly cast doubt on government disabilities imposed as a result of sexual orientation (homosexuality), sometimes finding them to be wholly lacking in any rational basis.[49] State constitutional bans on gay-rights laws have mixed results in the courts.[50] Many states and localities protect gays against discrimination and hate crimes,[51] and the federal government requires states to compile data on hate crimes against gays.[52] A pending federal hate-crimes sentence-enhancement law includes gay-bashing as a proscribed category.

---

[48]*Bowers* v. *Hardwick*, 478 U.S. 176 (1986).

[49]See, most recently, *Able* v. *U.S.*, CV 94-0974 (E.D.N.Y. 1994). (Overturning ban on gays in the military).

[50]See, e.g., *Evans* v. *Romer*, 854 P.2d 1270 (Col. 1993); *Baehr* v. *Lewin*, 852 P.2 49 (1993).

[51]See Anti-Defamation League, *Hate Crimes Laws: A Comprehensive Guide* (New York: Anti-Defamation League, 1994).

[52]Hate Crimes Statistics Act, P.L. 101-275, 104 Stat. 140; 28 U.S.C. §534 (1994).

Leave aside, for the moment, the question of whether *halakhah* requires opposition to gay-rights laws, a point much mooted lately.[53] Assume that it does, and assume further that gay-rights laws will ultimately be enacted in most states where large numbers of Jews live. We then face a situation in which a choice must be made between fighting gay-rights laws without a religious exemption (or without an adequate one), or, alternatively, finding some way to swallow the objection (or enunciate it without opposing the bill) and negotiating a far stronger exemption for religious institutions. Indeed, it is precisely non-Orthodox groups that support a gay-rights bill in general who are today battling for an exemption for religious institutions, so far with greater than expected success. Orthodox groups have, as of the writing of this paper, refused to participate in the effort, preferring scorched-earth opposition to the bill. It is, I think, a short-sighted policy. Heroic, selfless manning of the ramparts is often counterproductive, even if it does make some people feel good about their moral bravery in defending a politically incorrect position.

Naturally, matters are not so simple. Even if one is inclined to be pragmatic, or if one concludes that *halakhah* does not require, say, employment discrimination against homosexuals, one cannot ignore the need to make a moral statement at a time when the moral principle itself is under attack—a sort of *"makkin ve-oneshin shelo min-ha-din . . . ela la'asot seyag la-Torah."*[54] That tendency is plainly observable in R. Moshe Feinstein's responsa on birth control,[55] which display a marked reluctance to allow even that which is permitted by strict law in order to avoid misapprehension about the fundamental halakhic principle when the underlying principle is under attack in the society at large.

Even this does not end the matter. The principle of tolerating people who are different—at least part of what gay-rights laws are about—is well-ingrained in American thought. Jews are not the least of its beneficia-

---

[53]Compare Marc Angel, Hillel Goldberg, and Pinchas Stolper, "Here the Bullets Really Go," *Jewish Action* 54:1 (Fall 1993):53; 80–82 with Michael Broyde, "Bullets that Kill on the Rebound" in the same issue of *Jewish Action*, 52; 74–78.

[54]*Hagigah* 5b.

[55]*Iggerot Moshe, Even ha-Ezer* I, #64, p. 163.

ries. In intangible ways—but ways that are real nonetheless—preventing crimes against people because of who they are, or what they believe, or permitting people to choose for themselves how they will dress or even who they sleep with creates an atmosphere that helps Jews, especially Orthodox Jews, live in freedom and without fear of persecution.

These are not easy questions to answer. Reasonable people can disagree about what weight ought to be assigned to each of these values and to the costs and benefits of each element. No one can predict with accuracy how courts will react to a particular claim or what long-term impact a law will have on society, either in constituting an endorsement of activity Orthodox Jews regard as immoral or its impact on the broad principles, such as tolerance, on which the well-being of Jews depends.

IV

To return to the questions about the content of a Jewish politics, it is probably most useful to focus first on the question of whether all Orthodox activity must be grounded in *halakhah* or whether extra-halakhic values are possible. This is hardly a novel question.[56] Rav Aharon Lichtenstein has devoted a comprehensive essay to this question. Although he hedges a little at the end,[57] the upshot is that there is such an ethic; that human reason can ground ethical decisions apart from revealed *halakhah*, indeed that it could be itself halakhically obligatory to further these ethical values. This view is implicit in the Rav's position in "Confrontation" that the duty to confront evil in the world is a universal obligation that Jews and non-Jews share. A universal obligation cannot be dependent on revelation in the Torah, which, especially for the Rav, was the quintessential covenantal act.

---

[56] Aharon Lichtenstein, "Does Jewish Tradition Recognize an Ethic Independent of Halacha?" in *Modern Jewish Ethics*, ed. Marvin Fox (Ohio State University, 1975), 62–88.

[57] The hedge is that it is possible that the *halakhah* itself commands resort to an extra-halakhic morality. See Rabbi J. B. Bleich, "Is There an Ethic Beyond Halacha?" *Proceedings of the 9th World Congress of Jewish Studies*, (1986), 55–62. I do not think that Rabbi Lichtenstein's hedge changes matters for present purposes, because the source of this ethic is not itself halakhic.

There is a second way of looking at this question: to ask whether the revealed Torah is the only possible way to achieve a just world. Does the Torah exhaustively catalogue the universe of necessary means to that end, or is it simply the way Jews have been commanded to act? Popular opinion has the former view, which is incompatible with a variety of uncontested halakhic principles including the extra-judicial power of the king to punish, the principle of extra-legal action by the court, and the power of *takkanah*, of communal enactment.

A clear repudiation of the Torah's exclusive role is expressed in the eleventh of the *Derashot ha-Ran*.[58] Rabbeinu Nissim there addresses the respective roles of the king and the *Sanhedrin*. The Ran's position is that the *Sanhedrin* enforces the Torah. The Torah represents ideal justice, and is designed to increase the *shefa Elohi*. The king enforces practical or political justice. Moreover, "our Torah is distinguished from the customs of the nations with commandments and decrees [*hukkim*] and their purpose [i.e. the commandments and decrees] have nothing at all to do with the improvement of the community."[59]

As the Ran acknowledges, this limited role for *mitzvot* would leave a lacuna in the functioning of the day-to-day community—"because the political order cannot be fulfilled with [the ideal] alone, God completed [the political order's] work with [the establishment of the king]."[60]

Some commandments, the Ran concedes, might be a mix of political and spiritual improvement. But because of the emphasis on the spiritual in the Torah generally, "it is possible that some of the rules and laws of the nation will be found closer to perfecting the communal [or political] order from that which is found in some of the laws of the Torah. . . . And we are not lacking in this regard, because whatever is missing from the above mentioned perfection the king would complete."[61]

---

[58]*Derashot ha-Ran*, ed. L. Feldman (Jerusalem, 1977), #11. See Gerald Blidstein, "'Ideal' and 'Real' In Classical Jewish Political Theory," in *The Quest for Utopia: Jewish Political Ideas and Institutions Through the Ages*, ed. Z. Gitelman (University of Michigan Press, 1992).

[59]Ibid., 191.

[60]Ibid. The notion that the Torah does not cover every contingency is already found in Nahmanides, *Commentary on the Torah*, Deut. 6:18, discussed below.

[61]Ibid., 191.

Here, then, is a complete dichotomy between Torah and political law, one suggesting that political rules are to be based on the needs of the community. There is also an unambiguous acknowledgment that the political and spiritual orders are distinct. What is more important (and surprising) is the Ran's acknowledgment that the spiritual order might be unsuitable for the political order, that the political order, within its sphere, might be superior to the spiritual order.

The American political order is a decidedly political order (not a spiritual one), empowered to "establish Justice, insure domestic Tranquility . . . promote the General Welfare, and secure the Blessings of Liberty."[62] Those portions of the Torah intended to secure spiritual perfection or ideal justice (including, the Ran says, such apparently secular rules as that requiring a warning as a condition of punishing criminal law violations) are simply irrelevant to the political order. Rabbeinu Nissim does not purport to give us a detailed list of which *mitzvot* further *"tikkun ha-midini"* and which are designed to encourage the *shefa Elohi*. The *hukkim* (a category including many of the *arayot*) fall into the latter category, but beyond that we are on our own. In any event, the Ran provides further support for the notion that not every *halakhah* relevant to an ongoing political debate is necessarily appropriate for the twentieth-century secular community.

Moreover, it is not a long stretch from this principle to the conclusion that what is appropriate for the perfection of one community at one time or place might not be appropriate at another.[63] To take a famous example from the *rishonim*: the Talmud records the general rule that a wife is not permitted to transact business on behalf of her husband without his consent and that people doing business with her must be presumed to know that they are possibly participating in a theft of the husband's property.[64] By the Middle Ages, social realities had changed so that the *rishonim* laid down the reverse rule.[65] It is this departure from talmudic principle that is authoritatively codified in *Shulkhan Arukh*.[66]

---

[62]Preamble to the United States Constitution.

[63]See, on this, the justly famous introduction of *Ketzot ha-Hoshen*.

[64]*Bava Batra* 51b.

[65]See Ravan.

[66]*Even ha-Ezer* 81, comments of the Rama.

Similar changes have taken place with regard to rules regarding the collection of debts from personal property.

A third way of looking at the question is in terms of whether human reason is a reliable guide to action or whether only revealed truth may serve as the basis for action. Nahmanides, whose comments to Deut. 6:18 form the springboard for Rabbi Lichtenstein's conclusion that there is an ethic independent of *halakhah*,[67] is explicit in stating that the revealed Torah could not deal with every contingency and, therefore, that it embodies a general command to do that which is "good and straight" to cover these contingencies. Elsewhere in the Torah, Nahmanides likewise sees calls for human legislation and judgment on moral issues over and above specific revealed commandments.[68] For Maimonides, imitatio dei consists of acquiring broad character traits modelled after attributes of God,[69] but these contain little empirical content. We are commanded to train ourselves to be merciful, but that hardly provides a specific resolution of concrete problems.

Not all authorities were willing to accept a role for independent human reason. The Hazon Ish, in his attack on the Musar movement in *Emunah u-Bittahon,* can be read as denying the existence of any non-halakhic ethic.[70] In his commentary, Rashi evinces a marked preference for specific halakhic norms in those cases in which the Torah expresses itself in apparently broad terms. In those same cases, Nahmanides expresses what might be termed a more humanistic view.[71]

From the foregoing discussion, one may conclude that, within the confines of tradition, one can legitimately argue that there is no necessary one-to-one correspondence between *halakhah* and what is appropriate for the civil political order; that, in some respects, some *halakhot* are unsuited for the civil political order; that other arrangements might even be superior; and that, at the very least, where *halakhah* is silent, there is a general obligation to do that which is "just and good" based on

---

[67]See note 60 above.

[68]See his commentary on, e.g., Gen. 18:19; Ex. 17:5; Lev. 19:1; Deut. 6:18.

[69]*Yad, Hilkhot De'ot,* 2:1. Compare *Hilkhot Aveilut* 14:1. And see J. B. Soloveitchik, *Shi'urim le-Zekher Abba Mari* I (Jerusalem, 5743), 57.

[70]Hazon Ish (Rabbi A. I. Karelitz), *Emunah u-Bittahon,* 21–23.

[71]Compare Rashi's comments on the verses cited in n. 68.

human perception, experiences and reasoning. This means that much of what Orthodox Jews do in the political arena can be, from a legal point of view, wholly secular. I do not contend that this is the only view, just that it is a possible one.

One can immediately list areas that fall in the political-perfection class: whether the United States should adopt a single-payer system of medical care; whether to let market mechanics have a role in setting environmental-protection policies; the details of foreign policy (e.g., should the United States invade Haiti or Bosnia?). It is difficult to envision what halakhic sources would be controlling here, except perhaps in the most general way, and surely it is difficult to envision those that might prove compelling to people who do not accept the authority of *halakhah*. These are the types of issue that fall quite clearly into the political-perfection category, even if at the margins there are halakhic issues to be resolved.

I do not mean to suggest that we need Orthodox positions on all these issues. Being all things to all people is a quick route to political irrelevance. But being concerned solely with one's own immediate needs is, likewise, irreconcilable with the Jewish tradition.[72]

Perhaps because so much of the non-Orthodox community has reduced Judaism to knee-jerking obeisance to the (left-wing of the) Democratic Party, the Orthodox community has tended to reject all the positions emerging from that side of the political spectrum, and to resort in likewise knee-jerk fashion to right-wing agendas, either ignoring social-justice issues or mechanically opposing any politically liberal position. It sometimes appears as if Hazal never spoke of *tzedakah*, Maimonides never condemned those who gorge themselves while ignoring the poor,[73] or the entire calendar were not rearranged so that Purim would not fall on Shabbat in order to avoid disappointing the poor, who expect gifts on Purim.[74] It is no less a distortion of the Torah to assert reactionary

---

[72]Hillel's famous aphorism, "If I am not for myself, who am I; and if I am only for myself, what am I" (*Avot* 1:14), captures the dilemma perfectly. Unfortunately, it does not help in deciding concrete cases. How do we decide when the interest of the Jewish community should yield to the interest of the larger community? Some say never; some say always. Neither extreme is true to Hillel's teaching.

[73]*Yad, Hilkhot Yom Tov*, 6:18; *Hilkhot Hagigah* 2:8.

[74]"*Anei aniyim teluyim bo.*" (*Megillah* 4b).

positions on, say, the problems of the underclass as it is to allow Judaism to be reduced to left-liberalism.

Among the public issues that generate the most excitement in the Orthodox community are those that, one or the other way, involve sex—birth control for teenagers, public distribution of condoms, abortion, and homosexuality. These issues, in fact, are hot-button items, serving to demarcate between liberals and conservatives generally and liberal and conservative church people in particular. As Professor Robert Wuthenow[75] has demonstrated, these issues mark a border between religious liberals and religious conservatives. Contemporary religious liberals envision religion as concerned with social justice, not with regulating private behavior. Religious conservatives emphasize individual spiritual perfection, God's command and dominion over individuals. They accordingly de-emphasize regulation of social and economic life.

Because several of these issues of sexual behavior raise problems under the Noahide commandments, it is necessary to consider the possibility that intervention here is mandatory, a point addressed by Rabbis Bleich and Broyde in their contributions to this volume. Unfortunately, they do not arrive at identical conclusions. The fact that these issues are in contention in the larger society, with Reform and Conservative Jews asserting that Judaism adopts a permissive view on abortion, homosexuality or teenage sex, does call for some Orthodox response—if for no other reason, than to set the record straight—although that response need not be in the political arena.

Finally, precisely because we are full partners in this society and its government—in Pogo's immortal words "I have met the enemy and it is us"—what is said or done around us by *our* society speaks in *our* name. To be sure, we could renounce American society and its many benefits. We could create our own ghettoes, read no newspapers, not listen to the radio and television, not ride on buses and trains, and wholly ignore public debates. We could all become Jewish Amish. This is, for some, an untenable position. As the Rav put it in "Confrontation," "[we] are opposed to a philosophy of isolationism or esotericism which would see the Jews living in a culturally closed society."[76] Even if we were to adopt that policy,

---

[75]R. Wuthenow, *The Restructuring of American Religion* (Princeton, N.J.: Princeton University Press, 1988).

[76]Rabbi J. B. Soloveitchik, "Confrontation" (addendum), 28–29.

we could not wholly escape the surrounding society. This society is not something separate from us as it plausibly was for Jews in the Pale of Settlement.

Asserting public positions in these matters is not only an effort to impose these views on others (although it cannot be forgotten that it does) but a desire to protect ourselves. Thus, although Nahmanides disclaims any obligation on the *Sanhedrin* to put an end to prostitution so long as it does not involve Jews,[77] our social circumstances might not permit us the luxury of that hands-off attitude. On the other hand, his recognition that, in regard to at least some matters of sexual morality, Torah principles need not be universally applied coercively suggests caution before Orthodox Jews run to enlist in the ranks of the Moral Majority.

V

Whether or not Orthodox Jews are religiously obligated to engage in social betterment, they will on occasion participate in these activities. Some portion of the latter will have no justification other than revealed (and hence are for constitutional purposes, religious) truth. Many activities will be wholly secular, or can be plausibly explained in secular terms even if Jews are subjectively motivated by religious justifications in asserting them. Some positions will be a mix of the religious and the secular. The question is whether this state of affairs is problematic in a democracy that is by fundamental agreement secular, prohibited from furthering particular religious agendas.[78]

It is important at the outset to make a distinction between activities that are either sponsored by the government (i.e. a grant funded by the National Endowment for the Humanities) or policies that are adopted by the government as its own and activities that are directed toward the

---

[77]Commentary to Deut. 23:18.

[78]This is not the place for a full blown defense of the Establishment Clause. Despite the assertion by one participant in the Forum that Jews would do as well with no Establishment Clause, and a strong Free Exercise Clause, history, at least, demonstrates that American Jews have seen it differently from the outset. See sources quoted in note 1 above. I think that American Jews have it quite right, although there is substantial room for disagreement about just what ought to be prohibited by the Establishment Clause.

public at large by private persons or institutions.[79] Only the former class of activity comes under Establishment Clause scrutiny. The latter is wholly free of such limits and is entitled to constitutional protection under the Free Speech or Free Exercise Clauses.

Freedom to speak in the pulpit, to practice one's religion, the freedom to be different in fundamental ways, and the statutory exemption of churches from many regulations, are common examples of the freedom of churches to address the public. So is the now-all-but-settled rule that menorahs (and crèches, KKK crosses, or busts of Hitler) may be displayed in publicly owned places, where secular displays may be erected.[80] Similarly, a unanimous Supreme Court in 1993 held that a public school may not exclude a religious group from showing a movie about family values in a rented school building when that same topic may be addressed in that forum from a secular point of view.[81] Student religious clubs may meet after hours on the same basis as secular student clubs, both in the nation's high schools and in its universities.[82]

These rules, and others like them, guarantee free access to the private "public square." This provides an opportunity for people of conservative (and liberal) religious views ample room to persuade, to challenge, to set examples, and to encourage, for example, a new look at permissive sexuality—in other words, to put beliefs into action. If these practices prove superior to existing practices, they will soon prove themselves as such. All of this quotidian activity lacks glamour, often fails to attract media attention, and unfortunately is accordingly unattractive to much of Orthodoxy. Claims that the public square is "naked" of religion tend to overlook these principles guaranteeing a substantial role for religion in shaping the nation's life.[83]

---

[79]This requirement is known as "state (governmental) action." With the exception of the Thirteenth Amendment's ban on slavery, all constitutional limitations apply only to governmental action.

[80]See, e.g., *Chabad of Georgia* v. *Miller*, 3 F.3d 1383 (11th Cir. 1993) (private display of menorah in public space in state capitol building constitutional).

[81]*Lamb's Chapel* v. *Center Moriches School District*, 113 S.Ct. 2141 (1993).

[82]Equal Access Act, 20 U.S.C. § 471, et seq.; *West Side Bd. of Educ.* v. *Mergens*, 496 U.S. 226 (1990); *Widmar* v. *Vincent*, 454 U.S. 263 (1981).

[83]See my essay (untitled) in *American Jews and the Separationist Faith: The New Debate on Religion in Public Life*, ed. D. Dalin, (Lanham, MD: distributed by University Press of America, 1992), 130–34.

Moreover, those, such as Fr. Richard John Neuhaus, who bemoan the "naked public square,"[84] are curiously silent about the fact that this realm of activity is not as successful as one would expect. The unfortunate fact is that religion sometimes fails to persuade. If religion could persuade women not to have abortions after all, it would matter far less whether abortion was or was not legal. The fact is that many churches opposed to abortion have not convinced their adherents to live their lives according to church teachings.[85]

Complaints that the public squares are naked and that religion, particularly politically incorrect religion, is ignored in the public square, could mean one of several things. First, it could mean that the electronic and cultural media, the universities, and the public presses do not pay fair attention to religion; religious voices, therefore, are unfairly silenced. I think that complaint is valid in large part, although it is unlikely that developments in either law or political theory are primarily responsible. Some of the silence is due to an exaggerated fear of controversy. The more likely explanation is that elites responsible for that which is acceptable in "high culture" are themselves not religious in a serious, constraining way and have difficulty believing that anyone else (or anybody whose views are worth considering) takes religion seriously.

A second possible explanation of the absence of serious religious discussion in many manifestations of private culture is the following: those institutions that constitute the intellectual sector have intuitively grasped that which serious students of the subject are only now coming to realize—that the figures for church attendance, the most accessible measure of religiosity, are greatly overstated, and that Americans are nowhere nearly as religious as has been thought.[86] A recent study shows that a majority of American Catholics, for example, do not share the hierarchy's views on abortion or birth control not only in terms of supporting pro-

---

[84]R. J. Neuhaus, *The Naked Public Square* (Grand Rapids, Mich.: Eerdmans, 1984).

[85]See Princeton Religious Research Center, *Emerging Trends* (October, 1993).

[86]C. V. Hadaway, et al., "What the Polls Don't Show: A Closer Look at U.S. Church Attendance," *American Sociological Review* 58:6 (1993):741–52; Mark Chaves, "More Evidence on U.S. Catholic Church Attendance," *Journal for the Scientific Study of Religion* 33 (1994):376–81.

choice legislation, but in their own lives.[87] The Church can exert itself vigorously in opposition to abortion, but if politicians know that rank and file Catholics do not vote that way, they are not going to legislate the Church's way—not from animosity towards religion, but in fulfillment of their task to represent their constituents.

Thus, the political weakness of religion does not stem exclusively from systematic problems with the political system and built-in anti-religious bias in the system, but the real weakness of religion. It is possible, of course, that some of that weakness is a response to signals sent by our current legal system and political thinkers. Although this could be a chicken-and-egg problem, I tend to think that it is not to be laid at the door of the modern Supreme Court. In the first place, some of the problem's roots are as old as the United States, many of the Founders being Deists, and others frankly thought religion useful only for the uneducated lower classes.[88]

In any event, it is one thing to explain away the lack of religion's political influence as a product of Establishment Clause decisions, but how does one explain away the erosion in church attendance, a practice fully protected by the Constitution? Nor does the hypothesis that Establishment Clause jurisprudence is responsible for the decline of religion readily explain poll evidence demonstrating that many people do not put the views of their faith into practice in their own lives.

In short, "the culture" does not express itself only through government. We must carefully guard against the assumption that it does. In this vast culture, there is significant room for religion to persuade, to shape attitudes, and to shape the culture and lives of people who function in that culture. It is hard to imagine an Orthodox Jew steeped in talmudic literature, for example, enlisting in the critical legal-studies movement, because that movement's attitude toward law and text are so strikingly different from the talmudic tradition. But no one would treat the rejection of critical legal studies as religiously motivated.[89]

---

[87]See note 86.

[88]See, e.g., Leonard Levy, *Blasphemy: Verbal Offenses Against the Sacred* (New York: Knopf, 1993), 400–424; Gordon S. Wood, *The Radicalism of the American Revolution*, (New York: Knopf, 1992), 327–29.

[89]See M. Stern & J. Robison, *Church Involvement in Political Activity* (American Jewish Congress, 1980).

On a more practical level, there is now a growing willingness in society to consider programs that urge chastity on teenagers. The model for that willingness is a religious model, not one imposed by law but by example. The origin of the program could well be religious; its manifestation and adoption by the state would be secular.[90] Orthodox Jews should have no trouble urging secular reasons for their behavior, in the same way as the *monei ha-mitzvot* gave "rational" reasons for many of the *mitzvot* while recognizing their revealed character.[91] Doing so obviates any theoretical or legal difficulties that might arise from advocating public policies on purely religious grounds. In any event, advancing "secular" arguments is likely to be more effective.

The problem of whether religion may directly influence governmental affairs has attained much visibility lately. There are those, including legal theorists such as Bruce Ackerman,[92] Thomas Nagel,[93] and John Rawls,[94] who urge that only secular reasons are legitimate in public (read: governmental, legislative) debates, though each reached his conclusion by a different reasoning. These thinkers are apparently not advocating legal restrictions on political speech founded in religion. They merely urge self-restraint by citizens as a matter of what ought to be proper behavior for citizens in a democracy. Formal restrictions on the speech of citizens on the basis of religious content or motivation of content would be either unenforceable or unconstitutional, or both.[95]

Ackerman argues that only those positions that are equally available to others in the polity are acceptable in a liberal democracy.[96] Because

---

[90]See *Bowen* v. *Kendrick*, 487 U.S. 589 (1988), noting that promoting teenage chastity is a valid secular concern.

[91]See, generally, A. Heinemann, *Ta'amei ha-Mitzvot be-Siferut Yisra'el*, 5th ed. (Jerusalem: World Zionist Organization, 1966), 1:1.

[92]Bruce Ackerman, *Social Justice in the Liberal State* (Cambridge, Mass.: Harvard University Press, 1980).

[93]Thomas Nagel, "Moral Conflict and Political Legitimacy," *Philosophy and Public Affairs* 16 (1987): 215–40. As M. Perry, *Love and Power* (Oxford University Press, 1991), 151, 40 n. 28 (1991), reports that Nagel no longer stands by this essay, it is unnecessary here to consider it further.

[94]John Rawls, *A Theory of Justice* (Cambridge, Mass.: Harvard University Press, 1971), 208–09.

[95]*Paty* v. *McDaniel*, 435 U.S. 618 (1978).

[96]Ackerman, *supra*, at n. 92.

there are conflicting claims of divine revelation, and because one who does not share a particular revelation cannot participate *equally* in a discussion of these "revealed principles," Ackerman argues that reliance on religious revelation is improper in determining public policy.

Rawls, in general, urges that we must promote only those positions that we would support if we did not know who we were (the so-called "veil of ignorance"). Because religions vary, we cannot legitimately urge a particular religious position on the society at large; if we were other people, after all, we would embrace a different position. Indeed, Rawls explicitly excludes churches from those entitled to participate in the "behind-the-veil" setting of fundamental principles.[97] Both Ackerman and Rawls are strong egalitarians, and their positions reflect those commitments.

Implicit in their views as well is a conception of religion as purely individual and private, and revealed morality as inferior in rank to individual choice. David A. J. Richards, a constitutional philosopher, largely agrees with the positions of Ackerman and Rawls on the ground that ethical independence is the highest good. "[A]n ethical independence of the believer may better express the spirit of . . . religion than the attitude of the conventional religious believer."[98] Obviously, this principled denigration of revealed religious authority is wholly antithetical to Jewish thought.

Kent Greenawalt rejects any absolute rule that religion has no role to play in public debate. He urges instead what amounts to a rule of preference: when rational grounds are available these should take precedence and should exclude purely revealed religious views from use in political debate. But when no position can be rationally grounded, when questions of judgment, values and aesthetics are necessarily involved—e.g. animal rights or abortion—any position lacks firm rational basis. If so, there is no ground to exclude religious views from the marketplace of political views.[99]

---

[97]Rawls, 146.

[98]David A. J. Richards, "Religion, Public Morality and Constitutional Law" in *Religion, Morality and the Law* (*Nomos XXX*), ed. J. R. Pennock and J. W. Chapman, (New York: New York University Press, 1988).

[99]Kent Greenawalt, *Religious Conviction and Political Choice*, (Oxford University Press, 1988).

Michael Perry's views are not, on the whole, dissimilar to Greenawalt's, although he would not limit the permission to participate to matters insoluble by reason. In essence, he urges that religious groups may participate in public dialogue at the level of general principles (which he calls "religious faith") but not at the level of specifics (which he calls "religious belief"). He would require that religious arguments be accessible to the public—that is, not based on pure religious authority.[100]

To some extent, Professor Perry's proposal depends on religious groups being willing to accept principles of dialogue and fallibility—the possibility that they might be wrong. In response to criticism, Perry has acknowledged that this latter requirement could exclude Orthodox Jews and evangelical Christians who are not prepared to make a concession of fallibility.[101] (Apparently, he is concerned with the fallibility of religious faith, not of the application of religious principles to a particular set of facts. To illustrate, Orthodox Jews cannot admit that they might be wrong about the undesirability of extra-marital sex; they need not claim infallibility, however, as to the claim that sex education encourages this activity in teens. Several studies indicate the opposite is true.)[102]

On the other extreme, and from a decidedly and explicitly Christian point of view, Richard John Neuhaus vigorously condemns the differentiation of government and American culture, a culture that he sees as fundamentally religious.[103] Religion is necessary, says Neuhaus, as a source of ultimate concerns for the culture, absent which other ultimate concerns will fill the void ("the naked public square"), such as communism or fascism. Neuhaus blames the exclusion of religion on the prevailing interpretation of the Establishment Clause and insists that the Court has erred in treating the Establishment Clause as demanding a secular society, a view recently endorsed by moderate Orthodox Jewish groups.[104] Neuhaus himself assumes that the United States is properly a

---

[100]Perry, *Love and Power.*

[101]Ibid., 139–45.

[102]See, e.g., "Sex Education and Sexual Experience Among Adolescents," *American Journal of Public Health* 75 (1995).

[103]Neuhaus.

[104]Brief *Amici Curiae* of the Union of Orthodox Jewish Congregations, in *Board of Education* v. *Grumet,* 93-519 (U. S. Supreme Court).

Christian country, a conclusion tempered by Neuhaus with references to the *Judeo*-Christian tradition and with calls for tolerance.

Neuhaus' view that fascism or communism will fill the void left by the exclusion of religion from the public square is premised on an all-or-nothing view of the public square, a view that downplays the importance of the "private" public square. The spectres he evokes are not likely on the American scene. Nazism came to power despite the existence of functioning churches and with required prayer in the public schools. The Nazis simply assimilated the churches into the state. That evil is unlikely as long as a rigorous version of church-state separation prevails. Communism vigorously suppressed churches, even in the "private public" square, a result prohibited in the United States by the Establishment and Free Exercises Clause.

More recently, Stephen Carter has echoed Neuhaus' complaints, albeit without the Christian references and not without a fair amount of obscurity about whether he is complaining primarily about the exclusion of religion from the "private public" culture or from the public one. He does say, sounding quite confident about the ability of legislatures to resist bad public policy, that religion should be free to urge whatever policies it wishes and that bad religious policies should be defeated on the merits of arguments. Carter, however, believes that the country ought to be moderately pro-choice, make anti-gay discrimination illicit, and reject creation science, thus avoiding for himself all of the difficult questions that divide the country along religious lines.[105]

By way of contrast to Neuhaus and Carter, Stanley Hauerwas urges that Christians as Christians disclaim responsibility for the political order. Following in the tradition of Roger Williams, he urges that involvement is a danger to the church, corrupting it with hubris, and distorting its teachings.[106]

In summary, Nagel and Ackerman would impose on citizens a non-enforceable duty to discuss public issues on a secular basis. Greenawalt and Perry would permit explicitly religious advocacy but under serious constraints, with Perry's probably being objectionable to Orthodox Jews.

---

[105]Stephen Carter, *The Culture of Disbelief* (New York: Basic Books, 1993).

[106]S. Hauerwas, "A Christian Critique of Christian America," in *Religion, Morality and the Law*, ed. J. R. Pennock and J. W. Chapman, 110.

Neuhaus would permit hard-edged religious advocacy, including some views that are recognizably sectarian. Carter is more concerned, I think, with the "private public" square, but to the extent he would permit religious advocacy directed to the legislature, he would rely on the public's good sense more than on either legal or citizenship constraints.

None of these views is wholly persuasive, and yet none is without persuasive force. Nagel and Ackerman presume that people can stand outside themselves and construct a world-view free of self-interest (a position referred to as right-prior-to-good), which I think is highly improbable. Although we cannot wholly escape subjectivity, not every idea is a subjective, self-constructed reality colored by the accident of history and birth. Orthodox Jews cannot dismiss their commitment to Torah as simply an accident of history that must be set aside in establishing fundamental rules for society.

Moreover, as Greenawalt and Perry discuss at length, the views of Ackerman and Rawls condemn religion to the margins of life, and treat it as a set of purely personal beliefs, a position that probably reflects the hostility and disdain of intellectuals for religion. All but Neuhaus require a sort of schizophrenia for the deeply religious person, a putting aside of who one is in order to participate in public life. (It should be noted, however, that Rabbi Soloveitchik in much of his work contemplates these two distinct and clashing pulls, the secular and the religious, the particular and the universal. Far from regretting or condemning the clash, he regards it as a natural part of man's lot.) Hauerwas is plainly right about the danger of involvement in public affairs to the church, but his pursuit of religious perfection deprives society of much of value and assumes that religious perfection is not possible on a large scale. This is a pessimism[107] that Judaism does not share.

On the other hand, Neuhaus offers little but pious hopes for tolerance of those who speak views with which he disagrees. His own views subsequent to the publication of his book are revealing. Neuhaus has declared that atheists cannot be good citizens,[108] and he opposed the

---

[107]M. DeWolfe Howe, *The Garden and the Wilderness: Religion and Government in American Constitutional History* (Chicago: University of Chicago Press, 1964).

[108]R. J. Neuhaus, "Can Atheists Be Good Citizens," *First Things*, (August-September 1991):17–21.

Religious Freedom Restoration Act on the ground that it could be invoked to permit abortions that are religiously required (e.g, by Jews) thus demonstrating exactly by whom the naked square is to be clothed.[109] And in his book, *The Naked Public Square*, Neuhaus cannot quite bring himself to explain what role there is for religious minorities (e.g., Jews) in the nation's political life. In short, each of these views has its shortcomings either as a matter of principle or as a practical matter of Jewish self interest.

The theoretical debate, however, is just that—theoretical. As a practical matter, a consensus has emerged. Church, synagogue, and mosque are each entitled to play an active role in the political process. Except for some evangelical Christians, religious groups do not speak ex cathedra when they participate in public debates. It is rare that church groups advocate policies that cannot be defended on secular grounds. There are odd exceptions—such as the school district that banned dancing at the behest of the local churches acting out of pure religious conviction[110]—but these have not had a major impact on the law. Perhaps there is no ideal solution, but the practical problems with the de facto solution seem minimal. The value of the theoretical debate is cautionary. It warns of dangers that await religious involvement in public affairs.

VI

Pared down to its legitimate core, the complaint about the law creating a naked public square comes down to two points: that (1) the prohibition on establishing religion as construed by the Supreme Court disadvantages religion; and (2) that religion may not seek to have its agenda enacted into law as other competing ideologies can. The first problem focuses largely, but not entirely, on the questions of financial subsidies for religious education and prohibiting public schools from advocating religion.[111] It should be noted that even when a narrower test than cur-

---

[109]R. J. Neuhaus, "A New Order of Religious Freedom," *First Things* (February, 1992):13–17.

[110]*Clayton v. Place*, 884 F.2d 376 (8th Cir. 1989).

[111]See, e.g., *Grand Rapids County Board of Education v. Ball*, 473 U.S. 373 (1985).

rently governs is applied to prohibit a religious practice under public auspices—e.g., in the case of prayers at high school graduation ceremonies[112]—the complaints about discrimination against religion do not subside. It is on the second complaint, however, that I wish to focus.

The Supreme Court has repeatedly held that religious groups have the same legal right as any others to urge public policy positions on government. Thus, in *Walz* v. *Tax Commission*, the Court said: "Adherents of particular faiths and individual churches frequently take strong positions on public issues including . . . vigorous advocacy of legal or constitutional positions. Of course, churches as much as secular bodies and private citizens have that right. No perfect or absolute separation is really possible; the very existence of the Religion Clauses is an involvement of sorts—one that seeks to mark boundaries to avoid excessive entanglement."[113]

Similarly in *Lemon* v. *Kurtzman*, the case in which the Court consolidated its prior Establishment Clause decisions into the so-called three-part *Lemon* test (of which more below), Chief Justice Burger confirmed: "Of course, as the Court noted in Walz, '[a]dherents of particular faiths and individual churches frequently take strong positions on public issues.' We could not expect otherwise, for religious values pervade the fabric of our national life."[114]

In another case, the Court unanimously invalidated a statutory relic of the Revolutionary era, which excluded ordained clergymen from the legislature. One of the rationales offered in defense of the statute was that this rule was necessary to protect the separation of church and state. Clergymen-legislators, it was asserted, would not separate their religious obligations from their civil ones. The Supreme Court brushed this argument aside.[115]

Justice Brennan, who surely was as sturdy an advocate of church-state separation (as well as a sturdy defender of freedom of religious practice) as ever graced the Court went further than the Court did, reaffirming the right of religious individuals to speak about public issues on a religious basis:

---

[112]*Lee* v. *Weisman*, 112 S. Ct. 2141 (1992).

[113]397 U.S. 669, 670 (1970).

[114]403 U.S. 604, 623 (1971).

[115]*McDaniel* v. *Paty*, 435 U.S. 618 (1978).

The mere fact that a purpose of the Establishment Clause is to reduce or eliminate religious divisiveness or strife, does not place religious discussion, association, or political participation in a status less preferred than rights of discussion, association, and political participation generally. "Adherents of particular faiths and individual churches frequently take strong positions on public issues including . . . vigorous advocacy of legal or constitutional positions. Of course, churches as much as secular bodies and private citizens have that right.". . .

Religionists no less than members of any other group enjoy the full measure of protection afforded speech, association, and political activity generally. The Establishment Clause . . . is a shield against any attempt by government to inhibit religion as it has done here. . . . It may not be used as a sword to justify repression of religion or its adherents from any aspect of public life.

In a footnote, Justice Brennan cited Professor Laurence Tribe:

In much the same spirit, American courts have not thought the separation of church and state to require that religion be totally oblivious to government or politics; church and religious groups in the United States have long exerted powerful political pressures on state and national legislatures, on subjects as diverse as slavery, war, gambling, drinking, prostitution, marriage, and education. To view such religious activity as suspect, or to regard its political results as automatically tainted, might be inconsistent with first amendment freedoms of religious and political expression—and might not even succeed in keeping religious controversy out of public life, given the "political ruptures caused by the alienation of segments of the religious community."[116]

Notwithstanding the Court's declarations, the problem of elites who often publicly assert in opposition to religious initiatives that the Establishment Clause outlaws religious advocacy, remains a real and substantial one. The charge of improper religious intrusion into politics carries political weight even though it is legally trivial. It is also tainted with hypocrisy, as Professor Carter has pointed out,[117] because religious views advancing liberal positions are often welcomed by the same circles that criticize religious pro-life and anti-gay activists for injecting religion into public life.

---

[116]Ibid., 642.
[117]Carter, 44–69.

Second, while what has been said so far is fully applicable to individuals who speak on public issues, there are statutory restrictions on the speech of institutional religious speakers if they choose tax exemption. The tax code denies exemption to those institutions that expend a substantial percentage of their resources on lobbying or that endorse or oppose political candidates.[118] These restrictions (which are not stringently enforced) are applicable to any not-for-profit group claiming tax exemption. They do not uniquely disadvantage religion.[119] If the public square is spiritually naked, it is not because of the tax laws.[120]

The major legal obstacle to religious activity in the political marketplace lies in the details of the three-part test of *Lemon v. Kurtzman*.[121] The test says that a government practice violates the Establishment Clause if it (1) has a sectarian purpose, (2) has the effect of advancing or inhibiting religion, or (3) entangles government with religion.

The first portion of the Lemon test calls for an inquiry into whether a challenged practice has a secular or sectarian purpose. It is argued that application of this branch of the test demands that religion can speak only if it is unsuccessful or if it masks its true religious motivations, the ones on which it speaks with greatest authority. If a church speaks honestly, from genuine religious conviction, and it succeeds, the resulting legislation will be unconstitutional for want of a secular purpose.

After some hesitation, the Court has announced that only practices wholly lacking in a secular purpose will be invalidated under the purpose branch of the test.[122] So long as there is some legitimate secular purpose, even if there are accompanying sectarian purposes as well, the Court will not invalidate a practice on purpose grounds. Thus, even an openly expressed religious motive will not be fatal if there exists some recognizable secular justification for a particular policy.

---

[118]26 U.S.C. § 501(c)(3).

[119]*Taxation with Representation v. Blumenthal*, 461 U.S. 540 (1982).

[120]The Supreme Court, incidentally, has held in the context of a secular tax-exempt organization that Congress has the right to refuse to subsidize lobbying through tax exemption. There is no reason to think the result would be different in the case of religious organizations. Indeed, the Court has elsewhere suggested that it would be improper to favor religious speech over secular speech.

[121]403 U.S. 604 (1971).

[122]*Bowen v. Kendrick*, 487 U.S. 589 (1989).

The Supreme Court has been indulgent in applying this branch of the Lemon test. Thus, it has found secular purposes in aid-to-parochial-schools cases.[123] Even those justices who reject aid on other grounds agree that it has the secular purpose of assisting school children.[124] About the only statutes the Court has found invalid under the purpose test are pregnant with religion: school prayer statutes,[125] statutes requiring the display of the Ten Commandments in public schools,[126] or the teaching of scientific creationism,[127] a doctrine firmly rooted in some Christian readings of Genesis.

In some of these cases (e.g., the Ten Commandments case) the Court has found sufficient evidence of illicit religious purpose in the subject matter of the statute itself, which in the Court's view admitted of only one purpose to be achieved. That is, the Court's inquiry was forward looking, regardless of whether the goal was religious or secular. This use of the purpose test has had until recently little impact on the naked public square argument, a subject beyond the scope of this paper.

The well-known legal philosopher Ronald Dworkin's latest book, *Life's Dominion*,[128] is a philosophical-jurisprudential defense of *Roe v. Wade* and its pre-Rehnquist Court pro-choice progeny. Stripped to its essentials, Dworkin's argument is that any restriction on abortion (prior to viability) can be only religious, and hence is prohibited by the Establishment Clause. We cannot, he says, make sense of the "bizarre" claim that the fetus has intrinsic worth, that it is fully human, but only the derivative claim that the fetus will become a human life and hence is entitled to some degree of respect in order to cultivate respect for life generally.[129] Although Dworkin does not specify why advocacy of the contrary view is unconstitutional, it is possible to understand his argument as being premised on the purpose branch of the *Lemon* inquiry—that is, that the legislation is directed to a religious goal.

The argument fails, I think, for several reasons. First, Dworkin assumes

---

[123]*Pearl v. Nyquist*, 413 U.S. 756 (1973).

[124]*Mueller v. Allen*, 463 U.S. 388, 405–06 (1983), Marshall, J., dissenting.

[125]*Wallace v. Jaffree*, 472 U.S. 38 (1985).

[126]*Stone v. Graham*, 449 U.S. 39 (1982).

[127]*Edwards v. Agullard*, 482 U.S. 578 (1987).

[128]R. Dworkin, *Life's Dominion* (Cambridge, Mass.: Harvard University Press, 1993).

[129]Ibid.

(contrary to settled law) a definition of religion that is far broader than anything the Court has suggested in over twenty years. In his argument, religion means any set of deeply held views that fill the place of traditional religion.[130] The Supreme Court had once adopted this view in a Vietnam War-era conscientious objection case,[131] but quickly repudiated it.[132] Dworkin also purports to prove that a ban on abortion is too stringent a remedy for protecting the value of potential human life.[133] This value judgment is the stuff of politics in a democracy, however, not an inexorable philosophic certainty. Finally, it is a fact that intelligent and alert atheists (e.g., Nat Hentoff) are consciously not religious and nevertheless distinctly pro-life. Unless these people delude themselves, I think that their existence is a sufficient rebuttal to Dworkin, particularly on the view that for constitutional purposes religion requires a belief in a deity. (Dworkin would respond that a firmly held but not rationally grounded opposition to abortion is religious, but this rejoinder is contrary to authoritative Supreme Court decisions.)

The Supreme Court has explicitly rejected the argument that restrictive abortion laws establish religion.[134] It correctly saw no more than a coincidence between religious law and the secular—a coincidence no more troubling than, say, the parallel between the law against murder and the Sixth Commandment. Although there were dissents on other parts of the case, no justice objected to this part of the holding.

In *Webster* v. *Reproductive Rights*,[135] the Court considered a challenge to a Missouri anti-abortion law, whose preamble declared that human life began at conception. A majority of the Court refused to pass on the constitutionality of that declaration because it was of no practical effect as long as *Roe* v. *Wade* remained good law. Justice Stevens, however, opined in a dissent that the preamble unconstitutionally established religion:

> I am persuaded that the absence of any secular purpose for the legislative declarations that life begins at conception and that conception occurs at

---

[130]Ibid.

[131]*Walsh* v. *U.S.*, 398 U.S. 333 (1970).

[132]*Wisconsin* v. *Yoder*, 406 U.S. 205 (1971).

[133]Dworkin, *Life's Dominion*.

[134]*Harris* v. *McRae*, 448 U.S. 297 (1981).

[135]492 U.S. 490 (1989).

fertilization makes the relevant portion of the preamble invalid under the Establishment Clause of the First Amendment to the Federal Constitution. This conclusion does not, and could not, rest on the fact that the statement happens to coincide with the tenets of certain religions . . . or in the fact that the legislators who voted to enact it may have been motivated by religious considerations. . . . Rather, it rests on the fact that the preamble, an unequivocal endorsement of a religious tenet of some, but by no means all, Christian faiths, serves no identifiable secular purpose. [footnotes omitted][136]

More problematically, Justice Stevens found that the preamble was unconstitutional because it injected the state into a religious debate: "Bolstering my conclusion that the preamble violates the First Amendment is the fact that the intensely divisive character of much of the national debate over the abortion issue reflects the deeply held religious convictions of many participants in the debate. The Missouri Legislature may not inject its endorsement of a particular religious tradition into this debate, for '[t]he Establishment Clause does not allow public bodies to foment such disagreement.'"[137]

This latter argument has roots in the third branch of the *Lemon* test, the so-called entanglement branch. As originally stated in *Lemon*, the entanglement branch of the test asked whether a particular practice was likely to fuel political debate and controversy along religious lines.[138] I have always had difficulty with this aspect of the test, because the no-funding rule is also politically and religiously divisive. The Court in any event has all but repudiated this branch of the test.[139] It now exists, if at all, only in regard to programs requiring annual appropriations to religious institutions.

But what of Justice Stevens' other ground—that the definition of human life as beginning with conception has no other purpose, no goal in view, other than the furtherance of religion and hence is invalid? He was clearly correct that not all religious authorities teach that human life begins with conception. Indeed, without attempting to rehash the entire abortion controversy in *halakhah*, it is at least safe to say that not

---

[136]492 U.S. at 566 (1989).
[137]492 U.S. at 571.
[138]403 U.S. at 622–23.
[139]*Mueller* v. *Allen*, 463 U.S. 388 (1983).

all halakhic authorities would agree with the Missouri definition as a halakhically authentic one.[140] Assume for the moment, then, that no secular justification exists for adopting Missouri's definition of fetal life as human from the moment of conception. I think that Justice Stevens would be quite right that the adoption of an exclusively religious definition of life into law would be unconstitutional and that Orthodox Jews should, as a matter of self-interest, agree. This does mean that some views (i.e., religious ones) are impermissible as the sole grounds for legislation and other ones are not; and this means that religion is disadvantaged vis-a-vis other beliefs or political ideologies. I think this is an inescapable meaning of the Establishment Clause. It is good that it is so.

By what right did the Missouri legislature decide that a Christian definition of life was superior to a Jewish one? The problem does not limit itself to just abstract questions of definition. Agudath Israel filed a brief in the Webster case urging the Court to overturn *Roe v. Wade* and require the states to permit only those abortions religiously mandated. Leaving aside questions about the legal viability of this approach, one is astounded by its sheer *hutzpah.*

By what right, on whose authority, and with whose consent did Agudah delegates to the various state legislatures, including such halakhic experts as those who compose the legislature of South Dakota, receive the power to decide that only those abortions necessary to save the life of the mother (a phrase almost always read more narrowly by Christian pro-life groups than by Orthodox Jews) were constitutionally protected but not those designed to abort Tay-Sachs babies or early (first 40 days) abortion in the case of rape, which are not halakhically necessary but nevertheless permissible? In each of the last two cases, there are competent *rabbanim* who permit these abortions.[141] And what, other than political happen-

---

[140]See, e.g., the commentary of R. Ovadyah mi-Bartenura to Mishnah *Ohalot* 7,6. See, generally, J. D. Bleich, "Abortion in Halachic Literature," in *Jewish Bioethics*, ed. F. Rosner and J. D. Bleich (New York: Hebrew Publishing, 1979), 134–77.

[141]As to Tay-Sachs babies, see ibid., 160–61. Rabbi J. B. Soloveitchik once told me that, in principle, he agreed with the ruling permitting the abortion of a Tay-Sachs fetus. Subsequent to the Forum, Professor David Berger suggested to me that the Aguda's position can be defended on the ground that avoiding the greater harm of aborting literally hundreds of thousands of fetuses is more

stance, is to stop the legislature of a largely Catholic state such as Rhode Island from prohibiting even abortions to save the life of the mother in keeping with Catholic doctrine? And if abortion is too sensitive a subject, then what of Sunday blue laws, which imposed substantial economic hardship on Orthodox Jews and which they fought with every means at their disposal (including the Establishment Clause), but which were defended as necessary to protect social morality?[142]

The second aspect of the purpose test is not forward looking, but backward looking. It inquires into what motivated the legislature to adopt a particular rule. Theoretically, any law could be invalidated on this ground, though in practice only those with religious overtones are scrutinized under this branch of the test because it is only in these cases that legislatures are likely to express religious views.[143] It was on this basis that the Supreme Court invalidated Louisiana's equal-time-for-creation statute and Alabama's silent-prayer statute.[144]

The issue of improper motivation by the lawmaker as a justification for invalidating a governmental action is not limited to establishments of religion. That doctrine has been invoked in freedom-of-the-press cases (where a tax is imposed with the purpose of punishing a newspaper[145]) or in the case of race (where statutes or governmental action are invalidated because motivated by racial bias).[146] Indeed, it is required to prove a claim under the Equal Protection Clause that an invidious motivation be shown.[147] Similarly, the presence of an explicitly anti-religious motiva-

---

important than permitting an abortion in the case of Tay-Sachs fetuses, especially because it is likely that at least some states will continue to permit such abortions and Jewish women who want abortions can travel to these states. His point is a powerful one, and I have no decisive answer to it. On balance, I think that it is more important to maintain the viability of a full range of halakhic positions, and leave the Orthodox community able to demonstrate its response to a full range of issues.

[142]N. W. Cohen, *Jews in Christian America.*

[143]*Edwards v. Aguillard*, 482 U.S. 578 (1987).

[144]*Wallace v. Jeffries*, 472 U.S. 38 (1985).

[145]*Minneapolis Star Tribune v. Commissioner of Revenue, Minn.*, 460 U.S. 575 (1983).

[146]*Hunter v. Underwood*, 471 U.S. 222 (1985).

[147]*Washington v. Davis*, 426 U.S. 229 (1976).

tion against all or some religions will invalidate an otherwise constitutional statute.[148]

Moreover, illicit motivation is not proven from the fact that the relevant decisionmaker adheres to a particular religion. Abortion laws are not suspect because Catholic legislators vote for them. The courts look rather to what is said during the course of official public debate by decision makers.

Even so, this inquiry has been subject to searching criticism, never better expressed than by Justice Scalia in the Louisiana scientific creationism case:

> But the difficulty of knowing what vitiating purpose one is looking for is as nothing compared with the difficulty of knowing how or where to find it. For while it is possible to discern the objective "purpose" of a statute (i.e., the public good at which its provisions appear to be directed) or even the formal motivation for a statute where that is explicitly set forth (as it was, to no avail, here) discerning the subjective motivation of those enacting the statute is, to be honest, almost always an impossible task. The number of possible motivations, to begin with, is not binary, for example, a particular legislator need not have voted for the Act either because he wanted to foster religion or because he wanted to improve education. He may have thought the bill would provide jobs for his district, or may have wanted to make amends with a faction of his party he had alienated on another vote, or he may have been a close friend of the bill's sponsor, or he may have been repaying a favor he owed the Majority Leader, or he may have hoped the Governor would appreciate his vote and make a fundraising appearance for him, or he may have been pressured to vote for a bill he disliked by a wealthy contributor or by a flood of constituent mail, or he may have been seeking favorable publicity, or he may have been reluctant to hurt the feelings of a loyal staff member who worked on the bill, or he may have been settling an old score with a legislator who opposed the bill, or he may have been mad at his wife who opposed the bill, or he may have been intoxicated and utterly *un*motivated when the vote was called, or he may have accidentally voted "yes" instead of "no," or, of course, he may have had (and very likely did have) a combination of some of the above and many other motivations. To look for the *sole purpose* of even a single legislator is probably to look for something that does not exist.[149]

---

[148]*Church of the Lukumi Bablu Aye v. City of Hialeah*, 112 S. Ct. 2217 (1993).
[149]*Edwards v. Aguilard* 482 U.S. 578 (1982).

Putting that problem aside, however, where ought we to look for the individual legislator's purpose? We cannot of course assume that every member present (if, as is unlikely, we know who or even how many there were) agreed with the motivation expressed in a particular legislator's pre-enactment floor or committee statement. Quite obviously, "[w]hat motivates one legislator to make a speech about a statute is not necessarily what motivates scores of others to enact it."

Justice Scalia concludes by insisting that motive is irrelevant to constitutionality, a position with ancient roots but little modern resonance. As already noted, in a variety of areas, from freedom of religion and speech to equal protection, motive is highly relevant.

These are not easy questions that Justice Scalia poses. Although answers may be difficult, ultimately Justice Scalia's challenge does not escape the response of Justice O'Connor in an earlier school prayer case:

It is not a trivial matter, however, to require that the legislature manifest a secular purpose and omit all sectarian endorsements from its laws. That requirement is precisely tailored to the Establishment Clause's purpose of assuring that government not intentionally endorse religion or a religious practice. It is of course possible that a legislature will enunciate a sham secular purpose for a statute. I have little doubt that our courts are capable of distinguishing a sham secular purpose from a sincere one, or that the Lemon inquiry into the effect of an enactment would help decide those close cases where the validity of an expressed secular purpose is in doubt. While the secular purpose requirement alone may rarely be determinative in striking down a statute, it nevertheless serves an important function. It reminds government that when it acts it should do so without endorsing a particular religious belief or practice that all citizens do not share. In this sense the secular purpose requirement is squarely based in the text of the Establishment Clause it helps to enforce.[150]

As a practical matter, then, there will be some small class of cases in which the expressed religious motives of the legislators will invalidate a statute. But this rule does not silence religious persons outside the legislature, only those charged with actually making laws.

A group of Orthodox groups, most of whom are not associated with so-called right-wing Orthodoxy, filed a brief in the case of *Kiryas Joel*

---

[150]*Wallace v. Jaffree* 472 U.S. 38 (1985).

School District v. *Grumet*, the Monroe, New York school district created to accommodate the Satmar Hasidic children. The groups supported the constitutionality of the district, a perfectly legitimate position. But what was startling about the brief was that it opened with an attack on the notion that the United States is a secular democracy.

American Jews—and Orthodox Jews—have done astoundingly well under secular democracy, far better in most ways than they did under the not-so-secular regimes of eastern Europe. Western culture is not by any means an unmitigated good, nor is it possible to ignore the challenge it poses. But the secular nature of the political structure should not be a problem for Orthodoxy. On the contrary, it is the very secular nature of the government that is responsible for the ability of Orthodox Jews to participate on equal terms with our fellow citizens and to do so free of any serious threat of religious persecution.

Perhaps the rejection of the secular state reflects bitterness at the denial of aid to parochial schools. More likely, it reflects an unfortunate tendency to reject all Western values, including, for example, the Enlightenment and Emancipation. Better persecution and isolation, goes the argument, than the risks of an open society.

One need not accept with equanimity every decision favoring the separation of church and state to accept the fundamental notion that American democracy is secular. There are risks to that acceptance, but there are surely greater costs to the policy of attempting to turn the clock back to the identity of church and state, which inexorably led to the religious persecution of the Middle Ages. Nostalgia for the *shtetl* is no substitute for clear-headed analysis. Rejection of real progress is not a religious virtue.

6

Liberal Theory
and Jewish Politics

Martin P. Golding

On December 23, 1789, Comte Stanislas de Clermont-Tonnerre stood before the National Assembly of France to defend the extension of full equality to Jews, a status he regarded as implied in the Declaration of the Rights of Man and Citizen. In a somewhat ominous fashion, he also stated the assumption on which that extension should be based. "The Jews," he said, "should be denied everything as a nation, but granted everything as individuals . . ." and that "it should not be tolerated that the Jews become a separate political formation or class in the country."

Clermont-Tonnerre's statement, I think, encapsulates a central problem in our topic, "*Tikkun Olam*: Jewish Responsibilities to Society." As much as Jews are tolerated and even find themselves comfortable in the liberal democratic societies of which they are full citizens, do they, *as Jews*, have anything to contribute to the questions of principle and policy that those societies currently face? (This question has in view Jews resident in the Western liberal democracies, especially the United States; presumably, for reasons that deserve separate treatment, the State of Israel is a different case.) If there exists the possibility of a "Jewish politics" under these conditions, of course, it would be very different from anything like that of pre-World War II Poland, when delegates of Jew-

201

ish political parties sat in the Sejm.[1] But can such a politics be anything
more than more than a Jewish version of the Social Gospel?

Papers in this volume demonstrate (though sometimes with serious
qualification, as in Michael Broyde's contribution) the wealth of resources
in the Jewish spiritual and halakhic tradition that bear on a variety of
important social issues. Aside from the numerous rabbinic enactments
instituted for purposes of *tikkun olam* and *darkhei shalom* (the ways of
peace), the authoritative sources evince a broad concern for human well-
being.[2] Various speakers have indicated the universalistic as well as the
particularistic elements of the tradition.

It is an apparent assumption of theorists of the liberal democratic state,
however, that its members confront each other in the debate over questions of principle and policy in their capacity as citizens only, rather than
as members of particular groups. It is assumed that its members are free
and equal persons who will speak in a language of shared political and
social values rather than particularistic ones. The midrashic literature
tells us that the Jews in Egypt kept their distinctive identity; two of the
reasons why they were redeemed are that they did not change their names
or their language.[3] In an important symbolic sense, however, the change
of language, if not of name, is precisely what citizenship is said to imply
in a liberal democracy, according to much of recent American political
and legal theory.

I want to explain very briefly how this position comes about and consider some of its consequences for the Orthodox community in its attempt to engage itself in *tikkun olam*. (Obviously, I cannot survey all the
versions of liberal democratic theory, with their distinctive nuances;
I am concerned with a general tendency of thought, best represented,

---

[1]See Ezra Mendelsohn, *On Modern Jewish Politics* (New York: Oxford University Press, 1993), on the varieties of Jewish politics in the diaspora, with
particular attention to the United States and Poland.

[2]For examples of enactments for *tikkun olam* see, e.g., *Gittin* chapter 4. As
far as I can tell all the enactments in this category apply to Jews only, while the
category of *darkhei shalom* includes enactments that also apply to non-Jews. See,
e.g., *Gittin* 61a. Presumably, though I am not sure, these concepts are extend-
able beyond the enactments specifically mentioned in the *posekim*; the sources
contain legions of enactments for purposes of social improvement.

[3]*Lev. Rabbah*, 32.

I believe, by John Rawls). It could well be the case that there remains an inevitable, foundational conflict at the theoretical level between Judaism and liberal democracy. It should be mentioned, on the other side, that liberal democratic theory is not the only player on the field of American thought. Liberal theory has recently come under fire from communitarianism, about which I shall also say a little. I find some of this attack convincing, but I am not sure that, as developed, communitarianism, even so-called liberal communitarianism, resolves the foundational conflict. All this at the theoretical level, and here I shall be going over some of the same ground covered by Marc Stern. It should not be thought that such theoretical considerations are insignificant, for they will affect the terms on which Jews can participate in the debate over policy matters. At the practical, working-relationship level, any foundational conflict, if one exists, can perhaps be mitigated. Later on I shall briefly comment on Michael Broyde's paper[4] and, further on, Marc Stern's.[5]

Let me start with some general features of the liberal democratic state in its American manifestation. The two most obvious are (indirect) majority rule and the protection of minorities from illegitimate intrusions by the majority. This protection is expressed in the U.S. Constitution in various provisions of the Bill of Rights. The principle underlying this protection of minorities, however, is not, in the first instance, derived from a concern for minority *groups*, as such. Rather, the underlying principle is one of regard for individual self-determination, the rights of individuals; and the protection of groups, insofar as it exists, is reached through the idea of freedom of association.[6] Of course, these features of liberal democracy—majority rule and protection of individuals and

---

[4]Michael J. Broyde, "The Obligation of Jews to Seek Observance of Noahide Laws by Gentiles," in this volume.

[5]Marc D. Stern, "Jews and Public Morality," in this volume.

[6]I find a problem here, but I shall not be able to take it up. See my paper "Communities and the Liberal Community: Some Comments and Questions," in *Democratic Community*, ed. J. W. Chapman and I. Shapiro, *Nomos* 35 (New York: New York University Press, 1993), 115–125. I think that Marc Stern's "religious exemption" or "religious accommodation" approach to handling some of the interests of Jews, which I accept, requires a more substantial account of freedom of association than the one currently adopted by the Supreme Court.

minorities from the tyranny of the majority—are often in a tension that
threatens one or the other attribute. Moreover, regard for individual self-
determination is not an entirely uncontested concept in liberal theory,
once the sphere of economic activity is taken into account. Here, lib-
eralisms range from modern welfare liberalism to libertarianism.

Of an importance equal to that of majority rule and the protection
of individuals' rights is "liberty of conscience," to use an old-fashioned
phrase. In the U.S. Constitution, again, liberty of conscience is protected primarily in the Establishment and Free Exercise Clauses of the
First Amendment. ("Congress shall make no law respecting an establishment of religion, or prohibiting the free exercise thereof. . .") These
provisions reflect the deep wisdom of the Founding Generation as to
the condition necessary for the viability of a religiously plural society—
that government (initially only the national government, but various
eighteenth-century state constitutions had similar provisions) should
be neutral on matters of religion and stay out of religion's way. Without question, the "toleration" of religion(s) enshrined in the Constitution had its origins in the religious conflicts of the preceding centuries, and it is not surprising that political liberalism is seen as a corollary
of the rise of religious tolerance.[7] But the Founders' wisdom also rested,
I believe, on a perceptive understanding of religion; they understood
that one's religion constituted a more fundamental loyalty than loyalty to the state.

It is not clear how far this understanding of religious loyalty still prevails, for liberal theorists have in effect introduced what might be called
the idea of "constitutional citizenship" by extending the requirement of
religious neutrality to citizens in their participation in the most important
of public activities, that is, participation in the debates over questions of
principle and policy. It is clear that this neutrality is bound to leave seriously committed religious believer in a rather uncomfortable position. One
can appreciate, therefore, the near anguish of Kent Greenawalt in his
important book, *Religious Convictions and Political Choice*. Greenawalt, who
is a committed Christian and a liberal democrat, seeks to find a space for
religious convictions in the public debate. He finds this space for ordinary
citizens in the area in which "competing publicly accessible reasons" are

---

[7]See, e.g., John Rawls, *Political Liberalism* (New York: Columbia University
Press, 1993), xxiv ff.

radically inconclusive,[8] examples of which are such borderline questions as the moral status of the fetus and animals' rights. And although it is plain to him that legislation must be justified in terms of secular objectives, "legislators in similar instances," he says, "may also rely on their own religious convictions and those of their constituents, and occasionally such reliance is warranted even for judges."[9]

As limited and severely qualified as Greenawalt's position is, many liberal theorists find it unacceptable nevertheless.[10] Their position reminds one of the Erastianism of the seventeenth-century philosopher, Thomas Hobbes. As part of his absolutistic solution to the English Civil War, which was in great measure a religious war, Hobbes proposed that there be a public religion that would be determined by the sovereign; in the privacy of their own hearts, ordinary citizens could believe whatever they liked. Though hardly any committed religious person would accept Hobbes's solution, its parallel is found in liberal thought wherein a comparable public-private distinction is maintained. Religion is relegated to the realm of the private, with the secular put in the place of Hobbes's public religion. In part, it might be argued, the liberals' position reflects a failure to understand the nature of religious loyalties. But this accusation liberals would deny. They would claim, I think, that they understand the depth and strength of religious bonds only too well. For that very reason, they would say, they see the need, in a religiously plural society, to institute the American Founders' notion of religious neutrality at the level of democratic citizenship, and not merely at the level of government—that is, a more thorough desacralization of politics. Many religiously committed people, on the other hand, would see the liberals as going beyond the Founders; what the liberals propose is secularism, a tendency of thought that is hostile to religion.

Be all this as it may, the basic contention of modern liberal theory concerns the character and conditions of debate over questions of principle and policy in the liberal state. It is well understood that parties to

---

[8]Kent Greenawalt, *Religious Convictions and Political Choice* (New York: Oxford University Press, 1988), 147.

[9]Ibid.,12.

[10]For a critical notice of Greenawalt from a liberal perspective, see Kenneth I. Winston, "The Religious Convictions of Public Officials," *Canadian Journal of Law and Jurisprudence*, 3 (1990): 129–143.

the debate enter into it from different perspectives, special interests and biases, and with opposed values. Liberal theory insists that these personal standpoints must be superseded by a public, impersonal point of view. Essentially, this means that only "publicly accessible reasons" (Greenawalt, above) or "common modes of reasoning" be used in the public debate.[11]

This stipulation raises deep metaphysical and epistemological issues that cannot be discussed here. The underlying motive for the stipulation, however, is readily understandable. If society is going to be able to reach a relatively broad consensus on matters of public concern, for purposes of public action, it would seem, firstly, that the debate must be conducted in terms that are common to the parties and, secondly, that the parties should be prepared to change their minds as a result of the debate. According to many liberal theorists, it is not always enough that the parties agree on the answers to the factual questions relevant to the matter under discussion and that they share various values. It is necessary that they ultimately accept the same kinds of *grounds* for their factual and normative convictions. It is basically for this reason, in a religiously plural society (in which some people have no religion at all) that propositions, whether factual or normative, that are rested by an interlocutor on religious convictions are excluded from the debate, although any party could put them forward insofar as they might be asserted on grounds of so-called common modes of reasoning.

It is also plain that this stipulation presents serious difficulties for Orthodox Jews (despite the universalistic elements in Jewish tradition), as well as for others who maintain a "comprehensive" religious, philosophical, or moral conception, as John Rawls calls it in his 1993 book *Political Liberalism*. A conception is comprehensive "when it includes conceptions of what is of value in human life, as well as ideals of personal virtue and character, that are to inform much of our nonpolitical conduct (in the limit our life as a whole)."[12] Rawls, in fact, acknowledges that it seems paradoxical that citizens thinking about "the most funda-

---

[11] The latter expression comes from John Rawls, *A Theory of Justice* (Cambridge, Mass.: Harvard University Press, 1971), 215. See, also, Rawls, *Political Liberalism*, 224.

[12] Rawls, *Liberalism*, p. 175.

mental political questions" should "honor the limits of public reason" and cannot appeal to "the whole truth as they see it."[13]

Rawls's development of liberal theory and his answer to the paradox deserve attention here, however brief. In the above mentioned book, Rawls brings together the modifications developed in numerous articles subsequent to his 1971 work *A Theory of Justice*, which is rightfully regarded as one of the most significant American contributions to ethical theory and social philosophy in this century. He no longer purports to be presenting a universal theory of social and economic justice, however, but rather a political theory that expresses the essential elements of a liberal democratic state.

The focus of Rawls's enquiry is how to settle the principles and basic structure of a society that contains groups with a variety of comprehensive doctrines. And though he still retains the idea of a "veil of ignorance," which was integral to his argument in *A Theory of Justice*,[14] in *Political Liberalism* this idea is modified because, realistically speaking, modern democracies inevitably contain a plurality of comprehensive conceptions, a diversity of conflicting theories of the good. In the determination of the principles and basic social structure, therefore, Rawls seeks an "overlapping consensus" of *reasonable* comprehensive conceptions. In Rawls's view, ideal moral agents do have, and do rationally pursue, a theory of the good; but they also have a capacity for an effective sense of justice, which is exercised by being reasonable, acting on a conception of the fair terms of cooperation. The overlapping consensus and the constitutional principles of justice and basic rights in which it

---

[13]Rawls, *Liberalism*, 216.

[14]Rawls argues that there are certain universal principles of justice, which would be chosen by rational, self-interested contractors as a basis for social cooperation, where this choice is made from behind a "veil of ignorance." Among the essential features of this situation, says Rawls (p. 12), "is that no one knows his place in society, his class position or social status, nor does anyone know his fortune in the distribution of natural assets and abilities, his strength, intelligence, and the like. I shall even assume that the parties do not know their conception of the good or their special psychological tendencies." To which one might add, they do not know their religion either. The purpose of these stipulations is to insure utter impartiality, so that universal principles of justice will be chosen.

results are not just a modus vivendi; they reflect a higher capacity for reasonableness and intelligent moderation.

According to Rawls, the diverse theories of the good provide the content of the "nonpublic reasons" that citizens hold. But, as he continues to maintain, conceptions of the good are "irrelevant from the standpoint of justice."[15] In Rawls's terms, the citizens of the liberal state, who are reasonable, will accept the priority of the Right over the Good.[16] In settling on principles of justice and basic rights, citizens will accept "public reason," whose content is given by the Right and could be rationally accepted by everyone who is reasonable, and they will ignore nonpublic reasons. It is for this reason that the above-mentioned paradox arises, namely, that citizens thinking about "the most fundamental political questions" should "honor the limits of public reason" and cannot appeal to "the whole truth as they see it."

Rawls attempts to dissolve the paradox by appealing to the liberal principle of political legitimacy and the ideal of democratic citizenship.[17] In effect, he maintains, citizens should be reasonable, for otherwise the exercise of public power is not justifiable: advancing a single comprehensive theory requires oppression. (This is reminiscent of his claim that if we can agree on any principle regarding religion, it must be liberty of conscience.)[18] Moreover, it is not only public officials who are restricted to using public rather than private reason. A duty of civility, which is endorsed from within citizens' reasonable convictions, too, requires that one should not vote, or participate in policy debates either, apparently, with the motive of expressing one's distinctive view of the good life or any sectarian interest. Although Rawls insists in many places that he is concerned only with "the most fundamental political questions," he seems to go beyond them in the dissolution of the paradox. He leaves a narrow space, if any space at all, for the operation of individual convictions in the public arena.

Although there is much that appeals to me in Rawls's theory, and one cannot but appreciate the brilliance of his argument, I find it ultimately

---

[15]Rawls, A *Theory of Justice*, p. 18.

[16]Rawls's argument is apparently circular here. See Bruce W. Brower, "The Limits of Public Reason," *Journal of Philosophy*, 91 (1994): 5–26.

[17]See Rawls, *Liberalism*, 216–220.

[18]Rawls, *Justice*, 208.

unsatisfactory. This is not the place for an extensive analysis, and I must confine myself to a few very brief remarks. In the end, it is unclear as to what can coexist with liberalism's overlapping consensus. Rawls is greatly motivated by a concern for stability, and he argues that political liberalism promotes stability, which explains the centrality of the idea of reasonableness in his theory. Now it is plain that a willingness to be reasonable, to cooperate with others on fair terms of cooperation, is extremely important in a democracy. But reasonableness and stability are matters of degree. The choice for a democracy is not between pure liberalism and stability, on the one side, and coercion or instability, on the other, for there are relatively stable intermediate stages. A variety of religious and ethnic traditions can be governmentally promoted without threatening stability. Many liberals, and Rawls too, object to public support for religious schools, for instance, but such support is available in the United Kingdom without threatening its stability. (How much the Jewish community has benefited as a result is questionable; England could have the highest rate of assimilation in the Western world.) There is also a significant omission in Rawls's discussion. What role is there for real politics? Although Rawls intends his *Political Liberalism* to be a more realistic treatment, by taking into account the "fact of pluralism," this vital question is not considered. Finally, Rawls's appeal to an ideal self ignores, to a degree, actual selves and what they deeply care about.

There is no doubt in my mind that Jews have good reason to be appreciative of liberal democracy, especially in America (as the saying goes, "Only in America . . ."). But it does seem that there is a foundational incompatibility between liberal theory, at least insofar as it represented in Rawls and theories like his, and the participation of Jews, as Jews, in a liberal society. On a practical level, of course, Jews will be "reasonable" and cooperative, be self-restrained in the promotion of Jewish interests. As a matter of tactics and sincere conviction, Jews can share in much of the common language of liberal values, but they cannot entirely give up their own. However, their self-image as free and equal members of the society will be different from that rendered by liberal theory. But the subject of self-image is one that I cannot take up here.

Even though Rawls apparently would limit Jewish participation in public debate for reasons external to Judaism, Broyde would seem to limit it for internal reasons; he questions whether there is an obligation, under the *halakhah*, to seek the enforcement of the Noahide Law. His learned and intricate paper is more focused than the broad topic of *tikkun olam*, and I shall proceed by briefly discussing an example.

Consider, for instance, whether it should be a crime to assist in a suicide. All sorts of reasons, pro and con, of a non-religious nature have been given on the question, some of which might well be accepted by Jews. Ultimately, however, one's view on the matter will be affected by whether suicide itself is morally permissible. Secular philosophers (Hume and Kant, for instance) have disagreed on the issue, and I imagine that the arguments for one or the other position, taken in their own terms, could be found compelling by an Orthodox Jew. But suppose the Noahide Law forbids suicide and that (contrary to Broyde's conclusion) there is an obligation to seek the enforcement of the Noahide Law by the civil state. Jews might then consider it an obligation to participate in the public debate, yet they would seem to be debarred from any resort to the Noahide Law as a ground for the propositions they put forward in the public forum. Of course, the status of the Noahide Law as an independent "rational morality" has been widely discussed in the Jewish sources. Still in all, whatever its status, it is hard to see how a Jew (or a religious non-Jew, for that matter) could regard theological considerations as irrelevant to the case of assisted suicide. He cannot simply dismiss, for instance, the statement of the Radbaz on another, but related matter (not inflicting corporal punishment on the basis of a confession), that "Man is not the owner of his life, God is."[19] But whether or not a Jew has an obligation to participate in the debate on the criminalization of assisted suicide, liberal democratic theory disallows him use of the theological premise.[20]

---

[19]Radbaz, commenting on Rambam, *Mishneh Torah*, Sanhedrin 18:6. Compare Rambam, *Mishneh Torah*, Rotze'ah, 1:4: *she-ein nafsho shel zeh ha-neherag kinyan go'el ha-dam ela kinyan ha-Kadosh barukh Hu.*

[20]In a *New York Times* op ed article (17 May 1994, A 15), "When Is It Right to Die?," Ronald Dworkin, a leading liberal theorist, gives the theological premise an interesting twist. He takes the premise, that human life is a divine gift, to mean that life has objective, intrinsic value. "But it would be wrong to think," he says, "that those who are more permissive about abortion and euthanasia are indifferent to the value of life. Rather, they disagree about what respecting that value means." To the extent that the latter point can be debated without resort to any theological premises, there could be common ground for discussion between religious adherents and secularists.

Here it might be mentioned that Broyde concludes, if I understand him correctly, that Jews may assist in the violation of the Noahide Law when a Noahide will certainly violate it. Of course, one reason for wanting to make assisted suicide a crime is that without such assistance the suicide is less likely to occur; if so, we may have an instance of *terei ibbera de-nahara*, and a Jew would be prohibited to assist in the suicide of a *ben No'ah* (assuming that suicide is forbidden to a *ben No'ah*). In a footnote (n. 142), Broyde suggests that "merely because one is under no obligation to teach a person that murder is wrong, [it] does not mean that one can sell a person a gun to commit a murder . . . ." Perhaps there is a parallel here to assisted suicide. But from the tenor of his discussion it appears that there is no analog to *lifnei ivver* for a non-Jew, and a *ben No'ah* may assist in a suicide. If this is the case, a Jew need not participate in the debate on criminalization of assisted suicide even if there is an obligation to seek the enforcement of Noahide Law. On the other hand, Broyde allows that it might be right and proper, if not technically obligatory, to seek its enforcement. In that case, Jews certainly could participate in the debate, but according to liberal theorists they may not do so *as Jews*.

The case of suicide and assisted suicide exemplifies a feature of the *halakhah* that is significant here: the *halakhah* is decidedly *paternalistic*; an individual may be forbidden (under penalty of disciplinary flogging) to do things that are harmful to himself.[21] When it comes down to concrete cases, paternalism is an issue over which liberals sometimes divide, but liberalism's general tendency is clear: it is anti-paternalistic. This stance follows from a general presumption in favor of individual liberty and it is related to (though not identical with) a notion mentioned earlier, namely, the priority of the Right over the Good. Put in other terms, the liberal state is required to eschew *perfectionism* of any kind; it may not seek to promote a particular "life style" on the grounds that it is morally superior to any other, nor may it seek to promote a particular comprehensive conception, according to Rawls. Individuals should be free to pursue their own "experiments in living" subject to the limitations of John Stuart Mill's harm-to-others principle or a near relative of it. Put in still other terms, the liberal state should not seek to bring about a moral utopia. And, in general, I think it would be a mistake for Jews in

---

[21]See, e.g., Rambam, *Mishneh Torah*, Rotzeah 11:5.

a liberal society to seek it governmentally either. Jews should be very cautious about the mixing of religion and politics.

Rawls's theory, and liberal theories generally, have been attacked by the communitarians. Communitarian approaches might seem more promising in providing a theoretical underpinning for the participation of Jews, as Jews, in the debate over principle and policy in a liberal democracy. (Some communitarians, I might note, do align themselves with a welfare state. Here, I should say that although I have no principled objection to welfare liberalism, I tend in the direction of libertarianism, because I am skeptical of the capacity of the state to do anything well.) According to communitarians, there is no theory of justice or the good that can be abstracted from, and that exists independently of, concrete communities and traditions. The attacks follow various lines, ranging from an account of the nature of social goods, for instance, to a form of relativism about rationality itself.[22] (The latter approach does not appeal to me.) The most plausible approach, in my opinion, turns on the nature of the self. The life of the active, participating self should be thought of as possessing a "narrative unity" about which a meaningful story can be told.[23] Ends and desires, historically based in a community, and the process of balancing between these ends and desires, are constitutive parts of the self.[24]

This last approach, by way of an account of the self, of actual selves and what they deeply care about rather than a Rawlsian ideal self, is, I think, vital for a realistic understanding of the meaning of citizenship in a democratic society, such as the United States. But the way is fraught with difficulty. For the fact is that each of us is a member of many communities, which is something that (with some significant exceptions) communitarians tend to overlook. Because one has to function in so many communities, and because one has so many roles to play, the construc-

---

[22]For the former, see Michael Walzer, *Spheres of Justice* (New York: Basic Books, 1983); for the latter, see Alasdair MacIntyre, *Whose Justice? Which Rationality?* (Notre Dame, IN: University of Notre Dame Press, 1988).

[23]See Alasdair MacIntyre, *After Virtue* 2nd ed. (Notre Dame, IN: University of Notre Dame Press, 1984).

[24]This formulation is derived from Michael Sandel, *Liberalism and the Limits of Justice* (Cambridge: Cambridge University Press, 1982), though I would not go quite as far with it as he does.

tion of a unified self becomes a difficult matter. It is true that, because each one of us performs in so many capacities, one is able to achieve a measure of distance from any one role and thereby achieve a level of impartiality and, almost, impersonality. This is a condition that we expect someone who occupies the office of a judge to attain.

But is there such a thing as a role of "constitutional citizenship" as described by liberal theorists, to which all other roles become subordinated in the process of debate on social issues? I do not think there is. There certainly is not for Jews, whose fundamental loyalties do not permit any such subordination. (I should mention that there is a variety of liberalism called communitarian liberalism, which denies that liberalism assumes a notion of the "unencumbered self"—and so does Rawls, in fact—that Michael Sandel accuses it of. But I do not think that liberal communitarians have adequately faced up to the significance of the plurality of communities in a democratic state.)[25]

What is the practical alternative, then, for Jews? Stanley Hauerwas and William Willimon, in their book *Resident Aliens: Life in the Christian Colony* (1989),[26] describe the Christian community as embattled and surrounded, with no place to withdraw to. A possible response to that situation is: live like aliens from another planet; do not reach out into the world; cluster in little colonies, and take care of your own. Some Orthodox Jews have taken this kind of route, though they are not above seeking benefits for themselves from the largess of the modern welfare state. Nevertheless, it is clear that Marc Stern and others represented in this volume believe that Jews have a mandate of concern for society at large thrust upon them. Stern holds that this concern is dictated by more than self interest, but rather as a consequence of full membership in the society. He finds a religious justification for civic involvement. And in any event, the "resident alien" option, becoming Jewish Amish, is not a feasible one, if only for reasons of self-protection, as Stern makes clear.

The issue that troubles Stern is the contents of a Jewish politics in a democratic society, whether all Orthodox activity must be grounded in *halakhah* or whether extra-halakhic values are possible. If I understand him correctly, he leans toward the latter view. Moreover, he maintains

---

[25]See my paper referred to above, n. 6.

[26]Stanley Hauerwas and William Willimon, *Resident Aliens: Life in the Christian Colony* (Nashville: Abingdon Press, 1989).

that there might be social questions for which there is no controlling *halakhah*. In a sense, his problem is the reverse of Greenawalt's. The question is not whether there is a role for religious conviction in a liberal democracy, but rather whether there is a role for secular politics within the Jewish tradition. Stern concludes that American Jews, and Orthodox Jews, have done astoundingly well under secular democracy. "[I]t is the very secular nature of the government," he says, "that is responsible for our ability to participate on equal terms with our fellow citizens and to do so free of any serious threat of religious persecution."[27]

Marc Stern surveys the writings of several liberal theorists who would push to the margins people who speak on public issues out of a religious perspective. He dismisses their theory as just that: theory. In practice the Court has affirmed the right of religious individuals to speak to public issues on a religious basis. On this point, Stern surely is correct. But I think he dismisses too quickly the theoretical question of the terms on which Jews should participate in the debate. In the area in which the *halakhah*, or the tradition taken broadly, is not controlling, how do Jews participate *as Jews*? It is all well and good to say that we should pursue *ha-yashar ve-ha-tov*, but how do we give that Jewish content? Or do we in the end simply speak in the language of shared values as free and equal citizens of the liberal democratic polity? I am not sure of his answer.

The problem discussed here has its analog in another area. In a discussion of multiethnic societies, in a different context, Nathan Glazer points out that responses to that situation by a nation (for instance, on the questions of an official national language and bilingual education) will depend upon whether it sees the different groups as remaining "permanent and distinct constituents of a federated society" or whether it sees these groups as "ideally integrating into, and eventually assimilating, into a common society."[28] Clearly, Jews cannot accept the second alternative for themselves. Clermont-Tonnerre might have been right in being cautious.

I think Jews and all citizens need a better theory of citizenship in a religiously plural democracy than has yet been offered. But I am prepared to concede that the compromise that democratic practice has produced might be better than any theory that might be constructed.

---

[27]Marc D. Stern, "Jews and Public Morality," this volume, p. 200.

[28]Nathan Glazer, "Individual Rights against Group Rights," in *Human Rights*, ed. E. Kamenka and A. E.-S. Tay (New York: St. Martin's Press, 1978), 98.

7

A Comment on *Tikkun Olam*
and Political Activity

Nathan J. Diament

The American attitude toward political and civic activity by religious citizens and groups in our society's public sphere is currently the subject of heated debate. The essay by Marc Stern in this volume makes the case historically adopted by the Jewish community; namely, that the United States Constitution[1] requires strict separation between church and state and that religious minorities, such as Jews, benefit most from a secular society. According to this view, a secular society is one in which religion is principally relegated to the private sphere and any public manifestations of religious ideas must be clearly divorced from any possible connection to "the state." Any state support of religion (which is defined in broad terms) is viewed as a breach of the proscription against the establishment of religion.

In the closing paragraph of his essay, Mr. Stern takes to task those Orthodox Jewish groups that filed a brief with the United States Supreme

---

[1]The First Amendment of the Bill of Rights provides that "Congress shall make no law respecting an establishment of religion or prohibiting the free exercise thereof . . ."

Court in support of the Satmar Hasidim in the *Kiryas Joel* case.[2] Mr. Stern suggests that their advocacy for a reversal of Supreme Court precedent and a shift toward a view of religious pluralism as opposed to strict secularism was advanced out of "bitterness at the denial of aid to parochial schools" or a "tendency to reject all Western values including . . . Enlightenment and Emancipation" and a sense that "persecution and isolation" is "better . . . than the risks of an open society." It is to this suggestion as well as Mr. Stern's underlying theory that this note briefly responds.

As demonstrated by Martin Golding's essay, underlying Mr. Stern's view of the Constitutional attitude toward religion is the liberal demand that only "common modes of reasoning" based in secular rationalism are appropriate for use in the debates we have in our "public square." This underlying theory, however, has been severely critiqued by scholars.[3]

---

[2]Briefly, that case dealt with the following set of facts. The Village of Kiryas Joel, located in New York State, was a duly incorporated village populated almost exclusively by Satmar Hasidim. Many children of that community had various learning disabilities requiring a level of special education that the community *yeshivot* could not provide. After several different methods for providing special education through the public school system were unsuccessful, the New York Legislature with the approval of Governor Cuomo created a school district whose boundaries were coterminous with the Village of Kiryas Joel. That school district consisted of one school (because most children attended private *yeshivot*) that would provide wholly secular special education to the handicapped children of that and other local villages. The creation of this school district was challenged as a violating the First Amendment's proscription of the establishment of religion. New York State courts, including its highest court, found the school district's creation an unconstitutional establishment of religion. These rulings were principally based upon precedents rendered by the Supreme Court, which demanded a high degree of separation between church and state. (The courts employed the test set forth by the Court in *Lemon v. Kurtzman*, 403 U.S. 602 [1971]. This test requires that for a statute to survive an Establishment Clause challenge it must [1] have a primarily secular purpose, [2] with a primarily secular effect, and [3] not entangle the state with religion.) The case was appealed to the Supreme Court which similarly found the creation of the Kiryas Joel school district to violate the Establishment Clause. However, it must be noted, the Court did not base its determination upon the *Lemon* test.

[3]For the presentation of the liberal position, see John Rawls, *A Theory of Justice* (Cambridge, Mass.: Harvard University Press, 1971), 215. For a presentation

As noted in this volume's introduction, Chief Rabbi Jonathan Sacks has written that "one of the most powerful assumptions of the twentieth century is that faith . . . belongs to private life. Religion and society are two independent entities, so that we can edit God out of the language and leave our social world unchanged."[4] In a more general context, Alasdair MacIntyre described this phenomenon more elaborately:

> Any contemporary attempt to envisage a human life as a whole, as a unity . . . encounters two different obstacles . . . The social obstacles derive from the way in which modernity partitions each human life into a variety of segments, each with its own norms and modes of behaviour. So work is divided from leisure, private life from public, the corporate from the personal . . . The philosophical obstacles derive from . . . the tendency to think atomistically about human action and to analyze complex actions and transactions in terms of simple components . . . [as well as the tendency to make a] sharp separation . . . between the individual and the roles that he or she plays . . .[5]

The converse of these understandings of human personality and existence underlies the position taken by Mr. Stern or, in a more stark illustration, that taken by the French Assembly as noted in Martin Golding's essay; namely, that which the French National Assembly offered the Jews in 1789: nothing as Jews but citizenship as Frenchmen. It must be recognized, however, that asking religious citizens to suppress that aspect of their personality and cast their religious modes of reasoning and knowing the world aside in order to permit their participation in the public discourse is improper, if not impossible. This bifurcated view of the religious citizen contradicts the insight offered by MacIntyre above, along with the integrationist view of Modern Orthodoxy, and would be scorned if demanded of any other group of citizens.

There is another view of the First Amendment and the role of religion in our republic; a view contrary to Mr. Stern's, which is based upon an understanding of what the First Amendment's provisions were designed to achieve and which accounts for the insights of Sacks and

---

of the critique from a variety of philosophical standpoints, see Michael Sandel, ed. *Liberalism and Its Critics,* (New York: New York University Press, 1984).

[4]Jonathan Sacks, *The Persistence of Faith,* (Jews College, 1990), 27.

[5]Alasdair MacIntyre, *After Virtue,* 2nd. Ed. (Notre Dame, IN: University of Notre Dame Press 1981), 204.

MacIntyre as well. This view sees religion as a balancing force against the secular government and the Free Exercise and Establishment Clauses designed to protect religion from the state so that it may fulfill this role. It holds that the religion clauses are not to protect the state from religion, but religion from the state. Scholars of American history and law have demonstrated the foundational role that religion played in the early years after the Revolution and the role for religion envisioned by the Framers.[6] Alexis DeTocqeville recognized this as well when he described religion as "the first of [America's] political institutions."[7]

Currently, in the wake of some thirty years of Supreme Court jurisprudence that sought to separate church and state by constructing a wall of separation that was high and wide under the euphemism of "state neutrality toward religion", lawyers,[8] legal scholars,[9] and Justices of the Supreme Court[10] have questioned the current doctrine. It is, to say the least, in a state of flux. In brief, the argument advanced by those who dispute the current doctrine of strict separation is as follows. The Founders sought to ensure that the United States would be a religiously pluralistic society (rather than a secular society)[11] in which many religions could practice their faiths freely. Thus, the First Amendment pro-

---

[6]See, for example, Gordon S. Wood, *The Creation of the American Republic; 1776–1787* (New York: Norton, 1969); Akhil Amar, "The Bill of Rights as a Constitution," *Yale Law Journal* 100 (1991): 1131–1210; Phillip Kurland, "The Origins of the Religion Clauses of Constitution," *William and Mary Law Review* 27 (1986): 839–861; Michael McConnell, "Coercion: The Lost Element of Establishment," *William and Mary Law Review* 27 (1986): 933–941.

[7]Tocqueville, *Democracy in America*, ed. J. P. Mayer (New York: Harper & Row, 1988), 292.

[8]See, for example, *Brief for the National Jewish Commission on Law and Public Affairs* ("COLPA"), *as Amicus Curiae* filed in support of the Board of Education of the Kiryas Joel Village School District before the U.S. Supreme Court in 1994.

[9]For the most recent and sweeping presentation of this critique and the argument outlined below, see Stephen L. Carter, *The Culture of Disbelief* (New York: Basic Books, 1993).

[10]In 1993, for example, Justice Antonin Scalia cited the many instances in which then sitting Justices had criticized the state of religion clause doctrine. See, *Lamb's Chapel* v. *Center Moriches U.F.S.D.*, 113 S.Ct. 2141, 2150 (1993).

[11]It is in this context that the brief cited by Mr. Stern criticized "secular society" as the goal of church and state jurisprudence.

scribes the establishment of a state religion and mandates the accommodation of all religious groups and their faiths. It seeks, in short, to make the United States free *for* religion rather than free *from* religion. As presented by Professor Stephen Carter:

> The ideal of neutrality [toward religion] might provide useful protection for religious freedom in a society of relatively few laws, one in which most of the social order is privately determined. That was the society the Founders knew. In such a society, it is enough to say that the law leaves religion alone. It is difficult, however, to see how the law can protect religious freedom in the welfare state if it does not offer exemptions and special place for religion is the minimum it might be said that [the religion clauses do] . . . Neutrality treats religious belief as a matter of individual choice, an aspect of conscience, with which the government must not interfere but which it has no obligation to respect . . . indeed, it can be trampled by the state as long as it is trampled by accident.[12]

It is from this perspective that the recent development of constitutional doctrine, which reads the First Amendment as demanding a secular democratic order in which religious citizens may be denied some benefits to which citizens who profess other ideologies or beliefs are entitled, must be realized as incorrect. The religion clauses of the First Amendment are to be read as a coherent whole demanding the accommodation of religious beliefs and practices while ensuring that the state does not officially endorse or coerce religious activity.[13]

---

[12]Carter 133. A similar concern was noted by Justice Arthur Goldberg in *Abington v. Schempp*, 374 U.S. 203 at 306 (1963), wherein he warned against an "untutored devotion to the concept of neutrality" yielding an unconstitutional hostility toward religion.

[13]As mentioned, the discussion of this important issue in American civic life is ongoing and its resolution is yet to be determined. It is worth noting that, despite the rejection of the arguments advanced in the *Kiryas Joel* case outlined above, the Supreme Court did employ that theory (at least in part) the following term in *Rosenberger v. University of Virginia*, 115 S.Ct. 2510 (1995) (holding that a university subsidizing many student activity groups must also subsidize a Christian student newspaper and may not withhold funds based upon its religious viewpoint). Also, in July, 1995, President Clinton directed the Secretary of Education to issue guidelines to all public schools outlining the range of student religious activities permissible under current federal law.

Thus, the argument advanced in *Kiryas Joel*, for example, was advanced out of a belief diametrically opposite to Mr. Stern's characterization. It is a belief that religious citizens should be able to participate in all aspects of our open society to the same extent as non-religious citizens. Just as speech or ideas or actions may not be censored or restricted if they express racism, humanism, or environmentalism, expression and participation in society may not be restricted if they convey monotheism (or any other religious notion). Thus, went the argument, if the law provides for the public funding of schools for the disabled children of a community where all the residents believe in liberalism irrespective of their commonly held belief, then a community of Satmar Hasidim is just as entitled to have a publicly funded school (which teaches only secular subjects) to educate their disabled children.

It is worth noting that this understanding of the American constitutional view dovetails well with the Centrist Orthodox view described in the introduction to this volume. In "Confrontation," an essay cited frequently in this volume, the Rav posited an obligation upon Jews on the basis of their humanity to engage in the struggles that all people are involved in. He insisted that it is implicit in human existence that we must act as "human beings committed to the general welfare and progress of mankind . . . interested in combatting disease, in alleviating human suffering, in protecting man's rights, in helping the needy, *et cetera*." Again, as noted in the preface, Rav Soloveitchik, halakhist *par excellence*, did not marginalize the topic of Jewish participation in general society by seeking to define a specific imperative and the set of appropriate responses to narrowly fulfill that command. The Rav's language and rationale are reasonably understood as supporting a broad and ambitious conception of the nature of our obligations to society, and a similarly ambitious plan of action for the observant individual and his community to engage in. Mere peripheral engagement, or limited engagement for the sake of narrowly defined self interest is insufficient to meet this lofty standard.

In addressing the topic of political engagement by the Jewish community, Rabbi Aharon Lichtenstein has pointed to *Shabbat* 54b as an indication that our level of obligation is a function of our capability. There the Talmud states: "Any person who is able to rebuke the members of his household and fails to, is accountable for [the misdeeds] of the members of his household; [if he is able to rebuke] the citizens of his city, he is accountable for the [misdeeds of the] members of his city; [if he is able to rebuke] the entire world, he is accountable for the [misdeeds of the] entire world." Rabbi Lichtenstein reasoned that if responsibility falls upon those who are in a position to chastise potential misdoers with words, how much more responsibility falls upon those who can actually influence and shape the course of society's conduct.[14] As noted in the essays by Marc Stern and Jeffrey Ballabon, the American Jewish community in the closing decades of the twentieth century enjoys unprecedented opportunities to engage in political activity and thereby influence and shape society's conduct. The possibilities are of a magnitude unimaginable even by the generation of Jews that immigrated to these shores from Europe a scant fifty years ago. Jews, including Orthodox Jews, are "insiders" in the policy making process at local, state, and national levels. Thus, in Rabbi Lichtenstein's terms as well as the Rav's, these great opportunities generate equally great responsibilities.

Lastly, it is worth considering that political and civic activity is uniquely suited to achieving integrationist goals and to allowing the notion of *tikkum olam* to serve as the bridge between the secular and the religious.[15] Toward these ends, it must first be noted that "politics" must be thought of in broad terms. It is not confined to serving in government, whether in elected or appointed positions, nor is it confined to lobbying government entities. Rather, participation in the *polis*—the community—is manifested in non-governmental "mediating institutions" such as community councils, social action organizations, and other fora where citizens come together to address common problems. It is also manifested in civic-minded private sector activity such as corporate environmentalism, pro bono legal representation of the poor, and supporting services for the homeless. In the United States in particular, political activity in the non-governmental realms is encouraged.

The philosophy of limited government, which underlies American constitutional theory,[16] has as one of its key assumptions that citizens

---

[14]Aharon Lichtenstein, *The Interface of Torah and Politics* (1992). Audiotape on file with the author.

[15]It may serve other goals as well including the material self interest of the community and creating a context in which otherwise disconnected segments of the Jewish community can come together.

[16]This topic was recently discussed by the Supreme Court (although in a different context) in *United States v. Lopez*, 115 S.Ct. 1624 (April 26, 1995).

will join together without the prodding of the state to achieve commonly desired goals. It is expected that citizens of all backgrounds and persuasions, whether religious, atheistic, or agnostic, come together in the public square to shape this nation's public life. The constitutional position as well as the integrationist view of the Centrist Orthodox community clearly exhort us to participate fully in the political life of our city, state, and nation.

8

A View of *Tikkun Olam* from Capitol Hill

Jeffrey H. Ballabon

The Hebrews have done more to civilize men than any other nation. . . .The doctrine of a supreme intelligent . . . sovereign of the universe . . . I believe to be the great essential principle of all morality, and consequently of all civilization. —*John Adams, 1809*

[1] *TIKKUN OLAM*

Some introduction is in order to explain my approach to this paper. I have been asked to introduce into a theoretical discussion some thoughts on a practical model for the Modern Orthodox community to become involved in government policy-making in order to promote *tikkun olam*. I emphasize this last qualification because, although the words *tikkun olam* are not explicitly mentioned in the formula of the questions presented to me, it is my understanding that this entire forum is geared toward the promotion of that goal or something very similar to it.[1]

---

[1][Editors' note: At the time this paper was authored, Mr. Ballabon served as Legislative Counsel to Senator John Danforth (R. Mo.). The conveners of the Forum asked him (as well as Jack Bieler) to address the following questions:

223

For a variety of reasons, I am not convinced that *tikkun olam* is a viable source for policy-making to improve "society-at-large." Hazal's use of *tikkun olam* was extremely sparing. It is my sense that none of the talmudic *takkanot mi-penei tikkun ha-olam* had any application to gentile society, or even to gentile individuals. The argument that, as citizens in an egalitarian democracy, we now have both the unprecedented luxury and the burden of being able to influence the lives of outsiders can be made, but I am not sanguine that this was the reason that Hazal never extended *takkanot mipnei tikkun ha-olam*. Certainly, if *tikkun olam* were just a catch-all, it would have been used far more frequently by Hazal to legislate for Jewish society in accordance with their individual philosophies of social improvement and reform.

Thus, there are grounds to argue that it would be imprudent (and, perhaps, intellectually dishonest) to appropriate Hazal's own invention while ignoring its proper context and their circumspect application of the concept.[2] Moreover, there is no doubt that had Hazal conceived of this broad an application of the concept, the Gemara would be fraught with arguments between opposing *amoraim* about how to use the law to be *metakken*. Because—and this is a second flaw of the *tikkun olam* rationale—*tikkun* lacks normative substance, it is insufficient to dictate the form of *halakhah*.

It is also flawed as a prescriptive model because in its fundamental form, *le-takken olam be-malkhut shakkai* is not an exhortation to Israel; quite the contrary, it is in the context of "*al ken nekaveh lekha*." This, I would not characterize as a disqualifying flaw, although it is a discouraging one. It is not disqualifying despite the apparent lack of imperative to Israel, because an activist approach could be consistent with the aggres-

---

"What role can/should Jews play in the formation of government policy, both foreign and domestic? In what ways and to what extent do Jewish interests and the interests of the rest of society converge and to what extent do they conflict? How ought Jews in government positions make professional decisions, in terms of Jewish interests alone or in terms of general societal needs? What has the experience been of those Jews who have been active in political affairs?"]

[2]It is true that *tikkun* has been used in other than a *halakhic* context in traditional literature. Even in its kabbalistic sense, however, *tikkun* is used in reference to *Kelal Yisrael* alone and has to do with spiritual correction and *gilui malkhut Shamayim* rather than social amelioration.

sive stance adopted by Modern Orthodoxy and religious Zionism to set the stage for redemption and return. It is nonetheless discouraging because, as I will discuss more fully below, while there is much agreement relating to Israel and Zionism in the Modern Orthodox community, it is far more difficult to arrive at consensus on issues of domestic social policy.

Finally, *tikkun olam* is a deficient source because, even if there were agreement as to the best course to strengthen American society and make it more ethical, it is by no means clear that this is what is meant by *malkhut shakkai*. That goal, it seems, would require at the least overt acknowledgment that our policies are firmly Orthodox Jewish or, perhaps, rooted in Noahide ethical monotheism.[3] Any severing of this linkage, and the stated purpose of *tikkun* is lost. The impulse to ameliorate society which underlies this forum seems more oriented toward offering unilateral material and social assistance and ethical direction than to requiring a theological or religious concession in return.

Undeniably, the concept of *tikkun* is today in vogue, but its star seems to ascend from the Reform movement's promotion of a social, non-*halakhic* role for Judaism. As *halakhic* Jews, we can admire and share their social conscience. But if we purport to act as a community, we may be required to find a more compelling authority to guide our own actions.

[2] OTHER POSSIBLE SOURCES

Because there is no explicit scriptural or rabbinic imperative, the search for other possible *mekorot* is likely to result only in a derivative duty suggested by such phrases as *"or la-goyim"* or *"mamlekhet kohanim"* describing Israel's national status, or a duty by analogy from *ma'aseh avot*. We can also derive if not a duty then at least (to use a recently popular political term) "empowerment" to engage in social betterment policy from the general moral and ethical adjurations in *Tanakh*.

Certainly, in the Jewish society prescribed, for example, in Ex. 22:20–23 ("And a stranger you shall not wrong, neither shall you oppress him; for you were strangers in the land of Egypt. You shall not afflict any widow, or orphan. If you afflict them in any way—if he cries out to Me,

---

[3]This premise is assumed by Rabbi Bleich and Professor Broyde in their essays.

I will hear his cry.") and Deut. 14:29 ("And the Levite will come, because he has no portion in the land with you, and the stranger, and the orphan, and the widow, that are within your gates, and they will eat and be satisfied; so that the Lord your God will bless all the produce of your hands that you will do."), and elsewhere, Israel is commanded to implement ethical, just, and kind treatment for the oppressed, for widows, orphans, and aliens. As the *Gemara* in *Bava Metzia*, 59b, notes, Israel is warned no fewer than thirty-three (according to some, forty-six) times to ensure that its society does not mistreat gentiles. Similarly, in at least two places, *Avodah Zarah* 6b and *Nedarim* 62b, Hazal make it clear that it is a *de-oraita* transgression of *lifnei ivver* to lead a gentile to transgress that which is forbidden to him. *Avodah Zarah* states: "From whence do we derive that one should present a cup of wine to nazirite and a limb [torn] from a living creature to a Noahide? The verse states 'do not place a stumbling block before the blind.'"

The prophets, too, are often hailed as thunderous agitators for ethical society (see, e.g., Is. 58:6–8, Amos 5:12–15 and Micah 5:8), although their reputations seem to me to outpace the actual amount of energy they spent on "social justice" issues. In any event, as noted almost two decades ago, "although there is ample evidence to show that the ancient Hebrew prophets were striving for a just order of society, there is no evidence whatsoever that they laid down a concrete and detailed blueprint of how exactly such a just order of society is to come into existence, and how it is to be administered."[4]

Searching elsewhere for evidence of a duty of concern for the welfare of non-Jews, we find that Rambam asserts an affirmative duty in *Hilkhot Melakhim* 8:10,11 to influence gentiles to accept the Noahide code of laws: ". . . and so commanded Moses our teacher from [Divine Command] to force (*kofin*) all of the world's inhabitants to accept the *mitzvot* that the sons of Noah were commanded, and any person who did not accept them is to be put to death."

Ultimately, if all textual and traditional rabbinic sources fail to persuade, or if they can be distinguished by context, there remains the

---

[4]Jakob Petuchowski, "The Limits of Self Sacrifice," in *Modern Jewish Ethics*, ed. M. Fox (Ohio State University Press, 1975), 104–105.

argument from "*sekhel.*" This argument, which I believe to be the most convincing, is elegantly presented by R. Avraham Grodzinski of Slobodka in *Torat Avraham* based on a passage by R. Nissim Gaon: "All of those *mitzvot* which are contingent upon the *sevarah* (reasoning) and the insight of the heart; we were liable to fulfill them from the day that God created man on the earth . . . and those *mitzvot* which are known through revelation and prophecy . . ." As R. Grodzinski explains: "This is *Torat ha-adam*: everything that the *sekhel* of man is able to grasp, man is obligated to do and is punished for if he transgresses it, and according to its closeness to *sekhel*, so the [level of] obligation and punishment increases, for dear is man who was created in the image of God, his wisdom is derived from divine wisdom." And, lest *sekhel* be seen as a source inferior to the Torah, *Torat Avraham* quotes R. Yonah, who states in *Sha'arei Teshuvah*: "And I call the credible witnesses, *ha-sekhel, ve-hamikra'ot, ve-divrei hakhamim*; the *sekhel* is prior to the [latter two] because our rabbis knew of the nature and depth of logic, that it is heavenly."

Perhaps, then, this "*sekhel*" attribute is the ultimate source for the desire of some individuals to become involved in social-betterment projects. If so, perhaps they need look no further for support—unless these individuals are unwilling to permit "*sekhel*" to be the acknowledged source because they recognize that others might arrive at different conclusions about what needs to be done if left to their own *sekhel*'s devices. Hence this campaign to contrive an objective textual source.

Moreover, as powerful as is the argument of the *Torat Avraham* for the duty of every person—and, no less, every observant Jew—it leads to no imperative regarding Orthodox Jews as a faith community to act together and exclusively.[5] On the contrary, I would argue that it leads Jews as individuals to join with other individuals, regardless of faith or background, to accomplish good works. It should prompt leaders from within

---

[5]Of course, one reason to act as a community is to get credit for the achievement; another is to help uplift the community. Each of these justifications raises its own problem. The former rationale is pure self-interest and justifies social action without accepting the *tikkun olam* rationale. The latter's bears the additional tension of treating non-Jews as objects to use as means to better Israel. Neither of these objections exists in a model reliant upon the individual human *sekhel* imperative rather than communal halakhic imperative.

our community to encourage and promote such activity, but it is in no way a "Jewish" undertaking. Rather, it is a human undertaking.[6]

To conclude, because I have both the luxury and the burden of assuming that participants at the earlier session have agreed that normative Judaism dictates some political action can, should, or must be taken, it is not expected that I take a position on the threshhold matter. I will assume it as a given.

However, whether the *"sekhel"* construct of the *Torat Avraham* is the ultimate mandate or one is persuaded that the answer lies in some text or ordinance, the Jew embarking on a course of social amelioration will find little guidance other than the dictates of his conscience.

But to respond constructively to my assigned questions, it will not suffice to conclude that we should do "good" or be "upright" or "just" and "righteous." These terms are insufficient to form the basis of political philosophy and political action. Regardless of our commitment to furthering those ideals through the political process, we must first arrive at a far more definite set of principles.

[3] EXISTING MODELS

Perhaps the best—in the sense of most appropriate as well as effective— model for Modern Orthodoxy to consider is that of Agudath Israel of America. Agudath Israel has established a respected and known presence in Washington, as well as with the state and local governments where its constituency is concentrated. Agudah is known both for its effective advocacy for its constituency as well as for its firm stances on many social/ethical issues in American society at large.

A glance at Agudath Israel's methods for setting policy, however, will demonstrate immediately why Modern Orthodoxy faces a far greater (I

---

[6]Arguments inevitably will be made that Jews invite assimilation and other evils from prolonged contact with others. For those who fear these results, engaging in initiatives with other Jews alone (and even primarily benefiting Jews) is clearly preferable to no good works and, after all, *"aniyei irkha kodemin."* Still, I think that these fears are less prominent among Modern Orthodox Jews. If bettering humanity vests in our humanity and not in our revelation from Sinai, therefore, why is it "Jewish" at all?

believe insurmountable) challenge to establishing as strong a presence on social/ethical issues:

> The Moetzes Gedolei HaTorah and the Nesius of Agudath Israel of America are guided by three considerations when issues of public policy arise: (1) Does Torah Judaism have a position that is either not expressed by or contrary to the public policies of the mainstream Jewish organizations? (2) If so, do the interests of the Orthodox community require that they take a position and fight for it? (3) Even if there is no direct impact on Orthodox interests, or no realistic chance that Orthodox advocacy will change public policy, does *k'vod Shamayim* nonetheless require that the Torah view on an issue be made known?[7]

It is immediately clear that Agudath Israel considers its operation to have two roles—advocate for its own community's interests and spokes-man for the Torah view. Both of these, I will argue, are important roles for the Modern Orthodox community as well. However, the first (which is given short shrift by some idealists) will be far easier to achieve than the second.

In a previous Orthodox Forum, R. Aharon Lichtenstein explicated the difference between the "modern Orthodox Jew and his *haredi* coun-terpart." According to Rav Lichtenstein: "Few elements distinguish the typical modern Orthodox Jew from his *haredi* counterpart more than their respective instinctive relations to authority. To the latter, authority . . . is a wholly unmixed blessing. . . . the authority of *gedolim* is not only ac-cepted but relished. They are regarded—indeed, experienced—as both fountains of wisdom and towers of strength. . . . The modern Orthodox Jew's relation, by contrast, is far more circumspect—if not, indeed am-bivalent. . . .[He] bridles at the thought of constricting his autonomy."[8]

Viewed in this light, it is clear that determining a communal stance on public policy matters, though a relatively straightforward task for Agudath Israel's public affairs department, might be impossible for a simi-

---

[7]R. Nosson Scherman, "Spokesman in the Halls of Government: Agudath Israel's Evolving Public Role in Shtadlonus and Advocacy," *The Jewish Observer* 25,4 (May 1992): 28–37.

[8]R. Lichtenstein's paper appears in volume 5 of the Orthodox Forum Series, ed. Moshe Sokol.

lar modern Orthodox entity. For the Agudah, a small group of *gedolim* create policy when they arrive at a consensus. This ex cathedra consensus determines, with force of law, *the* Torah approach as well as the requirements of "*kevod Shamayim.*" The decision is not subject to popular debate. This is not to suggest that there is never dissent or grumbling within what R. Lichtenstein calls the "haredi" camp, due to a position adopted by its leaders. But, on a practical operational level, the system brooks no defiance or deviance.

Who can do the same for Modern Orthodoxy? This is clearly a rhetorical question, because it is not a lack of learning, but a fundamental departure in approach which renders Modern Orthodoxy incapable of asserting a universal social/ethical position on almost any issue of public policy that is likely to arise. Paradoxically, what distinguishes Modern Orthodox Jews and binds them together is their diversity (within, of course, the parameters of *halakhah*). Indeed, in a perfect example of the exception that proves the rule, there is one issue on which Modern Orthodoxy and *haredim* switch shoes: *Medinat Yisra'el*. Where American Modern Orthodoxy communally and ardently lobbies in Washington and gathers in support of the State of Israel, the *haredi* camp is divided and, therefore, usually silent. Modern Orthodox Jews are outspoken and activist for Israel as they are for no other issue.

[4] A MODEL FOR MODERN ORTHODOX INVOLVEMENT

Communal

I have no doubt that the above prognosis for Modern Orthodox political involvement will be resisted. It sounds uncomfortably fatalistic. But that is only half the analysis—there is good news as well.

Despite the fractious philosophies of the Modern Orthodox constituency, there are some widely held, if not universal, tenets. First, as noted above, is a commitment to the flourishing of the State of Israel. This does not mean that Modern Orthodox Jews will never dispute how to approach a policy or action of the Israeli government (e.g., the September 13, 1993 Declaration of Principles). For most purposes, however, there will be agreement as to United States policy toward Israel sufficient to articulate a communal position. In the arena of domestic and international human rights, as well, Jews, including Modern Orthodox Jews, have through the travails of our history acquired a special sensitivity to abusive governments. Similarly, on many constitutional issues, particularly the free exercise of religion and the separation of church and state, Modern Orthodox Jews can achieve some communal consensus.

No doubt, there are other issues on which communal agreement can be reached. These should be sought out and defined, because the first arena for Modern Orthodox involvement in policy is in those areas of general application that resonate universally in the community.

The second arena for political involvement is self-interest. I realize that this sounds less than edifying, and might even offend those who intend for us to make an unsullied ethical "*tikkun olam*." But I believe it is vital that Modern Orthodox Jews shed their disdain for . . . well, for (political) "pork."

Without digressing too far, I surmise that this discomfiture stems from two sources. First, is a misguided transfer of our ingrained relationship to God to our relationship with the government. Israel comes annually before *ha-Melekh ha-Kadosh* to lobby for ten days. During that time, the time that He is most accessible to us, and we are most vulnerable and aware of His power of absolute judgment, we are cautioned by Hazal not to ask for boons for the nation, or ourselves. Rather, we ask for His *malkhut* to become known. True, we ask that God grant respect for His nation, rejoicing for His land, and so on. But it is our clear intention that this be granted only because of the glory it reflects on Him. The notion that Israel's status reflects on God is well documented in the canon, as noted by Professor Blidstein in his paper. In fact, that is made explicit in the liturgy. It is this attitude that, when transferred to American government, is misguided. In America, the reverse obtains: the people are not the means to our government's end, rather it is the government that exists to serve the people.

One aspect of America's participatory democracy is that constituents have access to elected officials—who serve at their pleasure—to seek benefits for themselves. It is of great moment to elected officials that they keep their constituents happy. So, it is not only not wrong or ethically suspect; it is not only not subversive; lobbying for one's own community's interest is expected. It is as American as apple pie. Altruism is not a hallmark of respected and effective lobbying.

The second reason that Jews might be reluctant is a little more difficult to refute, because it is not actually an explanation of why Jews seek
to help others at their own expense. Instead, it is the thought that this
selflessness is actually a defense mechanism—a preemptive strike against
claims of Jewish grasping selfishness and separatism that have plagued
us from Pharaoh to Haman to Hitler. In this light, voting for the interests of others at our own expense is actually a circuitous way of voting
our own interests. If that is the rationale, I have no fundamental disagreement, except that it might not actually be effective.

I do not mean to be cavalier about the issue of self-interest. I believe
there is a significant amount to be accomplished for the Jewish community, which is certainly not a lesser responsibility for the modern Orthodox community than is working for society-at-large. I also believe that
the two interests are complementary rather than exclusive. It is my observation that Agudath Israel's very strong reputation on Capitol Hill is
one of conservatism with thoughtfulness, integrity, straightforwardness,
and reasonableness. Much of that reputation was earned while Agudah
pursued very self-interested legislation. But its effects can be felt when
Agudah lobbies for a social issue as well.

Individual

But Modern Orthodox involvement need not end there. The truth about
politics is that policies seldom anticipate all contingencies. In other words,
"Many are the thoughts in a man's heart, but the counsel of the Lord
will prevail" (Prov. 19:21). The Torah assigns us only goals, not practical policy choices. We know that we want to make ours a just society
and a righteous society—we just do not know how. That does not mean
we are free to shirk the task as a community or as individuals.

Judaism anticipates our imperfections. With regard to perfection, we
are shown that God knows our limitations but will not let us off the hook.
We have a duty to act even if we cannot complete the task. Indeed, the
pursuit is itself the imperative: Deut. 16:20: "Justice, justice, shall you
pursue." And again: Prov. 21:21: "One who pursues charity, justice, and
lovingkindness will find life, justice, and honor." Ps. 34:14: "Turn from
evil and do good; seek justice and pursue it." And again: *Avot*, 1:12: "Be
among the disciples of Aaron: a lover of peace and a pursuer of peace . . ."

The Modern Orthodox Jew need not be excluded by virtue of his independence. On the contrary, when there is communal agreement as to a policy, halakhic Jews should act in concert. We should lobby, write to our legislators, pass resolutions. But where there is no special divine revelation, and reasonable Jews disagree, they must act as individuals.

Indeed, Modern Orthodoxy can (and does) coexist with both liberal and conservative, Democrat and Republican philosophies. A wide divergence of opinion is possible on issues from crime and punishment to education to civil rights to health care to trade to foreign policy. There is no revealed truth about welfare reform. I might argue that we need immediate workfare to end the cycle of dependency that plagues the inner city and drains our resources and moral fiber. I might cite Rambam to support this argument as the highest form of *tzedakah*. You might argue that workfare is too demanding and too many of society's neediest and weakest would fall through the cracks without welfare. Indeed, you, too, could cite Rambam to show that it is better to give even a lower form of *tzedakah* to those individuals than to give only superior *tzedakah* to fewer people. Both of us could be arguing *le-shem Shamayim*, but we have no way of determining which of us is correct. That is the plight of the Modern Orthodox. But it need not end in inaction.

The Torah requires that we pursue the just and peaceful society, not that we attain it. "It is not upon you to finish the task, yet you are not free to withdraw from it" (*Avot* 2:21). The task is worthy, and the pursuit, ennobling.

[5] A PLAN OF ACTION

The modern Orthodox community is educated, interested and involved in affairs of the world. It must recognize its capacity to affect policy and legislation on matters of communal concern and agreement. This can be accomplished by establishing and supporting presences in Washington and at the state level. These presences must establish a reputation and working relationships with policymakers who are interested in the well-being of our communities as well as earn respect as intelligent advocates.

To some extent, this is already being done. Institutions such as the Union of Orthodox Jewish Congregations have a sophisticated understanding of the system and use it to preserve very important communal interests, particularly relating to Israel, *kashrut*, *get* laws and the like. Existing Modern Orthodox Jewish institutions should stop excusing inaction based on the existence of other organizations—notably the American Israel Public Affairs Committee (AIPAC)—which already represent their positions. Certainly, AIPAC is becoming more sensitive to Orthodox Jewry, but the best way to become effective as Orthodox Jews is to become involved. No matter how confluent our agendas (and, since September 1993, their public position has been questioned by many in the Orthodox community), AIPAC is not committed to the same values and ideals as we. Our positions should reflect this either through AIPAC or side-by-side with AIPAC.

Clergy and other leaders can undertake to keep their congregants informed and aware of policy issues of interest to the Jewish community and to all Americans. If there is a clear halakhic consensus, then the communities should be mobilized to act, at the least to contact their representatives and express their opinions. When there is an important debate about which there is no clear halakhic mandate, then community leaders should urge individuals to lobby or vote or agitate for whatever solution those individuals believe to be most beneficial to society.

[6] CONFLICTS OF INTEREST

It is hard to imagine a scenario in which a policy would be unmitigated evil for society and unmitigated good for Jews (or vice versa). Most policies have costs and benefits and require balancing of competing interests. Were such an initiative to arise, there is little question that our community must act out of self-preservation. Of course, self-preservation is often a complicated calculus that takes *darkhei shalom* into account.

One recent example was the 1992 sale of F-15 fighter jets to Saudi Arabia. Early on, in anticipation of the sale, the pro-Israel community began to press Congress to reject the sale. As the sale date grew nearer, however, it was realized that approval of the sale meant literally tens of thousands of jobs for several years in the suffering defense industry. A successful assault on the sale would surely result in backlash against Israel and its friends in America. Instead, political leaders and the defense industry worked out concessions from the Saudis that guaranteed a qualitative edge would remain with Israel and that the Saudis would base the F-15s further away from Israel than they would have based jets they purchased from the British or French. Under these terms, Israel received a little more security than she would have had the Saudis simply bought from another country, and Israel did not have to test its friendship with America against a very important boost for America's economy. Were such an arrangement not made, or were the weapons enough to make Israel fear for her survival, then the results would no doubt have been different. An even more dramatic illustration of this principle took place not in America, but in Israel during the Gulf War. Israel's excruciating decision to allow itself to be the passive target of Scuds is a perfect demonstration of the fact that conflicts of interest are seldom all-or-nothing propositions.

However, it might be more interesting to consider the more troubling conflicts that arise between Jewish interests and ethical interests. Consider a bill in the 103d Congress, S. 1677, proposed by Senator Hatfield, which would prohibit the United States from providing military assistance and arms transfers to foreign governments "that are undemocratic, do not adequately protect human rights, are engaged in acts of armed aggression, or are not fully participating in the United Nations Register of Conventional Arms." The bill happens to vest in the State Department the discretion to determine which governments do not meet the enumerated standards. Assuming, as we have, that Judaism holds some mandate to assist society to become more ethical, it would seem clear that we should support this initiative. In practice, however, especially given historic tendencies of the State Department, Israel might find itself listed as a country that does not adequately protect human rights. Perhaps Israel would be forced to take a preemptive strike, as in 1967, and find itself in an act of armed aggression. There is little room for doubt that a politically activist Orthodox community would have to oppose this initiative, or at least remain silent and unsupportive. Supporters of Israel would lobby hard to keep Israel off the black list. But to address the conflict-of-interest question, I do not think the situation will ever appear to us to be a true conflict. Whether accurately or myopically, the Modern Orthodox community accepts almost as an article of faith the moral superiority of a world with a strong State of Israel.

Thus, as intriguing as the inquiry is, the conflict-of-interest question will seldom arise in a purely moral or philosophical setting for the Jewish activist. Rather, some concession to public opinion will be made, while self-interest is pursued.

[7] A FINAL WORD

We convene, as members of a community, to determine whether we have a communal duty. Regardless of our discourse today, there are likely to be individuals sharing our commitment and concern for *halakhah* who are thrust by circumstances or choice into positions where they are able to influence American public policy or, indeed, are charged with influencing policy. But the far more salient question is communal. It implicates our role as a *kelal*, our need to prioritize, to husband resources and, perhaps most difficult, to contrive and represent communal policy consensus.

Certainly, there are unique and interesting halakhic questions that arise in the course of employment as a public servant with the ability to influence policy and law. For example, as one who draws salary from the state coffers, do you violate the trust of your employers, not to mention your oath to defend the Constitution, if you promulgate (albeit anonymously) a church agenda? Is it proper on the basis of personal religious commitment to champion a policy, perhaps inferior to another in some respects, but nonetheless reasonable and defensible on legitimate, non-church grounds? How do you balance the desire and mandate to avoid establishing state religion as you strive to protect the free exercise of religion? Is there a response in *halakhah* to the classical question of the elected official: Do I do what my constituents think is best or what I think is best for them?

There are also unique opportunities. To present just one example, although it was hotly debated in the House of Representatives (it ultimately passed), an amendment which I drafted, condemning the anti-Semitic diatribe of Nation of Islam spokesman Khalid Mohammed, passed the Senate 97-0. It is nothing more than a "Sense of the Senate" resolution. On the other hand, the United States government had never responded in this way to mere speech. It could be argued that this resolution was a mistake, because it had a chilling effect on free speech. It could be argued that it was a mistake, because it merely stoked Mohammed's fire to speak out more. In fact, in the House of Representatives, those arguments were made. On the other hand, it was also argued that a diatribe of this magnitude and this notoriety emanating from an organization that was engaged in a "sacred covenant" with members of Congress, deserved unequivocal condemnation. That Congress can and should speak out for what is right and against evil.

The balancing of these issues is a challenge and it is impossible to foresee the outcomes of policies made to impact hundreds of millions of people. Perhaps, therefore, I conclude where I began—with a reliance on the imperative of "*sekhel.*"

In the American political system constituencies are expected to petition their government for their own needs while being mindful of the competition for resources and other limitations inherent in a pluralistic nation. The Orthodox community is clearly able to engage in these activities and is as entitled to do so as any other constituency. And, while I believe that inherent in the nature of Modern Orthodoxy and its insistence on autonomy are barriers to communal policy decisions, it is equally evident that, as individuals, members of the Modern Orthodox community, who are broadly engaged in all other aspects of American life, who balance the private and public on a regular basis, and who integrate *halakhic* principles into everyday life, are uniquely qualified to engage in the political aspect of American life as well.

9

Social Responsibilities of the Jewish Individual*

Meir Tamari

I. INTRODUCTION

The topic of the provision of welfare, like any other socio-economic subject, is by definition inter-disciplinary. It creates, therefore, special didactic problems arising out of the admixture of ostensibly objective subjects such as economics, accounting, and public policy, with subjective ones such as philosophy, social values, and political institutions. In this process, personal bias, the prevailing socio-economic philosophies, and hidden agendas distort the discussion, unless these biases are made clear and the agenda specifically presented. In the case of a Jewish perspective, there is an even greater danger, which requires constant vigilance if we are not to present an intellectually dishonest perspective. Specifically, one might be predetermined to present Judaism not in its authenticity, but rather in a way that makes it palatable and publicly acceptable. However, both the halakhic rulings and the philosophic or moral parameters of Judaism are primarily concerned with case law, op-

---

*This paper is based on the detailed study which forms part 2 of my book *The Challenge of Wealth: A Jewish Perspective on Earning and Spending Money* (Northvale, NJ: Jason Aronson, 1994).

erating within a clearly defined communal structure, with recourse to
rabbinic courts to adjudicate the conflicting claims that exist in welfare
presentation. Hence the possible introduction of foreign non-Jewish and
perhaps anti-Jewish thought into this perspective is a major concern.

In the early years of this century, Judaism was equated with socialism
and communism. The teachings of the Prophets, along with halakhic
rulings with regard to the rights of workers and society's intervention in
the market place, were seized upon by the majority, or masses, of Jews to
present the Torah falsely as a handmaid or a vehicle for socialism in its
various forms.[1] So, too, the present-day fascination with the free market
seems to be leading to a blurring of the social obligations, unashamedly
presented by Judaism, that curtail the creation of wealth both at the
individual and the communal level, and/or determine the use of that
wealth in order to, inter alia, achieve definite patterns of social justice.
The truth is that both seem to be a perversion of Judaism's role in the
marketplace, which is neither socialist nor capitalist, but an "ism" of its
own.

Personal biases are unfortunately almost impossible to eradicate. Nevertheless, cognizance must be taken of the existence of these biases, and
attempts to limit them constantly pursued. There is no doubt in my mind
that my presentation is, inter alia, a reflection of experience and knowledge gained from non-Jewish circles or sources. I can only atone for them
by stressing the dangers of biases and hoping that I have kept them to a
minimum.

At the same time, it is essential to remember that despite the presentation by many economists of their subject as a value-free discipline,
similar to the physical sciences, it is easy to demonstrate that, in fact,
all forms of economics, from the purest free-market to the most stringent of planned economies, are partially the result of moral, religious, or
social values. The statistical presentation of economic data and the mathematical structure of econometrics, serves, all too often, only to hide the
value structure of the proponents, as though what is being presented are
economic laws rather than a system dependent inter alia on the particu-

---

[1]A. Wolfson, "Jewish Cultural Sources for the Israeli Welfare Ideology," (Heb.)
Journal of Welfare and Social Security Studies 3, 1 (1977) 16. See also D. Ben
Gurion, *Development and Security* (Heb.) (Tel Aviv: Hoveret Bittahon, 1954).

lar values of the authors. The same applies to the economic discussion of welfare and social policies. There is no need, therefore, for us to be overly concerned with the introduction of spiritual and religious values flowing from Torah into this discussion. This is no less legitimate than the ideological concepts that lie behind orthodox and acceptable welfare economics. One example should suffice to demonstrate that applying a Jewish perspective to welfare, is intellectually and practically, no different from any of the theories and policies advocated today in the general world.

Economic regulation and government intervention in the market place in order to achieve a desired social safety net or the provision of health, social services, education, and so on, are, in fact, reflections of theological or philosophical questions regarding the nature of the human being. Enlightened self-interest, the ideological basis for morally correct self-regulation and free markets, seem to flow primarily from a Christian concept of the sufficiency of faith and grace to prevent evil acts or to promote charity and welfare.[2] Couched in secular terms, the same economic issue is really only an aspect of different attitudes to freedom and uncertainty, both ideological or spiritual concepts. F. A. Hayek, M. Friedman and I. Kirzner, although discussing economic matters, are actually presenting a case for the supremacy of individual freedom.[3] In planned economies, and perhaps even in aspects of present-day Japanese economy, the protection of the individual against the uncertainties of life in general, and economic hardship in particular, is actually being purchased in exchange for the loss of individual freedom. The sovereignty of the consumer, which is the basis of the market place, is really a value judgement regarding the ability of the individual to make his own decisions wisely and to suffer or enjoy the consequences thereof. Planned economies, on the other hand, are basically an implementation of the philosophical idea that the planner is able to better provide for the individual a desired quality of life, social security, old age, and so on, than the individual. The issue, therefore, of more or less bureaucracy in

---

[2] R. H. Tawney, *Religion and the Rise of Capitalism* (Harmondsworth, Eng.: Pelican Books, 1964), ch. 2.

[3] B. Griffiths, *Morality and the Market Place* (London: Hodder and Stoughton, 1980).

the market place, more or less public intervention to achieve social welfare, is not only an economic one but also a reflection of attitudes to society's own ideas of democracy.

In contrast to all these attitudes, the Judaic view of human acts as a solution to immorality, through a divine or revealed code of law, severely limits the scope of self-regulation and the efficiency of enlightened self-interest. Judaism's emphasis on the community and the national entity, as a framework for individual redemption, will therefore enhance or encourage an economy aimed at achieving or providing welfare of different sorts and at different levels through the agencies of state and group control. At the same time, though, public intervention and regulation are also limited and controlled, as is evidenced in the laws of kingship. This role of the public sectors would stand in contradiction not only to Christian thought, but also to those of the religious or social philosophies of the Far East, which are quite dominantly concerned with individual spiritual redemption.[4] It is interesting to point out the similarities between Islam and Judaism in the acceptance of communal intervention and legislation in the field of welfare.

Naturally, the understanding that welfare policies are not only economic policies but also a reflection of spiritual, religious, and philosophical ideas, does not do away with real problems of costs, of allocations and of limits. But it is necessary to reject the idea that, in some form or other, the Jewish perspective based on religion is in any way less legitimate than welfare economics, supposedly based on pure unadulterated economic thinking.

II. SOCIAL RESPONSIBILITY AS AN INTEGRAL PART OF JUDAISM

Jews and non-Jews alike, have consistently recognized that caring for others, providing for the needs of the poor, the weak, the orphan, and the stranger, and the necessity to use one's wealth for this purpose, is a hallmark of Jewish thought and practice. It is therefore without any apology and without any attempt to present a low-key attitude, that any Jewish perspective must be presented.

---

[4] J. Trevian, *The Middle Way: Buddhist Economics* (Villanova University Press, 1983).

Law and philosophy, education and biblical commentary, have all combined to make acts of mercy and righteousness the model for the Jew. We use the full power of the law to enforce charitable acts, and we consider one who does not do favors or assist another to have cast doubt on his ancestry as the son of Avraham, Father of Israel. The *Sefer ha-Hinukh* sees the purpose of the agricultural gifts to the poor, *leket, shikehah* and *pe'ah*, the sabbatical year, as well as injunctions to make interest-free loans, all as means of educating the Jew towards mercy and kindness to others. God Himself is seen as the provider of welfare. At the beginning of the Torah, He clothes the naked, Adam and Eve. At the end of *Devarim*, He buries Moshe, an act of *hesed*, of righteousness. Because man, in the Jewish perspective, is to be taught to achieve holiness in imitation of the deity, these acts must be made an integral part of Jewish life.

But this kindness, this welfare, if one wishes to call it such, is not merely a spiritual obligation. Its neglect can be the cause of political and social destruction of Jew and Gentile alike. Pestilence comes to the world, destruction comes to the world, because of neglect of the tithes and the gifts to the poor.[5] Seventy years, our ancestors spent in Babylon to pay recompense for neglect of the sabbatical year. The Talmud tells us that Jerusalem and the Temple were destroyed because Jewish religious leaders did not prevent the people from insisting on legal rights rather than forgoing those same rights in the interests of charity and kindness.[6] The people of Sodom were destroyed for a sin that is not clear in the Torah. Their evil acts are stated without being described, and many of the commentators show that what was involved was a rejection of the Jewish teaching of welfare and *hesed*. Malbim tells that the people of Sodom were wealthy and that their real sin consisted of acts that were aimed at preventing the poor among the surrounding peoples from coming in and sharing their wealth.[7] It is noteworthy perhaps, that although we teach our children of the Sodomites' objection to visitors and to *hakhnasat orehim*, Lot was quite welcoming in Sodom, the only difference being that Lot was wealthy. There is a parallel today: migrant workers, people seeking employment, and the oppressed have great difficulty in entering the

---

[5]Mishnah, *Avot* 5:13.
[6]*Bava Metzia* 30b.
[7]Malbim, *Bereshit* 13:13.

wealthy Western societies, while capitalist visas are provided easily and quickly. In Sodom, they even covered the fruit of the trees in order to prevent the birds having their share of wealth. Once this egotism and selfishness became institutionalized and legal, Sodom had to be destroyed. Sodom constituted a threat to the very soul of *Eretz Yisrael*, promised to Abraham. After all, he is characterized by human kindness, by concepts of mercy and acts of *hesed*, which constitute Judaism's understanding of the use of wealth.[8]

It is suggested here that this social responsibility flows from three separate concepts: guardianship; the brotherhood of man; and the economics of enough.

a) Guardianship

God could have provided for the needs of the poor, the weak, the strangers, and the afflicted, directly. Instead of that, He provided individuals with the ability, the knowledge, and the facilities to create wealth. That wealth serves many purposes, such as the needs of one's family and one's children, yet at the same time it is also provided in order to fulfill another aspect of human life, namely assistance to others. Samson Raphael Hirsch points out that one may not charge interest and is obligated to provide interest-free loans, because one purpose of the wealth given to us is to assist another; that part of the wealth does not really belong to us, so to speak, and therefore we may not earn interest on it. This is not a negation of private property. On the contrary, protection of private property is clearly and repeatedly enunciated in halakhic rulings regarding theft, damages, and so forth. At the same time, however, there is nothing unlimited in Judaism; therefore, there is no such thing as unlimited private property. It is legitimate to earn and to have this property, it is not legitimate to use this property solely for the satisfaction of one's own selfish needs.

b) The Brotherhood of Man

Because a human being is created in God's image and, originally, only one human being was created, the belief in divine creation must of

---

[8]*Shem Mi-Shmuel, Parshat va-Era.*

necessity support the belief in the brotherhood of all human beings. There is not only a vertical relationship in Judaism between man and God, but also a horizontal one, between individuals. This horizontal relationship is expressed in many different aspects of Torah and is possibly the only moral justification for holding people responsible for inhumane acts, callousness, and unkindness to each other. It is interesting to notice in this regard, that the first chapters of Amos, which deal with expressions of callousness and disregard, are pertinent to relationships between two non-Jewish peoples. It is only later that the same yardstick is applied to relationships within the Jewish kingdom, between one Jew and another.[9] It is true that there exists a special relationship among Jews as members of a religious ethnic group. However, this does not detract from or in any way obviate the relationships or social obligations regarding those who are non-Jews.

Acts of charity and kindness are therefore obligatory for the Jew with regard to non-Jews as well, a corollary to the concept that all men were created in God's image. Therefore, it is halakhically necessary to support the poor of the nations, together with the Jewish poor.[10] It is necessary to bring in the implements of non-Jews from the fields in order to protect them. There were authorities who frowned heavily on lending money at interest to non-Jews, even though this is permissible.[11] The fact that these citations explain that these actions should be performed "for the sake of peace," does not detract in any way from the social obligation extended to all men. So, too, the limitations expressed on non-Jewish charity are simply extensions of the accepted notion that there are limitations even on charity. The differences are those of degree, not kind.

Furthermore, the concept of the sanctification of God's name, *kiddush ha-Shem*, through acts of undeserved kindness and righteousness, with regard to non-Jews, is repeated in rabbinic sources.[12] One must bear in mind that the positive obligation to sanctify God's name

---

[9]Amos 1–5.

[10]*Mishneh Torah, Hilkhot Melakhim* 10:12. Also *Hilkhot Mattenot Aniyyim*, 1:9; 6:7.

[11]*Mekhilta*, 22:24; Rab Hiyya in *Bava Metzia* 70b–71a.

[12]*Talmud Yerushalmi, Bava Metzia* 4:5.

applies to all Jews at all times, including men and women, as explained by the Rambam.[13]

c) Economics of Enough

All acts of kindness, the fulfillment of social obligations, and the acceptance of responsibility for the needs of others entail, in the last resort, giving away some portion of our wealth. A society in which "more is always better than less" is the individual's credo, will find it hard to implement any socially motivated policy. Only when people can accept the concept that there is a stage of enough can they share their wealth with others. There can be no doubt that Judaism presents exactly this concept. Maimonides, describing the lifestyle of the *talmid hakham*, Judaism's role model, presents a picture of modesty and restraint in consumption.[14] The patriarch Jacob, answers his brother Esau's "I have much" with "I have enough."[15] The other examples of economic modesty, found in all sources, amply support this point.

Fear that the "economics of enough" could lead to recession and economic stagnation through a reduction in demand, shortage of funds for development, and the substitution of social criteria in investment for economically viable principles seems to be based both on an error in economics and on a misreading of Jewish social teachings.

Economic modesty is not the same thing as a negation of things material, nor is it the embracing of a religion of poverty. Both of these can lead to the dire economic conditions feared, because they deny the validity of wealth creation and the legitimacy of economic needs. Primitive communism, monastic life, and the otherworldliness of the Eastern religions and possibly of some forms of Christianity, in fact, bring economic stagnation. However, the Judaism of Maimonides' *talmid hakham* has as its founders rich men. All the patriarchs were rich with flocks and herds, men and maidservants, gold and silver, while the nazarite brought a sin offering for his rejection of the material things of life.

Judaism's economics of enough is simply a realignment of patterns of demand and investment, not a negation of either. It is not comparable

---

[13]*Mishneh Torah, Hilkhot Yesodei ha-Torah* 5:6.
[14]Ibid., *Hilkhot De'ot* 5.
[15]*Bereshit* 33:24.

to the decline of demand or negative growth that characterizes economies during periods of recession; then, it is fear of uncertainty that causes demand and investment to dry up. Transfer of wealth, either voluntary or through taxation, to solve social problems is, in fact, often a major stimulant to growth. The waves of immigration to Israel always placed severe strains on its social budget, yet they led to periods of great economic growth; the recent *aliyah* of Russians and Ethiopians is only one example.[16] The social budget is an investment in infrastructure (housing, education, and health) that ultimately pays economic dividends. By and large, it has been factors such as low productivity, non-cost-related welfare and exaggerated populism, rather than a serious commitment to welfare, that has been the cause of recession and stagnation.

III. INDIVIDUAL AND COMMUNAL

It is not possible to present a Jewish perspective on welfare restricted only to the individual, because the duality that exists in many aspects of Judaism exists here also. There are two concepts operating in Jewish welfare. There is the biblical commandment that one is obligated to open one's hand to the poor, but there is also a negative injunction in the verse: "thou shalt not close thy hand." Thus we have acts of individual kindness and righteousness, which are voluntary and flow from a sense of personal involvement, but also a power given to society to enforce legislation aimed at creating these acts. The former, on its own, all too often becomes mere rhetoric remaining primarily good intention; the latter would result in a soulless bureaucratic administration.

The power of enforcement given to the state or the community by *halakhah* to provide for welfare creates in the individual the obligation to see that society provides the necessary charitable acts. One is obligated to give to the poor all his needs, *dei mahsoro*. The Rama notes that the individual cannot fund all these needs, but fulfills this obligation by drawing the attention of leaders, legislators, and bureaucrats at the state or communal level, so that they will provide those needs that the individual, with his limited resources, is unable to do.

---

[16]Bank of Israel, *Annual Reports* 1991, 1992.

So, throughout the centuries, the Jewish communities, operating as autonomous mini-states rather than as religious communities in the modern sense of the word, had and implemented the right to tax their members in order to provide social needs, education, assisting the poor, public health services, and so on.[17] In addition, they had the power to regulate the market in order to achieve social justice and to provide welfare. This was done through a system of price controls, through subsidies, and through restraints on competition when these were found harmful to the community as a whole. At the same time, those restraints on competition that were adverse to communal welfare were not recognized; they were deemed halakhically inoperative. The *Shulkhan Arukh* and the other codes rule that the community appoints overseers to control prices of basic goods in accordance with Rav and contrary to Shmuel, who saw these overseers as needed only to represent supervision over weights and measures.[18] It is interesting to note that Shmuel's argument, that the market would adjust inequitable rises in prices, was not accepted.[19] Communities, according to the same codes, legislated taxes that were obligatory on all; failure to pay these social taxes was considered theft.[20] The landmark decision of ibn Migash, permitting the competition posed by an outsider, is couched in the phrase that "how could I approve the welfare of the few, namely the few local merchants, at the expense of the many, namely the community, who would thus be able to benefit from reduced prices."[21] Where no communal benefit was produced by the competition, however, the same and other responsa forbade the competition. All the codes claimed that the local townspeople did not have the right to prevent free entry of merchants from another town, provided the new entrants paid their taxes. Nevertheless, in medieval, Christian, western Europe, the *herem ha-yishuv*, whereby there existed a property right of the local merchants to operate and prevent the entry of people from other towns, became an accepted principle.[22] It

---

[17]*Shulhan Arukh, Hoshen Mishpat* 163.

[18]Ibid. 231:27. Also *Mishneh Torah, Hilkhot Mekhirah* 14:1–2.

[19]*Bava Batra* 89a.

[20]Maharshdam on *Hoshen Mishpat* 442.

[21]Hiddushim *Bava Batra* 21b. See also Meiri, *Beit ha-Behirah* to *Bava Metzia* 40b; Rosh, *Bava Metzia* 16; *Tur, Hoshen Mishpat* 231:26.

[22]T. I. Rabinowitz, *Herem Ha-Yishuv* (London: Goldston, 1945).

would seem that the fragile basis of the western European Jewish economy during the Middle Ages meant that competition would lead not only to a reduced income for the local merchants but to the destruction of the whole community, something that runs counter to the concepts of Jewish welfare.

Non-Jews too, have an obligation under Noahide laws to establish courts of law and to provide a moral and a just society. In host societies, we, as citizens, participate through the polls and through the fiscal system in the social policies and economic legislation of our society. It would seem incumbent upon us, therefore, to guide our participation along the lines now discussed in the following sections.

All these examples of the collective implementation of welfare do not flow from the social contract of Hobbes, which held that in order to enable the governor, which is the state, to rule, individuals gave up some of their rights in order to enjoy the mutual benefits of rule.[23] This attitude, which influenced much Protestant thought and later that of capitalistic economic thinking, is simply an expression that sees a benefit being gained by allowing the implementation of legislation regulating the market (egotistical, selfish thought). Nor was the Jewish involvement of the community in welfare an expression of altruism. It is the acceptance of collective responsibility that obligates government, as the agent of individuals constituting society, to implement the social justice that the individual is commanded to, but cannot pursue because of limited means. The national, communal nature of Judaism, aiming at the creation of a holy nation, in contradiction to the individual salvation emphasized by other religions, places society's intervention, as an integral part of the individual's social obligations.

IV. CHARITY, NOT WELFARE

Despite the centrality of social responsibility to Judaism and the wide spectrum of actions demanded of the individual to enhance the care of weaker, unfortunate, even lazy members of society, the emphasis is on charity rather than on entitlement or welfare. The acts enjoined on us by *halakhah* are obligations on the possessor of wealth to share part of

---

[23]Thomas Hobbes, *Leviathan* (London: Oxford University Press, 1929).

that wealth with others and to shoulder the responsibilities that come
with wealth. They do not entitle the recipient of those acts. I suggest
that this is a major consideration in achieving the balance between the
obligation to extend assistance and the moral, economic and social abuses
that can develop from that self same desire to achieve a socially responsible society. The significance of Judaism's insistence on charity rather
than on the alternative concepts of welfare, human resources, or social
egalitarianism, can be summed up as follows:

1. Charity has negative overtones. There is a shame attached to receiving assistance from other individuals or from society. The Hatam
Sofer once mentioned that this was the price the poor paid for that assistance. It is this price that militates against the creation of a welfare mentality, which leads to social disarray. The concept that one has only rights
to obtain from society, without concurrent obligations, would seem to
be not only economically dangerous, but also immoral.

There is no justification in the Jewish system for living off welfare,
because this is not a right but an obligation of the giver. The rabbis told
us that "a man should flog a carcass in public, a degrading form of work,
rather than come to take assistance from others."[24] It would seem that
this price concept, this shame, would have prevented much of the overshooting of the welfare provisions in the 1960s and 1970s in most Western economies. Because communities' economic resources are limited,
this overshooting led to economic stagnation and placed on the public
purse a burden that it could not maintain.

It is interesting to remember that the poor, also, are required to give
charity. Their exemption from the taxes levied to provide welfare did
not absolve their moral obligation; it was simply a pragmatic understanding that they did not have the wherewithal to pay for it.

2. If the assistance given by the individual to other individuals is his
obligation rather than an entitlement, then recipients may not abuse it.
This abuse is not the exploitation of an anonymously funded service, but
constitutes theft from a group or an individual. Those who obtain charity through false means or who pretend to difficulties they do not have
are, according to the Rambam and the *Shulkhan Arukh*, guilty of theft
from the public purse, a theft far more serious than the theft from pri-

---

[24]*Pesahim* 112–113.

vate individuals.[25] The recipient of an interest-free loan receives the loan because of the Torah's injunction on the lender to give it to him; it is not the recipient's by right or his private property. So the codes makes it clear that one who receives a loan may not squander it, may not waste it, may not procrastinate in its repayment.[26] The Torah, which obligates the lender, obligates the borrower as well. In case of non-payment of this loan, the full power of the law in the courts are brought to make the debtor pay in full, even at the expense of selling much of his personal property.[27]

3. Charity is an important component, yet it is only one component of the Jewish social system, and its implementation is limited by the demands of justice. Just as it is not permitted to distort the law before the fear of the rich and the mighty, so, too, it is not permitted to pervert justice in favor of the poor. The social actions to which we are commanded are consistently acts of charity within which the limitations imposed by the rights of others must be enforced. Taxation for funding communal needs may not, in general be confiscatory.[28] So, too, those who were given *pe'ah* could not harvest the *pe'ah* till the farmer had harvested his field, lest they trample and destroy his property.[29] The rights of employers and creditors will be upheld against the unjustified or illegal claims of workers and debtors, even if these are poor. It is interesting to note that when dealing with the subject of the repayment of debts, the Rambam is careful to point out that even if the lender is rich and the borrower poor, we still enforce these rights.[30] We encourage the lender to waive his rights voluntarily—this is charity—but we do not deny the creditor his rights. It must be stressed that this is not a limitation on cost, but a limitation on claims and rights.

It is in accordance with this limitation that we have communal enactments such as that of Padua, which ordered the recipients of welfare to perform communal work as part of the preservation, so to speak, of the rights of the communal tax payers. This places Judaism in favor of

---

[25]*Mishneh Torah, Hilkhot Mattenot Aniyyim*, 10:19.

[26]Ibid., *Hilkhot Malveh ve-Loveh* 1:1–8.

[27]*Shulkhan Arukh, Hoshen Mishpat* 96:23–25.

[28]*Terumat ha-Deshen* 342.

[29]*Mishneh Torah, Hilkhot Mattenot Aniyyim* 2:12.

[30]Ibid., *Hilkhot Malveh ve-Loveh*, 1:3.

policies that make all those on the welfare rolls or the recipients of assistance in any other form liable to pay back these benefits or to perform various communal services in order to qualify for financial assistance.

4. Where assistance is regarded as charity, given either freely or in accordance with communal legislation, the giver is entitled to his set of priorities. Were this an entitlement or a right, what should be included in charity or welfare, and who should be included would be unlimited. So we find in the Jewish system a definite set of priorities, clearly adjudicating the conflict between charity and the rights of the givers.

Not all are equally in need or equally able to participate in the obligation to give charity. This obligation is graded. The most meritorious method of fulfilling it is to give a person a job, or advice, or a loan; the least meritorious way to fulfill this obligation is directly, brutally and cruelly. This gradation provides the giver with a structured program or budget, as it were, for the fulfillment of his obligation. Feeding the poor and other life-saving measures have top priority. For this purpose, it is not permitted to conduct a means test, nor is it permitted to check the veracity of the claims. By the time the claim is processed, after all, the recipient might be dead. However, with regard to clothing and other benefits which can be postponed, those providing it have both the right and the obligation to see to the legitimacy of the claims of the recipient.[31] Means tests, supervision by communal organizations and other formal and informal means of controlling and preventing fraud, would seem consistent with this policy.

But an economic policy that thwarts the purpose of Jewish charity, to break the poverty cycle, would seem contrary to the Jewish perspective. Unemployment benefits at a level almost equal to the average wage level, for example, make it unprofitable for the recipient to receive work or force him to operate in the underground economy in order to continue receiving the benefit. These negative results would not occur in the Jewish system.

Of far greater importance than any of these examples of concern for the rights of the giver, however, is that there does not seem to be any Jewish support for the concept of welfare as a means of achieving an egalitarian distribution of wealth. Maimonides rules that it is not the duty

---

[31]Ibid., *Hilkhot Mattenot Aniyyim* 7:6.

of the giver of charity to enrich the recipient, merely to sustain him.[32] The *Shulkhan Arukh*, reflecting earlier codes and various responsa makes the giving of charity limited to minimal needs; two meals per day, clothes for a year, and a bed to sleep on. One who has assets of more than two hundred *zuz*, the equivalent of funding the minimal needs for a year, is always barred from public assistance.[33] I was unable to find support for any provision for an average standard of living as distinct from this minimal standard. The emphasis on protecting the rights of the giver, by limiting provision to minimal needs, calls into question the present-day use of a poverty line based not on objective indicators of need, but rather on subjective ones such as reasonable, average or acceptable standards of living. This is not merely an economic concern. It is of great moral importance in preserving the equity between justice and charity.

5. One is not obligated to impoverish oneself in order to give charity. This perceptively caps the obligation, both of the individual as well as of society, to divert resources to the satisfaction of unlimited needs. The exchange of one impoverished individual for another, through an exaggeration of caring, giving, and support, is not very clever. In the long run, it is also not achievable, because this is a demand contrary to the possibilities of human nature. Irrespective of whether we accept a ruling of a tithing, or of a 20 percent limit, and even accepting that these limits do not apply to very wealthy individuals (who would not suffer any impoverishment)[34] they clearly indicate Jewish support for a budgetary limitation on provision of social needs. The limit must be reviewed seriously and constantly, however, within the size of the gross national product and the allocation of funds through the government budget. It would be un-Jewish for wealthy societies or those with discriminatory fiscal policies to ignore their social obligations. One must hasten to point out, furthermore, that there is no limitation on the amount of money one is expected to spend rather than transgress negative precepts. Therefore, this limitation does not seem to be applicable when welfare needs are in actual fact life-saving situations, as in some medical situations, or the question of the redemption of captives who might otherwise be put to death, flooding, hunger, refugees, and so on.

---

[32]Ibid. 7:3.

[33]*Shulhan Arukh, Yoreh De'ah,* 252.

[34]Ibid., 249:1.

This means that in wealthy societies, the restriction on spending for medical needs, or the allocation of scarce resources, may not be divorced from the total budget or gross national product and the other priorities to which the public purse is pledged. It would be difficult to find Jewish support for anti-social curbs on education, health, or provision of basic food and clothing for a society that enacts a minimal tax base or permits heavy spending on an infrastructure that benefits only the wealthy. This is true also of the individual, whose limitations on charitable spending have to be viewed in regard to his income and his life style. This is clearly shown in numerous responsa regarding the income that has to be tithed. One responsum, for example, requires a person to add back money spent in earning that income, which are exaggerated. So, one would be required to add to one's taxable income, the difference between a medium hotel and a five star hotel, between a reasonable car and a luxury one, or between first class travel and economy class, even when these are spent in the pursuit or earning of an income and recognized by the I.R.S.[35] The poor are not required to fund luxury living.

6. There does not seem to be any Jewish support for distinguishing between deserving and undeserving poor. This distinction was a mainstay for most welfare systems in western Europe till the modern period and its thinking still permeates the socio-economic patterns of most countries. The actual situation of the recipient is what counts in Judaism, rather than the means whereby he arrived there. So while the poor, the aged, the infirm, the widow, and the orphan are automatically eligible, so, too, are the lazy, the addicted, and the inefficient members of society. Perhaps the best illustration of this, is the ruling that a man who borrowed money from gentiles, and then was placed in jail by them because he could not repay it, had to be redeemed under the injunction of the redemption of captives—notwithstanding the fact that it was his own fault. Interestingly enough, this applied even if he did it a second time. It was only after it became clear that this was a pattern, whereby he was using the welfare system, that the benefit of redemption was withheld. However, if there was a threat to his life and there was a reasonable fear that his imprisonment would lead to his death, he had to be redeemed

---

[35]M. Sternbuch, *Am ha-Torah* (Tze'erei Agudat Yisra'el of America), vol. 2 no. 5 (1982–1983).

again, and again, and again.[36] This has important implications for a welfare system, regarding those who are entering into it through a fault of their own, such as drug addicts, AIDS patients, delinquents, and so forth. They cannot claim innocence; at the same time, the possessors of wealth cannot abdicate their obligations.

V. IMPLEMENTING CHARITY

1 Unemployment

The major social problem facing all Western economies today is the persistent high rate of unemployment. Despite the signs of emerging growth in the American economy, and to a lesser extent, the levelling out of the recession in western Europe, they have not been accompanied by substantial changes in the unemployment rate. South Africa, despite its jettisoning of apartheid, is still faced with a major social problem because of the over 50 percent unemployment rate of its labor force. Even Japan, with its traditional policies of absorbing and retaining redundant workers, has nevertheless seen a substantial rise in this rate, although the actual figures are lower than that of other countries. It would seem fitting, therefore, that a Jewish perspective on alleviating such a situation should be accorded pride of place. Unemployment presents a twofold problem. First, there is the need to provide the economic base both for the workers made redundant and for younger people who cannot enter the labor force. The second aspect, however, is a psychological one that is of equal importance. For people to be told that they are redundant, that society has no need of them, must leave severe psychological scars. So, too, is the case in many Western countries today, where young people leaving school or academia are finding that they have no place in society due to pervasive unemployment. The issue has to be seen not in purely monetary terms, therefore, but in its wider implications.

The primary issue can be summed up very simply: Does the corporation, or the individual employer, have an obligation to continue to provide employment for workers, even though economic conditions deter-

---

[36]*Mishneh Torah, Hilkhot Mattenot Aniyyim* 8:13.

mining sales and profits, are such that this is not viable? Does the worker have a right to lifelong employment? Does the employer, simply on the basis of having employed people, now have a moral or legal obligation to continue doing so? May firms relocate to areas of low cost, even though this means that those previously employed in their plants will now be redundant? All these are expressions of the simple issue stated at the beginning of this paragraph.

The present Secretary of Labor in the United States of America is one of the vociferous exponents of the stakeholder theory of corporate organization, which puts this social obligation squarely on the shoulders of the employer.[37] This presents relationships among shareholders, workers, creditors, debtors, and the community that override the previous concept of the corporation's purpose being the creation of wealth for its shareholders alone. There seems to be no place in Judaism, however, for the abrogation of the legal rights and ownership of the shareholders. Workers do not acquire a right in a firm simply by working there; for that they receive salaries. So, too, creditors and banks, which extend credit or loan capital, incur risks in doing so, for which their judgment is responsible and for which they must bear the costs. At the same time, however, Judaism would state categorically that even though, in the absence of custom or legal agreement to the contrary, the employer does not have a legal obligation to provide employment or to maintain a plant when it is no longer profitable for him, yet there does exist a moral obligation of charity to do so. This brings with it responsibilities beyond those of legal relationships, and it is this responsibility that would require the individual entrepreneur or the corporation to assist workers made redundant and even competitors displaced by more efficient firms.

It has already been mentioned that the obligation of charity is a limited one, which applies to this scenario as well. If the number of workers to be dismissed, or the number of workers to be employed on a purely charitable basis as an expression of the highest form of charity, were to cost only a reasonable part of the profits, it would seem that this obligation would exist. After all, any form of monetary charity, is in effect, a surrender of part of the profit or part of the wealth of the donor. Just as

---

[37] R. B. Reich, *Tales of a New America* (New York: New York Times Books, 1987).

in the case of the individual giving charity, there does not seem to be a place in Judaism for corporate retrenchment simply to yield abnormal profits. The issue becomes more complicated when large scale retrenchment or relocation is necessary to maintain a viable profitability rate.

There are other non-financial aspects of charity that are definitely possible for the employer to pursue, however, because their cost is marginal. In my survey of Israeli corporations, I found that the vast majority paid severance pay in excess of the contractual obligations flowing from wage agreements or legal requirements. Because an action that enables the redundant worker to start a business on his own is the highest form of charity, it is conceivable that these severance payments or interest-free loans created out of accumulated profits should be used for achieving this halakhically mandated purpose. It is pertinent to point out that in Thatcherite England, corporate funding available for small business start-ups, in partnership with private banking institutions, was responsible for a growth rate of new small firms unparalleled either in British history or other Western economies. The same mandatory degree of charity can be fulfilled through the giving of advice, the provision of technical training, and the financial assistance to find alternative employment.[38] This means that the individual employer or corporation should use its facilities to provide training for its redundant workers, which would enable them to find alternative employment. So, too, collation of data on alternative employment within the area or beyond it, and dissemination of this data to redundant workers, together with assistance in writing resumes and so on would provide a non-financial form of charity, easily within the ability of the corporation to meet.

2 Education

The Talmud states, and this is repeated in the codes, that a man is obligated to teach his children a trade; he who does not teaches them, in effect, to become robbers.[39] This is similar to the parental obligation of a man to teach his son Torah. However, although this obligation early on became a communal obligation, I have not been able to find a similar ruling in regard to providing vocational guidance and technical educa-

---

[38]*Shulkhan Arukh, Yoreh De'ah,* 249:6.
[39]Talmud Bavli, *Kiddushin* 29a–30a.

tion aimed at enabling people to enter the labor force. It is true that there exist communal enactments regarding apprenticeship, and the education and living conditions of apprentices.[40] But this is not the same as enjoining communal effort in regard to providing technical education.

It could well be that creating a halakhic obligation of charity on the individual entrepreneur or corporation to foster this education is an example of the distortions due to bias that were mentioned in the introduction to this paper. At the same time, bearing in mind the many examples of rabbinic legislation fostering *tikkun olam* and the philosophical underpinnings of numerous *mitzvot* regarding theft and murder, this obligation would seem necessary—especially in view of the fact that in the modern technological society in which we live skill and training are prerequisites for entry into the labor force. The provision of skill or education, therefore, is tantamount to the provision of employment, assistance, or advice, considered by the codes to be the highest forms of charity. So the creation of bursaries out of undistributed profits, for the encouragement of vocational and technical education, should well be within the parameters of a legitimate Jewish perspective. Combined with the parental obligation to provide education, the reason behind the ritual of the *eglah arufah*, provides a philosophical basis. In reply to the question as to whether we imagine that the *Sanhedrin* and the priests were guilty of shedding innocent blood, which is part of the confession made over the *eglah arufah*, the sages of the Talmud point out that the lack of hospitality and the lack of provision of means of earning a livelihood, or acquiring the training for it, make the community in some way responsible for the murder for which they have come to atone.[41] Because this is a form of assistance, which the private purse can easily provide for small numbers of individuals, there seems to be no reason why this educational obligation should not also fall within the parameters of individual charity.

I found further support for this idea when, in the winter of 1981, I heard that the Rebbe of Lubavitch called for public-funded assistance for educational facilities for African American youth and other gentile

---

[40]For example, *The Shoemakers' Guild of Saragossa*, reproduced in N. Wischnitzer, *A History of Jewish Crafts and Guilds* (New York: Jonathan David, 1965).

[41]Mishnah, *Sotah* 6:9; *Sotah* 45b, (see also Rashi on 46b); Talmud Yerushalmi, *Sotah* 9.

ethnic groups, in order to enable them to become productive citizens. This would enable them to observe more easily the Noahide laws. The Rebbe's call was in effect, an admission of the Jew's obligation to assist or educate the non-Jew towards the observance of these laws and for the latter to participate actively in them himself.

3 Food, Shelter, Clothing and Health

In all these areas, the individual Jew has always been called upon to provide for the communal funds needed to provide these basic minimal needs. Just as the individual contributed to those funds, so to it would seem that in our own day, the individual is obligated to provide part of his *ma'aser* money or more for this purpose, as explained previously. The *tamhui* and the *kupah* described in the Talmud provided daily and weekly for food and basic needs.[42] Rambam tells us that there was no town, no community, that did not provide for these needs.[43] So, too, there is evidence of health services provided by the community through voluntary donations and/or taxes. We find reference from the days of the Temple to *heder ha-shayish* and in later times to the *hekdesh*, which served in various periods of history as a hostel, a sick room, or sick clinic. The rabbis were insistent that one may not live in a town that does not have a doctor.[44] There are innumerable examples of the public employment of doctors, whether it was to gauge the amount of damage caused under bodily assault so that the courts could adjudicate claims, or whether it was for ordinary medical needs.[45] Because food, health, and clothing are essential to keeping people alive, these were seen as enabling the individual to fulfill his obligations, as acts of *dinei nefashot*; not monetary matters, but matters of life and death. There is no reason to argue or to assume that this would not be true in our own day.

The public funds to be so allocated were raised through taxation, and it would seem that in any Jewish frame of individual welfare, payment of

---

[42]*Sanhedrin* 17b and *Bava Batra* 8b.

[43]*Mishneh Torah, Mattenot Aniyyim* 9:3; also 43:22.

[44]*Sanhedrin* 17b.

[45]*Sanhedrin* 78a. For examples of communal funding in this regard see Pinkhas Padua, enactments of 1585. S. W. Baron, *The Jewish Community* (Philadelphia: Jewish Publication Society of America, 1945) 2:329.

taxes for this purpose would be a religious obligation, as they have been throughout the centuries. One who does not pay his taxes is regarded as a thief, not only because he causes others to have to pay more than their legal share, but also because he has stolen as it were from the budget of welfare participants.[46] Here, too, however, the Jewish perspective is different from that of present-day welfare economics. The former would entail a negative income tax, or direct payments to participants in order to provide them with a minimum standard of living. Subsidizing the needy is preferable to subsidizing the basket of goods and services, a common practice, because the former is implementing charity and not a transfer payment. For similar reasons, a means test may be applied, except in the case of those in life-threatening situations requiring food and medical assistance. In many cases, there would be nothing wrong in allowing recipients to continue getting assistance and to find employment as long as the income from that employment did not raise them above the minimum standard considered to make one eligible for charity (200 *zuz*). This would eliminate much of the fraud and illegal employment, so prevalent under many modern welfare systems, whereby the recipient is not allowed to work.

4 Public Funding

It is obvious that the individual is unable to fund all the manifold services necessitated by the Jewish perspective on charity. This difficulty does not free society from its obligations, however, and the individual may be taxed in order to fund these social needs.[47] I have been unable to find any halakhic limitation on the taxes that may be levelled as a percentage of gross national produce, or of income, or of any other indicator of wealth. It is true that Hirsch would like us to accept the level of 20 percent as a maximum based on Joseph's tax on the Egyptians.[48] Interestingly enough, an Israeli economist has argued that 20 percent is the maximum tax rate that an economy can handle; taxes above this are accompanied by massive tax evasion.[49] The fear of tax evasion or

---

[46]*Teshuvot Maharshdam* 453.

[47]*Shulkhan Arukh, Yoreh De'ah* 248:1.

[48]*BeReshit* 47:43–44.

[49]G. Ofer, *Fiscal Policy* (Heb.) (Jerusalem: Falk Institute, 1970).

consideration of the community's readiness to pay the taxes levied, is in all probability the major limitation on taxes levied by the state or the community. However, it can be demonstrated easily, when there is public support for the purpose of taxes, and the individual believes that his money is not being wasted and that the tax burden is being equally spread, there is readiness to shoulder a greater burden. In Jewish communities throughout the centuries, possession of the right to tax was a treasured civil right, very often being the basis for the charters that these communities demanded from gentile governments. Although statistics are not readily available as to what percentage of the collective income was raised by taxes, we find by and large that individuals fulfilled their obligations to the communal treasury. It would be naive to assume that there was no evasion of taxes; nevertheless, the ramified social structure provided by these communities—covering education, defense, sewage, public health, care of the poor, and so on—amply testify to the abilities of the communities to raise the tax funds needed; after all, the non-Jewish government certainly did not contribute to these funds. My survey in Israel showed a similar pattern. Manufacturers asked to indicate the tax rate that was acceptable in their opinion, presented a 20 percent limitation. However, on the assumption that the government would cut its spending by 25 percent, or reduce its labor force by 30 percent, the vast majority of the respondents indicated that they assumed that higher tax rates could be levied. The long tradition of communal assistance persists even in secular and modern Israel.

If the government is to use its funds to provide those aspects of welfare that the individual is unable to do on his own, the principles of Jewish charity should be able to guide economic policy and the use of public funds. In all democratic countries, the individual influences and participates in policies through voting and lobbying. It would seem, therefore, that the following could constitute a Jewish perspective for which Jews could agitate even in a non-Jewish society.

a. Government funding would be given for interest-free loans to establish new enterprises. This would be preferable to the accepted socioeconomic practice of government aid to large firms in order to provide employment. In almost all modern economies, both those of the developed and underdeveloped countries, the practice over the last fifty years has been to provide subsidized capital, tariff protection and tax holidays for encouraging rapid industrialization and the establishment of large corporations—the primary public interest being the creation of jobs. Experience of the past seventy years, however, has shown that this form of assistance, as often as not, is morally and economically a negative one. It is true that it is easier and more convenient for governments to handle large units, which provide visible, physical evidence of their social intentions. Nevertheless, these have led to a distortion in the allocation of economic resources, to widespread fraud and mismanagement, together with the creation of unsuccessful economic enterprises. The need to create jobs later means that these uneconomic projects have to be bailed out, incurring a further waste of taxpayer money.

b. Government policies aimed at creating jobs are expressions of the Jewish belief that this is the highest form of charity. Here, too, however, the Jewish value system to be proposed by the individuals has important implications. It could be argued that public-sector jobs are preferable to the subsidy, tariff, and fiscal assistance of existing private firms or whole industries, so widely practiced in most countries. This raises the bogey of socialism. But if it is clearly demonstrated that these are not economic undertakings but charity, then it could be considered more moral and effective. Charity extended through job creation by state agencies can be measured and the cost known and monitored; this would prevent exploitation of the public purse, as is common when private enterprise is used as a middle man. The shame attached to being helped by sheltered workshops, would motivate people to seek real employment; in the alternative system, the illusion of real employment is created. State-owned corporations, a bloated civil service, and bailed-out privately owned corporations in all countries provide the workers with a fig-leaf to pretend that they are employed in viable economic institutions. This illusion exists even though no relation links their productivity, their wages, and the market demand for their goods. This basically creates an immoral attitude: receiving wages without making a real economic contribution. At the same time, entrepreneurs are able to obtain public funds for "white elephants" and nonviable projects. A charitable public-work project, on the other hand, makes it quite clear that those employed there are recipients of charity.

c. All monopolies, agreements on restraint of trade, and associations of workers or producers halakhically require the supervision of an *adam hashuv*.[50] When Rava disallowed an agreement between two butchers

---

[50]*Shulkhan Arukh, Hoshen Mishpat* 231.

on the grounds that it did not have his seal of approval, he was expressing a ruling that became codified as law in all the codes.[51] A mediator would be able to adjudicate between the costs and the benefits of the welfare policies mentioned throughout this paper. Taxation for implementing social programs means a transfer of wealth from one set of citizens to another. This process can become excessive and can be corrupted by the existence of pressure groups and lobbies. The implementation of policies using these funds, moreover, can be wasteful or fraudulent. It is necessary, therefore, to supervise the use of the holy money raised to provide charity in all its aspects. But there is a further element in this cost-benefit relation. Restrictive practices aimed at preventing imports can save jobs but they can also saddle the average citizen with the cost of inferior goods or, which in economic terms is exactly the same, higher prices. At what stage does the protection of jobs become socially immoral? The same question arises from policies aimed at preventing closure of inefficient firms, from allowing the feather bedding practiced by unions, and from the closed-shop principle that protects the jobs of those inside against those outside. So, too, does this question apply to monopoly arrangements allowing for the use of natural resources. All these pose the same moral question: how much welfare and at what price? The halakhic concept of the *adam hashuv*, an independent judiciary, free from the political pressures, could be used to provide the solution.

VI. CONCLUSION

Throughout any discussion of the individual's social obligations, the question of attitudes and ideology affects both decisions and their implementation. Kindness, concern for the feelings of the recipient, and the understanding that acts of charity are among the purposes of wealth, both private and communal, could prevent the creation of soulless or corrupt welfare-dispensing mechanisms. It must be remembered that, in Judaism, charity is not given but done.

---

[51]*Bava Batra* 9a. For additional examples, see Tosefta *Bava Metzia*, 11:12; also Vilna Gaon to *Hoshen Mishpat* 231:28.

10

Aspects of the Ideology of Capitalism and Judaism

*Aaron Levine**

INTRODUCTION

Capitalism is no less an ideology than a system of economic organization. Its most salient features are private ownership of the means of production and economic freedom. To be an effective engine for the creation of wealth, participants in the capitalist system must be committed to a work ethic. The work ethic takes the form of a devotion to income-generating activities. Moreover, capitalism preaches that allowing the self-interest motive free expression in the economic sphere will result in society maximizing its material well being. What brings this result about is the price system. Specifically, if a particular good or service is in relative scarcity, its price will rise. A rising price signals resource owners that a differential reward can be obtained by moving to the advantaged area.

*I wish to express gratitude to Rabbi Shalom Carmy for formulating the issues discussed in this paper and for his helpful comments on conspicuous consumption; to Dr. Moses Pava for his helpful comments on corporate social responsibility; to Jeffrey Frankel for his research and technical assistance; to Dr. Mareleyn Schneider for her assistance in computer technology; and to Joshua Blacher for technical assistance.

This shifting of resources to the advantaged area increases its supply, but at the same time reduces its scarcity value and hence reduces its price. An "invisible hand" hence guides the self-interest motive to expand production of the goods and services that society desires most and makes these outputs available at their lowest possible price.

Another feature of capitalism is the belief that society reaps benefits from competition. The more intense competitive pressures are in the marketplace, the less likely an individual seller will adulterate his product, pay lower wages than rivals, or charge a higher price than competitors. A competitive marketplace hence serves as an automatic check against fraud and exploitation.

Finally, capitalism believes in a limited role for government. Most importantly, government's operation should not interfere with or distort the incentive system of the marketplace.

My purpose here is to investigate several issues revolving around economic freedom, the profit motive, and the role of government from the perspective of Torah values.

THE INHERENT WORTHINESS
OF ECONOMIC ACTIVITY

In the capitalist system, the profit motive is what drives production. This is desirable because when production is driven by profit considerations society's economic well being, as discussed earlier, is maximized. Capitalism, however, provides no mechanism that forces market participants to give pause and consider the worthiness of their economic activity by anything other than an economic criterion.

In contrast to the capitalist ethic, Torah idealism requires an economic actor to consider the inherent worthiness of his actions. We begin development of this thesis with Rabbi Joseph B. Soloveitchik's insights into the blessing God conferred Adam the first: ". . . be fruitful and multiply and fill the earth and subdue it . . ." (Gen. 1:28). R. Soloveitchik understands this blessing as a divine *mandate* to mankind to subdue the earth and master the environment (henceforth, *kibbush*). Consider that the psalmist describes man as both a being crowned with glory and dignity[1]

---

[1]Ps. 8:6.

and also as a being made by God to have dominion over His works.[2] The *kibbush* mandate hence amounts to a charge to man for self-actualization in realizing his Godlike potential as a creative being.[3]

For R. Soloveitchik, man achieves dignity when he reclaims himself from co-existence with nature, rising from a degrading helpless existence to a powerful existence that is intelligent, planned, and majestic.

Coexistence with nature is undignified because man is incapable of discharging his responsibilities in a state of bondage. The more man masters nature, the freer he is to discharge his responsibilities. Therefore, dignity is not an end in itself. Without raising man's sense of responsibility, dignity has no value.[4]

Before the *kibbush* mandate can become operational as an evaluative criterion, the importance of the economic system in actuating the *kibbush* mandate must be noted. The most fundamental point to be made here is that progress in subduing nature and in mastering the environment cannot take place in an economic vacuum. Given the specialization and division of labor characteristic of modern society, production is impossible without the cooperative voluntary exchange of countless economic units. Professional services are the product of society's educational and research institutions. The financial underpinning of these institutions, in turn, depends on the efficiency of commerce and industry. The import of these interlocking relations is to make the subduing of nature and the mastering of the environment the work of the economic system as a whole.

Moreover, dignity manifests itself in the access one has to the available technical progress. This makes income the means of securing dignity. The higher the per capita income, the more widely accessible this technical progress will be. But the single most important factor in determining society's per capita income is labor productivity. Improvements in labor productivity, in turn, result from such factors as harder work, better training, more or better equipment, and innovative technology. Economic growth, in short, works to propel human dignity to greater and greater heights.

---

[2]Ps. 8:7.

[3]R. Joseph B. Soloveitchik, *The Lonely Man of Faith* (New York: Doubleday, 1992) 14–17. Originally published in *Tradition* 7:2 (1965).

[4]Ibid. 16–20.

The role that the economic system plays in the dignity-responsibility formulation of the *kibbush* mandate makes ordinary livelihood activities a fulfillment of this mandate. This is so because the income earned gives the economic actor a measure of command over the technical progress of society and thus contributes to his own dignity. In addition, participation in the economic system frees an individual from the shackles of dependency[5] and thus raises his sense of responsibility as well.

The proposition that work enhances one's sense of responsibility finds support in Rashi's comment on Rabban Gamaliel ben R. Yehudah ha-Nasi's oft-quoted dictum: "It is seemly to combine the study of Torah with an occupation for the wearying labor of both keep sin forgotten. All Torah study that does not have work accompanying it must in the end come to nothing and bring sin in its wake."[6] Commenting on this dictum, Rashi explains that the combined striving of Torah study and livelihood activities predisposes an individual against coveting and engaging in theft. Pursuit of a livelihood, in Rashi's understanding, raises one's sense of responsibility.

Further support for the above thesis can be found in Ulla's dictum: "A man who lives from the labor [of his hands] is greater than the one who fears heaven" (*mi-yire Shamayim*).[7] Commentators understand the intent here to compare two individuals, A and B. A spends his entire day in Torah study relying on his fellow man's largess for his material support. B, on the other hand, devotes himself to Torah study but engages himself in a worldly occupation for his support. Both people are *yir'ei Shamayim* but the latter's *yi'rat Shamayim* is greater.[8] We take it as axiomatic that *yir'at Shamayim* must be equated with a *rarified* sense of responsibility to both God and to one's fellow man. The underlying rationale for Ulla's dictum, therefore, is that Torah study combined with livelihood activities catapults one to a higher sense of responsibility than would be the case when one is exclusively involved in *patron*-supported Torah study.

---

[5]For the deplorable attitude the sages regarded a state of human dependency, see, *Shabbat* 118a; *Eruvin* 18b; *Pesahim* 113a; *Betzah* 32b; *Bava Batra* 110a.

[6]Mishnah, *Avot* 2:2.

[7]*Berakhot* 8a.

[8]R. Josiah Joseph Pinto, *ha-Rif* in R. Jacob ben Solomon Ibn Habib, *Ein Ya'akov*; R. Joseph Hayyim ben Elijah Al-Hakam, *Ben Yehoyada*, *Berakhot* 8a (second explanation).

RANKING LIVELIHOOD ACTIVITIES
AND THE *KIBBUSH* MANDATE

Proceeding as a corollary from the proposition that ordinary livelihood activities represent a fulfillment of the *kibbush* mandate is the impossibility of making a *kibbush* ranking of jobs on the basis of their dignity-enhancing feature. To be sure, medical research ranks above silver production as far as advancing the cause of human dignity. But dignity without responsibility is a perversion of the *kibbush* mandate. It is in this vein that R. Hanokh Zundel ben Joseph interprets the dictum *tov she-ba-rofe'im le-Gehinnom*.[9] Use of the phrase *tov she-ba-rofe'im* (the best among physicians) instead of the more apt phrase *kasher she-ba-rofe'im* (the most *competent* of physicians) indicates that the intent here is not to condemn the medical profession. Rather, this case deals with the physician who deludes himself into believing that he is the best practitioner around and sees therefore no reason to consult medical texts or colleagues. Conceit in this context carries the potential of exerting much harm. The physician is accordingly warned that *conceit* in his profession makes him particularly *prone* to a fate of Gehinnom.[10]

This dictum lends itself to the generalization that the more God like one's work is, the more one must guard himself against the sin of arrogance. Without cultivating proper humility, the loftiness of the work itself can work, ironically, to divest the practitioner of any *real* sense of responsibility to others.

What the aforementioned points to is that the *kibbush* mandate has an intangible aspect to it. This is the element of a raised sense of responsibility to others. Without intense cultivation, this character trait will be subject over time to erosion and distortion. Nurturing this character trait over time will, on the other hand, pay off in the form of a deeper and more refined sense of responsibility to others.

Proceeding from the above analysis is that the silver-production worker is not automatically relegated to a lower ranking in the fulfillment of the *kibbush* mandate compared to the medical researcher. What matters most

---

[9]Mishnah, *Kiddushin* 4:14.

[10]R. Hanokh Zundel ben Joseph, *Etz Yosef*, in R. Jacob ben Solomon Ibn Habib, *Ein Ya'akov*. For a similar interpretation see, R. Samuel Eliezer ben Judah ha-Levi Edels, *Maharsha*, *Kiddushin* 82a.

is the dignity-responsibility combination the work generates. Harboring a demeaning attitude toward someone on account of the type of work that person does, therefore, is morally repugnant.

INCOME PRODUCTION AND SOCIAL BENEFACTION

Formulating the *kibbush* mandate in terms of the dignity-responsibility criterion points to a basic difference in attitude between the capitalist ethic and Torah idealism in respect to economic activity. In the capitalist ethic, the *income producer is a social benefactor.* This is so because A's spending is B's income, and B's income results in an increase in spending for B, which, in turn, increases C's income, and so on. In terms of *kibbush* terminology, A's spending puts into motion a series of rounds of income creation and spending, which makes the technical progress of society available to a whole number of people. Moreover, when the economy is operating at full employment, the saver is also the social benefactor. This is so because an increase in saving, other things being equal, reduces interest rates, which, in turn, increases investment spending. The act of saving hence also sets into motion a series of rounds of spending and income creation, thereby spreading the availability of the technical progress to a whole number of people.

In sharp contrast, from the standpoint of Torah idealism, A's dignity-enhancing activity, whether it works to promote his own dignity or someone else's, does not rise to the level of fulfillment of the *kibbush* mandate unless it raises A's sense of responsibility.

Supporting the notion that a dignity-enhancing activity that is not accompanied by a raised sense of responsibility is not a fulfillment of the *kibbush* mandate is the following Talmudic passage at *Avodah Zarah* 2b:

> In times to come, the Holy One, blessed be He, will take a scroll of the Law in His embrace and proclaim: "Let him who has occupied himself herewith, come and take his reward." . . . the Kingdom of Edom [Rome] will enter first before Him . . . the Holy One, blessed be He, will then say to them: "Wherewith have you occupied yourselves?" They will reply: . . . "we have established many marketplaces, we have erected many baths, we have accumulated much gold and silver, and all this we did only for he sake of Israel, that they might [have leisure] for occupying themselves with the study of Torah." The Holy One, blessed be He, will say in reply: "You foolish ones among peoples, all that which you have done, you have only done to satisfy your

own desires. You have established marketplaces to place courtesans therein; baths to revel in them; [as to the accumulation of] silver and gold, that is Mine, as it is written: Mine is the silver and Mine is the gold, saith the Lord of Hosts [Hag 2:8]. Are there any among you who have been declaring this [that everything was done for the sake of Israel]?"

In modern economic terms, Rome's claim for a reward consisted of the assertion that it had created a prosperous and efficient economic system. The enormous purchasing power in the hand of the economy (*kesef ve-zahav hirbinu*) made it possible for the Jewish people to eke out a livelihood with only minimal participation in the economic system, leaving them free to make Torah study their main preoccupation. But, God summarily dismisses their claim. The contempt God has for their economic institutions, as *Tosafot* point out (*ad loc, s. v. "shevakim"*), is mentioned only for good measure. Most basically, their claim is rejected because their economic activities were pursued purely out of self-interest. Wealth brought with it neither a recognition of the divine element in their success nor a raised sense of responsibility. Economic viability meant one thing and one thing only to them, namely, *self-gratification*.

PERVERSIONS OF THE *KIBBUSH* MANDATE

Evaluation of the permissibility of a particular economic activity is routinely decided on the basis of *technical halakhah*. The import of the dignity-responsibility formulation of the *kibbush* mandate is to add an ideological dimension, however, to this analysis. The following are several illustrations of this ideological component.

Let us suppose that on the basis of technical *halakhah* a clear-cut prohibition against smoking cannot be established.[11] Nonetheless, the causative link medical science has established between cigarette smoking and various dreadful diseases is undeniable.[12] Far from advancing human

---

[11] This is the position taken by Rabbis S.Z. Auerbach and Ovadiah Yosef, quoted in A.S. Abraham, *Medical Halachah for Everyone* (New York: Feldheim, 1980), 6. See also Rabbi J. David Bleich, *Tradition* 16:4 (Summer 1977): 121–3; 17:3 (Summer 1978):140–2.

[12] For a summary of the evidence, see, Robert E. Goodin, *No Smoking: the Ethical Issues* (Chicago: University of Chicago Press, 1989), 8–15.

dignity, the tobacco industry degrades human existence by causing disease, misery and pain. Its very existence perverts the *kibbush* mandate.
The tobacco industry's perversion of the *kibbush* mandate puts into question the inherent worthiness of the production of cigarettes, working in
the industry, and investing in tobacco stocks. It should even put into
question the inherent worthiness of the economic activity of the tobacco
farmer.

Another illustration of the perversion of the *kibbush* mandate is the
gambling industry. This can be seen from an analysis of why the sages
disqualified a professional gambler from serving as a witness. Preliminarily,
we note that the disqualification obtains only when the gambler is engaged in no other gainful employment.[13] The rationale behind this
caveat is a matter of dispute. Maimonides and R. Joseph Caro regard the
earnings from a game of chance as theft by dint of rabbinical law (*avak
gezel*).[14] Earnings are not regarded as legitimate unless it can be presumed
that the income was conferred on him with perfect resolve. Given the
climate of levity and sport under which games of chance are played, satisfaction of the condition of perfect resolve is doubtful. This factor alone
does not disqualify the gambler, however, from serving as witness. The
penalty is not imposed unless the advantage the gambler derives from
his winnings rises to the level of being the means of his support. In the
event the gambler is not at the same time engaged in legitimate employment, the presumption that his gambling income is what supports him is
reasonable. Under the latter circumstance, the gambler is disqualified
from serving as a witness.[15]

Rashi, however, adopts a different tack in explaining the rationale for
the professional gambler's disqualification. In his view, earnings from a
game of chance are not *avak gezel*.[16] What is objectionable about gam-

---

[13]R. Judah, Mishnah, *Sanhedrin* 3:3; Isaac ben Jacob Alfasi, Rif, ad loc.;
Maimonides, *Yad, Hilkhot Edut* 10:4; Asher ben Jehiel, Rosh, *Sanhedrin* 3:7; Jacob
ben Asher, *Tur, Hoshen Mishpat* 34:10; R. Joseph Caro, *Shulhan Arukh., Hoshen
Mishpat* 34:16; R. Jehiel Michel Epstein, *Arukh ha-Shulhan, Hoshen Mishpat*
34:18.

[14]*Yad*, loc. cit.; *Shulhan Arukh.*, loc cit.

[15]R. Joshua ha-Kohen Falk, *Sefer Meirot Enayim, Shulhan Arukh.*, op. cit.
n. 40.

[16]Ibid.

bling is that it does not contribute toward the settlement of the world (*yishuv ha-olam*). Because the gambler makes no contribution to *yishuv ha-olam*, he is not knowledgeable regarding either the nature of commercial enterprise or business law and is not God fearing.[17]

The connection Rashi makes between ignorance of commercial affairs and the God fearing personality requires an explanation. Recognition of the essential difference between a commercial and a gambling transaction provides the missing link. In a commercial transaction, A's reward is predicated on his ability to satisfy B's wants. A's gambling winnings, on the other hand, are entirely predicated on B's *losses*. Because gambling earnings are in no way predicated on a necessity to satisfy someone else's needs in the form of a product or service, the activity has no inherent capacity to raise man's sense of responsibility to either God or to his fellow man. It is reasonable to doubt, therefore, that the gambler is a God fearing person.

Following Rashi's line, R. Jacob ben Asher formulates the disqualification of the gambler in terms of his non-contribution toward *yishuv ha-olam*. What the gambler lacks, in his view, is an appreciation for the toil and effort that commercial activity entails. Because the gambler entertains an attitude of levity in respect to monetary matters, he cannot be trusted to testify truthfully in a monetary dispute.[18]

R. Jacob's rationale provides support for the proposition that worldly occupation carries with it the potential of raising one's sense of responsibility. This is so because training to be a responsible person begins with the lesson that earning a reward is predicated upon supplying a product or service. Commercial experience thus serves as a base from which to advance to the notion that responsibility should be assumed even when there is no reward for taking on the burden.

Irrespective of whether a player in a game of chance becomes thereby disqualified to serve as a witness, nevertheless, gambling is an unredeeming activity. It is either *avak gezel* or an activity that contributes nothing to *yishuv ha-olam*. The gambling industry, therefore, should be regarded as a perversion of the *kibbush* mandate. To be sure, *halakhah* might be incapable of making a case to prohibit an accountant from tak-

---

[17]Rashi at Mishnah, *Sanhedrin* 3:3.

[18]*Tur*, op. cit.

ing on a gambling casino as a client, to prohibit investing in the stock of a gambling corporation, or to prohibit the manufacture and sale of gambling equipment. But the *kibbush* mandate would recommend a definite shifting away from these activities.

One final illustration of the perversion of the *kibbush* mandate is the manufacture and sale of war toys. These toys glorify violence, and studies have indicated that they have the effect of fostering aggression and antisocial behavior in children.[19] Here again, technical *halakhah* might be hard put to find a clear-cut prohibition in the production and sale of these toys. But toys that glorify violence and foster antisocial conduct counteract the ethos of responsibility. Dropping the product line, therefore, is indicated on the basis of the *kibbush* mandate.

CORPORATE SOCIAL RESPONSIBILITY

Critics of the capitalist ethic think that the profit maximization goal of the firm should be modified to accommodate a proactive social role. In the next few sections we will examine the ethics of a business corporation using its wealth to engage in altruistic projects for the general good of society. Referred to in the literature as "corporate social responsibility," some social critics regard the phenomenon as highly meritorious and would like to see much more of it.

Toys for Guns

ASL is a large furniture store located in the Washington Heights section of New York City. The company was originally organized as a partnership. But, the good fortune of tremendous growth, combined with a desire to secure the advantages of perpetual life and limited liability, convinced the owners to reorganize the company as a corporation. The company can now best be described as a *closely held private corporation*. It consists of fifteen shareholders, with its C.E.O., I.M. Dagesh, owning 20 percent of the outstanding shares.

---

[19]For a listing of these studies, see, George A. Steiner, John F. Steiner, *Business Government and Society* (New York: McGraw-Hill, 1991), 150.

Dagesh believes that the pursuit of profit should not be the only goal of his firm. Instead, the profit-maximization goal should be modified to accommodate a proactive social role. Toward this end, Dagesh, without consulting fellow shareholders, launches a program designed to make a dent in the local crime rate. Working with the local police precinct, he inaugurates a "toys for guns" program. The program offers amnesty, along with a $100 voucher redeemable at Toys "R" Us, to anyone who turns in a weapon. Dagesh commits $10,000 of corporate funds for the voucher certificates. At the same time, he believes that without an intensive educational and promotional effort, the program will not make a significant impact on the crime rate. Towards this end, he gives lectures on corporate time to and/or arranges meetings with local public schools and community groups. Dagesh is very enthusiastic about his project. Fewer guns in dresser drawers should translate into fewer accidental shootings, fewer crimes of passion, and fewer guns stolen for later use in crime.

Corporate Social Responsibility in Secular Society— A Critical View

In implementing "toys for guns," Dagesh joins a phenomenon on the American scene called "corporate social responsibility." What it entails is the use of corporate wealth to engage in projects for the general good of society. This phenomenon finds its greatest frequency in the public corporate sector. The following provide illustrations of altruistic projects undertaken by public corporations. (1) Dow Chemical Company runs a multimillion dollar project to educate the public regarding organ transplants and to encourage more donations of organs. A notable aspect of the program is that it is unrelated to any of Dow's commercial interests. (2) Merck and Co. has given away millions of dollars worth of a drug to fight the world's leading cause of blindness. (3) Sixteen of the nation's largest corporations have opened their own private school for pupils in the Lowndale area of Chicago aged two to nine. The aim of the program is to show that children raised in poverty and in drug- and crime-plagued urban communities can learn as well as suburban children.[20]

The problem that corporate social programs present is that the diversion of corporate funds for these purposes conflicts with the presump-

---

[20]Steiner 117–119, 122.

tive shareholder desire to maximize profits. Corporate altruism, according to Milton Friedman, undermines the foundation of the capitalist system. This is so because the business corporation is not organized for a charitable purpose, but rather to make as much money as possible for the shareholders within the limits set by law and ethical custom. Given the agency relationship between the executive and the shareholders the executive is mandated to run the business with the aim of maximizing profits for the shareholders.

What makes the notion of corporate social responsibility subversive to capitalism is its introduction of a political mechanism into the marketplace. By means of self-selection or some form of appointment, the executive becomes simultaneously a legislator, executive, and jurist. He decides whom to tax, by how much, and for what purpose.

The political principle that underlies the political mechanism is *conformity*. This means that the individual has a say in what is being done, but he must conform if overruled. In sharp contrast, the political principle that underlies the market mechanism is *unanimity*. In an ideal free market resting on private property, no individual can coerce any other; all cooperation is voluntary. All parties to this cooperation benefit, or they need not participate. By rescuing social responsibility from the corporate executive and putting it in the hands of individuals, we will be preventing coercion for purely *unselfish* reasons.

Friedman's final salvo against corporate social responsibility is that it is often totally futile. The executive is presumably an expert in running his company—in producing a product, selling it, or financing it. But nothing about his selection makes him an expert in curing such systemic ills as inflation, environmental pollution, or hard core unemployment. Will holding down the price of his product reduce inflationary pressures or, by leaving more spending power in the hands of his customers, simply divert it elsewhere? Or, by forcing him to produce less because of the lower price, will it simply contribute to shortages?[21]

Friedman's critics believe that corporate social responsibility is compatible with the capitalist ethic. Mulligan, for instance, points out that Friedman's model of the "lone ranger" executive is not typical in corporate America. Far more realistic is the consultative type, who under-

---

[21]Milton Friedman, "The Social Responsibility of Business Is to Increase Its Profits," *New York Times Magazine*, Sept. 13, 1970, pp. 32–33, 122–128, 132–135.

takes corporate responsible projects only after building the necessary consensus.[22]

Another flaw in Friedman's analysis is his conceptualization of corporately responsible actions in the form of committing resources to combat society's systemic ills. This presentation ignores the reality that corporate social responsibility is more a matter of targeting "do-able" projects.[23]

Advocates of corporate social responsibility reject the notion that executives are merely agents of the shareholders. Consideration that the corporation is a legal personality, separate and apart from its owners, has led some to conceptualize the corporation in terms of stakeholders. Stakeholders are groups and individuals who benefit from or are harmed by corporate actions. These include suppliers, customers, employers, stockholders, and the local community. Managers bear a fiduciary relationship to stakeholders. Their duty is to balance the multiple claims of conflicting stakeholders. The stakeholder theory does not give primacy to one stakeholder group over another, though there will surely be times when one group will benefit at the expense of the others.

In the traditional stockholder theory of the firm, the purpose of the firm is to maximize the welfare of the stockholders, subject to the constraints set by law and ethical custom. In the stakeholder theory of the firm, the very purpose of the firm is to serve as a vehicle for coordinating stakeholder interest.[24]

Corporate Social Responsibility and *Halakhah*

In extrapolating *halakhah*'s attitude toward ASL's venture into corporate altruism, perhaps the most fundamental point to make is that *halakhah*

---

[22]Thomas Mulligan, "A Critique of Milton Friedman's Essay, 'The Social Responsibility of Business Is to Increase Its Profits,'" *Journal of Business Ethics* 5 (1986): 265–69.

[23]Bill Shaw, "A Reply to Thomas Mulligan's Critique of Milton Friedman's Essay, 'The Social Responsibility of Business Is to Increase Its Profits,'" *Journal of Business Ethics* 7 (1988): 541.

[24]William M. Evan and R. Edward Freeman, "A Stakeholder Theory of the Modern Corporation: Kantian Capitalism," in Tom L. Beauchamp and Norman Bowie, *Ethical Theory of Business*, 3rd ed. (Englewood Cliffs, N.J.: Prentice Hall, 1988), 97–106.

does not recognize the corporation as a legal personality, separate and apart from its shareholders and employees.[25] This piercing of the corporate veil makes the stakeholder theory of the corporation alien to *halakhah*. In the hands of *halakhah*, the corporation becomes a nexus of contracts between the owners of the factors of production and their customers.

For *halakhah*, the ethics of corporate altruism revolves around the legal relationship between the shareholders and the managers in respect to the corporate wealth. Bearing on this issue is a Talmudic passage at *Bava Metziah* 104b. This text deals with *iska*. *Iska* is a special type of business partnership that *halakhah* regulates.[26] The distinctive feature of *iska* is that the financier plays no operational or managerial role in the business enterprise. In the event no stipulation has been made between the active partner (A) and the silent partner (B) regarding the division of profits and losses, *halakhah* calls for profits and losses to be divided equally. The portion of the capital for which A assumes responsibility takes on the character of a loan (*milveh*), and the remaining portion takes on the character of a deposit (*pikkadon*). Commenting on the dual character of

---

[25]R. Solomon b. Joseph Ganzfried, *Kitzur Shulhan Arukh*, 65:28; R. Mosheh Feinstein, *Iggerot Mosheh, Orah Hayyim* 1:90; R. Shlomo Zalman Auerbach, *Ha-Ne'eman*, Tishrei 5723 (1963): 6–10, 12; R. Menasheh Klein, *Mishneh Halakhot*, 6:277; R. Ezra Basri, *Dinei Mamonot* (Jerusalem: Sukkat David, 1976), vol. 2, chap. 4, sec. 3, n. 16.

Following the above line, R. Yitzhak Ya'akov Weisz, *Teshuvot Minhat Yitzhak*, vol. 3, no. 1, draws a distinction between voting and nonvoting shareholders. Only voting shareholders, in his view, should be regarded as owners; nonvoting shareholders are to be regarded merely as creditors of the voting shareholders. Disputing R. Weisz, R. Mosheh Sternbuch, *Mo'adim u-Zemanim* 3:269, pp. 160–163, treats both classes of shareholder alike, regarding them as partners in the business.

A minority position in this matter holds that the *halakhah* regards the corporation as a legal personality, separate and distinct from the shareholders. See R. Joseph Rozin, *Tzofnat Pane'ah* 184; R. Saul Weingart, *Yad Sha'ul*, 35–49; R. David Hoffmann, *Melamed le-Ho'il, Orah Hayyim* 91.

[26]The purpose of these regulations is to avoid violation of the rabbinic interdict of *ribbit*, called *avak ribbit*. For a description of these regulations, see, Aaron Levine, *Free Enterprise and Jewish Law: Aspects of Jewish Business Ethics* (New York: Ktav; Yeshiva University Press, 1980), 165–170.

iska, the Talmud states: "Now that we say that it is a semi loan and a semi trust, if he [the trader] wishes to drink beer therewith [i.e., for the loan part] he can do so. Rava said: [No.] It is therefore called *iska* [business] because he can say to him, 'I gave it to you for trading, not for drinking beer.'"

Talmudic decisors regard Rava's position as normative.[27] Insofar as no *explicit* restriction was agreed to regarding the disposition of the *milveh* portion of the *iska,* Rava's position requires an explanation. Addressing himself to this issue, Rashi regards the restriction to proceed from the implicit mandate A is operating under to manage the *iska* in a manner that maximizes B's return on his investment. Since putting the *milveh* portion of the *iska* at risk in the venture effectively drives A to be more diligent in his management of the enterprise, *the requirement to do so* is self-evident in the agreement.[28] In a similar vein, Tosafot point out that the consequence of not investing the *milveh* in the venture is to immediately expose B's entire capital to loss, with no additional capital to draw upon if needed. The implicit mandate to operate the *iska* to maximize B's gain requires A, therefore, to invest the *milveh* portion of the *iska* in the venture.[29] We should note that in respect to the *pikkadon* portion of the *iska,* a bailor-bailee (*mafkid-nifkad*) relationship exists between the financier and the active partner. A's use of the funds in a manner which departs from B's mandate constitutes misappropriation (*shelihut yad*).[30]

Several principles are able to be generalized from the preceding discussion. First, if A furnishes B with capital for the purpose of investing it for him, a *mafkid-nifkad* relationship is thereby established between the parties in respect to the capital furnished. Moreover, A's *nifkad* status places him under an implicit mandate to manage the funds with the aim of maximizing profits for B. Committing corporate resources for altruistic projects hence constitutes *shelihut yad* on the part of the managers.

Reinforcing the *shelihut yad* case against corporate altruism is the consideration that *halakhah* specifically imposes the charity obligation on the individual on a personal level. A business entity as such bears no

---

[27]*Yad, Sheluhin ve-Shufetin* 7:4; *Tur, Yoreh De'ah* 177:30; *Shulhan Arukh, Yoreh De'ah* 177:30.

[28]Rashi at *Bava Mezia* 104b.

[29]Tosafot, *Bava Mezia* 104b.

[30]R. Moses Isserles, Rama, *Shulhan Arukh, Yoreh De'ah* 177:5.

responsibility to engage in charity. Committing the resources of a business corporation to philanthropy amounts therefore to co-opting the shareholders' prerogative to discharge their charity duty in a manner of their own choosing.

The above argument finds support in the law of charity as it pertains to *iska* profits. Suppose it is the widespread custom for business partners to devote 10 percent of their *iska* profits to charity. Here, the active partner, according to R. Moses Isserles, has no right to take it upon himself to donate 10 percent of the *iska* profits to charity. Instead, the financier is entitled to receive his full pre-tithing share of the profits and be given the opportunity to allocate his charity funds in a manner of his own choosing.[31]

Proceeding clearly from R. Isserles' ruling is that even when a business entity operates under an implicit mandate to devote a specific percentage of its profits to charity, the *disposition* of the charity funds is a matter of individual shareholder prerogative and does not fall under the purview of the business entity. How much more so does this judgment hold when the business entity operates without any understanding that a portion of its profits shall be devoted to charity.

Further support for the co-opting rationale against corporate altruism can be found in Nahmanides' ruling in connection with the issue of freedom of entry in the marketplace. Specifically, the issue dealt with the right of out-of-town, non-taxpaying merchants to enter the local area on the basis of their promise to undercut the local competition. Insofar as competition here decidedly benefits local consumers, R. Joseph ibn mi-Gash sided with the outside merchants and ignored the protectionist pleas of the local merchants.[32] Nahmanides disputes his position on various grounds. One argument he adduces, which has particular relevance for the case at hand, is that the local community has the legislative authority to fix prices. Now if the community believes that local prices are too high, it is within its authority to directly mandate a reduction of prices. The community must not, therefore, allow anyone to usurp their authority in this matter. Allowing outside merchants to enter on the basis of their promise to undercut the local competition does just this.[33]

---

[31]Rama, op. cit. 177:22.

[32]R. Joseph ibn miGash, *Bava Batra* 21b.

[33]Ramban, *Hiddushei ha-Ramban* (Jerusalem, 5689), to *Bava Batra* 21b.

In a similar vein, corporate altruism co-opts the prerogative of shareholders to discharge their charity duty in the manner of their own choosing. The business corporation should therefore be operating under an implicit mandate not to commit corporate wealth for altruistic projects.

The *shelihut yad* basis for opposing corporate altruism in no way conflicts with any particular secular law on this matter. Secular law does not *mandate* a corporation to engage in altruism. Expanded rights for consumers, workers, and the community, which have resulted from recent legislative and judicial actions, have the effect only of adding additional constraints on the pursuit of profit. Secular law says nothing to vitiate the bailor-bailee relationship that *halakhah* regards as being operative between the shareholders and employees vis-à-vis the wealth of the corporation.

What the aforementioned points to is a halakhic objection to ASL's venture into corporate altruism. Committing corporate funds for the "toys for guns" project violates for Dagesh his mandate to operate the business in the interest of maximizing the shareholder's profits.

Another feature of the "toys for guns" project was the time and energy Dagesh devoted to the educational and promotional phase of the program. Given that the project itself violates the shareholders' mandate, the company time he devoted to the project breaches his halakhic obligation not to idle on the employer's time.[34] Idling on the employer's time forfeits for the worker the wages he would have earned for that time period.[35]

Proceeding as a corollary from the above arguments is that a majority vote by the shareholders in favor of an altruistic project does not halakhically validate the undertaking. Because the entity was organized for profit, majority vote determines policy only in respect to the means of achieving this goal. But majority rule cannot change the ends themselves.

---

[34]*Yad*, Sekhirut 13:7; *Tur*, Hoshen Mishpat 337:20; *Shulhan Arukh, Hoshen Mishpat* 337:20; *Arukh ha-Shulhan, Hoshen Mishpat* 337:26.

For various aspects of the productivity standard *halakhah* sets for the worker, see Aaron Levine, *Economics and Jewish Law* (Hoboken, NJ: Ktav; Yeshiva University Press, 1987), 178–82.

[35]See, Shillem Warhaftig, *Dinei Avodah ba-Mishepat ha-Ivri* (Jerusalem: Moreshet, 1968), 1:324.

Supporting the above assertion is R. Solomon ben Abraham Adret's comment regarding the limits of communal legislative authority. The specifics involved the validity of a communal practice of taxing a resident on the basis of his ownership of assets located in a different town. Since the edict effectively subjects a segment of the community to "double taxation," R. Adret ruled that the provision amounted to outright robbery.[36] Proceeding from his ruling is that majority decision violates minority rights when the body making the decision has no authority to deal with the issue at hand. Similarly, a majority vote by shareholders of a business corporation to commit corporate resources for an altruistic project violates the rights of the minority shareholders as undertaking the project changes the goals of the organization.

Corporate Altruism Masquerading as Business Investment

One variant of corporate altruism occurs when the project at hand is packaged by its sponsors as a business investment that incidentally promotes social welfare. Dagesh's "toys for guns" project conveniently illustrates this genre of corporate altruism. To be sure, "toys for guns" can be presented in purely altruistic terms, but it can also be packaged as an investment opportunity. All that is needed here is to project benefits the firm will reap from the expenditure. It is only the imagination that sets limits as to what these benefits might be. For starters, Dagesh can claim that "toys for guns" will put ASL on the commercial map. Media publicity for its social benefaction will incidentally draw attention to the firm's products and services. This will do more for sales than $100,000 worth of straight advertising. Moreover, it is not unreasonable to expect a bandwagon effect for the "toys for guns" project in the form of other firms joining the effort. A real dent in the crime rate will be made. Increased neighborhood safety will generate many tangible benefits for ASL. Employee morale, for one, will be boosted. This will translate into increased productivity. The perception of a safer neighborhood will attract a whole new clientele into the store. "Toys for guns," in short, is consistent with a *long-run* profit maximization goal for the firm.

---

[36]R. Solomon ben Abraham Adret, *Responsa Rashba* 1:788 (Jerusalem: Makhon Tiferet, 1989).

The legal treatment of corporate altruism of the "toys for guns" genre reveals a large gap between secular law and *halakhah*. Under the "business-judgment rule," secular law recognizes wide latitude for the executive in not second-guessing his business decisions. Judicial review of either the bona fides or the reasonableness of a business management judgment is quite narrow. As a practical matter, the business-judgment defense is unlikely to fail in the absence of conflicts of interest, extraordinary amounts of profit foregone, or some other *affirmative* suggestion of bad faith.[37] Dagesh's unilateral venture into corporate altruism would thus have no trouble meeting the "business-judgment rule."

From the standpoint of *halakhah*, the ethics of Dagesh's project turns on the issue of whether the expenditure should be regarded as corporate altruism masquerading as a business investment. If the shareholders regard the project as corporate altruism, then the expenditure constitutes *shelihut yad* on the part of Dagesh. Given the latter possibility, moving along the project without first consulting the shareholders is untenable. For the shareholders, the first order of business is to determine whether "toys for guns" is corporate altruism or a business investment. Should a majority decision decide that it falls into the category of corporate altruism, the item immediately moves off the firm's agenda. Validating the project requires a two-tier majority vote.

Corporate Altruism and Coercion

Another halakhic concern in connection with corporate altruism is that this practice sets into motion a likely scenario that entails unlawful coercion. By way of illustrating this moral pitfall, let us return to the "toys for guns" scenario. Suppose that "toys for guns" is ASL's first foray into corporate altruism. Dagesh presents his proposal to the shareholders. To his chagrin, he finds much opposition to the plan.

Some dissenters are convinced that only those who are least attached to their weapons will be attracted by the trade-in offer. Inherited guns and the spare weapons of criminals fall into this category. Those whose lifestyles require them to carry guns, such as drug dealers and gang mem-

---

[37]David L. Engel, "An Approach to Corporate Social Responsibility, *Stanford Law Review*, 32:1 (Nov. 1979): 16.

bers, will not be induced by the offer to trade in their basic arsenal. The program will at best only nibble at the edges of gun violence.

Critics, with both a penchant for quoting authorities and a flare for economic analysis, assert that the gun buybacks, to be effective, would have to be coupled with a national ban on new sales of handguns. Otherwise, taking guns out of circulation in the face of constant market demand unwittingly subsidizes the gun industry.[38] Moreover, it would be naive to imagine that the gun buyback program is exempt from normal market processes. Specifically, if the buyback price rises above the retail price for guns, the program could very well encourage gun thefts, with government serving, in effect, as a reliable fence.[39]

After listening intently to the arguments against "toys for guns," cynics began to quip that the only certain benefit of the program is the *personal one* Dagesh realizes as a result of the media attention. The consensus is that "toys for guns" is neither a prudent investment nor an optional way of dealing with the crime problem. Taking the opposition very personally, Dagesh threatens to resign if his proposal is not accepted. Out of fear that ASL will plunge into turmoil without Dagesh's leadership, the shareholders turn around and vote in favor of the project.

Dagesh's conduct here is morally objectionable. One issue his conduct raises is that it might constitute extortion. In developing this point, consider the classical case of *teluhu ve-zavin* (lit. he was [threatened] to be hanged and [because of this] sold), discussed at *Bava Kamma* 62a : A coerces B to sell him property he owns at its "fair market" value. Considering both the duress B is subject to and his receipt and acceptance of the cash representing the "fair market" value of the property, it is evident that the latter desires to transfer the article to A.[40] The sale,

---

[38]Lawrence W. Sherman, professor at the University of Maryland and President of the Crime Control Institute, quoted in Erik Eckholm, "Add Gun Buybacks to the Public Wish List," *New York Times*, 2 Jan. 1994:3.

[39]Philip J. Cook, professor of public policy at Duke University, quoted in "Add Gun Buybacks to the Public Wish List," op. cit. 3.

[40]R. Samuel ben Meir, Rashbam, *Bava Batra* 48a.

A "fair market value" duress sale, according to R. Isaac Alfasi, on the interpretation of R. Abraham ben David of Posquières (quoted in *Beit Yosef, Tur*, op. cit. 205:l, and Rama, *Shulhan Arukh*, op. cit. 205:l), is valid only when the buyer makes full payment at the time the transaction is entered into. Should the duress sale have been entered into by means of a deed, the sale is invalid, despite its fair market value price.

although immoral,[41] is nevertheless, legally binding.[42] To this, the Talmud adds that to be valid B must in the end declare "I am willing" (*rotzeh ani*).[43] Decisors regard B's acceptance of the purchasing price *without protest* as equivalent to declaring *rotzeh ani*.[44] A variation of this case occurs when A snatches away B's article but leaves him with its fair market value. With the duress element absent here, B's acquiescence to the exchange does not become objectively evident until B explicitly verbalizes his consent.[45]

Let us now move to another variant which has direct relevance to the case at hand. In this variant, A coerces B to make him a gift or sell his property below "fair market" value. Here, the transaction, according

---

R. Joshua ha-Kohen Falk (*Sema, Shulhan Arukh*, ad loc. n. 5) interprets this view to void a "fair market value" duress sale consummated by means of *kinyan* but accompanied only by the buyer's promissory note instead of actual payment.

Disputing this interpretation of R. Isaac Alfasi's view, R. Shabbetai ben Me'ir ha-Kohen (*Siftei Kohen, Shulhan Arukh*, ad loc. n. 2) posits that what the latter refers to is the circumstance where the "fair market value" duress sale was consummated by means of *kinyan shetar* and the purchasing price was not paid at the time of the transaction. Here, the duress element renders the transaction void.

R. Isaac Alfasi, on the interpretation of R. Joseph Caro (*Beit Yosef*, loc. cit.), and R. Asher b. Jehiel, on the interpretation of R. Joseph Caro (*Beit Yosef*, loc. cit.), validate a "fair market value" duress sales provided it was consummated by means of proper *kinyan*. The cash transfer, in this view, is not at all essential.

With authorities in dispute regarding the validity of a "fair market value" duress sale not accompanied by the necessary cash transfer, the party in physical possession of the disputed article has the advantage. See *Dinei Mamonot* 2:70.

[41] The pressure tactics A uses to acquire B's property violates for A the *lo tahmod* interdict. See, *Dinei Mamonot* 2:70, n. 1.

[42] R. Huna, *Bava Kamma* 62a; *Rif, Bava Batra* 48a; *Yad, Mekhirah* 10:1; *Rosh, Bava Batra* 3:51; *Tur*, op. cit. 205:1; *Shulhan Arukh*, op. cit. 205:1; R. Jehiel Michel Epstein (Belorussia, 1829–1908), *Arukh ha-Shulhan, Hoshen Mishpat* 205:2

[43] *Bava Kamma* 62a.

[44] R. Joseph Caro, *Beit Yosef, Tur*, op. cit.; *Sema, Shulhan Arukh*, op. cit. n. 2; R. Eliyahu ben Solomon Zalman, *Gra, Shulhan Arukh*, op. cit. n. 1.

[45] R. Jacob b. Jacob Moses Lorbeerbaum, *Netivot ha-Mishpat, Shulhan Arukh*, op. cit. 205, n. 1.

to R. Jacob ben Asher and R. Joseph Caro, is invalid.[46] These same decisors define coercion in terms of either physical duress or monetary threats.[47]

Applying these latter two rulings to the case at hand renders Dagesh's conduct extortion. Given the initial majority opposition to the plan, the above judgment holds even if the dissenters concede that the project will likely generate some benefits to the firm.

In opposition to the school of thought that regards monetary threats as a form of coercion, R. Joseph Colon would not invalidate a commercial transaction on this basis.[48] Dagesh's conduct does not constitute extortion, therefore, according to R. Colon. Nonetheless, his behavior could very well violate the Torah's prohibition against coveting (*lo tahmod*).[49] Violation of the interdict entails the following elements: A desires to acquire an item B owns. B refuses A's offer. As a means of overcoming B's initial resistance A pesters B or pressures B to accept his offer. Alternatively, A petitions B's friend to induce him to change his mind. Acquiring B's item by means of these pressure tactics violates for A the prohibition against coveting.[50] A declaration on the part of B of *rotzeh ani* at the time he parts with the article removes for A, according to R. Abraham ben David of Posquières (Ravad) the *lo tahmod* interdict.[51] In his formulation of the interdict, however, Maimonides offers no such caveat.[52]

---

[46]*Tur*, op. cit.; *Shulhan Arukh*, op. cit. 205:4.

[47]*Tur*, op. cit.; *Shulhan Arukh*, op. cit. 205:7.

[48]R. Joseph Colon, *Responsa Maharik*, 184, quoted in Rama, *Shulhan Arukh*, op. cit. 205:7.

[49]Ex. 20:13–4, Deut. 10:18.

[50]*Yad, Gezelah* 1:9; *Tur*, op. cit. 359:9; *Shulhan Arukh*, op. cit. 359:10–12; *Arukh ha-Shulhan.*, op. cit. 359:8.

[51]R. Abraham ben David, Rabad, at *Yad*, loc. cit.

[52]*Yad*, loc. cit. The dispute between Maimonides and Rabad is explained by R. Vidal Yom Tov of Toloso (Maggid Mishneh, *Yad*, ad loc.) as follows: Maimonides regards the prohibition of *lo tahmod* to consist of the *exertion of effort* to overcome B's resistance to part with his article. B's declaration of *rotzeh ani* at the end of the process hence does not remove *lo tahmod*. Rabad, however, regards the prohibition to consist of *acquiring* B's article when he is initially unwilling to sell it. B's declaration of *rotzeh ani* at the moment of transfer hence removes *lo tahmod*.

The prohibition against coveting is formulated in the codes in terms of the behavior of the buyer. By logical extension, posits R. Ya'akov Yeshayahu Bloi, the prohibition should apply to the conduct of the seller as well. Accordingly, the use of pressure tactics to induce someone to buy an item violates for the seller *lo tahmod*.[53]

R. Bloi's line finds ready application in the "toys for guns" scenario. To be sure, the *rotzeh ani* caveat is satisfied here. This is so because the expenditure is approved only after the shareholders formally vote in favor of the project. Dagesh's threat to resign as a means of inducing shareholders to turn around and approve the project violates *lo tahmod* only according to Maimonides, but it is free of violating this interdict according to R. Abraham ben David.

Another mitigating factor here is that Dagesh seeks the corporate funds not for his personal use but rather for the benefit of the corporation and for the benefit of society at large. This circumstance should not, however, work to vitiate *lo tahmod* unless the shareholders are in agreement with Dagesh that the project is an ingenious way of drawing attention to the products and services of the firm, and disagree only whether the expenditure is the optimal investment for the firm. Before investing in ASL, shareholders should have been aware that business policy issues would at times be hotly contested and in the end decided by majority vote. If Dagesh believes that "toys for guns" is in the best long-term interest of the firm, he has every right to fight for its approval, even to the extent of putting his job on the line.

But suppose the majority of the shareholders view "toys for guns" as purely corporate altruism and do not believe that the resulting publicity will draw any significant attention to their products or services. Then, "toys for guns" is for the majority shareholders a misplaced agenda item; it diverts profits for a non-business purpose and or co-opts the shareholders' personal prerogatives in respect to charity giving. Within this context, threatening to resign as means of securing passage of the project puts Dagesh at risk in respect to *lo tahmod*. That Dagesh seeks the funds not for his personal use, but rather for the benefit of the company and for the benefit of society, should not be a saving factor here. *Lo tahmod*,

---

[53]R. Ya'akov Yeshayahu Bloi, *Pithei Hoshen, Hilkhot Genevah ve-Ona'ah*, p. 30, at 26.

according to R. Bezalel Stern, is violated whether the acquirer seeks the article for himself or for someone else.[54]

Corporate Altruism and Misplaced Priorities

Another concern corporate altruism raises in *halakhah* is the issue of misplaced priorities. Of critical importance here is the prohibition against false religious pride (*yohara*).[55]

In his exposition of the concept of *yohara*, Rabbi Moshe Meiselman identifies it as occurring when an individual who is presumably not proficient in basic religious observance engages in a religious practice that is expected only of people of the highest level of piety. Illustrating this concept is the objection R. Moses Isserles[56] raises against a woman wearing a *tallit* and reciting a blessing over it. The objection begins by noting that even for a man, the *mitzvah* of *tzitzit* is not an absolute requirement. This is so because the *mitzvah* is triggered only if one chooses to wear a four-cornered garment. There is no obligation for a man to go out and buy a four-cornered garment, however, so as to make the *mitzvah* incumbent upon himself. Nevertheless, men have taken it upon themselves to perform the *mitzvah* of *tzitzit*. The observance of this *mitzvah* is thus a matter of extra piety. For a woman, the obligation is even more remote since she has the further option of wearing a four cornered garment without even placing *tzitzit* on it. Because *tallit* for a woman is a "doubly optional" *mitzvah*, wearing a *tallit* communicates that she is punctilious of even the highest forms of piety. Because this communication presumably belies the reality of the situation, this conduct constitutes *yohara*.

Yohara is basically objectionable, in R. Meiselmans' view, because the motives of the individual are suspect. Had the individual's motives been pure, he would certainly have first become proficient in basic observance before leaping to conduct expected only of the religious elite. The fact that he has not done so brands the conduct religious exhibitionism.[57]

---

[54]R. Bezalel Stern, *Be-tzel ha-Hokhamah*, 3:45.

[55]Cf. *Berakhot* 17b, *Pesahim* 55b.

[56]Rama, *Shulhan Arukh, Orah Hayyim* 17:2.

[57]R. Moshe Meiselman, *Jewish Woman in Jewish Law* (New York: Ktav; Yeshiva University Press, 1978), 152–154.

By way of illustrating the issue of *yohara* in connection with corporate altruism, let's return again to the "toys for guns" scenario. For the purpose of focusing on the issue at hand, assume that ASL owes some outstanding debt to its suppliers at the time it ventures into its project of corporate altruism. In secular society, creditors would have no basis for challenging the legality of ASL's "toys for guns" project.[58] But *halakhah* would have grounds of objecting here. Leaping into acts of *hesed* with the community at large, without first discharging its basic duties to one of its stakeholders, amounts to the practice of *yohara* on the part of the shareholders. Altruism of this sort would be objectionable even if it were *unanimously* agreed to by the shareholders.

Corporate Giving and *Halakhah*

One form of socially responsible conduct that secular law authorizes is corporate giving. Indeed, a business firm's incorporation charter expressly authorizes this practice. Contributions to universities and charitable organizations are examples of qualified expenditures of this type. Because the entity was not set up for altruistic purposes, but rather to earn profits for its shareholders, corporate giving in the face of minority opposition to the practice violates *halakhah*. Corporate giving represents a conflict between the law of the land (*dina de-malkhuta*) and *halakhah*.

Dina de-malkhuta cannot, of course, set aside Jewish ritual law. But, in the area of civil law, decisors dispute the degree of validity it is given. Representing the view that gives the widest scope to *dina de-malkhuta* in civil law is R. Moses Isserles (Rama). Conflict between *halakhah* and *dina de-malkhuta*, in his view, is generally decided in favor of *dina de-malkhuta*.[59] Exceptions to this rule, however, apply. It does not hold in relation to the law of inheritance;[60] nor does it give Jews the option of taking their dispute to secular courts,[61] or to have the secular court's evidentiary procedure imposed on them.[62] Moreover, *dina de-malkhuta*

---

[58]Engel, op. cit. p. 17, n. 52.

[59]Rama, *Shulhan Arukh, Hoshen Mishpat* 369:11.

[60]Ibid.

[61]Rama, op. cit. 26:1.

[62]Rama, on the understanding of R. Mordecai ben Abraham Jaffe, *Ir Shushan,* Hoshen Mishpat 369.

is recognized only where the law involved either benefits the government or was enacted for the benefit of the people of the land.[63]

Disputing R. Isserles, R. Shabbetai ben Me'ir ha-Kohen avers that in litigation between Jews, the law of the land finds its validity only when the non-Jewish law does not contradict Torah law, or in a case when the practical application of Torah law is not clear.[64] Following R. Shabbetai Ben Me'ir ha-Kohen's line, R. Abraham Isaiah Karelitz sharply disputes the notion that *lacunae* exits in *halakhah*. A halakhic position can be extrapolated for any issue. If *dina de-malkhuta* contradicts *halakhah*, even if the *halakhah* was derived by means of extrapolation, the law of the land must be set aside.[65] Many decisors regard R. Moses Isserles' position as normative.[66] Nonetheless, it is doubtful whether Rama's position can serve as a basis for validating corporate giving. One consideration here is the tax-deductibility feature of corporate giving. Corporate giving results in the government losing tax revenues it would otherwise get and hence works to its detriment. Moreover, it is by no means clear that this law works to the benefit of society. Recall Milton Friedman's argument: introducing a political mechanism into the marketplace sets up the possibility for people in positions of power to exploit others for *unselfish* purposes.

What the aforementioned indicates is that majority-decision rule may not force minority shareholders to participate in corporate giving.

Business Social Responsibility—Several Caveats

Business social responsibility is treated in the secular literature in a context much broader than the boundaries of the previous discussion. Several caveats, therefore, should be noted.

Discussion was confined to the small business organized as a closely held corporation. The analysis could be extended to the limited part-

---

[63]Rama, op. cit. 369:11.

[64]R. Shabbetai ben Me'ir ha-Kohen, *Siftei Kohen, Shulhan Arukh, Hoshen Mishpat* 73, n. 39. In litigation between Jew and non-Jew, *dina demalkhuta* is operative (*Siftei Kohen*, ad loc).

[65]R. Abraham Isaiah Karelitz, *Hazon Ish, Hoshen Mishpat, Likutim* 16, alef.

[66]*Iggerot Mosheh, Hoshen Mishpat* 2:62; R. Yosef Elihayu Henkin, *Teshuvot Ivra*, vol. 2, p. 176; See also list of authorities cited by Shmuel Shilo, *Dina de-Malkhuta Dina* (Jerusalem: Hebrew University Press, 1974), 157, n. 26.

nership as well. Some of the objections raised earlier in respect to business altruism might not apply to the publicly traded corporation. Because social benefaction is not an uncommon practice for the publicly traded company, this practice cannot be said to dash the legitimate expectations of an investor. In addition, a decision to engage in social benefaction reached only after acrimonious debate and high-handed pressure does not violate *lo tahmod*. Once social benefaction is on the corporate agenda, the investor should be no more surprised if the company undertakes a socially responsible project after heated debates than he would be if the company arrived at purely business decisions through a similar route.

The issue of *yohora*, however, remains intact. Engaging in do-good projects for society at large, while paying its workers below industry-average wages and falling behind in paying its bills, evidences skewed priorities on the part of the firm. This can engender only cynicism by the underprivileged or mistreated parties, contaminating the moral climate of society. In response, media and insider pressure for the firm to set its own house straight before engaging in altruism for society at large is warranted.

Another caveat should be noted. This discussion has related only to do-good projects for society at large. Socially responsible conduct directed toward employees, customers, and suppliers, however, is a different matter. In respect to these and other stakeholders of the firm, *halakhah* imposes definite duties and responsibilities. Beyond legalities, *halakhah* imposed a *moral duty* to treat people with decency and generosity extending beyond the strict letter of the law (*lifnim mi-shurat ha-din*). The agency relationship between a manager and the firm implicitly authorizes the manager to conduct business with a measure of *lifnim mi-shurat ha-din*. To what extent this obligation pertains and to what extent the owners have a right to override it requiress exploration. These issues, however, are beyond the scope of this paper.

Conspicuous Consumption

The central tenet of capitalism is economic freedom. In the realm of consumer behavior, this ethos translates into a non-judgmental attitude towards the pattern of consumption the economic system produces. It is only in the extreme instance when a good poses a physical danger to the consumer that government intervention in the marketplace is indicated. But the preferred approach even then is not to ban the product, but only to require the manufacturer to certify the risk involved to the consumer.

Illustrating the gulf between the capitalist ethic and Torah values in the area of consumer behavior is the phenomenon of conspicuous consumption. What is involved here is the consumption of goods not for their functional utility, but rather for their display or status value. In the capitalist ethic nothing objectionable would be found in this practice. This phenomenon, however, clearly assaults Torah values.

One objection to conspicuous consumption is that it is a form of conduct that generates envy. The prohibition against envy-generating conduct is spelled out in the following talmudic text:

> Our rabbis taught: . . . If one journeys from a place where they do not fast to a place where they do, he should fast with them . . . If he forgot and ate and drank, let him not make it patent in public, nor may he indulge in delicacies, as it is written, "And Jacob said to his sons, 'Why should you show yourself?' ['*lama titra'u*', Gen. 42:1]." Jacob conveyed thereby to his sons, "When you are fully sated, do not show yourselves before Esau or before Ishmael, that they should not envy you."[67]

Differential living standards inevitably produce feelings of inadequacy, embarrassment, and envy among those of limited means. With the aim of reducing the intensity of these ill feelings, the sages in talmudic times, regulated the lifestyles of the wealthy in various ways. Mourning customs provide a case in point:

> Formerly, they were wont to convey [victuals] to the house of mourning, the rich in silver and gold baskets, and the poor in osier baskets of peeled willow twigs, and the poor felt shamed: they therefore instituted that all should convey [victuals] in osier baskets of peeled willow twigs out of deference to the poor.
>
> Formerly, they were wont to serve drinks in the house of mourning, the rich in white glass vessels, the poor in colored glass, and the poor felt shamed:

---

[67]*Taanit* 10b; Rif, ad loc.; *Yad, Taanit* 1:15; Rosh, *Taanit* 1:7; *Tur, Orah Hayyim* 574:1; *Shulhan Arukh, Orah Hayyim* 574:2–3; *Arukh ha-Shulhan, Orah Hayyim* 574:2–3.

they instituted therefore that all should serve drinks in colored glasses out of deference to the poor.[68]

Out of concern that conspicuous consumption would ignite both internal discord and envy among neighboring non-Jews, autonomous Jewish communities in the Middle Ages regulated living standards. The medieval sumptuary laws typically imposed limitations on the type of dress residents could wear and restricted expenditures for weddings and other social festivities.[69]

Another halakhic objection to conspicuous consumption is that it adversely affects the margin on the choice between Torah study and *gemilut hasadim* on the one hand and marketplace activities on the other. This is so because a conspicuous consumption lifestyle heightens an individual's concept of what constitutes an adequate income to support a family. The more numerous conspicuous-consumption items appear in an individual's budget the more that person is driven to choose work over leisure at the margin. This, in turn, translates into less Torah study, less parenting, and less *gemilut hasadim*.

Robert Mason's research indicates that the real incidence of status-linked purchases can be considerably understated. One indication of the correctness of this assertion is that advertising today often stresses the social along with the practical benefits of goods and services. To this end, heavy emphasis is placed on style and visual attributes so as to cause the consumer to become preoccupied with appearance rather than with functional utility of any sort. Although it is impossible to measure the importance of secondary status-linked considerations in consumption decisions, its significance increases in consumer oriented societies as status-linked consumption is more effectively exploited.

Another consideration is the price-expectations effect. This concept entails the principle that people's purchasing behavior at any time is determined not only by the current market price, but also by the expectation as to what the future price will be. If the consumer believes that prices will rise, for instance, he can be expected to accelerate his normal

---

[68]*Moed Katan* 27a; Rif, ad locum; *Yad*, Avel 13:7; *Tur, Yoreh De'ah* 378:12; *Arukh ha-Shulhan, Yoreh De'ah* 378:7.

[69]R. Bezalel Landau, "Takanot Neged ha-Motarot," *Niv ha-Midrashiya* (Spring–Summer, 1971): 213–26.

demand pattern and to buy the goods in question immediately even if current prices are already high. Consequently, in times of high inflation and considerable uncertainty as to the future, consumers have been observed to increase their purchases of some commodities as prices themselves increase.

Although the price-expectations effect could be considered the most convincing explanation for positive demand/price correlations, it is also true that any increase in price of a particular product makes that product potentially more attractive to the conspicuous consumer. Part of the increased demand, therefore, can be ascribed to its relative increase in status.

Another price-related factor that can effectively mask conspicuous consumption is the price-quality relation consumers operate under when they have no first hand knowledge of the product they wish to purchase. Higher prices are taken to reflect better quality. But higher prices can also increase the status value of products, and it is possible that any increase in demand at the higher price includes an element of conspicuous consumption.[70]

Strategies to Reduce Conspicuous Consumption

Conspicuous consumption, as discussed earlier, assaults Torah values. Contemporary rabbinical initiatives to reduce this phenomenon have typically taken the form of promulgating decrees to circumscribe consumption of various forms.[71]

An alternative to this essentially negative approach is suggested by the research finding of cross-cultural studies on conspicuous consumption. Perhaps, the most vital finding of these studies is the rejection of the notion that conspicuous consumption is socially uncontrolled and motivated solely by self- indulgence and vanity. Quite to the contrary, these studies provide solid support for the notion that conspicuous consumption is primarily conditioned by social and economic factors. This behavior is most in evidence in those communities that actively encour-

---

[70]Robert Mason, *Conspicuous Consumption* (New York: St. Martin's Press, 1981), 122–3, 144–6.

[71]Cf. Meir Tamari, *With All Your Possessions* (New York: Free Press, 1987), 58.

age and promote the display of material and pecuniary advantage as a means of securing social status. Moreover, the tendency to consume conspicuously is strongest for those individuals who live in a subculture that reinforces the general societal approval of this conduct. Finally, the evidence indicates that conspicuous consumption is horizontally rather than vertically directed and appears to be motivated more by a desire to conform than to make significant status advances.[72]

These findings have important implications for the development of a positive strategy to reduce conspicuous consumption. The strength of this phenomenon indicates a corresponding weakness in status attached to Torah study, scholarship, piety, and *gemilut hasadim*. The existence of conspicuous consumption in the Jewish community indicates a measure of failure of both the parental and educational institutions to impart the primacy of spiritual values over material striving. This primacy will not triumph until the Torah personality replaces the pop-culture figure as the hero and role model for both youth and adults.

Another component in the thrust against conspicuous consumption is a role for the Jewish mass media. Their job is to attach glamour and glitter to the world of spiritual achievement and striving. They do this by exalting Torah authorities and publicizing extraordinary acts of nobility. No less important is the playing up of the spiritual triumphs and striving of children and ordinary people.

Another component in the attack against conspicuous consumption is the need to make Torah leisure activities competitive with the objectionable forms of the secular leisure industry. The more attractive the Torah leisure product is, the less people will relate to and be exposed to the secular counterpart, which embodies the conspicuous consumption ethic and other moral pitfalls.[73]

Conspicuous Consumption and Macroeconomics

Modern economic theory teaches that it is the level of aggregate spending that determines the level of income. For the United States economy, consumption spending constitutes approximately three-quarters of the

---

[72]Robert Mason, op. cit. 1–31.

[73]For the development of a theory for the Jewish ethic of leisure, see, R. Norman Lamm, *Faith and Doubt*, 2nd ed. (New York: Ktav), 187–212.

total expenditures that go into the Gross Domestic Product (GDP). What part of consumption spending is conspicuous consumption is impossible to measure. But any significant reduction in consumption spending, other things equal, would have the effect of dragging down the economy to a lower level of income. Job opportunities and earnings, therefore, would shrink. What this implies for the thrust to reduce conspicuous consumption is that it should be limited to the Jewish community itself. Turning the initiative outward to society at large would represent a dangerous item for the Jewish *tikkun olam* agenda.

The above analysis, however, is faulty. Within the context of the modern managed economy, the slack created by the reduction in consumption spending would be made up by a corresponding increase in either investment and or in government spending. To see why this is so, consider that the flip side of a reduction in consumption spending is an increase in saving. An increase in saving should, other things being equal, lead to lower interest rates. Lower interest rates, in turn, induce additional investment spending.

A reduction in conspicuous consumption spending might not be offset, however, by an increase in private investment spending. The main reason to doubt this is the possibility that the new trend in lower conspicuous consumption spending could generate waves of pessimism in the investment community, causing the investment-demand schedule to shift downward to the left. But government could step in here and borrow in the capital markets, increasing investment spending. The appropriateness of this action would depend on its evaluation of how the increased spending would affect on the dual but somewhat conflicting goals of full employment and price stability.[74]

Note that capital formation and expenditures on research and development are essential ingredients for economic growth. Any change in the composition of aggregate demand in the direction of more investment spending and less consumption could result in higher living standards for future generations.

---

[74]In Jewish society, the obligation of government to devise policies with the aim of achieving full employment and price stability is a matter of religious duty. For the development of this thesis see, Aaron Levine, *Economic Public Policy and Jewish Law* (Hoboken, NJ: Ktav; Yeshiva University Press, 1993), 201–207.

Within the context of the current economic environment, an increased saving rate is generally favored by economists.[75] If Americans would save more, we could finance more of our government budget deficit at home and would not need, therefore, to borrow so much abroad. This, too, would lead to a cheaper dollar and a smaller trade deficit. Any decrease in consumption spending would be offset, therefore, by a combination of an increase in investment spending and export demand.

What the aforementioned has demonstrated is that reducing conspicuous consumption is not only desirable from a moral standpoint, but it represents sound macroeconomic policy as well.

Social Welfare and *Halakhah*

In the capitalist ethic, charity giving is best left to individual decision making in the private sector. Government taxation for this purpose both violates economic freedom and interferes with the incentive system of the marketplace. In sharp contrast, Judaism calls for a dual system to deal with the social welfare issue. It consists of both public and private components.

In talmudic times, the public component consisted of a variety of coercive levies for the purpose of attending to the full range of needs of the poor.[76] However, public communal levies were never entirely relied upon to relieve poverty. People followed the dictum that one who becomes needy does not immediately apply for public relief.[77] First, his relatives and neighbors would attend to his needs; only then would the community be required to make up the discrepancy.

Providing a rationale for the dual system is R. Hayyim Soloveitchik. To begin, he notes that the charity obligation in the Torah is repeated twice: once in Lev. 25:35 and once in Deut. 15:7–8. The former pas-

---

[75]William J. Baumol and Alan S. Blinder, *Economic Principles and Policy*, 5th ed., (New York: Harcourt Brace Jovanovich, 1991), 431–2; see also Robert J. Gordon, *Macroeconomics*, 6th ed. (New York: HarperCollins, 1993), 373.

[76]Rama, *Shulhan Arukh, Hoshen Mishpat* 163:1; *Arukh ha-Shulhan, Hoshen Mishpat* 163:1. For a description of these levies, see Aaron Levine, *Free Enterprise and Jewish Law: Aspects of Jewish Business Ethics*, (New York: Ktav; Yeshiva University Press, 1980), 155.

[77]*Nedarim* 65b; *Shulhan Arukh, Yoreh De'ah* 257:8.

sage, in R. Soloveitchik's view, refers to society's collective responsibility to relieve poverty; the latter speaks of the individual's personal charity obligation. Noting that the reward for charity giving, expressed in the biblical phrase, "for the Lord your God will bless you for this in all your works and in whatever you undertake," is mentioned in connection with Deut. 15:10, R. Soloveitchik posits that coercion may not be applied to the individual's personal charity obligation. This follows from the general talmudic principle that when a reward is mentioned in connection with a biblical positive precept, the Jewish court will not force compliance, but instead, will rely upon voluntarism. Because no reward is mentioned in connection with the Leviticus passage, coercion is applied to the individual to force him to finance society's collective charity responsibility.[78] Coercion is rarely resorted to as a means of ensuring compliance with the Torah's dictates. So why is there coercion with respect to the Torah's charity obligation? Permit me to suggest two alternative approaches.

One possibility is that reliance on voluntarism possesses the danger that the needs of the poor would not adequately be attended to. Judaism requires an individual to give priority in his charity to his needy relatives. Without a government tax, indigents without relatives would surely suffer. Moreover, reliance on private measures to combat poverty could prove disappointing. Individuals, unless coerced (by a government charity tax), might choose to be free riders. This involves the following paradox: On an abstract level, people find poverty and misery appalling and are driven to alleviate these conditions; in practice, meaningful anti-poverty action fails to materialize as people rely on the collective efforts of others to do the job.[79]

Another possible rationale for the anti-poverty tax is the desire to elevate the quality of the individual's charity giving. Judaism teaches that charity in its most noble form consists of preventing a faltering individual from falling into the throes of poverty. The position of this person must

---

[78]R. Hayyim Soloveitchik, quoted in the name of R. Joseph B. Soloveitchik by R. Daniel Lander, "be-Inyan dei Mahsoro," in *Kevod ha-Rav* (New York: Student Organization of Yeshiva University, Rabbi Isaac Elchanan Theological Seminary, 1984), 202–6.

[79]H. M. Hochman and J. D. Rogers, "Pareto Optimal Redistribution," *American Economic Review* 59 (1969):542–3.

be stabilized and his dignity preserved, whether by making him a gift, extending him a loan, entering into a partnership with him, or creating a job for him.[80] Poverty prevention, in short, ranks as a higher priority than poverty relief.

The poverty prevention obligation is derived by *Torat Kohanim* from the phrase "you shall maintain him" employed in the Leviticus passage. Understanding the Leviticus passage to refer to society's collective responsibility to relieve poverty, as R. Soloveitchik does, adds a societal component to the poverty prevention obligation.

There is an enormous potential in public sector taxation for social welfare programs to elevate charity-giving to the level of prevention. Left to their own devices, private citizens might have few opportunities to disguise their charitable intent or prevent someone from sinking into poverty. A government levy, on the other hand, pools part of society's charitable resources. This fund could be used creatively by the public sector for such programs as job training and improving the efficiency of the labor market. Government subsidization of the working poor by means of such programs as the earned income tax credit and the wage rate subsidy also promote the goal of poverty prevention. Public sector involvement of the sort described above also removes the stigma that beneficiaries might otherwise feel in receiving charity.

Applying the obligation to prevent poverty to the public sector generates a responsibility to pursue policies that would foster a favorable economic environment. These policies would prevent the economy from falling into a recession. Public sector investment in the development of society's infrastructure, in the form of road, bridge, school, plant, mass transit, and hospital construction, represents one type of initiative that promotes this end. Investment in basic research is another area of vital concern for long-term economic growth. Reliance on the profit motive to bring forth an optimal level of investment in the above areas invariably results in an underallocation of resources.

Meeting its obligation to create a favorable economic environment requires the government to build "automatic stabilizers" into the economic system for the purpose of softening the impact of any sharp economic downturn in the private sector. An adequate unemployment compensation system and a progressive income tax serve this function. The

---

[80]*Yad, Mattenot Aniyyim* 10:7.

operation of these automatic stabilizers guarantees that the federal budget will automatically increase the government deficit when the economy
experiences a tailspin. Similarly, automatic stabilizers reduce the federal
deficit and hence retard the rate of government spending when the private sector is expanding at too rapid a pace. *Restoration* of a favorable
economic environment in the face of a severe economic downturn requires discretionary expansionary monetary and fiscal policy initiatives
to supplement the automatic stabilizers. Implementation of any measures
currently regarded as necessary to promote a depression-free economy
is also indicated. Mandatory insurance on bank deposits and margin
requirements on the purchase of financial assets provide examples of
these measures.

If the public sector limited its involvement in poverty relief out of
concern that it would be at the expense of economic growth, this would
represent a clear-cut *abdication* of its charity obligation. Nonetheless, once
society has already devoted 10 percent or more of its income[81] to a combination of poverty prevention and poverty-relief measures, the possible
conflict between these two objectives must be taken into account. To
illustrate, suppose conventional economic wisdom insists that any further substantial increase in government spending, regardless of how it is
financed, threatens the efficiency of the economy. If the spending were
financed by increasing the tax burden, a work-disincentive signal would
be generated to the marketplace. On the other hand, financing the increased spending by means of new money supply creation and/or bor-
rowing would run the risk of both increasing inflation and causing a surge
in interest rates. Within the context of this assessment, unless the federal government is willing to restructure its priorities, further poverty-
relief efforts must be shifted to the private sector. Deferring to voluntarism
here follows from the public sector's responsibility to give poverty prevention primacy over poverty relief.

The Role of the Private Sector

Notwithstanding the advantages of an anti-poverty tax, Judaism does
not saddle the entire burden of anti-poverty efforts on the public sector.

---

[81]See infra text accompanying notes 96–101.

Doing so would ignore Judaism's call for relatives and neighbors to bear greater responsibility for their poor. Moreover, exclusive reliance on the public sector impedes fulfillment of the charity obligation. Jewish charity law requires more than financial outlay; it compels an emotional contribution in the form of relieving for the indigent his feelings of isolation and hopelessness. Public assistance decreases both the opportunity for, and the sensitivity to, easing a poor man's emotional burden.

In the Talmud, R. Issac stated that "he who gives a small coin to a poor man obtains six blessings, and he who addresses to him words of comfort obtains eleven blessings."[82] Although the financial aspect of the charity obligation is subject to an upward limit, there is no limit on one's obligation to devote time to the performance of good deeds.[83] Sharing the companionship of the poor and affording them social equality represents a high level of charity and merits special blessings.[84]

R. Isadore Twersky points out that according to the Jewish theory of philanthropy, personal contact with, and exposure to the needy is essential. R. Twersky observes that "the individual can never really isolate himself from the needy, especially in times of euphoria, pleasure and indulgence. The very nature of rejoicing and festivity includes sharing with others."

In accordance with this thought, Maimonides formulated the biblical command to rejoice with others during the festivals: "While one eats and drinks by himself, it is his duty to feed the stranger, the orphan, the widow, along with other despondent poor people. But he who locks the doors to his courtyard and eats and drinks with his wife and family, without giving anything to eat and drink to the poor and the bitter of soul—his meal is not a rejoicing in a divine commandment, but a rejoicing in his own stomach. . . . Rejoicing of this kind is a disgrace to those who indulge in it."[85]

In addition, *halakhah* prohibits a Jew from taking action that would dull his sensitivities to the suffering of his fellow man. This prohibition is derived by the *Sifrei*, which relates the biblical phrase "thou shalt not harden thy heart nor shut thy hand" (Deut. 15:7) not only to consciously

---

[82]*Bava Batra* 9b.
[83]R. Ovadiah Yarei Bartenura at Mishnah *Pe'ah* 1:1; *Yad, Avel* 14:1.
[84]*Yad, Mattenot Aniyyim* 10:16.
[85]*Yad, Yom Tov* 6:18.

hardening one's heart and suppressing the inclination towards kindness, but also to the omission of the positive.[86]

Reliance on public charity carries with it the danger of creating the misperception that the total needs of the disadvantaged, both material and emotional, are being attended to by "others." The more society relies on public assistance to combat poverty, the less aware independent citizens will be of individual poverty cases. Although anonymity preserves the dignity of the disadvantaged, it also isolates them and desensitizes the public to their plight. In a state reliant completely on government assistance for the poor, citizens will begin to concentrate their *gemilut hasadim* (acts of kindness) only on their inner circle of friends, creating social stratification.

Income Redistribution and *Halakhah*

Liberals have always sought to expand the social welfare role for government. The proper role in that tradition is to go beyond poverty relief and effect a fairer distribution of income. My purpose here is to demonstrate that income redistribution is a foreign concept to Jewish charity law.

Although *halakhah* prescribes personal and communal responsibilities vis-à-vis the poor, it does not mandate income redistribution. Specific aspects of Jewish charity law that point to this conclusion include: (1) the *dei mahsoro* imperative; (2) the eligibility requirement to receive assistance; and (3) floors and ceilings on individual charity rates.

Dei Mahsoro

Jewish law imposes an obligation to satisfy fully the needs of the poor (*dei mahsoro*).[87] According to talmudic explanation, codified by later halakhic decisors, *dei mahsoro* requires the community to supply the poor man only with his basic requirements; society is not obligated to make him rich.[88]

---

[86]R. Isadore Twersky, "Some Aspects of the Jewish Attitude toward the Welfare State," *Tradition* 5:2 (1963): 140–149.

[87]Deut. 15:8; *Ketuvot* 67b; *Yad, Mattenot Aniyyim* 7:1–5; *Rosh, Ketuvot* 6:8; *Tur, Yoreh De'ah* 250; *Shulhan Arukh, Yoreh De'ah* 250:1; *Arukh ha-Shulhan, Yoreh De'ah*, 250:1–5. Literally, *dei mahsoro* means "sufficient for his needs."

[88]*Ketuvot* 67b; *Yad*, op. cit. 7:3.

At the same time, *dei mahsoro* extends to basic psychological needs, and might compel the community to provide luxuries for a poor person temporarily. For example, the Talmud relates that Hillel the Elder provided a poor man with a horse on which to ride and a slave to run before him, because the individual had been accustomed to these luxuries in wealthier times.[89]

The *Geonim* explain that *dei mahsoro* imposes communal sensitivity to a specific psychological need: the humiliation accompanying public revelation of a fall from wealth to poverty. To prevent or delay a person's destitution from becoming public knowledge, society creates a facade of affluence for him. The *Geonim* further point out that once the indigence becomes public knowledge, *dei mahsoro* no longer obligates the community to provide luxuries to maintain a pretence of affluence. At this stage, society fulfills its obligation by supplying basic needs alone.[90]

Once understood as a sensitivity to an indigent's psychological trauma, the *dei mahsoro* requirement to provide luxuries cannot be described as an income-redistribution plan. Except to mitigate temporarily the degradation accompanying an economic disaster, *dei mahsoro* compels satisfying only an indigent's basic needs; if a person is not actually impoverished, there is no obligation to lavish luxuries upon him, even if he had enjoyed them in better days.

Eligibility Criteria for Public Assistance

Wealth and its liquidity formed the two basic elements of the talmudic eligibility criterion for public assistance. In establishing eligibility standards for receiving the agricultural gifts,[91] the Talmud classified a household as poor if its net worth fell below 200 *zuz*. When net worth consisted of capital invested in business transactions, the minimum net worth sum shrank to 50 *zuz*, on the assumption than an active capital of this size would generate subsistence for a year.[92]

---

[89]*Ketuvot* 67b; *Yad*, op. cit. 7:3; *Arukh ha-Shulhan*, op. cit. 250:2.

[90]Gaonim, quoted in R. Bezalel Ashkenazi, *Shittah Mekubbezet, Ketuvot* 67b.

[91]Biblically prescribed charities included *leket, shikhhah and pe'ah*: gleanings, forgotten produce, and the corner of the field, respectively, as well as agricultural tithe. For a description of the operation of these agricultural gifts, see *Encyclopedia Judaica*, 5:343.

[92]Mishnah *Pe'ah* 8:8–9; Bartenora, ad loc.

Liquidity of a family's assets affected the 200-*zuz* criterion. Usually, claims for assistance on the basis of inadequate cash flow were denied when net worth exceeded the poverty line. Instead of relying on the public purse, the household was expected to liquidate its assets to increase cash flow to an adequate level.[93] There were several exceptions, however, to the general liquidity rule. First, the law did not require an individual to sell his apparel, home, or any essential household article in order to obtain cash for basic subsistence,[94] unless those items were made of gold or silver. In the case of gold or silver utensils, an indigent was required to sell the articles and replace them with less costly ones.[95] Net worth was then recalculated, excluding the new and cheaper household items from total assets. If his net worth then reached 200 *zuz*, the individual did not qualify for public assistance.[96]

Second, the liquidity of farmland received special treatment. Jewish law recognized that the market value of farmland was subject to seasonal fluctuation.[97] Close to harvest-time, during the summer months, land value was relatively high; immediately after the harvest, during the autumn, its market value was relatively low. If the liquidity of the household was calculated during the depressed autumn market, the family would qualify for public assistance unless it could sell its land for at least one-half its harvest-time value.[98]

In addition, Jewish law was sensitive to the disadvantageous bargaining position faced by a pauper forced to sell his land. If the household's low liquidity compromised its bargaining position to such an extent that it could not sell its holdings at the prevailing market price, the household qualified for public assistance until it could find a buyer at the pre-

---

[93]Mishnah *Pe'ah* 8:8; *Yad*, op.cit 9:14; *Shulhan Arukh.*, op. cit. 253:1; *Arukh ha-Shulhan*, op. cit. 253:5.

[94]*Shulhan Arukh.*, op.cit 153:1.

[95]Ibid. Selling more expensive utensils was only a condition for the receipt of public assistance; eligibility for private assistance did not depend on such a sale (*Shulhan Arukh.*, loc.cit.).

[96]Ibid.

[97]Tosafot, *Bava Kamma* 7b, claim that the realty market in general is subject to the same fluctuation.

[98]Tosafot, *Bava Kamma* 7a; *Tur*, op. cit. 253. For a different view, see *Yad*, op. cit. 9:1; *Shulhan Arukh*, op. cit. 253:1.

vailing market price.[99] When real estate values were generally depressed, however, the low price offered an indigent family did not entitle the household to public assistance while it waited for property values to rise.[100]

Another consideration that points to halakhic opposition to income redistribution is the requirement set to qualify for weekly disbursements of the public food fund (*kuppah*). In order to qualify, a person had to be unable to provide himself with fourteen meals; funds for two meals per day for one week disqualified the individual from becoming a public charge for that week.[101] The Talmud (*Shabbat* 118a) refused to liberalize the eligibility requirement to fifteen meals in order to accommodate the religious obligation of eating three meals on the Sabbath. Instead, it observed Rabbi Akiva's maxim: Treat your Sabbath like a weekday rather than be dependent on your fellow-beings. Commenting on this passage, Rashi explains that a person may not "impose on others the honor of his Sabbaths."[102]

Post-Talmudic Era

Although some authorities extend the Talmudic 200-*zuz* criterion for eligibility to modern times,[103] R. Yitzhak of Corbeil broke new ground

---

[99]*Bava Kamma* 7a; *Yad*, op. cit. 9:17; *Shulhan Arukh.*, op.cit 253:3; *Arukh ha-Shulhan*, op. cit. 253:5.

[100]R. Joseph Caro, *Kesef Mishneh*, *Yad*, op. cit. 9:17; *Arukh ha-Shulhan*, op. cit. 253:8.

A third aspect of liquidity, unrelated to income redistribution, is the location of a person's assets. For inclusion in net work, an asset must be accessible to its owner. Thus, a traveler, whose holdings were situated near his permanent residence, qualified for public assistance as soon as his funds ran out. Upon his return home, the law did not require him to return any charity he received while on his travels. In the modern banking era, when electronic transfer of funds is commonplace, location, it appears to me, would not render a cash asset inaccessible.

[101]*Shabbat* 118a; *Yad*, op. cit. 9:13; *Shulhan Arukh*, op. cit. 253:1; *Arukh ha-Shulhan*, op. cit. 253:1.

[102]Rashi, *Shabbat* 118a.

[103]R. Ephraim of Regensberg and R. Yizhak of Vienna quoted in *Beit Yosef*, *Tur*, op. cit. 253.

by rejecting this identification. In his view, the 200 *zuz* minimum applied only to former times, when agricultural gifts, as well as institutionalized public welfare in the form of the charity chest (*kuppah*), and the charity plate (*tamhuy*),[104] were regularly available to people whose net worth dropped below the minimum. A person could sell his assets today with the assurance that the community would provide for him tomorrow. However, in a world in which these gifts are less certain, the standard shifts from capital inadequacy (based on net worth) to income inadequacy. So long as a person's income (from all sources) for a given period remains below subsistence level, he is eligible for public assistance.[105] R. Joseph Caro records R. Yitzhak's view approvingly.[106]

Seemingly following R. Yitzhak's approach, the late contemporary scholar R. Shlomo Zalman Auerbach applies the income inadequacy standard to modern society, positing that an unemployed person, whose total income, including income from capital and transfer payments from the government, does not afford him a "reasonable" standard of living, qualifies for public assistance. What is "reasonable" will depend upon the neighborhood in which he resides and the level of wealth to which he was formerly accustomed.[107]

Although R. Auerbach would seem to adopt the approach of R. Yitzhak of Corbeil, closer examination of R. Yitzhak's reasoning indicates the possibility that he would apply the Talmudic capital inadequacy standard to contemporary society. R. Yitzhak based his distinction between Talmudic society and his own on the guarantee of agricultural gifts and communal support in Talmudic times. So long as the community secured an indigent's future, he could reasonably by expected to deplete his capital for support. However, when society provides no safety net, requiring a pauper to exhaust his assets would leave him with a completely insecure future. The modern social welfare state, with its regular support payments, closely resembles the Talmudic community. Because the modern poor can rely on government contributions in the way Talmu-

---

[104]For the operation of these communal charity functions, see, *Encyclopedia Judaica*, 5:346–7, n. 13.

[105]*Shulhan Arukh*, op. cit. 253:2; *Arukh ha-Shulhan*, op. cit. 253:2.

[106]*Shulhan Arukh*, op. cit.

[107]Interview with R. S. Z. Auerbach, quoted in Cyril Domb, *Ma'aser Kesafim* (New York: Feldheim, 1980), appendix 9:19.

dic indigents could depend on the various agricultural gifts, *halakhah* could very well require them to deplete their capital before applying for public assistance.

Defining poverty in terms of income inadequacy, as R. Auerbach does, leads to a work disincentive for those who have a small amount of capital but cannot survive on the income from that capital. Following an income inadequacy standard, these indigents receive public assistance and thus have little incentive to work. Under a capital inadequacy standard, however, these paupers become eligible for public assistance only after depleting their capital. Faced with the choice of losing their savings, many might choose to earn a living instead. In a society providing the poor with a safety net to secure their basic needs, it could very well be fairer to follow the talmudic capital-inadequacy standard and establish strong work incentives.

Individual Charity Rates

Jewish law establishes a 10 percent (of net income) minimum and a 20 percent maximum rate for individual charity donations. Both the minimum and maximum rates demonstrate that halakhic charity law intends to supply the poor with only basic needs, not to redistribute income throughout society.

Talmudic decisors differ as to whether the 10 percent charity obligation imposed by the Torah on agricultural produce[108] applies to income as well.[109] Opinions in the matter range from an income tithe requirement arising from Biblical law to one that requires the tithe only by dint of custom. In his survey of the responsa literature, R. Ezra Basri concludes that the majority opinion regards the 10 percent level as a definite obligation, albeit by dint of rabbinical decree.[110] In any case, devoting less than 10 percent of one's income to charity is considered by the rabbis to reflect an ungenerous nature.[111]

---

[108]See Deut. 14:22.

[109]See *Ma'aser Kesafim*, op. cit. pp. 18–29.

[110]R. Ezra Basri, *Dinei Mamonot* (Jerusalem: Rubin Mass, 1974), 1:403.

[111]*Yad*, op. cit. 8:5; *Tur*, op. cit. 249:1; *Shulhan Arukh.*, op. cit. 249:1; *Arukh ha-Shulhan*, op. cit. 249:1.

Because Jewish law requires a person to donate only 10 percent of his net income to charity, any additional contribution is considered *lifenim mi-shurat ha-din*, beyond the letter of the law. Jewish law prohibits the community from coercing a person to act *lifenim mi-shurat ha-din*,[112] so it may not enact a general charity levy compelling donation of more than 10 percent. This protection of property rights prevents the community from accomplishing an income redistribution plan through the charity laws.

Fearing that over-generosity would make the donor himself vulnerable to poverty, the sages at Usha enacted a prohibition against donating more than 20 percent of one's income to charity.[113] There is some dispute as to the breadth of the prohibition. Some authorities apply the prohibition only to donations to the charity fund in the absence of requests for assistance but allow a person to exceed the maximum rate to comply with specific pleas for assistance. Others suspend the interdict only for bequests and situations in which aid is necessary to avert the loss of human life.[114] Neither school of interpretation allows use of the charity law to effect greater equity in society.

---

[112]Rosh, *Bava Metzia* 2:7; R. Shabbetai ben Meir ha-Kohen, *Siftei Kohen, Shulhan Arukh, Hoshen Mishpat* 259:5, n. 3; *Arukh ha-Shulhan, Hoshen Mishpat* 394:11. A minority view in the matter calls for a Jewish court to compel a person to relinquish his legal rights. Judicial coercion is, however, only appropriate if the individual is wealthy. See R. Mordekhai ben Hillel, *Mordekhai, Bava Metzia* 2:257; R. Joel Sirkes, Bah, *Tur, Hoshen Mishpat* 12, n. 4.

[113]*Ketubot* 50a; *Yad, Arakhin* 8:13; Rama, *Shulhan Arukh., Yoreh De'ah* 249:1; *Arukh ha-Shulhan, Yoreh De'ah* 249:1.

[114]See sources cited by R. Basri, op. cit. 408.

11

Health Care and *Tikkun Olam*

Barry Freundel

I. INTRODUCTION

Ever since the election of Bill Clinton as President of the United States, the issue of health care has been a central concern of the American body politic. Cost of the care is the most significant conundrum, with larger and larger segments of the gross national product and the federal budget deficit attributable to health-care-related items. As a logical extension of this problem, the capacity for poor or marginal people to obtain adequate health care declines as the costs rise. So, too, the number of people carrying adequate insurance coverage for themselves and their families goes down in response to the increased expense.

The seriousness of the problem evokes many suggested solutions. Models from other countries are proposed and studied, plans with intriguing sounding names are put on the table and high level committees are formed. All struggle with competing pressures—free market versus affordability, universal access versus timely availability, a personal doctor-patient relationship versus universal care, reward for professional excellence versus reasonable pricing, incentive and funding for research and development versus responding to the current need—that are extremely difficult, or perhaps, impossible to reconcile. In short, it is a Herculean task that awaits, and one that will, in all probability, never yield a perfect solution. Jewish communities through the ages struggled with similar concerns. Both in our years of sovereignty during the Second Commonwealth and as autonomous communities in many foreign lands, officials of the Jewish community attempted to provide adequate health care to their constituents. What follows is a discussion of the historic, halakhic and philosophical underpinnings of those attempts and a description of the model that emerges. The advantages and contemporary applications of the model will be highlighted.

All this will be preceded by a discussion of the imperatives that drive the Jewish community to assume the health-care burden. In addition, a discussion of a possible halakhic basis for our general involvement in public policy issues will be presented. This will serve to place the issue in its *tikkun olam* context.

Historically, the *or la-goyim* ("light unto the nations") role that the Jewish community has been proud to fill has included not only the teaching of ethical and moral constructs but also the showcasing of efficient and workable models. As an example, the American legal system owes much to the rabbinic court system. In that sense, health-care reform could provide another opportunity for the Jewish community to exercise appropriate influence on an area of fundamental concern to the lives of every single human being.

II. THE SOURCES OF THE IMPERATIVE—
WHY IS HEALTH CARE A JEWISH CONCERN?

In some ways, the answer to the question posed as the title to this section would seem obvious. The *Encyclopaedia Judaica* begins its entry on "Amenities, communal" with the statement, "From the beginnings of Jewish communal organization, the Jewish community 'held nothing human to be beyond its ken.' . . . Total care had to be taken of the community, especially of the less fortunate members."[1] As such, it is part of our intrinsic self-help *weltanschauung* for the Jewish community to ensure that needs of this kind be provided for members of the community.

If one wishes to formalize this cultural norm and conceptualize it within halakhic imperatives, one may begin with the general obligations to heal. These include the prohibition "Do not stand on your brother's

---

[1]*Encyclopaedia Judaica*, s.v. "Amenities, Communal."

blood"[2] and the affirmative requirement of returning a loss,[3] which is understood to include restoring a sick person's health.

Public officials have an additional and specific burden in this regard. They are charged with maintaining the infrastructure so that deaths and injuries do not result from broken bridges or roads or from thorns on the thoroughfares.[4] The Talmud, basing itself on the biblical phrase, "and blood shall be upon you,"[5] goes so far as to hold public officials who neglect this duty personally responsible for any blood shed through their negligence. This imperative is seen as significant enough to override some of the prohibitions attendant to work on the intermediate days of the holiday (*hol ha-mo'ed*). Certain types of work were permitted on *hol ha-mo'ed* when done for communal need, therefore, that would have been prohibited had they been done only for individual need.[6] As I shall show, licensing of doctors and regulation of medical practice were done by the rabbis as early as the talmudic period. Neglect of the system would surely have evoked the same burden of responsibility on the part of public officials for death or injury as did non-repair of a bridge.

A similar case of relaxing at least some prohibitions against work, this time on the Sabbath, could provide an underlying rationale for this heightened concern within the public domain. A red-hot piece of metal may not be extinguished on the Sabbath in a private domain, but it may be so treated in the public domain.[7] One can argue that the difference

---

[2]Lev. 19:16. See generally *Sanhedrin* 73a; Maimonides, *Mishneh Torah, Hilkhot Rotze'ah u-Shemirat ha-Nefesh*, 1:14, *Shulhan Arukh: Hoshen Mishpat* 426:1. See Num. 17 regarding personal involvement of communal leaders in stopping a plague.

[3]See generally Ex. 23:3, Deut. 22:1–3, *Sanhedrin* 73a, Maimonides, *Commentary to the Mishnah*, Nedarim 4,4.

[4]*Mo'ed Katan* 5a. See Maimonides, *Sefer Hamitzvot*, negative precept 298.

[5]Deut. 19:10. This verse is found in the section mandating the establishment of refuge cities. Deut. 19:3 reads "prepare the roads," so that the imperative requires public infrastructure maintenance. Maimonides, ibid., sees the removal of dangerous public conditions as one of the 613 Biblical commandments. See below for a suggestion of how liability might apply to a health care situation.

[6]Maimonides, *Hilkhot Shevitat Yom Tov* 7:10–12, *Shulhan Arukh: Orah Hayyim* 544:1–2. See *Shulhan Arukh: Orah Hayyim: 70:4–5* for discussion of whether one involved in communal needs should interrupt to recite *keriat Shema*.

[7]*Shabbat* 42a, *Zevahim* 91b, Maimonides: *Hilkhot Shabbat* 1:7 and 12:2, *Shulhan Arukh: Orah Hayyim* 334:27.

has a statistical basis. A danger that carries a one-in-one-thousand probability of occurring might be tolerable if only a few people are exposed to it. However, if it is in a public area where hundreds or thousands will happen upon it, the danger becomes intolerable. The likelihood of the accident happening has gone from one with only a slim possibility, to one with a virtual certainty because of the vastly increased number of times that the dice are being rolled.[8] Since the public health-care system deals with millions of individuals, many potential dangers will be amplified to the point of virtual certainty if the system is not adequately managed.

There may also be a more general imperative to involve oneself in issues of this type. In discussing the seven Noahide laws, Rambam sees the Jewish community as required to appoint judges for Noahides (or at least for resident aliens) to adjudicate cases related to the seven Noahide laws "that the world not be destroyed."[9] Although it is doubtful that Jews have an obligation to direct and control the moral acts of individual gentiles,[10] one needs to approach major public policy questions from a macro perspective instead of an individual perspective.

Rambam's concern about the potential destruction of the world is likely rooted in two things. The first is chronological. The revelation of these laws to Noah and his family occurs in the biblical story immediately after the Flood, which did, in fact destroy the world.[11] As such, the laws can be seen as a preventive measure against the repetition of that event.[12] This is supported by the second element: Rambam's use of the root "*shahet*," which parallels the Torah's account of the breakdown of morality in antediluvian society.[13] Rambam is reminding us, then, that macro-moral breakdown—societal moral breakdown—is a precursor to (or perhaps a definition of) worldwide destruction.

Preventing worldwide destruction is a matter of concern for us not only for the obvious reasons of self-interest. The world is precious to

---

[8]See S. Boylan, "Heshash Sakkanah le-Or ha-Halakhah," *Or Hamizrach* 32,1 (Tishrei 5744): 48–59, especially 58.

[9]Maimonides, *Hilkhot Melakhim* 10:11.

[10]See Rabbi J. David Bleich's paper in this volume.

[11]Gen. 9.

[12]See *Zevahim* 116a for an indication that such a possibility exists.

[13]Gen. 6:11.

God,[14] and He made a covenant to preserve it in the aftermath of the flood.[15] In fact, mankind's commitment to keep these seven laws is our concomitant obligation to God's pledge of non-destruction. As signatories to the covenant, on imitatio dei grounds as well as on the simple premise that what is precious to God is and should be precious to us, we have an obligation to preserve the world and therefore the world's morality.

Even if one holds that there is no obligation to the individual non-Jew, there is an obligation to the entire non-Jewish world. Clearly, when global nuclear war must be prevented or a worldwide environmental catastrophe must be averted, Jews, under this rationale, would need to be involved even if not a single Jew were affected. The question remains, however, regarding the undifferentiated middle. How big a segment of the world must be involved before "that the world not be destroyed" takes effect?

Although I can think of no specific guidelines (though it is true that Abraham felt compelled to intervene on behalf of four small gentile cities,[16] and Jonah was sent by God to save one[17]) contemporary public-policy issues can often have an impact far beyond what is first perceived. Health-care reform, for example, directly affects not only the health and well-being of hundreds of millions of people, but also one seventh of the U.S. gross national product. In a global economy, this can have world-wide ramifications.

In a moral sense, too, health-care reform has potential global consequences. If health-care reform results in encouraging active euthanasia, in enshrining the notion that people who have passed a certain age are less worthy of care than younger people, or in creating a destructive life-and-death competition between one person's health and another's job, then the moral tone of society will be seriously harmed with potential negative consequences. These issues surely evoke Rambam's imperative even for those who do not see a requirement to involve themselves in the moral life of individual gentiles.

Health care, therefore, is both a Jewish and a *tikkun olam* concern. Our concern for God's world, our cultural heritage, the demand that we

---

[14]Cf. Mishnah, *Avot* 5:1.

[15]Gen. 9:12 ff.

[16]Gen. 18.

[17]Jon.

restore what has been lost, and the demand that we not stand idly by when someone is in need—all require us to act. Further, the potential for truly world shattering events—mass epidemics or people dying due to lack of financial resources or adequate delivery systems from diseases whose cures exist—lies at the heart of our concern about health care.

On the other hand, society must also face the real problem of setting limits on public health-care expenditures. In some utopian sense, a fully appointed intensive-care-unit bed should be available for every man, woman, and child in this country in case we all become ill at once. Obviously we would bankrupt our society long before achieving that goal. Even if we used all available resources to set up as many beds as possible, we would not be acting appropriately, because we would be drawing resources away from other vital needs. Clearly a balance must be struck, and guidance in striking that balance must be found. Given the magnitude of the challenge and the consequences of failure if we do not involve ourselves, we should, *pace* the Talmud, hold ourselves responsible for any harm that comes.

III. THE MACRO QUESTION: HOW MUCH SHOULD A SOCIETY DEVOTE TO HEALTH CARE?

The question of limiting society's financial obligation to and support for its constituent members who are in need is morally wrenching and emotionally taxing. One need look only at the responses evoked by the Oregon Plan for Managing Health Care Resources to recognize how difficult these discussions can be. Under this plan, a priority list of medical needs was created and a cutoff point, defining which types of situations would receive governmental assistance and which would not, was determined. This is similar to policies found in some European national health plans, under which, for example, patients who have passed a particular age may no longer receive governmental subsidy for treatments such as dialysis. This is done to ration available financial resources in what is believed to be an ethical and reasonable fashion, so as to prevent the system from bankrupting itself.

Similar problems concern many public-policy planners. We have the technology to build aircraft that are so crash-survivable that virtually everyone would survive any conceivable incident. However, the cost of construction would be so high that, should these airplanes come to replace our current fleet, virtually no one would be able to afford a ticket. Similarly, automobiles could be manufactured to ensure survivability for passengers involved in accidents. Should this technology be included in automobiles on today's assembly lines, the technology would no longer serve a purpose, because so few cars would be on the road that accidents would almost never occur. (I am reminded of an apocryphal story, however, that tells of the first two motorcars in the State of Kansas in the early twentieth century managing to find a way to collide with one another. This is an interesting exception, though a statistical anomaly.) In all of these cases, a reasonable balance between need and economic realities must be struck.

How did Judaism strike that balance? First, and in direct opposition to contemporary American society, Judaism did not ask us to create a risk-free world. In requiring us to act to prevent negligent injury, the Torah requires only the following: "When you build a new house you shall make a parapet for your roof so that you not bring blood into your home when the faller falls from it."[18] Note that the biblical reason for building the parapet is not to prevent falling; when the faller falls, however, the homeowner is not responsible. The requirement is that reasonable precautions be taken, not that all risk be eliminated.

Similarly, the Talmud[19] gives license to people who work in somewhat hazardous professions to continue doing so in order to make a living.[20] R. Yehezkel Landau[21] permits hunting for those who do it to make a living, when it is essential, and prohibits the same activity for sport—specifically in light of this source. The dangers of entering a forest and encountering wild animals is tolerable in the one case, intolerable in the other. Again, the normal activities of living do not come risk-free. A community need do only that which is reasonable, therefore, and not take every possible precaution to solve communal problems even when

---

[18]Deut. 22:8.
[19]*Bava Metzia* 112a, *Sifrei*: Deut. 69.
[20]Based on Deut. 24:15.
[21]*Noda Be-Yehudah: Mahadura Tinyana: Yoreh De'ah* 10.

risk is involved. If we were absolutist in this regard, professions involving risk would have to be eliminated.

Second, as against both the Oregon Plan and the European models, Jewish tradition would eschew any attempt to withhold medical care based on age or similar criteria. This statement is best understood from within its philosophic framework, which closely parallels a formal mathematical construct. Some mathematicians define "infinity" (∞) as "a number, some of whose subsets are equal to the whole." To clarify that with a specific example, we all know that $\infty - 1 = \infty$. In precisely the same fashion, Jewish tradition views each human life as infinitely valuable. "One who saves one life, it is as if he has saved the entire world", says the Talmud.[22] The subset—the single life—is equivalent to the whole—the entire world.

This is not merely a theoretical formulation. It has significant practical implications that affect many legal conclusions codified by Jewish law. Perhaps the most dramatic is the law's refusal to permit the sacrificing of even a single life for the sake of the survival of the many. If criminals surround a group of people with the intent of killing one of them and demand that the group choose one who shall be put to death, no such choice may be made by the group. They should all die at the hands of the criminals rather than make the ethically impossible determination of who shall live and who shall die.[23] Because each soul is infinitely valuable—by definition, as valuable as the whole—no ethically correct choice can be made in the circumstances described. For this same reason, an eighty-year-old's life is not intrinsically any more or less valuable than an eighteen-year-old's. Both represent infinite value and cannot be compared and contrasted as to which is more appropriate to save.[24]

---

[22]Mishnah *Sanhedrin* 4:5.

[23]Cf. Maimonides, *Hilkhot Yesodei Ha-Torah* 5:5.

[24]We should cite the Mishnah in *Horayot* 3:7–8, which appears to give precedence to some people over others (e.g. Kohen before Levi, Levi before Yisra'el, etc.). These are formalistic statements that deal primarily with externals, not with essential value. Further, historically, they seem never to have been used in cases of life and death. See E. Rackman "Priorities in the Right to Life" in *Tradition and Transition: Essays Presented to Chief Rabbi Sir Immanuel Jakobovits to Celebrate Twenty-Five Years in Office*, ed. J. Sacks, (London: Jews' College Publications, 1986). R. Moses Feinstein, *Responsa Iggerot Moshe: Hoshen Mishpat*

Judaism does, however, make a distinction in issues of this type between a theoretical person in need and an actual person in need.[25] A contemporary model for this distinction was provided to me by a former naval-planning officer. It can cost as much as $100,000 to turn an aircraft carrier around and then around again to resume its original course. Although the navy could rationally and appropriately decide against adding a particular $100,000 safety device designed to prevent people from falling overboard as not being cost effective, no one would hesitate, even momentarily, to try to rescue a sailor who had actually fallen into the water because it could cost the same $100,000 to turn the boat around. At the point where drowning becomes a real rather than a theoretical concern, the infinite value of the sailor's life overwhelms any other considerations.

A final element that derives from the "infinity" principle is relevant to us here. Jewish law does allow for a distinction between a person who is terminally ill and one whose life is at least, theoretically, presently unbounded. When one is forced to choose by circumstance or lack of resources to institute treatment either for one who is terminally ill or for one whose illness is not terminal, the latter would be chosen,[26] because the unbounded nature of his life carries the full implications of infinite value while the former has lost at least some of them.

This last statement is true only so long as care has not been instituted. If care has begun, however, it may not be terminated even for someone with extreme morbidity.[27] Here, the Jewish response to a classic moral dilemma takes ethical control of the situation. Two travel the desert. One has a bottle of water. If both drink, both will die; if one drinks, he

---

2:74 states that it is impossible to follow these rules without great investigation and study and that they only apply if the needs present at precisely the same time—a virtual impossibility. In addition, Yerushalmi treats this as a case of who is fed first, not as the issue of whose life takes precedence.

[25]"Befaneinu" and "lo befaneinu." The principle reaches its fullest modern exposition in discussions of issues of autopsy and organ transplant, cf. J.D. Bleich, *Contemporary Halakhic Problems*, (New York: Ktav, 1983) v. II, p. 57, F. Rosner, *Modern Medicine and Jewish Law* (New York: 1972) p.164.

[26]Moses Feinstein: *Responsa Iggerot Moshe, Hoshen Mishpat*, 2:73, subsection b.

[27]Feinstein, loc. cit.

will live, though his partner will not survive. What is the ethically appropriate response? For Jewish tradition, despite some early debate, the one with the bottle drinks and lives.[28] So, too, the one for whom treatment has been instituted has that precious bottle of water in his hands, and the other does not. Even if the life so preserved is extremely limited in duration, one may not take the bottle from the one who has it for the sake of another.

One additional point must be mentioned. The Jewish community knew of many tragic cases of individual need affecting the general economy. The prototype in Jewish literature is actually not a medical issue, but rather a hostage situation. In these cases, Jewish law requires that excessive ransoms (of more than the slave-value of the person involved) not be paid.[29] Beyond the familiar concern that kidnappers and terrorists not be encouraged to see hostage-taking as a lucrative proposition, finding thereby reason to continue their criminal ways, a second concern was also expressed. This was the fear that other members of society, who were not directly involved in the hostage situation, would suffer so much economic deprivation (from society's payment of excessive ransoms) that they would replace the freed hostages as hostages to poverty.[30] A limit must be placed by society on its response to the financial demands of those who suffer from individual needs, therefore, regardless of how tragic those needs might be. The healthy members of society have the wellness bottle; others drinking too deeply from it could make those not affected by illness unable to survive the desert of life.

A most interesting exposition of these principles appears in the talmudic discussion[31] of competing claims to the waters of a spring between inhabitants of the city in which the spring is found vs. inhabitants of another city.

> With respect to a well belonging to townspeople, when it is a question of their own lives or the lives of strangers, their own lives take precedence; their cattle or the cattle of strangers, their cattle take precedence over those of strangers; their laundering or that of strangers, their laundering takes prece-

---

[28]*Bava Metzia* 62a.
[29]Mishnah, *Gittin* 4:6.
[30]*Gittin* 45a and Rashi s.v. *"mi'penei dohaka de-tzibura hu."*
[31]*Nedarim* 80b.

dence over that of strangers. But if the choice lies between the lives of strangers and their own laundering, the lives of the strangers take precedence over their own laundering. R. Jose ruled: Their laundering takes precedence over the lives of strangers. Now, if to [refrain merely from] washing one's garment is a hardship in R. Jose's view, how much more so with respect to the body?— I will tell you: In R. Jose's opinion laundering is indeed of greater importance than bathing. For Samuel said: Scabs of the head [caused by not washing] lead to blindness; scabs [arising through the wearing] of [unclean garments cause madness; scabs [due to neglect] of the body cause boils and ulcers.

The Talmud, without debate, concludes that the lives and needs of the citizens of the city that has the spring take precedence. The Talmud then presents a debate as to whether the laundry of the owners of the city takes precedence over the lives of others. The view of R. Jose, that this is indeed the case, is not quite as callous as it seems. R. Jose is concerned that unlaundered clothing would cause a health hazard that could lead to some kind of mental aberration.[32]

Interestingly, Rashi[33] understands the unchallenged ruling (that the lives of those who own the spring take precedence over the lives of others) to refer to a circumstance where a spring originates in one place and then produces a stream that flows to another place. Even if the citizens of the second city have become dependent on this water, it may be dammed by the inhabitants of the upper city for their use when the supply is insufficient for both.[34]

Again, the one (or the community) who has the resource need not share with another if sharing will seriously affect the former's ability to survive. R. Jose's opinion tells us that even indirect danger, or danger over time, allows for the withholding of resources. As there is a contra-

---

[32]Ibid., 81a. The Aramaic term "sha'amumita" is explained by Rashi as "shiga'on" and by Jastrow as "stupefaction." The parallel Yerushalmi passages, *Shevi'it* 8:5, 38B, and *Nedarim* 11:1, 42c simply call laundering an issue of *hayyei nefesh*—life or death. This strongly supports the idea that loss of sanity is tantamount to loss of life with obvious implications for issues such as violation of the Sabbath and abortion.

[33]Ad. loc.

[34]S. Lieberman based on *Tosafot*, disagrees. See S. Lieberman, *Tosefta ki-Peshuto*, (New York: Jewish Theological Seminary, 1988), *Bava Metziah*, p.326.

dictory opinion and no clear *pesak* in Rambam or *Shulhan Arukh*, the matter seems to remain undecided.[35]

However, *Beit Shmuel*[36] posits that Rambam does, in fact, accept R. Jose's opinion. He bases this contention on Maimonides' *pesak*,[37] that a nursing woman may eat as much as she desires and may not be prevented by her husband from doing so, on the claim that she is endangering the child. Maimonides' rationale is that her own pain comes first. This position is cited in *Shulhan Arukh*,[38] as is the opposing view.[39] *Beit Shmuel* expresses surprise that Rambam would follow R. Jose as opposed to the rabbis.

One can support Rambam's *pesak* by looking at the more complete version of the discussion of the spring, as it appears in the Tosefta where it originates.[40]

> With respect to a well belonging to townspeople, when it is a question of their own lives or the lives of strangers, their own lives take precedence; their cattle or the lives of strangers, the lives of strangers take precedence over their cattle; R. Jose ruled: Their cattle take precedence over the lives of strangers. Their cattle or the cattle of strangers, their cattle take precedence

---

[35]Meiri, ad. loc., decides as the rabbis that others' lives come before my laundry, for one entails life while the other entails only great need *tzorekh gadol*. On the other hand Shitah Mekubetzet, ad. loc., citing Eliezer of Metz, allows damming the water for either pain or economics even at the risk of other's lives as the city's need comes before all.

[36]To *Shulhan Arukh: Even Ha'ezer* 80:15. R. Hayyim Ozer Grodzinsky, "Responsa Ahiezer" 1:23 suggests that Rif and *Tur* also accept R. Jose's position. It is on that basis that they do not require one to place oneself in a possibly dangerous situation to save another who is clearly in danger, despite the Jerusalem Talmud's requiring this behavior. Grodzinski suggests that R. Jose disagrees with the Jerusalem Talmud and that Rif, Rambam, and *Tur* decide in his favor.

[37]Maimonides, *Hilkhot Ishut* 21:11.

[38]*Even Ha-ezer*, loc. cit.

[39]Presumably that of Ravad in *Hilkhot Ishut*, loc. cit., who claims that Rambam's position is not based on Talmudic sources. It is interesting to speculate how Ravad would have reacted to *Beit Shmuel*'s claim that Rambam's source is R. Jose in *Nedarim* 80b. So too *Tur*, *Even Ha'ezer* 80 disagrees with Rambam citing *Ketubot* 60b, but does not mention *Nedarim* 80b.

[40]Tosefta: *Bava Metzia*: 11:33—end, ed. Zukermandel (Jerusalem: Wahrmann, 1975), p. 397. All citations of Tosefta are from this edition.

over those of strangers; the lives of strangers and their own laundering, the lives of strangers take precedence over their own laundering; R. Jose ruled: Their laundering takes precedence over the lives of strangers. Their own laundering or the laundering of strangers, their own laundering takes precedence over the laundering of strangers; the cattle of strangers or their own laundering, the cattle of strangers takes precedence over their own laundering; their irrigated field or the cattle of strangers, their irrigated field takes precedence over the cattle of strangers. And all these items are included in the final accounting.

The Tosefta records the *mahloket* between R. Jose and the rabbis regarding laundry versus life. It then records a second *mahloket* not found in the Bavli[41] concerning whether the animals of those in the city take precedence over the lives of others. Again, R. Jose argues that they do, and the rabbis disagree. R. Jose presumably holds that economic deprivation as represented by the loss of the animals presents a long term danger, so it, too, takes precedence.

Another important element is the concluding section of the Tosefta not cited in the Gemara. The Tosefta states, without argument, that other's animals take precedence over my laundry and that the city's irrigated fields come before others' animals.

Let us then summarize the hierarchy of the rabbis and of R. Jose as we now understand them. According to the rabbis, the city that controls the water takes precedence only when competing needs are of similar magnitude. Given that rule, life then takes precedence over irrigated fields (economic concerns). Irrigated fields (which need water that cannot be easily replenished in the location where they are)[42] take precedence over animals (which can be moved and are more easily replenished). Animals then take precedence over laundry (danger of insanity). This last obviously makes no sense, because danger of insanity would come only slightly below the first item on the list (life) and well above the other two, which are only economic concerns.

R. Jose's list, too, is problematic. He clearly gives great precedence to the owners of the spring; any equivalent competing claim would certainly

---

[41]Nor is it in the Yerushalmi sources. See note 22 above. The Yerushalmi, though worded very differently, presents the same substance as the Bavli.

[42]Cf. Mishnah: *Mo'ed Katan* 1:1 and Tosafot, ad. loc.

be won by the people of the city. As for the rest—life, laundry (insanity), irrigated fields (non-replenishable resources), and animals (replenishable resources)—when the city is in need, all take precedence over even the lives of others. The only exception is that other's animals (replenishable economic needs) take precedence over my laundry (insanity). This is true even though others' lives do not take precedence over my laundry. This, too, makes no sense.

Returning for a moment to the source in the Bavli, the Gemara explains laundry as leading to insanity only in connection with R. Jose's view. If one were to suggest that the Rabbis disagree with R. Jose not only on the substance of the law, but also on whether one must be concerned that lack of clean clothes leads to insanity, all the problems disappear.

If the rabbis see laundry as representing not insanity, but creature comforts, our understanding of the Tosefta changes dramatically. For the rabbis, life, replenishable resources, non-replenishable resources, followed by creature comforts are the needs discussed in descending order by this source. At each level, the townspeople take precedence, but strangers would prevail if their need is at a higher level. This is true even to the extent that others' replenishable resources that can potentially be taken to another water source (animals) still take precedence over my creature comforts (laundry).

R. Jose, on the other hand, gives priority in all things (except creature comforts, which are not mentioned in the first part of the Tosefta) to the members of the city. Life, danger (which is his understanding of what laundry represents), and all serious economic concerns take precedence—even over others' lives. The unchallenged statement that others' animals take precedence over the city's laundry is not opposed by R. Jose, because the usage of laundry here is the rabbis' usage and cannot possibly mean danger of insanity. No one would assume that economic needs could possibly take priority over danger of insanity. Laundry, here, must mean creature comforts. As R. Jose apparently agrees that others' economic needs take precedence over my creature comforts, there is no reason to debate the position.[43] His understanding of the

---

[43]Lieberman, loc. cit., argues that a debate exists here, a fortiori, but fails to explain how the rabbis could possibly see economic needs as superior to danger of insanity.

dangers of unclean laundry are clear from the earlier part of the Tosefta and so stated by the Gemara.

If this analysis is correct, one other assumption must also be true. The rabbis see laundry as a creature comfort and thus disagree with R. Jose who sees it as a danger. However, if the rabbis were convinced that a situation involving insanity or even physical pain were involved, it would be reasonable to assume that they, too, would agree with R. Jose that one's own pain takes precedence even over the lives of others. Rambam is correct to adopt this *pesak*, because no one, in this analysis, disputes it. Thus *Beit Shmuel*'s conclusion is correct, and the problem he raises with that conclusion disappears.

Further, because the Bavli quotes the Tosefta in a context that deals with oaths involving *inuy nefesh*, pain, one can understand why only the section discussing laundry—which the rabbis see as dealing with creature comforts—is cited. The material dealing with animals and irrigated fields, except as mentioned inter alia in the topically relevant section, do not belong in the Bavli. The response of the Gemara is then to say that R. Jose does not see laundering as being in this category either, but in the category of danger.[44] Nonetheless, the rabbis can, and according to Rambam do, continue to see laundry as part of the discussion of *inuy nefesh* and creature comforts issue.

The Jerusalem Talmud's citation of this discussion[45] proves the point, as it includes the following statement: "R. Johanan said: Who is the *tanna* who views laundry as a matter of life and death? R. Jose." This clearly implies that the others do not.

I can suggest a rationale for accepting R. Jose's view with regard to the city's priority in economic areas.[46] Poor people are considered to exist in a state of physical danger: "Four are considered as dead: a poor person . . ."[47] The more literally one takes this statement, the more one can support R. Jose's view that even in the economic area, the city dwellers come before the lives of others.

---

[44]Cf. Tosafot and Ran, ad. loc.
[45]See note 22.
[46]As R. Eliezer of Metz, note 25.
[47]*Nedarim* 64b.

In any case, it is clear that vital resources may be shared with others only to the point that doing so does not seriously harm the one who possesses the resource. The principle of the bottle and the principle of the hostages hold true on a communal level[48] in the story of the spring owned by a city whose water is needed by others. Even when others lack necessities, the city cannot put its citizens in physical, or perhaps even economic danger, to help meet someone else's needs.

The values described above would seem to embody inviolable halakhic principles for dealing with the pivotal issues of respect for each individual human life, response to immediate versus theoretical need, limits of concern for one's fellow human being, and the extent to which a society may economically affect its constituents. Bringing these elements together results in the following public-policy posture.

1) Without reference to actual patients,[49] economists and other experts should determine a ceiling for health-care expenditure that responds as generously as possible to the need without causing impoverishment or loss of employment to others.[50]
2) This money should be pre-allocated[51] by the same type of expert, to provide equipment, facilities, and supplies for the various maladies that afflict mankind according to actuarial frequency of the following: need; efficacy, and survivability of a particular illness and its treatment; and whether the treatment is palliative or curative.[52] A reasonable percentage should be left for research.[53]

---

[48]Ran *Nedarim* 80b s.v. "ma'ayan," writes: "'*hayekha kodemin*' [Lev. 25:36]— 'your brother shall live with you'—your life comes first," thus quoting *Bava Metziah* 62a, where these exact words are used to explain why the individual with the bottle in the desert may drink and not share with his fellow traveler. See also Lieberman, loc. cit.

[49]"*Holeh shelo befaneinu*"; see n. 15 above.

[50]Based on Rashi: *Gittin* 45a, *Bava Metziah* 62a and the well controlled by one city and our analysis of the discussion surrounding it.

[51]To avoid "*befaneinu*" problems.

[52]A derivative of R. Feinstein's positions cited above, as well as of the hierarchy of needs in the discussion of the well.

[53]This can be seen as part of God's first imperative to mankind of "ve-*kivshuha*" ("and you shall conquer it"). Gen. 1:28. see also R. Judah Loew of Prague (Maharal mi-Prague), *Hiddushei Aggadot* to *Sanhedrin* 58b.

3) It should be stressed that these criteria would be used for prioritization,[54] not for exclusion. A reasonable balance must be struck in allocating the majority of the resources to those situations that best meet the criteria, while leaving a smaller, but significant amount, for those that do not yet rate as high. Priority does not, and should not, mean exclusivity.[55]

4) Once the health care system has been set up along these guidelines, care is to be given on a first-come, first-served basis. Older people are not precluded from treatment because of the theoretical younger person who might yet come through the door.[56]

5) If several patients need the same treatment at the same time, priority should be given to those who will be helped most to be healed from their present malady. (Again, age should not be a criterion.)[57]

6) Once a specific treatment has been instituted for a specific patient, it may not be terminated for financial reasons or to serve the needs of another patient or patients.[58]

---

[54]Talmudic sources often speak of one person or set of people having priority in cases of need. For example in the case of the well discussed above it is their lives (those of the people in the city) that are prior to those outside. So, too, *Bava Metzia* 71a tells us that the poor of our own city take precedence. Occasionally, priority results in totality, but given the huge amounts devoted to health care and the fact that the work is being done without a sick person before us, it would be counter-intuitive to find major categories of need that would be completely excluded from funding.

[55]Cf. Moses Feinstein, ibid., 49. "Priority" is most fully explicated in the context of the laws of charity and estates. This responsum deals with proper apportioning of the estate of a childless individual to relatives and charitable institutions. Though relatives have priority, Feinstein posits that only two thirds of the estate goes to them, while one third goes to charitable institutions.

[56]Feinstein, ibid., #75, subsection g, supporting our earlier statements that decisions cannot be made on this basis.

[57]Feinstein, ibid., 74, subsections a and b, and 75 subsections a and b. I have heard that R. Feinstein once ruled during World War II that a doctor entering a ward knowing that an inadequate supply of antibiotic was available and realizing that all in the ward needed what little he or she had, should simply inject arms at random until the supplies were exhausted without choosing anyone for any specific reason.

[58]See note 5 above.

7) Under a system such as this one, it is theoretically possible that some resources would be exhausted while patients are still in need.[59] It is to be hoped that society would do as much as possible within these guidelines to avoid reaching the point at which patients are turned away for lack of resources. The cost-containment effect of the items discussed in the other sections of this paper should keep medical care available to all, thus avoiding this dire extreme except in the most exceptional circumstances.

IV. WHO TAKES CARE OF THE POOR?

For those who have adequate financial resources, appropriate health care requires only that one find the proper medical practitioners to deal with one's needs. For those with limited resources, however, the challenge is much greater and can often be insurmountable. For this reason, countries and communities have tried various systems to provide universal access. These attempts have met with varying degrees of success.

Free-market models reward professional accomplishment, provide some measure of competition, promote research, and allow for prompt and personalized care. But they tend to exclude those at the bottom of the socioeconomic ladder. Socialized-medicine models, while being inclusive of all who are in need, tend to fail precisely where free-market models are strongest. Professional rewards are lower, access is slower, research is diminished or disappears, competition is limited, and physicians tend not to develop the types of personal relationship with patients that free-market models promote. Further, the dangers of overuse and exploitation of the system, along with the overall tax burden to society, can be onerous and damaging to national economic health.

Jewish practice took a mixed-model approach to the problem. During much of the medieval and early modern periods, many Jewish communities would hire doctors and even provide hospital or other medical facilities. In exchange for his salary, the physician would care for the poor of the community. Though the reimbursement was modest, it often included tax breaks and/or housing accommodations. When caring for those of sufficient financial means, the doctor was not paid by the community and could establish whatever fees he deemed appropriate, sub-

---

[59]See above, that life is not a risk-free experience.

ject to the limits that the market and Jewish law (see below) would allow. In this way, many, if not all, the advantages of the free-market model
could be maintained while providing access to even the poorest members of society.[60]

There may be a rabbinic precedent for this type of system. The Talmud[61] tells the following story:

> Abba was a cupper and daily he would receive greetings from the Heavenly
> Academy. Abaye received greetings on every Sabbath eve, Raba on the eve
> of every Day of Atonement. Abaye felt dejected because of [the signal honor
> shown to] Abba the Cupper. People said to him: This distinction is made
> because you cannot do what Abba does. What was the special merit of Abba
> the Cupper? . . . He also had a place out of public gaze where the patients
> deposited their fees which he would charge; those that could afford it put
> their fees there, and thus those who could not pay were not put to shame.
> Whenever a young scholar happened to consult him not only would he ac-
> cept no fee from him but on taking leave of him he also would give him some
> money at the same time adding, Go and regain strength therewith.

At least part of Abba's special status came from his creating a mixed
model for health care. This mixed model then led to community-wide
implementation as described above.

It should be noted that, unlike Abba's example, proposals to care for
the disadvantaged pro bono, even when made by doctors themselves,
were often rejected.[62] Unrecompensed work, so it was thought, would

---

[60]Many historians describe these arrangements. Some examples: *Encyclopaedia Judaica*, s.v. "Amenities, Communal." S. W. Baron, *The Jewish Community*, (Philadelphia: 1942), 2: 115, 328–329; A.A. Neuman, *Jews in Spain* (Philadelphia: Jewish Publication Society, 1948), 2: 110–111; I. Jakobovits, *Jewish
Medical Ethics*, (New York: Bloch, 1975) 225; H. J. Zimmels, *Magicians, Theo-
logians and Doctors*, (London: E. Goldston, 1952), pp. 18–19. Though the details differ from community to community, and occasionally from scholar to
scholar, the general descriptions are the same.

[61]*Ta'anit* 21b–22a.

[62]See Jakobovits, loc. cit., for differing local customs. Even in regions where
physicians were not paid for work with the poor, they did receive compensation in the form of tax breaks and other special privileges. Modern examples
such as forgiveness of student loans readily suggest themselves and might be
factored into the equation.

not be treated with the same seriousness and priority as would work that received even limited professional compensation. To paraphrase what the Talmud says in a slightly different context:[63] "A doctor who heals for nothing is worth what he charges." The quality of medical care for the poor was thus preserved by offering compensation for services.

There is a way to translate this health-care model to the contemporary reality of specialized medicine and advanced technology. If some amount of every doctor's time were devoted to service to the poor, either in the doctor's office, or in regional or neighborhood clinics, where physicians would be required to serve for a few hours a week, almost everyone would be covered. In return for a governmental salary that would be reasonable, though not particularly lucrative, the doctor would handle all of the indigent who came through the door requiring his expertise and specialty (except those sent to others of a similar specialty serving on the same day). For the rest of the work week, the physician would be free to pursue his usual private practice and establish fees and income in what we now consider to be the normal way.

Obviously, some coordination and regulation must be instituted to ensure that all doctors are involved, that scheduling allows for an adequate number of each specialty to be present at all appropriate times, and that patients are adequately means-tested. The added bureaucracy should function locally[64] and should neither be so onerous nor so expensive that it would preclude developing this eminently sustainable model. Realistically, one would expect that much of the best of both the free-market and socialized-medicine models would be preserved by this type of system.

Two last points should be highlighted. First, doctors would be paid by time, not per patient, thus minimizing many current abuses of the Medicare and Medicaid systems. Second, preventive medicine[65] was a

---

[63]*Bava Kamma* 85a.

[64]Most Jewish communal amenities functioned locally. This is a logical extension of "the poor of one's own city take priority." *Bava Metzia* 71a. Cf. sources in note 12 above and the description of the communal charity structure described in *Bava Batra* 7b–10a.

[65]Cf. Neuman, loc. cit. This has a biblical origin. Deut. 4:15 states, "You shall diligently preserve your souls," which was understood to be an affirmative obligation to act in ways which would promote health, cf. Maimonides, *Hilkhot De'ot* ch. 4. See also S. Boylan, op. cit (n. 8).

centerpiece of the Jewish system. The ancient communal doctors were required to see each of the poor on a regular basis and to prescribe proper diet and behavior. Preventive medicine was seen in medieval times as a good idea in keeping costs and needs low, and it is a good idea today.

V. HOW MUCH SHOULD MEDICAL CARE COST?

President Clinton has focused some attention on pharmaceutical companies for allegedly taking excessive profits. Depending on the economic realities, Jewish sources express precisely the same concern.

Jewish law approaches this issue initially from its regulation of contracts. The paradigm emerges from the following talmudic regulation.[66] One who is escaping pursuit comes upon a ferry master at a river that must be crossed in order to escape. Any offer of excessive payment, beyond the normal fee for passage, even if suggested by the pursued and accepted by the ferry master, need not be paid after transport. The pursued may claim that he was only fooling, that he was under duress, and that there was therefore no contract, no meeting of the minds. Only the normal transport fee need be paid by the passenger.

This principle was expanded by Jewish legal scholars to other similar cases of undue duress.[67] One such situation was understood to be that of a person who is ill and finds someone in possession of medicine that will heal him. Jewish economic law allows for any businessman to realize profits of no more than one sixth over costs.[68] However, prior informed agreement of payment above this ceiling may vitiate the prohibition.[69] This last rule finds an exception in the ferry master case, and later halakhic scholars[70] find precisely the same exception (due to duress) in the sale of drugs or medication to one who is ill. Pharmaceutical companies, as such, would not be entitled to profits beyond the one sixth ceiling. Obviously, a reasonable amount for research and development could

---

[66]*Bava Kamma* 116a.

[67]Cf. *Yevamot* 116a.

[68]Mishnah, *Bava Metzia* 4:3.

[69]Maimonides, *Hilkhot Mekhirah* 12:7.

[70]David Ben Abi Zimrah, *Responsa Radbaz*, 986 and Simon Duran, *Tashbetz*, 3:3, #20, codified in *Shulhan Arukh, Yoreh De'ah* 336:3.

be included in the costs column, but the one sixth ceiling would still keep prices under some measure of control. Logically, this could be extended to the use of all types of medical material, thus putting an end to the $8.00 aspirin tablet and the $25.00 bandage.

Physicians' fees are a far more complex issue, on the other hand, and are not treated by Jewish law in the same way. One must first understand that the healing arts are viewed by Judaism as a "*mitzvah*," a positive good and the fulfillment of a divine commandment and not as normal work.[71] Direct compensation for activity of this type is judged to be unseemly and delegitimatizing of the good that is being done.[72] Full compliance with this standard in health care would likely lead to a rise in the rate of illness as hospitals, doctors' offices, and medical schools would, of financial necessity shut down.

This was equally true in ancient times. Jewish law, therefore, provided the "*mitzvah*" practitioner with a repayment concept known as *sekhar battalah*, meaning the sum one would accept *not* to do work. Imagine an individual making $100,000 a year. What would this individual require to stay home and not go to work?[73] $80,000? $75,000? He would probably not accept $10,000 or even $25,000. Certainly, though, there is some number that we could rationally agree on as representing appropriate *sekhar battalah* that would then be paid to the "*mitzvah*" practitioner.[74]

This would be an appropriate, but utopian, payment for a physician's services.[75] But what if, as in our previous case, the doctor had contracted with the patient for a sum far in excess of the *sekhar batalah* number. Although this would appear to be a case of duress similar to those discussed previously, it is not. In the previous examples, the services or goods had a clearly acknowledged market price. Here, the "commodity" in question is the doctor's wisdom and training, which are priceless. Therefore, any price

---

[71] *Shulhan Arukh, Yoreh De'ah* 336:1. See also the discussions of "*lo ta'amod al dam re'akha*" and "*hashavat aveidah*" in section II above.

[72] Tosafot, *Nedarim* 39a, s.v. "*al.*"

[73] The fullest explication of the concept appears in discussions of tort law as it is the standard used to determine compensation for a victim's lost wages. Cf. Maimonides: *Hilkhot Hovel u-Mazzik* 2:11.

[74] The Talmud apparently knew of "Type A" personalities for whom not working is not a benefit. Therefore no concept of *sekhar battalah* existed in Mehoza, whose people became ill if they did not work. *Bava Metziah* 77a.

[75] *Shulhan Arukh, Yoreh De'ah* 336:2.

is, in effect, fair (subject to rabbinic regulation as described below), as long as it is agreed to by both parties before treatment.[76] Though this requirement would not directly limit health-care costs, doctors would need to disclose fees before services are rendered. This would prevent the megabuck bill given to the patient after he is well, which seems designed to make him sick all over again. It would also create some price competition for those who chose to shop around before choosing a doctor.

Finally, although Jewish economic law tends to favor a free market,[77] this ceases to be true when prices climb to levels that make essential goods and services unavailable to the average person. Jewish courts also served as regulatory agencies for the Jewish community. In that capacity, they regulated items of this type through the establishment of price ceilings (not price-fixing) as necessary.[78] The ceiling kept the commodity within the reach of the average person, but competition could exist under the maximum. Physicians' fees were also subject to controls if they rose too high. Probably, the threat of imposing a ceiling would be enough to ensure that prices would be kept at reasonable levels.

VI. MEDICAL MALPRACTICE

Medical malpractice costs, in both direct and indirect ways, are seen by many as serious drains on medical resources. Multimillion dollar judgments in malpractice cases are well known. Obviously, these judgments cannot be paid by individual practitioners. Therefore, the costs are spread throughout the system and ultimately throughout the patient base by the rising premiums for medical-malpractice insurance, which figures in a doctor's overhead. Costs have reached crisis level in some areas. Recently Florida suffered an ob/gyn shortage caused, in large measure, by practitioners leaving the field as a result of these financial pressures. Other physicians have simply refused to pay premiums, structured their finances to limit exposure, or bravely relied on patients to recognize their good

---

[76]Ibid. 336:3.

[77]See generally A. Levine, *Free Enterprise and Jewish Law* (New York: Ktav, 1980), and M. Tamari, *With All Your Possessions* (New York: The Free Press, 1987).

[78]*Shulhan Arukh, Hoshen Mishpat* 231:20, and generally regarding the courts regulatory function ibid. 231:2.

will and personal dedication, and not sue. Obviously, these are very risky positions from which to "operate."

Indirect costs could be even more significant. Large batteries of tests and procedural requirements structure the doctor's working environment even in those cases where his own experience and training identify these as excessive. This is done so as to cover the doctor and hospital legally from financial exposure on the off chance that some normally unexpected or outlandish condition exists that might be actionable if not diagnosed by the physician. The tests and procedures are unnecessary in the view of many experts, thus adding cost and draining resources for fear of potential malpractice liability.

Nearly two millennia ago, Judaism removed financial exposure of this kind from legitimate practitioners precisely because it was believed that potential liability of this type was detrimental to the workings of an effective health-care system. Jewish courts, as part of their regulatory role, licensed competent physicians and exempted physicians so licensed from liability for acts of simple negligence. This was understood to be an example of *tikkun olam* that would allow the community to find physicians willing to undertake the responsibility of health care. As a result, licensed physicians who made an "honest mistake"[79] were held financially blameless.[80] Only in cases of gross negligence, such as using unnecessary or untested procedures or personal incompetence, was the doctor held financially liable.[81]

It should be noted also that even in cases that resulted in financial liability, Jewish law acted to mitigate the penalty. A thorough treatment

---

[79]Tosefta, *Gittin* 3:13: "A skilled doctor who practiced with the permission of the bet din and accidentally did damage is not culpable; if he did it purposely, he is culpable . . ." and commentary *Minkhat Bikurim*, ad. loc.. This licensure system fell out of use only in relatively modern times when secular licensing procedures were found acceptable to the Jewish community. See A. Kahana, "Medicine in Halakhic Literature After the Compilation of the Talmud," *Sinai* #14 (1950): 222. This secular licensure carried liability limitations only when and if the secular authorities were to decide that it should, because the secular courts now held sway.

[80]See Perisha to *Yoreh De'ah* 336:7 and *Beit Yosef*, ad. loc.

[81]Tosefta, *Bava Kamma* 9:3; see also discussion of "accidental approaching purposeful," *Bava Kamma* 32b. Responses to "accident" are not the same when the action approaches "purposeful."

of Jewish tort law is beyond the scope of this paper, but one principle is clear: tort awards were limited to levels of compensation that could reasonably be paid by the perpetrator. Awards for pain and suffering or punitive damages that exceed the costs of reasonable medical care for the victim by amounts that no human being could spend in multiple lifetimes would never be granted by Jewish courts.[82]

To illustrate, I mention our old friend *sekhar battalah* again. The tortfeasor did not pay the total amount of lost wages. Rather, the "advantage" of staying home was factored into the award. Liability was calculated on the basis of the amount that an individual of similar circumstances to the victim prior to his injury would take to stay home rather than work.[83] This approach to tort judgments would also lower medical malpractice costs even in those relatively few cases where these costs must be paid.

Exemption from liability for malpractice poses the obvious risk of doctors creating malpractice tragedies throughout the land and never being held responsible. Two mechanisms were used within the Jewish community to control this potential problem. The first was removal of licensure (and therefore, of malpractice protection), along with removal from any public medical position that one held. Though R. Yosef Karo, who is more stringent, and Rama, who is more lenient, disagree as to whether one mistake is sufficient to invoke such drastic measures, all agree that a pattern of mistakes and/or a warning followed by an additional mistake, are grounds for dismissal and loss of licensure.[84]

Further—and this is an idea that the American public would love in a sort of "raw-meat-to-the lions" fashion—the licensing body could be held financially liable for any physician certified by it who was incompetent in a way discoverable within the scope of their investigative powers. Though a licensed doctor who proved himself incompetent but retained his license would retain his exemption, the licensing board or court would be potentially financially liable for the doctor's mistakes while under licensure, possibly even on a personal basis.[85]

---

[82]See generally the eighth chapter of *Bava Kamma*, especially 83b–87a.

[83]See note 64 above.

[84]*Shulhan Arukh, Hoshen Mishpat*, ch. 306 at #8.

[85]Nissim Abraham Ashkenazi, *Responsa Ma'aseh Avraham*, 14:55. The case involves misdiagnosis and use of wrong medicine in a case of smallpox by an incompetent practitioner who received licensure by a local rabbinic court. Though maintaining that the financial liability exemption applied, Ashkenazi

On a moral plane as well, the rabbis attempted to influence physicians to be on their best professional behavior. For the sake of *tikkun olam*, financial liability was removed from negligent behavior, but criminal penalties for negligent homicide were specifically not removed.[86] Instead, doctors were warned that causing the negligent death of a patient would result in banishment to an *ir miklat* (city of refuge). By the time of the editing of the Tosefta, in which this law appears, this was a threat without applicability, because refuge cities had not existed for many generations.[87] But retaining the form even without the substance would remind physicians that errors were truly a serious business and that making an error might put them in the position of having committed a serious violation without any possibility of proper expiation.

Finally, the medical and physical care of malpractice victims who fall under the "exclusion from liability" rule would need to be covered by society. However, this is a much smaller cost than that which is presently incurred by the system as a result of malpractice litigation and its attendant effects.

VII. A FINAL ELEMENT—PERSONAL RESPONSIBILITY

In the case of business partners, the *Shulhan Arukh* distinguishes between the sustainable claim on shared assets made by one who becomes ill with a behaviorally related illness, and the sustainable claim of one whose

---

lays blame on the court for not doing its work properly. Judicial malpractice is discussed in general terms in *Shulhan Arukh, Hoshen Mishpat*, 25. See also *Beit Yosef: Yoreh De'ah* ch. 336 who equates judges and doctors in this area. See also M. Dratch, "Suing your Rabbi: Clergy Malpractice in Jewish Law," *Journal of Halakhah and Contemporary Society*, 18 (Fall 1989): 61–75.

[86]Tosefta, *Makkot* 2:5. See also *Yoreh De'ah* 336:1, that even financial liability remains "in the hands of Heaven."

[87]The institution probably did not exist during Talmudic times. See *Encyclopaedia Judaica*, s.v. "City of Refuge." Possibly, this was because the three original cities established by Moses (Deut. 4:41) were not under Jewish control during the Second Temple period, and all needed to be functioning for any to be functioning. See Maimonides, *Hilkhot Rotze'ah u-Shemirat ha-Nefesh* 8:3–4.

illness was caused through outside happenstance beyond his control.[88] According to R. Yosef Karo a working member of a business partnership who becomes ill through personal negligence (e.g. volitional exposure to cold in winter or heat in summer) must use his own resources to pay for acute illness that results from his unhealthy behavior. However, if the illness so caused is chronic, he may draw on partnership funds for his needs.[89] On the other hand, if the illness occurs through an act of God, without negligence on the part of the patient, both chronic and acute illnesses are to be covered by joint funds.

Rama reports a more restrictive view on coverage of illness. According to this opinion, negligence eliminates coverage even in cases of chronic illness, though the non-negligent partner who becomes ill is covered by partnership funds only in cases of chronic illness, not acute illness. Rama is lenient, however, in one regard. Not only is a working partner covered for non-negligent chronic illness; so, too, is a capital partner whose basic livelihood[90] comes from the activities of the partnership.

Two points emerge from this discussion. First, it indicates the area where coverage presents the greatest need. Chronic or catastrophic[91] illness presents the most significant cause for concern. Some things have obviously not changed. In fact, some make the argument today that only illnesses of this type should be covered by government or insurance plans. In fact, some argue, most people would be financially better off carrying only this type of coverage and paying for routine procedures or acute illnesses from their available resources.

Second is the point with which I began. People who become ill through their own negligence are in a different category than those who become ill through no fault of their own. The former simply will receive less of the available resources than the latter. Judaism held that people bear

---

[88]*Hoshen Mishpat* 177:2–3.

[89]I translate the Hebrew *sheyesh la kitzvah* as acute and "*she-ein la kitzvah*" as chronic. The terms might incorporate the idea of set financial limits, however, rather than simply the idea of time constraints. In that case, catastrophic and non-catastrophic illness would be better translations. The comments on types of coverage apply whichever definition one uses.

[90]Heb. "*nizonin min ha-shutafut.*"

[91]See note 79.

some responsibility for their actions[92] and that this responsibility is to be reflected in the use of shared resources. It is but a small step to apply this principle to communal funds, where, after all, we are all partners. Translating this policy to the contemporary era, smoking-related diseases, drug-and-alcohol-related illnesses, obesity and cholesterol-related-conditions under one's control, and even behaviorally acquired AIDS would be treated differently from, for example, an illness caused by a genetic disorder.

I should point out that contemporary acceptance of this principle underlies and legitimizes sin taxes. In addition, many hospitals refuse heart transplants as a matter of policy to people who continue to smoke, or liver transplants to those who continue their alcohol consumption. Engaging in controllable behavior that may make one ill, once the etiology of a disease is known, should allow the victim less command of communal resources than would be allowed to one who becomes ill through no fault or action of his own.

VIII. SUMMARY

The historical Jewish health-care system is a fairly sophisticated and complex model incorporating all of the following principles:

1. A mixed model of communally retained, part—time physicians who also practice privately and bring care to rich and poor alike.
2. Controls on drug and medical paraphernalia costs.
3. Pre-treatment agreement between doctor and patient as to physician's fees.
4. Possible ceilings placed on physicians' fees to ensure both availability and competition.

---

[92]A close corollary of the principle that life is not risk-free, this is most fully articulated in the biblical verse, "I call heaven and earth to witness against you this day, that I have set before you life and death, the blessing and the curse, that you may live, you and your offspring . . ." (Deut. 30:19). Certainly, any system that bases itself on reward and punishment must assume that personal responsibility operates as a bedrock principle.

5. Reasonable limits on society's burden to provide health-care re-sources so that those who are presently well do not themselves become victims.
6. An elaborate ethos detailing how scarce resources and facilities are to be apportioned and which type of illnesses most need coverage.
7. Control of medical competence and professional standards within a framework that removes much of the burden of onerous malprac-tice claims.
8. An insistence that people take some measure of responsibility for their own unhealthy actions.

The Jewish health-care system was sensitive to many of the issues that trouble us today. Its solutions reflected a sincere attempt at *tikkun olam*, bringing compassion, realism, and moral values to bear on a very com-plex problem. Most importantly, it successfully embodies those bedrock principles of *halakhah* and societal morality that we dare not allow to be violated "that the world not be corrupted and destroyed." Because we are all halakhically compelled to stand up, even in the secular world, for at least some of these principles, we had better be prepared also to offer a model that will serve to embody them, and not just adopt a public posture of demand and moral outrage.

The system also carries 2,500 years of accumulated wisdom to rec-ommend it. At the very least, it deserves a few minutes of study as we begin to make the difficult decisions on how best to structure our health-care system to maximize its effectiveness. At best, we could find tomor-row's solutions in yesterday's prototype.

Notes on Contributors

Jeffrey Ballabon is vice president of government relations and public affairs for Court TV. Previously, he was legislative counsel to United States Senator John Danforth and Minority Counsel to the Senate Committee on Commerce, Science, and Transportation.

Jack Bieler is assistant principal of the Hebrew Academy of Greater Washington and rabbi of the Kemp Mill Synagogue. He has published articles on the integration of Judaism and general studies, as well as on the philosophy of Jewish education.

J. David Bleich is a *Rosh Yeshiva* and the *Rosh Kollel Le-Horaah* at the Rabbi Isaac Elchanan Theological Seminary, professor of Jewish law at the Benjamin N. Cardozo School of Law, and Herbert and Florence Tenzer Professor of Law and Ethics at Yeshiva University. He is the author of the four volumes of *Contemporary Halakhic Problems* and of *Be-Netivot ha-Halakhah*, as well as many other works on Jewish law, ethics, and philosophy.

Gerald J. Blidstein holds the Miriam Martha Hubert Chair in Jewish law at Ben-Gurion University of the Negev, where he has also served as Dean of the Faculty of Humanities and Social Sciences. Among his many publications are the Hebrew books *Prayer in Maimonidean Halakhah* and *Political Concepts in Maimonidean Halakhah*, which was awarded a Jerusalem Prize in 1985.

Michael J. Broyde is senior lecturer at Emory University School of Law, where he is also director of the Project on Law, Religion, and the Family and a member of the Law and Religion Program. Ordained *yoreh yoreh*

339

v-yadin yadin, he is author of *The Pursuit of Justice and Jewish Law: Halakhic Perspectives on the Legal Profession*, as well as numerous other works.

Nathan J. Diament is director of the Institute for Public Affairs of the Union of Orthodox Jewish Congregations of America, where he develops and coordinates public policy research and initiatives on behalf of the Jewish community. Previously, he practiced law in New York and taught political science at Yeshiva University. Mr. Diament served as a law clerk for Judge I. Leo Glasser of the United States District Court.

Barry Freundel is rabbi of the Kesher Israel Synagogue in Washington, DC, adjunct instructor at the University of Maryland and adjunct professor of law at Georgetown University. He serves as a consultant to the Ethics Review Board of the National Institute of Aging of the National Institute of Health and to the Theologic Committee of the Human Genome Project of Baylor University. Author of numerous articles and reviews, he has given many presentations on Halakhah and political ethics on Capitol Hill and at the National Institutes of Health.

Martin P. Golding is professor of philosophy and professor of law at Duke University. His many publications on jurisprudence and ethics include *The Nature of Law*, *The Philosophy of Law*, and *Legal Reasoning*. He is also editor of the anthology *Jewish Law and Legal Theory*.

Aaron Levine is Samson and Halina Bitensky Professor of Economics at Yeshiva University and rabbi of the Young Israel of Avenue J in Brooklyn. He is author of *Free Enterprise and Jewish Law: Aspects of Jewish Business Ethics*, *Business Ethics in Jewish Law* (with Leo Jung), *Economics and Jewish Law*, and *Economic Policy and Jewish Law*.

David Shatz is professor of philosophy at Yeshiva University. He has published many scholarly articles and reviews, on both general and Jewish philosophy. Dr. Shatz is also co-editor of *Contemporary Philosophy of Religion*, *Definitions and Definability*, and *Abraham Isaac Kook and Jewish Spirituality*.

Marc D. Stern is co-director of the Commission on Law and Social Action of the American Jewish Congress. Previously he was a law clerk for the United States Court of Appeals. He writes widely on religion and public policy.

Meir Tamari is director of the Centre for Business Ethics at the Jerusalem College of Technology and dean of the American Association for Jewish Business Ethics. A consultant to various governmental bodies, he has written numerous books and articles on business ethics, small firms, risk evaluation, and entrepeneurship. He also publishes the *Business Ethics Newsletter* in Jerusalem.

Chaim I. Waxman is professor of sociology at Rutgers University and visiting professor at the Azrieli Graduate Institute for Jewish Education and Administration of Yeshiva University. Among his books are *America's Jews in Transition, American Aliya: Portrait of an Innovative Migration Movement* and *Jewish Baby Boomers*. He is also editor of *Israel as a Religious Reality*, vol. 3 in the Orthodox Forum series.

Index

About the Editors

David Shatz is professor of philosophy at Yeshiva University. He has published over forty scholarly articles and reviews, dealing with both general and Jewish philosophy. His work in general philosophy focuses on the theory of knowledge, free will, ethics, and the philosophy of religion, while his work in Jewish philosophy focuses on Maimonides, Jewish ethics, and twentieth-century rabbinic figures. Dr. Shatz is also co-editor of *Contemporary Philosophy of Religion* (1982), *Definitions and Definability* (1991), and *Abraham Isaac Kook and Jewish Spirituality* (1995).

Chaim I. Waxman is professor of sociology at Rutgers University and visiting professor at the Azrieli Graduate Institute for Jewish Education and Administration of Yeshiva University. Among his books are *America's Jews in Transition* (1983), *American Aliya: Portrait of an Innovative Migration Movement* (1989) and *Jewish Baby Boomers* (1997). He is also editor of *Israel as a Religious Reality*, vol. 3 in the Orthodox Forum series.

Nathan J. Diament is director of the Institute for Public Affairs of the Union of Orthodox Jewish Congregations of America, where he develops and coordinates public policy research and initiatives on behalf of the Jewish community. Previously, he practiced law in New York and taught political science at Yeshiva University. Mr. Diament served as a law clerk for Judge I. Leo Glasser of the United States District Court.